SOUTHERN BUILT

Southern Built

AMERICAN ARCHITECTURE,
REGIONAL PRACTICE

Catherine W. Bishir

University of Virginia Press
Charlottesville and London

University of Virginia Press
© 2006 by the Rector and Visitors of the University of Virginia
All rights reserved
Printed in the United States of America on acid-free paper
First published 2006

9 8 7 6 5 4 3 2 1

LIBRARY OF CONGRESS CATALOGING-IN-PUBLICATION DATA
Bishir, Catherine W.
  Southern built : American architecture, regional practice / Catherine W. Bishir
    p. cm.
  Includes bibliographical references and index.
  ISBN 0-8139-2538-X (cloth : alk. paper) — ISBN 0-8139-2539-8 (pbk. : alk. paper)
  1. Architecture—Southern States—19th century. 2. Architecture—North Carolina—19th century. 3. Architecture and society—Southern States. 4. Architecture and society—North Carolina. 5. Historic preservation—Southern States. I. Title.
NA720.B57 2006
720.975'09034—dc22

2005037586

CONTENTS

Acknowledgments vii
Introduction 1

PART I. BUILDING CULTURE AND PRACTICE

1. Jacob W. Holt: An American Builder 11
2. Good and Sufficient Language for Building 53
3. Black Builders in Antebellum North Carolina 69

PART II. LOCAL, REGIONAL, NATIONAL:
PATHS OF INFLUENCE

4. Mr. Jones Goes to Richmond: A Note on the Influence of Alexander Parris's Wickham House 113
5. Philadelphia Bricks and the New Bern Jail 121
6. "Severe Survitude to House Building": The Construction of Hayes Plantation House, 1814–1817 126

PART III. CONSTRUCTING GROUP IDENTITY:
ARCHITECTURAL LANDSCAPES, COMMUNITY,
AND POWER

7. The Montmorenci–Prospect Hill School: A Study of High-Style Vernacular Architecture in the Roanoke Valley 159
8. The "Unpainted Aristocracy": The Beach Cottages of Old Nags Head 188
9. "A Strong Force of Ladies": Women, Politics, and Confederate Memorial Associations in Nineteenth-Century Raleigh 215
10. Landmarks of Power: Building a Southern Past, 1885–1915 254

PART IV. ISSUES IN HISTORIC PRESERVATION

11. Looking at North Carolina's History through Architecture 297
12. Yuppies, Bubbas, and the Politics of Culture 312

Index 323

ACKNOWLEDGMENTS

During the journeys over many miles and years, many friends and colleagues have helped shape and encourage this work. Notes to the individual articles recall the help and friendships involved in each of those.

For help in planning and assembling this volume, I am grateful to Louis Nelson, Dell Upton, and Boyd Zenner. Thanks to Michael Southern for creating the maps; to Chandrea Burch, Bill Garrett, and Steve Massengill for assistance with the illustrations; to Susan Myers for the index; and to Kate Hutchins and Mark Mones for their editing skills.

I owe a pleasurable debt of gratitude to the many companions whose collegial friendship, support, and insights have encouraged me at key stages and sustained me over the years, including Charlotte Brown, Claudia Brown, Robert Burns, Elizabeth Cromley, Jeffrey Crow, Renee Gledhill-Early, Myrick Howard, H. G. Jones, Ruth Little, Carl Lounsbury, Jennifer Martin, Bruce McDougal, Keith Morgan, David Perry, William Price, Janet Seapker, McKelden Smith, Michael Southern, Douglas Swaim, Edgar Thorne, Dell Upton, Camille Wells, Jack Zehmer, and others. My parents encouraged my work from its earliest days. My daughter Caroline has given me balance and joy since the times when I picked her up from preschool at the end of a day of fieldwork, and now my granddaughter Cate adds a whole new dimension of both. Throughout these many years and projects, my husband John has been my mainstay and delight, encourager, editor, and best friend.

My journeys in this field began long before I started working in historic preservation—with my father, guide, and teacher, William Smith Ward. A farm boy who became an English professor and scholar, he took our family on treks through the farm country of Kentucky where he grew up, visiting folks at "the farm" and in little towns; admiring the "pretty country" and noticing the farmhouses and barns, fields, fences, and creeks; and retelling stories of farm and town people of every economic situation and from times past and present. He also modeled and encouraged in me the pleasures of the scholarly life, in which research and writing offer challenge, joy, and satisfaction. And he showed by word and example his respect for the people and language of the worlds in which he moved with ease and enjoyment, from the country crossroads store in Oddville to the halls of the university in Lexington, and back again. This book is for Bill.

Most of the illustrations in these essays come from the North Carolina Division of Archives and History (NCDAH), Department of Cultural Resources, Raleigh. Illustrations that come from other sources are credited in the captions and used with permission. My thanks to Elizabeth Matheson and the Cherry Hill Historical Foundation, Inc., for permission to use the photograph (from my book *The House Marina Built: Cherry Hill, A Plantation House and its Family*, Warrenton: Cherry Hill Historical Foundation, Inc., 2004) which graces the paperback cover of this work.

SOUTHERN BUILT

INTRODUCTION

This book is about how people in an American region created their architecture—how their choices, relationships, sources of ideas, and building practices reflected and shaped the society in which they operated.

Much of American building springs from the interweaving of local and national patterns, from syntheses of old and new ideas and methods, and from the interaction of traditional practices and professional precepts. The essays in this book consider various aspects of architectural practice and historic preservation. Focused mainly in the nineteenth century, when the balance of old and new and local and national was shifting dramatically and unevenly, these stories depict these interactions through individual projects and expressions of a group or community.

While these local case studies illuminate how building worked among particular people in particular times and places, they also address larger questions and may stimulate further exploration of building practices in other periods and regions. In addition, they may encourage a greater understanding of, and respect for, the process and the participants in the making and keeping of American architecture.

A prevailing theme throughout the following chapters is that of people selecting, adapting, and transmuting new ideas—often from urban models and nationally popular sources—into forms useful and meaningful in local settings. Although some clients and builders adopted such models wholesale, many others adapted them, and did so selectively. Neither following the national notions slavishly nor misinterpreting them through provincial myopia, they operated with awareness of both the national concept and the local reality, and built accordingly. Such patterns occur in nearly every region of the nation, where (in the words of one nineteenth-century client) people made decisions about their buildings with an "eye to the latitude & longitude of the place for which they are intended."[1]

BACKGROUND AND PROVENANCE

These essays grew out of my experience in the North Carolina State Historic Preservation Office from the 1970s through the 1990s. In the first years of the Statewide Architectural Survey (mandated and partially funded as a result of the Historic Preservation Act of 1966), state historic preservation offices across the country undertook to locate and record the historically and architecturally significant buildings, districts, and sites across each state.

The typical pattern in the 1970s was to start with the obviously historic, oldest, and finest buildings. This was the approach in the North Carolina office when I began work there in 1971, and in many others. Key references were the records of the Historic American Buildings Survey (HABS), the work of local historians, and such books as Marcus Whiffen's *American Architecture Since 1780: A Guide to the Styles* (1969), the Federal Writers' Project *North Carolina Guide* (1939 and 1955), and Frances Benjamin Johnston and Thomas T. Waterman's *The Early Architecture of North Carolina* (1941).

There was a tremendous sense of adventure and discovery as each survey turned up buildings that embodied the types and styles seen in these and other books, but simultaneously revealed a greater range and diversity of architecture. Documentary research required to prepare nominations to the National Register of Historic Places drew upon local and family records to supply histories and context for more and more buildings of every type.

Survey and analysis of the architecture of entire counties began to suggest still larger patterns and connections between groups and types of buildings. These findings raised new questions about the broad national picture of architecture that lay outside the traditional canon. They also intersected with developments in folklore, social history, industrial archeology, urban history, and geography, where scholars were paying attention to the whole social fabric as well as the figureheads of society, to the people who built the houses as well as those who commissioned them, and to ordinary as well as extraordinary buildings.

In North Carolina, a watershed in the appreciation of vernacular architecture (as some termed the broader body of building) came with the publication of *Carolina Dwelling*, the 1978 student publication of the School of Design at North Carolina State University. Its editor, Douglas Swaim, invited fellow students, faculty, and State Historic Preservation Office staff and surveyors to present their findings in a popular volume that became one of the first of its kind in the emerging national picture.[2]

Another vital development was the establishment in 1979–80 of the Vernacular Architecture Forum. Responding to the growing interest in ordinary and regional architecture, this multidisciplinary organization brought together individuals from across the country to share and challenge findings and methods of fieldwork, research, and interpretation. Those studying the architecture of far distant communities and regions found compatriots eager to expand the understanding of how each place fit into the bigger picture.

The questions that most aroused my curiosity concerned the people who actually built the architecture. In the early 1980s, Charlotte Brown, Carl

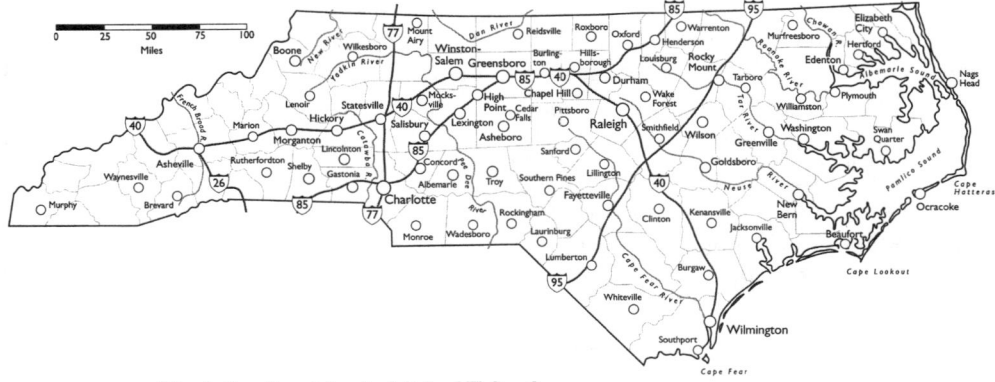

FIG. I.I. *North Carolina. Map by Michael T. Southern, 2005.*

Lounsbury, Ernest Wood, and I began a collaborative research project that addressed these issues and ultimately resulted in the publication of *Architects and Builders in North Carolina: A History of the Practice of Building* (1990). Additional research and synthesis have yielded numerous architectural survey books on communities and counties of North Carolina, statewide studies such as *North Carolina Architecture* (1990), and the regional *Guides* to the historic architecture of eastern, western, and piedmont North Carolina (1996–2003).[3]

The essays in this book, written over nearly thirty years, naturally reflect the experiences, research methods, and perspectives of their times. The earliest recall the first years of the heady discovery and description of a new world of buildings. They sprang directly from the architectural survey fieldwork and additional research for National Register nominations, and the stories that emerged from these: the "Unpainted Aristocracy" on the beach cottages of old Nags Head, and the ornate Federal style plantation houses of Warren and Halifax counties in "The Montmorenci–Prospect Hill School." The story of "Jacob W. Holt: An American Builder" likewise developed from the architectural survey of rural Piedmont counties, where history-minded residents shared family papers and memories.

Just as the fieldwork had turned up batches of buildings that posed stimulating questions, so the research for *Architects and Builders in North Carolina* uncovered lodes of documentary evidence that depicted revealing, specific events in building history—often in greater detail than could be presented in the book. Among the studies that resulted are "Black Builders in Antebellum North Carolina," whose stories poured out of documents from the antebellum era; "Mr. Jones Goes to Richmond," based on a letter found by research assistant J. Marshall Bullock; and "Severe Survitude to House Building," which originated in the papers of Hayes Plantation near Edenton.

The two essays about the building of public memory—"A Strong Force of Ladies" and "Landmarks of Power"—arose from a different set of circumstances. In this case a question spurred my search for evidence: I wanted to know how the version of Southern history I had grown up with had been created, and how that same history had affected the preservation philosophy of the historical agency where I worked. How did it happen that *this* account of Southern history—which skipped an entire chapter of the late nineteenth century—was still conveyed through monuments and memorials, Colonial Revival architecture, and the choices of historic buildings preserved from the past? With the support of the Winterthur Museum near Wilmington, Delaware, I began to explore these issues in 1987 in a research project that led me down different paths than I had anticipated.

Thus these essays are both deductive and inductive—going from the evidence to the concept and sometimes back again with a fresh question. Several sprang from the (often chance) discovery of a body of physical or written evidence—reinforcing a colleague's scholarly observation that sometimes the term "'research strategy' is an oxymoron."[4] Whatever the source of information or method of inquiry, the human story presented in one building project after another offered insights into how people created an architecture that was at once national and regional.

STRUCTURE OF THIS BOOK

This volume is organized around several overlapping topics.[5] The first section treats building culture and practice. The questions addressed there also pervade the entire volume: How do buildings get built? Who are the participants in design and construction? What knowledge do they share or alter? The second section raises related questions of how national and regional patterns interact: How do clients or builders in a locality adopt certain "national" models or ideas yet tailor them to suit local conditions? The third section treats the role of architecture in the formation of group identity and considers how people in power shape architectural forms and public landscapes to define or reinforce their position. The fourth and final section, similarly tied to the topic of group identity, concerns historic preservation, and how its activities address local and national values and practices.

Part I. Building Culture and Practice

In the opening essay, "Jacob W. Holt: An American Builder," the aforementioned themes weave through the career of a single prolific builder. Working from the 1820s through the 1870s, an era of dramatic change, Holt participated in a traditional building culture that depended on shared knowledge of types and methods of construction. He also accommodated the shift from handicraft to industrial production and updated his work by adapting new design ideas and methods to the local situation. He managed a work force of black and white men before and after emancipation. And he tailored his work to please and strengthen the identity of a clientele at once intensely localized and desirous of participating in national trends.

That so much of Holt's work has survived relates to preservation issues not addressed in the article. It stems partly from the lack of development in the once wealthy rural area in which he worked. It also reflects how well he suited the needs and identity of his client group, and how his buildings subsequently accommodated the altered economic situations and symbolic needs of subsequent generations, who remembered Holt's name with pride as part of antebellum history. Local preservationists have also employed his story to encourage appreciation and preservation of his buildings in recent times.

The other essays in this section treat broader aspects of regional building culture and practices. "Good and Sufficient Language for Building" examines the underlying assumptions in traditional practice through the language of contracts and specifications. Builders in North Carolina and throughout North America, like their predecessors across the centuries in Europe, relied on contractual language that sprang from a shared understanding of appropriate forms and methods of construction. Such language contrasts with the elaborate specifications generated by architectural professionalism and multiple rifts in building culture—which have become the norm in the last century. The continuity of old terms from medieval England through to nineteenth-century America suggests the resilience of the culture of building even amidst technological changes.[6]

"Black Builders in Antebellum North Carolina" documents the importance and multiple roles of black artisans in the building trades. Both free blacks and enslaved workmen played a central part in antebellum building throughout the South and elsewhere. The hiring of slaves by whites or free men of color was a standard practice, which gave economic flexibility to the hirer and the owner and sometimes a degree of autonomy to the worker. Slave artisans were often as highly skilled as free men, and their importance to the building industry increased in the 1840s and 1850s.

Part II. Local, Regional, National: Paths of Influence

Three tightly focused case studies depict specific ways in which people synthesized metropolitan and small-town or rural architectural elements and ideas. In one case, the path was clear, direct, and well recorded: "Mr. Jones Goes to Richmond: A Note on the Influence of Alexander Parris's Wickham House" tells how a well-traveled Raleigh man documented a fashionable new Richmond, Virginia, residence designed by a Boston architect, and then encouraged civic leaders in Raleigh to use it as a model for a governor's mansion—wherein local builders adapted some elements but ignored others.

Some clients decided to obtain actual building components from metropolitan sources. "Philadelphia Bricks and the New Bern Jail" recounts how, despite the presence of local brickworks, leaders in the port town of New Bern, North Carolina, chose to order costly bricks from a northern city and had them shipped to local docks, for use in building that most utilitarian of structures—a jail. Other finishing elements arrived by ship to create the town's elegant early-nineteenth-century architecture.

Multiple paths of influence and adaptation—client, artisan, and imported and local building materials—meet in a single story: "'Severe Survitude to House Building': The Construction of Hayes Plantation House, 1814–1817." An unusual house and an unusually complete set of family papers show how an independent-minded client and an ambitious English-born builder-architect blended a conservative form and plan with stylish elements from New York. It also highlights the roles of slave artisans—sawyers, masons, carpenters, plasterers—in multiple stages of the project, and illustrates the builder's self-propelled transition from artisan to architect.

Part III. Constructing Group Identity:
Architectural Landscapes, Community, and Power

Four community studies consider how specific groups of Southerners made use of national ideals and forms to create architectural and symbolic settings that affirmed their identity and position, values and goals.

A group of antebellum planter families takes a central role in "The Montmorenci–Prospect Hill School: A Study of High-Style Vernacular Architecture in the Roanoke Valley." Members of an elite kin group in an isolated plantation area employed (still elusive) artisans to create a distinctive group of houses. These houses, whether newly built or expanded from existing structures, followed various forms and plans, but all showed an attention to fashion and display that was novel to the immediate region. The lavish use of inventive Palladian and Adamesque motifs set these houses, and their owners, apart from their contemporaries and neighbors.

"The 'Unpainted Aristocracy': The Beach Cottages of Old Nags Head," examines a contrasting architectural ensemble in a once remote barrier island community. Here members of a larger regional elite built intentionally unpretentious beach cottages. In the late nineteenth and especially the early twentieth century, they employed local builders to adapt nationally popular shingled and craftsman forms to create a resilient row of summer houses. This community of buildings has withstood storms and defined the summer society of families who have gathered there for more than a century.

In the decades around 1900, other Southern leaders created a much larger and more public ensemble, a nationally understood vocabulary of architecture and memorials that asserted their renewed position in a reunified nation. "'A Strong Force of Ladies': Women, Politics, and Confederate Memorial Associations in Nineteenth-Century Raleigh" explores the strategies of a one city's elite white women, who rendered their narrative of the Lost Cause in lasting and public form despite political turmoil. In "Landmarks of Power: Building a Southern Past, 1885–1915," a broader study of Raleigh and Wilmington shows how women's groups and other Democratic social and political leaders drew upon national ideals—the revival of Colonial architectural models, the raising of memorial statuary, the emphasis on Anglo-Saxon American traditions—to assert sectional reunion on Southern Democratic terms. In this way, they gave symbolic and physical form to a racial, social, and political structure that would endure for more than half a century.

Part IV. Issues in Historic Preservation

In the final section, two brief essays highlight the interplay between national and professional ideals and local and traditional perspectives. "Looking at North Carolina's History through Architecture" stresses the value of commonplace architecture together with unique monuments. This discussion reflects the attention to vernacular architecture and the cultural landscape in the 1970s and 1980s. Yet despite increased scholarly attention, much of this common heritage—so directly affected by broad economic and technological and social change—remains even more endangered now than ever.

"Yuppies, Bubbas, and the Politics of Culture" considers the different value systems that characterize different groups involved in preservation issues. The essay examines "preservation professionals" and their cultural biases. It also returns to the overarching theme of the book—the notion that the practices of building and of preservation operate and can best be understood as a human process, which by its very nature occurs in a locale and a region as well as in a national setting.

WHAT NOW, WHAT NEXT?

What are the current issues facing those who study and hope to preserve our historic architecture? In North Carolina, current developments bode well for pursuing new research directions. The University of North Carolina at Greensboro and the University of North Carolina in Wilmington have established degree-granting programs in historic preservation and public history. Architectural historians in the public and private sectors are exploring a wide range of topics, from intensive studies of individual artisans and architects to the broad mapping of cultural zones. Some are devoting fresh attention and methods to the architecture of the eighteenth, nineteenth, and early twentieth centuries, such as traditional house forms of the coastal plain and the distinctive workmanship of regional artisans. A biographical dictionary of architects and builders in the state is a current collaborative project. A lively topic of current research addresses the architecture from the mid- and late twentieth century—an era when clients, architects, and builders used new architectural ideas to promote progressiveness in a conservative and long-impoverished state.[7] From these and other studies will come fresh understanding and new ideas about how our people and our architecture grew.

NOTES

1. James C. Johnston to Joseph Blount, July 15[?], 1817, Hayes Collection, Southern Historical Collection, University of North Carolina at Chapel Hill.

2. Doug Swaim, ed., *Carolina Dwelling: Towards Preservation of Place: In Celebration of the North Carolina Vernacular Landscape*, (Raleigh: North Carolina State University School of Design Student Publication 26, 1978).

3. Catherine W. Bishir, Charlotte V. Brown, Carl R. Lounsbury, and Ernest H. Wood III, *Architects and Builders in North Carolina: A History of the Practice of Building* (Chapel Hill: University of North Carolina Press, 1990). See also Bishir, *North Carolina Architecture* (Chapel Hill: University of North Carolina Press, 1990); Bishir and Michael T. Southern, *A Guide to the Historic Architecture of Eastern North Carolina* (Chapel Hill: University of North Carolina Press, 1996) and *A Guide to the Historic Architecture of Piedmont North Carolina* (Chapel Hill: University of North Carolina Press, 2003); and Bishir, Southern, and Jennifer F. Martin, *A Guide to the Historic Architecture of Western North Carolina* (Chapel Hill: University of North Carolina Press, 1999). For a list of numerous city and county survey publications see the web site of the North Carolina State Historic Preservation Office (http://www.hpo.dcr.state.nc.us/).

4. Carl R. Lounsbury, acceptance remarks for Founder's Award, Society of Architectural Historians Annual Meeting, 1988, for "'An Elegant and Commodious Building': William Buckland and the Design of the Prince William County Courthouse," *Journal of the Society of Architectural Historians* 46 (September 1987).

5. Thanks to Louis Nelson for his ideas and suggestions, here incorporated, about these themes during a tropical discussion in Barbados in October 2003 and subsequently.

6. See Howard Davis, *The Culture of Building* (New York: Oxford University Press, 1999), for a broad-ranging analysis of changes in building practices and culture, including language.

7. See, for example, M. Ruth Little, "Vernacular Hospitality in the Carolinas: The Tidewater Cottage and the Preacher Room," *Arris* 15 (2004); and Jo Leimenstoll, "Recent Discoveries in the Architectural Woodwork of Mr. Thomas Day" (unpublished paper, Historic Architecture Round Table, Preservation North Carolina, 2004). On the recent past see Claudia R. Brown, "Surveying the Suburbs: Back to the Future?" in Deborah Staton and Rebecca A. Schiffer, eds., *Preserving the Recent Past* (Washington: Historic Preservation Education Foundation, 1995); and Brown and Dan Becker, "Hyperbole in Parabolas: Preserving the Valuable Future of Raleigh's Modernist Visionaries," in *Forum Journal* (Fall 2000). On work in progress see, for example, Jennifer F. Martin, "Edward Jenkins, African American Architect in mid-Twentieth Century Greensboro" (unpublished paper, 2003 annual meeting of Preservation North Carolina); and Claudia R. Brown and Diane E. Lea, "A Bastion of Modernism in the Southern Part of Heaven: William Wurster and the Webbs of Chapel Hill" (unpublished paper, 2005 meeting of the Society of Architectural Historians).

PART I

Building Culture and Practice

One

JACOB W. HOLT
AN AMERICAN BUILDER

Jacob W. Holt, a builder who worked in North Carolina and Virginia in the mid-nineteenth century, is representative of an important group in the development of American architecture. He was one of the many practical builders—carpenters, housewrights, masons, and mechanics—who not only constructed but also shaped the design of much of the nation's architecture.

The study of American architecture has considered mostly the top and bottom layers with far less attention to the vast body of architecture in between or to the men responsible for it. Most architectural histories focus on the procession of elite, high-style buildings and their popular influence and, hence, upon the constellation of major architects and authors of architectural books that disseminated styles. Folk studies, on the other hand, examine the building patterns of the bedrock of traditional culture and thus the habits of craftsmen expressing ancient folkways. The buildings that lie between these two extremes are often dismissed as naive versions of academic models or as dilutions of traditional patterns. In either case, their importance on their own terms is not assessed.

But in fact the vast fabric of American architecture, stretching from elite to folk, contains a broad middle section where stylish and vernacular threads weave a lively pattern of national unity and regional diversity. The meaning of this mid-level architecture, which includes most American buildings, lies

---

"Jacob W. Holt: An American Builder" appeared in *Winterthur Portfolio* 16, no. 1 (Spring 1981): 1–31, and is reprinted by permission of the *Winterthur Portfolio*, Winterthur Museum, Winterthur, Delaware.

FIG. 1.1. *Reedy Rill, 1850s, Warren County, North Carolina. Photograph ca. 1890. (Courtesy of Panthea Twitty; NCDAH)*

in the diverse resolutions of popular and traditional forces and in the accommodation of aesthetic and practical demands. Its energy springs from the tension between continuity and change at work at different rates across the country.[1]

Such architecture was the work principally of practical builders. Trained in the apprentice system as carpenters or masons, these men worked closely with their clients in the unified process of design and construction. They used the models in popular architectural guides but translated them into locally appropriate forms that satisfied people of different regions, social situations, economic levels, and ethnic origins.

The creativity of these builders lay not so much in exploring new concepts as in finding workable syntheses of popular and traditional elements that expressed their communities' accommodation to these forces. In the proficient hands of these artisans, ideas promulgated by popular publications became livable, three-dimensional realities. The builders' design decisions as well as their skill with plane or trowel lay behind the regional variations on national themes that form the great body of mid-level American architecture.

Jacob W. Holt (1811–80) was such a builder. His career spanned the decades from the 1840s to the 1870s and illustrates how a builder worked to accommodate the changing demands of regional custom and current style. Because of his highly identifiable personal idiom (fig. 1.1), the survival of a high proportion of his work, and the continued presence of strong local and family traditions about him in a region little altered by economic growth, his career can be traced in considerable detail. The quantity of his work—as many as twenty buildings documented and about seventy more attributed to him—permits assessment not only of individual structures but also of broader patterns of his development. In his responses to the needs and tastes of his patrons, the possibilities as well as the limitations of local technology, the models of popular pattern books, and the dramatic changes of his period, Holt like thousands of his counterparts created his own synthesis of continuity and change.

HOLT'S CAREER

Jacob Holt was born and grew up in Prince Edward County, Virginia, a moderately prosperous agricultural, tobacco-producing region in the rolling southern piedmont section of the state (fig. 1.2). Remote from port cit-

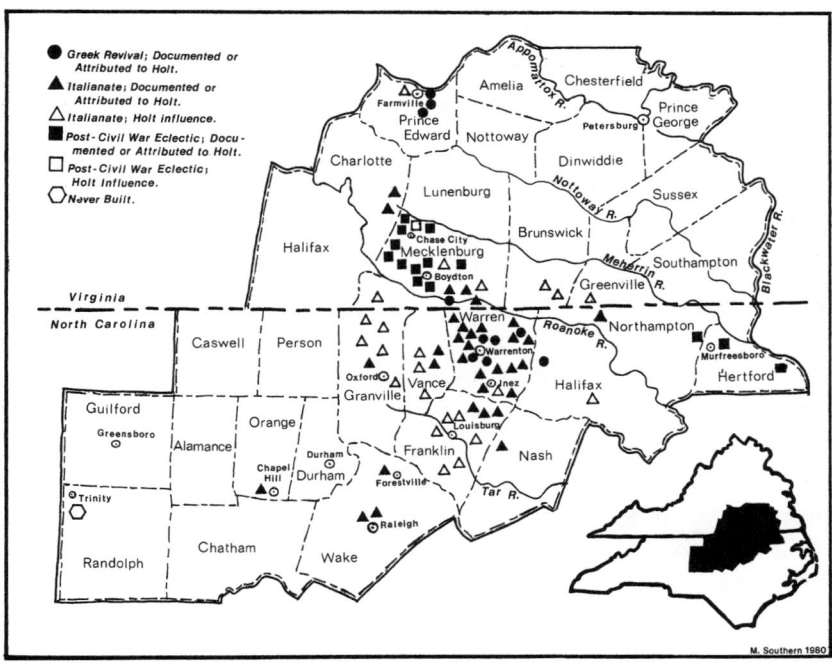

FIG. 1.2. *Distribution of buildings built by and attributed to Jacob W. Holt, as well as those reflecting influence of his work. Map by Michael T. Southern, 1980.*

Jacob W. Holt, An American Builder | 13

ies, the county's economic and political life focused on small trading towns and remained agrarian and conservative.[2]

Holt was the older son of David Holt, a carpenter, and Elizabeth McGehee Holt, daughter of a prominent planter family. At their mother's death in 1821, Jacob, his younger brother Thomas, and his two older sisters were entrusted by their father to the care of their maternal uncle John McGehee. Within three years David Holt died, leaving a poignantly meager estate of carpenter's tools "left at different places" about the community. Jacob and Thomas probably entered into apprenticeships, for this was the customary means of supporting and training orphans. The most likely master for Jacob and possibly Thomas is William A. Howard, a successful carpenter working in Prince Edward and nearby counties, who was the builder of Jeffersonian courthouses, colleges, and other buildings in the 1820s and 1830s.[3]

By his late twenties Jacob Holt had gained a solid place in the community. In 1837 he joined the Baptist church and the next year married sixteen-year-old Aurelia Phillips, also a new Baptist.[4] He began to acquire real estate and slaves and by 1840 commanded the second largest nonagricultural work force in the county—nineteen young freemen and twenty-nine young male slaves. By age thirty Holt had established a way of life that persisted throughout his career: strong family and church ties and his own unusually large and presumably self-sufficient work force.[5] Despite his large shop, little is known of Holt's work in Prince Edward County. There is no tradition of his role in the county's architecture, and comparison with his later work suggests only three houses as his, one of which, Rotherwood, circa 1840, is supported by documentary evidence.[6]

In the early 1840s Holt, his growing family, and his household of black and white workmen joined a throng of Prince Edward County craftsmen who abandoned their native Virginia to move south to Warrenton, North Carolina. Whatever the reason for their apparently abrupt mass departure, these skilled artisans soon gained wide success in their new community and reshaped the architectural character of the town and outlying county.

Warrenton offered much promise to ambitious young builders and cabinetmakers. Although isolated and rural like most of antebellum North Carolina, it had long been a fashionable little town, the trading and political center of Warren County, the wealthiest county in the South's poorest state.[7] The county's close-knit network of affluent planter families dominated a population of slightly more than 4,000 whites and 8,000 black slaves. The plantation system depended heavily upon slave labor and production of tobacco sold in Virginia markets. Mineral-spring spas and a famous racetrack lent panache to the social life of planters and town residents alike, and frequent trips to Petersburg, Richmond, Baltimore, Philadelphia, and New York whetted the gentry's appetite for stylish goods. Warrenton, with about 1,000 people, prided itself on its fine schools, fashionable shops, political leadership, and lively social season. Ambitious lawyers, doctors, and merchants lived alongside planters in the town and supported a surprisingly cosmopolitan collection of teachers, musicians, hotelkeepers, carriage makers, tailors, and artists from northern states and distant lands.[8]

With the coming of the railroad in the late 1830s, a general upswing after recovery from the panic of 1837, and increasing agricultural improvements, Warren County and Warrenton stood in the 1840s at the edge of a period of unprecedented prosperity. For a builder, a glance at the modest and, by 1840, old-fashioned dwellings that lined its streets confirmed a ready market for new and stylish construction. Memoirist Lizzie Wilson Montgomery later recalled:

> In the early forties the town of Warrenton began to improve in business and in numbers; new citizens moved in, and a colony of skilled mechanics and their families from Prince Edward County, Virginia, and adjoining counties, all Baptists, came there to reside. No community ever received a more valuable acquisition than did Warrenton in the settlement of that colony as her citizens. It embraced the callings of architecture, carpentry, brick-laying, lathing and plastering. They were all experienced and capable managers or workers. The individuals, without exception, were religious, sober, honest, truthful, orderly, and industrious. They were all intelligent, well informed, and possessed of sufficient education to meet the demands of their several callings.[9]

By 1845, Holt was at work in Warrenton along with Edward T. Rice and Francis Woodson, brickmasons and plasterers from Prince Edward. In 1849 Jacob's younger brother, Thomas, who had been in Lunenburg County, Virginia, joined him. The two brothers lived in neighboring households, and Thomas took responsibility for supervising some of Jacob's construction projects.[10] Rice and Woodson owned a small number of slaves, but Jacob Holt listed thirty-four male slaves and eighteen white carpenters in his workforce by 1850. His workshop was by far the largest in the building trades in the county and the state. His free employees included thirteen young men from Virginia, who had presumably come with him to Warrenton, and five others from North Carolina.[11] Holt's carpentry shop, sometimes working in association with Woodson and Rice or subcontracting with another mason, undertook the entire process of design and construction, as Holt's several extant contracts show. He assumed responsibility for every detail from cutting and curing the timber and sketching a ground plan to such finishing touches as window hardware or decorative painting and graining. Projects ranged from building a smokehouse for the Episcopal rectory to the construction of an entire plantation complex to the execution of the contract for carpentry for a large public building.[12]

The shop gained a broad practice and growing reputation in Warrenton and beyond. Working for the community's wealthiest families, Holt and his associates produced a series of substantial new buildings, first in a Greek Revival mode and, by the 1850s, in a more eclectic Italianate style. In Warrenton, Holt developed a distinctive architectural idiom that marked his work throughout his career. As many as twenty-seven Warrenton buildings from this period are attributed to Holt's shop through documents, family tradition, or stylistic evidence.[13] In less than a decade the town's small-scale streetscape gave way to the rapid construction of big new buildings, fronted by columned porches that lent sudden elegance and a more generous scale to the dusty old streets.

In the 1850s Holt reached into the county beyond Warrenton and then to more and more distant communities in North Carolina and Virginia (see fig. 1.2). His bold, personalized style appealed to the region's thriving planters and merchants, and his large work force enabled him to compete successfully for low bid on a series of major institutional buildings stimulated by the state's increasing prosperity. As many as twenty buildings in Warren County and about thirty more in eleven counties beyond demonstrate the dramatic expansion of his work in the antebellum period. Perhaps a dozen others exhibit similarities that suggest his influence or possibly the activity of former employees.

By the eve of the Civil War, Holt like many North Carolinians enjoyed unprecedented success. He had established a broad regional business and gained a degree of prosperity. At age forty-nine, he lived with his wife and six children in a towered villa he had built near the center of Warrenton. His oldest son and namesake worked with him, and his reputation as a builder attracted young artisans from distant communities to his shop. The 1860 census listed nineteen young men in his household, all different from those with him a decade earlier, natives of nine North Carolina and Virginia counties.[14]

Holt's brother, Thomas, after a decade in Warrenton, had moved south to Raleigh where he began to style himself "architect." He won first prize for architectural drawing at the 1860 state fair and became chief architect for the Raleigh and Gaston Railroad. His commissions included a massive railroad repair shop and the Peace Institute near the northern end of the city.[15]

Jacob Holt, in contrast to his brother, made no claim to the title "architect." He had called himself "carpenter" in 1850, and to the 1860 census taker he identified himself proudly as "master mechanic." In this role, he bid successfully on several big building projects in the region, enlarging his sphere of activity to Saint John's College in Oxford, Peace Institute in Raleigh, and Trinity College near Asheboro. Following a common builders' custom on major contracts, Holt served as contractor working from an architect's designs. At Saint John's, he took only the carpentry contract, with Hillsborough brickmason John Berry executing the masonry, but at Trinity and Peace he gained the contracts for both carpentry and masonry. In the meantime, he continued to undertake both design and construction on smaller jobs.[16]

Holt's increasing activity across the state won attention in the newspapers. One reporter observed in 1860, "Mr. Holt, the contractor [for Trinity] is one of the first architects in the state. He is a Virginian by birth, but has resided in Warrenton for several years. He has put up many fine residences and public buildings in the eastern part of the state."[17]

For Holt, as for so many others, the Civil War halted business. The Peace project stopped and work on Trinity never began.[18] Several plantation houses stood unfinished. After the war, Warrenton struggled to recover amid a county and region whose plantation economy was irretrievably wrecked. The builder found occasional repairs and modest construction jobs, as an 1868 issue of the Warrenton newspaper reported: "Our friend Jacob Holt, Esq., so well known in North Carolina and Virginia, is busily employed in repairing [Warrenton's Central Hotel]."[19] But the once-wealthy planters straining to retain their property could offer scant patronage to an ambitious builder.

So once again Holt, nearing sixty and with a grown family, moved to a more promising community. In and around the village of Christiansville in neighboring Mecklenburg County, Virginia, activity was stirring amid the ruins of the plantation economy. Two Pennsylvanians, John E. Boyd and George Endly, arrived in 1868, bought land cheaply, and advertised widely for immigrants and investors. People came from the North and established their farms on the plantation land bought at low prices from cash-poor owners. The village grew as new businesses were established. Christiansville, renamed Chase City in 1873, became one of the South's most successful postwar development efforts. Holt quickly recognized that Boyd, Endly, and the stream of energetic and ambitious immigrants would require—and could afford—new buildings. He moved there in 1869 and gained key patronage by erecting big new houses for the two entrepreneurs. More work followed rapidly as he established himself as leading builder for the growing community.[20] His slave work force gone, Holt hired hands as needed, and he adapted his work to reflect the growing ornateness demanded by current taste.

Soon Holt expanded his activity to remodeling and new construction in Boydton, the old Mecklenburg county seat. He erected a handsome new brick church and several dwellings. The local newspaper reported in 1870 that Holt, "master carpenter and genius," was "turning things upside down in Boydton," and continued, "We are satisfied that he can and does do more work than one can hire the labor by the day, and have it executed.... Yes, give us plenty of mechanics, and we will make Boydton and Mecklenburg County look like a new country. See what Mr. Holt and his brawny armed assistants have done for Christiansville." In March 1871, the paper observed, "We learn from Mr. J. W. Holt that he is being offered large quantities of work in the county. We have no idea that Mr. Holt will be able to do half of the carpenter's work that will be needed in the county this year. There is a fine field in the county for other house carpenters. Lands we think must now advance in some sections of the county."[21]

A firm base established, Holt again reached beyond the county for work. In the mid-1870s he undertook a number of houses in and around Murfreesboro, North Carolina, about ninety miles downriver from Chase City. There he erected his last and most floridly finished dwellings, including the David A. Barnes house. Holt's Murfreesboro reputation, however, extended beyond the houses he built. In 1877 one "J. P. Phillips, Builder," announced: "Having served my apprenticeship under the well-known Contractor and Builder, J. W. Holt, Esq., I hereby notify the [public] that I am prepared to execute all kinds of BUILDING, REPAIRING, &c., in the best and most modern styles."[22]

Holt died September 21, 1880, at age sixty-nine. His eldest son, Jacob Whitington Holt, continued in the trade in Petersburg. Another son, William Howard Kenneth Holt, practiced building in North Carolina and Virginia. At least three grandchildren also followed careers in building, making four generations of builders in the family.[23]

CONTINUITY AMID CHANGE

Holt's career spanned a period of tremendous social, technological, and economic change. He was part of a generation that grew up in an agrarian, still largely traditional, and, in the South, slave-dependent culture, but that survived—even thrived—in the late nineteenth century's increasingly urban and industrialized culture and a new economic and labor system.

For builders the period brought dramatic developments in the practice of building and in the character of popular styles. Rapid developments in building technology—the invention of the circular saw, the proliferation of sash and blind factories producing vast quantities of ready-made decoration, and the spread of the balloon frame—introduced new flexibility of form and decoration as well as new roles for the builder. Architectural publications shifted not only from classicism to eclecticism but also from builders' guides to the house pattern books with models for complete buildings and their settings. Growing separation of the processes of design and construction came with the emerging distinction between the professional architect and the contractor.

Holt's generation of builders had to adapt to all these changes and found different ways of surviving. Some clung to old ways and avoided the mainstream. Others, such as Holt's younger brother, Thomas, dismissed their traditional identity as carpenters or builders to lay claim to the title "architect," and, jettisoning all vestiges of earlier customs, plunged into the mainstream of new styles and practices.

Jacob Holt charted his own course through this turbulent transitional era, combining old and new elements to create for himself a workable synthesis. His long career exemplifies the persistence of traditional practices into the middle and late years of the nineteenth century, of antebellum culture into the postwar era, and of individualization into a period of growing standardization. He was no hidebound reactionary but a man of practical good sense who knew his market and his own capabilities. He combined reliance upon accustomed techniques with flexibility and accommodation to new ways. He began in a slave-dependent economy and relied upon slave labor for much of his career but quickly adapted to the labor situation of the postwar economy. He established himself as principal builder for one community yet left it in pursuit of new patronage when times changed. He undertook the entire process of design and construction in traditional fashion, but he bid successfully as contractor for other architects on major projects as well.

Just as his career reflected his resilience in the face of changing situations, so Holt's personal architectural idiom sprang from his resolutions of the disparate demands of his time and place. For builders the tension between traditional and popular forces found expression in the tenacity of traditional regional habits and the attraction of changing architectural fashions. Holt, like so many others, responded to both. He knew the architectural publications of his day, but he also knew his community. He used popular models to create buildings peculiarly suited to—and hence expressive of—his regional clientele. Although his work was more novel and fashionable than anything else in his vicinity, in a broader context it was nevertheless conservative. He executed popular motifs with boldness and vigor but nearly always within the framework of the vernacular artisan.

Holt's design process involved several components: use of popular publications, vernacular reliance on a conservative form and plan, the nature of his shop operation, and the character of his clientele.

The impact of popular architectural publications is obvious throughout

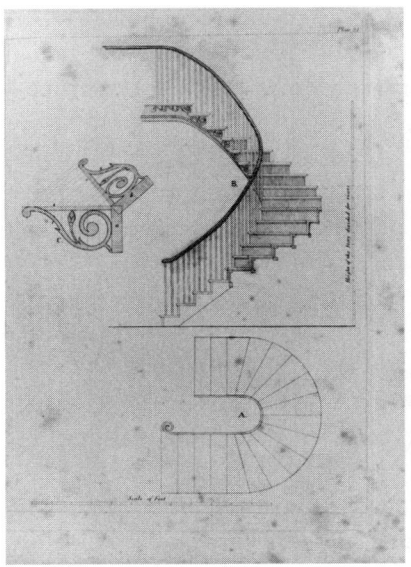 

FIG. 1.3. *Design for stair, Owen Biddle, Young Carpenter's Assistant (1805, pl. 31). (Courtesy of The Winterthur Library: Printed Book and Periodical Collection)*

FIG. 1.4. *Stair, Rotherwood, ca. 1840, Prince Edward County, Virginia. Attributed to Jacob W. Holt. Photograph by Catherine W. Bishir, 1978.* (NCDAH)

Holt's forty years of building. Like builders nearly everywhere, he relied on these volumes to keep his work current and appealing to the tastes of his wealthy patrons. He employed a sequence of widely circulated books that are credited with shaping the nation's architectural development.

Holt's earliest work reflected the influence of Owen Biddle's *Young Carpenter's Assistant* (1805).[24] He copied Biddle's restrained Federal style molding, foliated stair brackets, and design for stairs (figs. 1.3–1.5). In Prince Edward and in the imposing house of William Eaton in Warrenton (figs. 1.6, 1.7) he combined Biddle's Federal motifs with Asher Benjamin's Grecian designs which appeared in the widely circulated *Practical House Carpenter*, first published in 1830.[25]

In the 1840s Holt moved to a robust simplification of Benjamin's Grecian taste, executing Benjamin's motifs in a highly plastic, three-dimensional form. Holt built big, boxy houses fronted with broad porches whose columns and plain entablatures suggest Benjamin's 1835 economical hybrid Tuscan-Doric order of *The Practice of Architecture* (figs. 1.8, 1.9).[26] He emphasized the cubic forms of his buildings with broad, exaggerated linear strokes—wide water tables, heavy corner pilasters, and a plain frieze beneath the roofline. His *in antis* entrances reflected Minard Lafever's *The*

FIG. 1.5. *Rotherwood. Photograph by Catherine W. Bishir, 1978.* (NCDAH)

FIG. 1.6. *William Eaton House, ca. 1843, Warrenton, North Carolina. Carpentry attributed to Jacob W. Holt. Photograph by JoAnn Sieburg-Baker, 1976.* (NCDAH)

FIG. 1.7. *Stair hall, William Eaton House. Attributed to Jacob W. Holt. Photograph by JoAnn Sieburg-Baker, 1975.* (NCDAH)

Young Builder's General Instructor (figs. 1.10, 1.11).[27] The generous interiors boasted heavy woodwork typical of Greek Revival designs. Burly, Doric columned mantels reinterpreted Benjamin's models (figs. 1.12, 1.13). Also following Benjamin's example, Holt used Grecian key moldings at unexpected spots inside and out but not the floral decorativeness found in Lafever's or Benjamin's later anthemions and acanthus.[28] The large, boldly Grecian houses (fig. 1.14) rose rapidly throughout Warrenton and in the nearby countryside. Unified in their repetitive form and detail, no two were alike, as the builder played a series of recombinations on a theme.

In the early 1850s Holt introduced a new note, replacing the simple classicism of Benjamin's models with the more ornate and eclectic vocabulary taken from William Ranlett's *The Architect* (fig. 1.15) and possibly A. J. Downing's *Cottage Residences*.[29] He extracted from Ranlett's handsome plates of villas and cottages a series of brackets to punctuate the broad eaves of his houses, to clump in miniature at the caps of corner pilasters and porch posts, or to march up the raking cornices of temple-form public buildings. He filled his large rectangular windows with round, ogee, or lancet paired arches and enriched entrances with pinwheel and scallop motifs

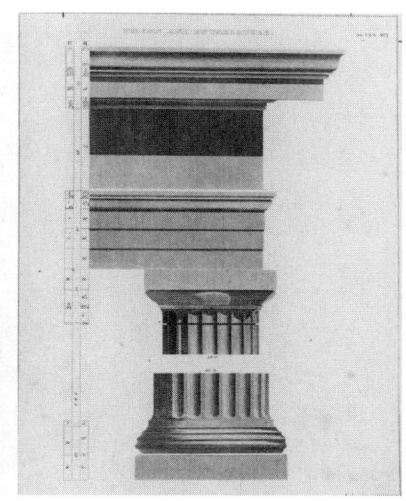

FIG. 1.8 (ABOVE LEFT). *Porch and entrance, Somerville House, ca. 1850, Warrenton. Attributed to Jacob W. Holt. Photograph by JoAnn Sieberg-Baker, 1976.* (NCDAH)

FIG. 1.9 (ABOVE RIGHT). *Design for column and entablature, Asher Benjamin,* The Practice of Architecture *(1833). (Courtesy of The Winterthur Library: Printed Book and Periodical Collection)*

FIG. 1.10. *Design for a front door, Minard Lafever,* The Young Builder's General Instructor *(1829). (Courtesy of the Thomas Lamb Collection, Avery Architectural and Fine Arts Library, Columbia University in the City of New York)*

FIG. 1.11. *Entrance, T. E. Wilson House, ca. 1850, Warrenton. Attributed to Jacob W. Holt. Photograph by JoAnn Sieburg-Baker, 1975.* (NCDAH)

FIG. 1.12. *Mantel, Reedy Rill, ca. 1850, Warren County. Attributed to Jacob W. Holt. Photograph by JoAnn Sieburg-Baker, 1978.* (NCDAH)

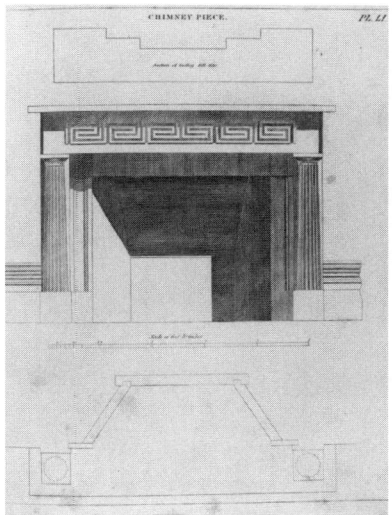

FIG. 1.13. *Design for chimney piece, Asher Benjamin,* The Practical House Carpenter *(1830, 1850). (Courtesy of The Winterthur Library: Printed Book and Periodical Collection)*

FIG. 1.14. *Somerville House, ca. 1850, Warrenton. Attributed to Jacob W. Holt. Photograph by JoAnn Sieburg-Baker, 1975.* (NCDAH)

(fig. 1.16). Instead of the Doric simplicity of his columned porches, he created luxuriant trellises of swags, pendants, arches, and brackets. He replaced his Doric mantels with an eclectic Ranlett model (fig. 1.17), and he lavished a series of Gothic trefoil and quatrefoil motifs on mantels, panels, and stair newels. He reshaped door and window moldings and gave arched heads to the panels of his doors (fig. 1.18). Sometimes handled with restraint as at

FIG. 1.15. *Exterior details accompanying design 20, William Ranlett,* The Architect *(1849), vol. 1, pl. 57. (Courtesy of The Winterthur Library: Printed Book and Periodical Collection)*

FIG. 1.16. *Details accompanying design 18, Ranlett,* The Architect, *vol. 1, pl. 52. (Courtesy of The Winterthur Library: Printed Book and Periodical Collection)*

FIG. 1.17. *Mantel, Engleside, John White House, ca. 1850, Warrenton. Attributed to Jacob W. Holt. Photograph by JoAnn Sieburg-Baker, 1975.* (NCDAH)

FIG. 1.18. *Entrance, Vine Hill, 1856, Franklin County, North Carolina. Jacob W. Holt, builder. Photograph by JoAnn Sieburg-Baker, 1976.* (NCDAH)

FIG. 1.19. *Engleside, John White House, Warrenton. Attributed to Jacob W. Holt. Photograph ca. 1876. Houses of the Holt school frequently had upper porch balustrades, but most have been lost.* (NCDAH)

FIG. 1.20. *Cherry Hill, 1859, Warren County. John A. Waddell, builder, shop or school of Jacob W. Holt. Photograph by Greer Suttlemyre, 1974.* (NCDAH)

Engleside in Warrenton (fig. 1.19) or at the more full-blown Cherry Hill (fig. 1.20), sometimes piled on extravagantly at every possible spot as at Reedy Rill (fig. 1.1), Holt's new collection of details when applied to his boldly outlined cube of a house created an eclectic and obviously modish idiom unique in the region.

Although at first straitened by economy, during the postwar period Holt continued the use of many of the 1850s elements. His penchant for incorporating new motifs kept his work current, and his buildings grew increasingly ornate in the 1870s. He took (postwar) motifs from various sources. He treated the roofline of his houses with a raised central gable, following the ubiquitous late nineteenth-century roofline feature seen in Ranlett's villas and in Downing's cottages. He adorned the gable with a cluster of sawn decorations (figs. 1.21, 1.22). Here and along raking cornices and at the brackets of porches, Holt introduced a tightly coiled spiral motif that he probably adapted from plates in new pattern books by A. J. Bicknell (fig. 1.23). He took from Ranlett's details an elongated quatrefoil to adorn porch brackets or compose a gallery balustrade. By his last work in the 1870s (figs. 1.24, 1.25) he had accumulated a wealth of wooden decoration to apply to his accustomed, firmly outlined cubic building form. The energetic design and copiousness of the brackets, coils, quatrefoils, faceted bosses, polygons, lattices, arches, and pendants expressed vividly the ornateness of the era.

FIG. 1.21. *Shadow Lawn, ca. 1869, Chase City, Virginia. Jacob W. Holt, builder. Photograph by Catherine W. Bishir, 1977.* (NCDAH)

FIG. 1.22. *House, 1870s, Boydton, Virginia. Attributed to Jacob W. Holt. Photograph by Catherine W. Bishir, 1977.* (NCDAH)

Holt's sequence of pattern-book motifs from the late Federal to the mid-Victorian era is precisely what the peruser of nineteenth-century architectural books might expect from a builder of his period. Yet comparison of the published plates with Holt's actual buildings shows immediately that these models were only one of many factors Holt considered in creating his architectural idiom.

FIG. 1.23. *Burwell House, 1870s, near Chase City, Virginia. Attributed to Jacob W. Holt. Photograph by Catherine W. Bishir, 1977.* (NCDAH)

FIG. 1.24. *David A. Barnes House, 1875, Murfreesboro, North Carolina. Jacob W. Holt, builder. Photograph ca. 1880.* (Courtesy of Frank and Margaret Stephenson; NCDAH)

FIG. 1.25. *Vinson House, 1870s, Murfreesboro. Attributed to Jacob W. Holt and his apprentice, J. P. Phillips. Photograph ca. 1890. (Courtesy of Frank Stephenson;* NCDAH)

As significant as what books he used is how he used them. He handled the entire sequence of publications in the conservative fashion established by the early builders' guides, thus working within the framework of the vernacular builder.

Holt began work with traditional builders' guides. Like their predecessors, Biddle, Lafever, and Benjamin aimed their books at the provincial builder who would take from their pages correct techniques for framing structures or for designing classical orders, as well as ideas for mantels, stairs, moldings, and the like. Seldom did these books present elevations or ground plans; they focused primarily on the presentation of details for application to various compositions. In the 1840s and 1850s, however, architectural propagandists like A. J. Downing, Calvert Vaux, Samuel Sloan, and William Ranlett redirected architectural publications. Their house pattern books, unlike the earlier builders' guides, promoted entire compositions of picturesque buildings with appropriate landscaping schemes, painting examples, and even furnishings for their users to emulate in toto with the object of improving the entire lifestyle of the prospective resident. Details like mantels, windows, brackets, and panels appeared to insure their proper execution as part of the exemplary picturesque whole.[30]

Holt, however, used the new pattern books not as their authors intended, nor perhaps as architectural historians depending on these volumes might assume, but selectively, as he had used the builders' guides. Rather than reproducing for his clients the glamorous villas of the plates, he chose a collection of appealing details, such as mantels, pinwheels, brackets, arches, trefoils, and the like, that he applied enthusiastically and repeatedly to his accustomed house form without substantially disturbing the basics.

Despite the changing character of detail, Holt's buildings remained essentially the same from the 1840s through the 1870s. The most extravagant application of decorative veneer never obscures the inherent conservatism of his work. The boxy three-dimensional double-pile form of the ornate 1875 Barnes House (fig. 1.26) is essentially identical to the Greek Revival Somerville House of 1850 (fig. 1.27) and the Italianate Vine Hill of 1856 (fig. 1.28).

Thus we can look through the fashionable veil to see Holt operating as a vernacular builder. Holt's approach embodied many characteristics considered to define the "folk" or vernacular artisan, whether furniture maker or builder. Folklorist Henry Glassie points out that the folk artisan, consciously or unconsciously, extracts from his tradition a few basic forms that are old at the time of his use and different from those promoted by popular culture. Working in his tradition he defines for himself a minimal concept of the essentials of the object and arrives at "a small set of rules that define the limits within which he can modify the concept according to his taste and talent and the taste and pocketbook of his clientele."[31] Within the concept thus defined the artisan can work freely, varying nonessential details as he chooses.

Typically the folk artisan responds to novelty or changing ideas by breaking down the new concept and translating it into terms compatible with the old. Usually this means that the artisan keeps the accustomed basic form and updates only the most obvious elements and those that are most easily changed.[32] The result is a composite of new and old, "a novel and synthetic idea ... a compromise of fashionable and unfashionable ideas." The fundamental rules of folk art—"the dominance of form and the desire for repetition"—rather than academic models govern the folk artisan.[33] However convoluted it may become, the ornament is characterized by symmetry and repetition; it never obscures and, in fact, emphasizes the basic form.

Holt gleaned from his tradition a "small set of rules" that defined his work. He relied on basic forms and plans that were old when he adopted them, and he continued them throughout his work without changing or obscuring them behind the increasingly abundant ornament. He took as his basic model the shallow-roofed, cubic house form, usually three bays wide and two deep, with a Georgian (double-pile) plan—a central hall with two rooms on either side. By the mid-nineteenth century this plan, origi-

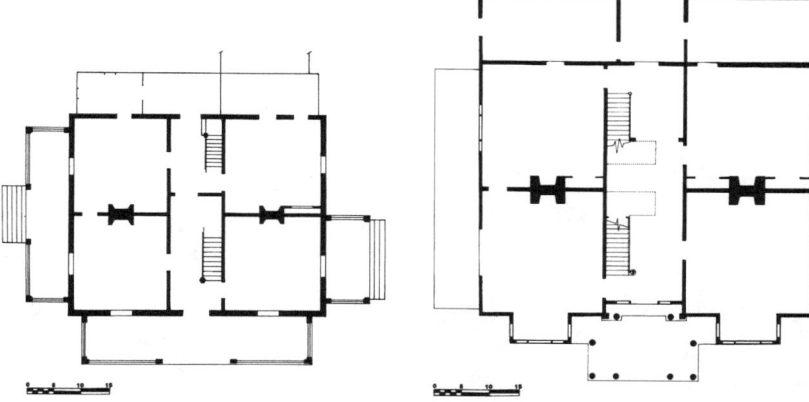

FIG. 1.26. *Ground plan, David A. Barnes House, 1875, Murfreesboro. Drawing by Margaret Stephenson, 1979.*

FIG. 1.27. *Ground plan, Somerville House, ca. 1850, Warrenton. Drawing by Carl R. Lounsbury, 1979.*

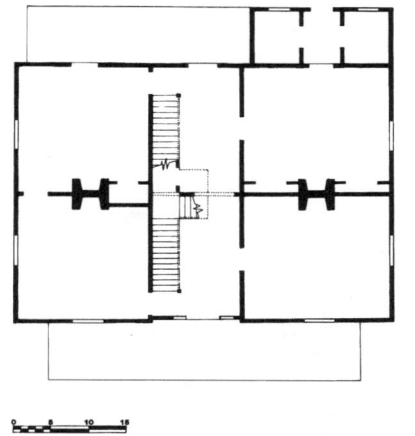

FIG. 1.28. *Ground plan, Vine Hill, 1856, Franklin County. Drawing by Carl R. Lounsbury, 1979.*

nally introduced in the eighteenth century in fashionable English houses, had supplanted the standard two-room vernacular house for middle- and upper-middle-class people in northeastern North Carolina and southern Virginia.[34] Well over half of Holt's houses follow this plan.

Holt used as well a few variations that also had been introduced to the region in fashionable eighteenth-century buildings but were antiquated by the mid-nineteenth century. He sometimes reduced the double pile to a single-room depth (the common I-house form), especially in less costly houses or in additions to existing dwellings (fig. 1.29). Occasionally he used a side-hall plan or a two-story central cross-hall block flanked by one-story wings—forms seen in modish Virginia and North Carolina houses of the eighteenth and early nineteenth centuries.[35] In all his public buildings (one

FIG. 1.29. *Pool Rock, early nineteenth century and 1850s, Vance County, North Carolina. Attributed to Jacob W. Holt. This is one of numerous examples of Holt's additions to existing dwellings. Photograph by Michael T. Southern, 1978.* (NCDAH)

FIG. 1.30. *Warren County Courthouse, 1853-57, Warrenton. Jacob W. Holt, builder, with brickmasons Francis Woodson and Edward Rice. Photograph ca. 1890-1900, from Lizzie Wilson Montgomery,* Sketches of Old Warrenton *(1924).* (NCDAH)

courthouse and five churches), Holt followed the simple rectangular temple form that had dominated Virginia and North Carolina public architecture since Jefferson introduced it in 1785 (figs. 1.30–1.32).

When Holt began building in the 1840s, these plans, although conservative, were still within the current Greek Revival vocabulary. However, his retention of the eighteenth-century plans through the 1850s, 1860s, and 1870s became increasingly conservative as the popular pattern books of the mid-century promulgated increasingly complex forms. Holt had extracted the set of rules that defined for him and his clients what the plan and form

FIG. 1.31. *Warrenton Presbyterian Church, 1855, Warrenton. Attributed to Jacob W. Holt, probably with brickmasons Francis Woodson and Edward Rice. Photograph by JoAnn Sieburg-Baker, 1975.* (NCDAH)

FIG. 1.32. *Boydton Methodist Episcopal Church, 1871, Boydton, Virginia. Jacob W. Holt, builder. Photograph by Catherine W. Bishir, 1977.* (NCDAH)

FIG. 1.33. *Archibald Taylor House, ca. 1857, Franklin County, North Carolina. Attributed to Jacob W. Holt. Photograph by Michael T. Southern, 1975.* (NCDAH)

FIG. 1.34. *Rear and side view, Archibald Taylor House. Photograph by JoAnn Sieburg-Baker, 1976.* (NCDAH)

of a house or public building should be, and he held to these rules with conservative tenacity. Within this framework, Holt was indeed free to work eclectically to suit the taste, comfort, and pocketbook of his client in addition to his own desires.

Respecting the budget of his client, Holt unabashedly adapted scale and ornamentation to economic requirements. On occasion he built plain, even old-fashioned houses—one for his own household, another for a farming family, and another for an associate, Warrenton cabinetmaker Samuel N. Mills, who had come with Holt and the other artisans from Prince Edward County. In 1846, Holt agreed to build for Warrenton carriage maker Thomas Burrows a plain frame house 28 by 18 feet, with only two rooms per floor. Burrows would pay the cost of $386.95 mainly in goods—including a horse, wagon, and equipment—and agreed to make a new carriage for Holt.[36] These inexpensive structures resembled their vernacular contemporaries more than they did Holt's distinctive and stylish work for the local elite. At the same time Holt applied to more pretentious buildings whatever degree of luxury properly announced the affluence of the client without straining his purse. He frankly concentrated costly decoration on the main facade (fig. 1.33) and front rooms where it would be most visible, restricting the finish of rear facade (fig. 1.34) and secondary rooms to cheaper components. Even in principal rooms, he used skillful woodgraining and marbleizing to enrich native pine doors, mantels, stairs, and sometimes plastered walls at far less cost than fine woods or marble (fig. 1.35).[37]

To accommodate the comfort and convenience of his patron, Holt improved the standard plan without making fundamental changes. Enhancing the air circulation already permitted by the central-hall plan, he partitioned the hall midway by adding a doorway filled with folding doors with movable louvers.[38] These could be adjusted to allow any degree of air flow and privacy. The two halls thus created each contained a stair, separating activity in the front and rear portions of the house so that guests, residents, children, and servants could move freely within the house (figs. 1.35, 1.36; see also figs. 1.26–1.28). He also inserted a series of closets, presses and cupboards flanking the fireplaces, providing unusually capacious storage space for the period. Often small service and storage rooms flanked an open rear porch, which is similar to regional vernacular use of shed rooms flanking rear central porches.[39]

All of Holt's variations of adjustable ornamentation, decorative painting, and functional improvements remained within the limits of the basic plan, from which in his work for his clients Holt never strayed, despite his familiarity with novel and often admirably functional pattern-book models. As with any vernacular artisan, the question arises: who defined the limitations, the artisan or the patron?[40] For Holt, it appears that both the practical requirements of his shop and the character of his clientele were involved.

Building technology obviously had an impact on Holt's design. Repetition of form and detail were singularly compatible with the operation of his prolific shop. Whether Holt expanded his operation so rapidly and undertook projects miles and miles apart because he had developed a standardized style or whether his method of production necessitated adopting a repetitive idiom is unclear. Certainly the two coincided conveniently.

Holt incorporated both traditional and innovative methods. Like his contemporaries, he relied on his own and on his clients' slave labor until the end of the Civil War.[41] He utilized traditional labor-intensive construction techniques, including heavy timber framing. (This old technique persisted in substantial construction until the late nineteenth century in many areas, notwithstanding the invention of the faster balloon frame in 1833, probably because of its obvious sturdiness, workers' familiarity with it, and the easier access to labor than to machinery.) The framing method, of course, restricted the complexity of Holt's building forms to those that could be framed with heavy timbers and thus dictated the composition of a cubical format.

In contrast with this conservative technology was Holt's somewhat unusual introduction of standardized, perhaps machine-made or mass-produced, decorative motifs long before his community boasted a sash and blind factory.[42] Little is known for certain about the technology of his production, but Mrs. Montgomery recalled that on the lot behind his Warrenton house "was located an old lumbering shop, in which the materials for the handsome homes and stores of the town and county were kept. The shaving pile outside of the building was the favorite place for the school boys of the town to play 'circus' and other games. On the lot was also the kiln, used by Mr. Holt for drying the lumber needed in his business. Large quantities of brick were burnt there."[43] Her description, plus the recurrence of the same details in building after building, and the standard itemization and pricing of components of woodwork in his contracts—bracket cornice by the foot, front doors at a set rate, various grades of mantels, cupboards, pilasters, windows, and so on—suggest that Holt employed an early system of mass producing the millwork required to complete the many buildings under way at any one time. That he did so with elements of his own idiosyncratic design represents an intermediate stage in building technology.

To produce items expediently, Holt typically adapted pattern-book motifs to forms that could be easily reproduced by his shop. For example, the paired arched windows and doorways of Ranlett's designs required arched openings far more difficult and unfamiliar than the customary rectangular openings. Holt simply placed Ranlett's forms within a rectangular frame and created a composite that was adequately stylish and far easier to execute. His style of building therefore accommodated, and indeed exploited, this standardization in its design. Thus, the vernacular penchant for repetition of ornament paralleled the demands of technological advance.

Not only the production of quantities of woodwork but also his reliance on a few basic plans enabled Holt to erect many buildings concurrently at widely separated sites. With many projects under way at a time in the late 1850s, Holt deployed workmen to several sites and entrusted their direction to his most experienced associates, including his brother, Thomas, and two employees from Prince Edward County, John A. Waddell and John C. McCraw. With buildings following familiar formulae in plan and detail and using standard components presumably sent from the Warrenton shop, workmen could construct buildings more quickly and reliably, and with less supervision, than if new decisions had to be made every day.

Beyond the practical requirements of shop technology, however, there lies the role of the taste of the client in the builder's designs. Was it merely

FIG. 1.35. *Stair hall, Archibald Taylor House, ca. 1857. Photograph by JoAnn Sieburg-Baker 1976. The plastered walls were painted to resemble blocks of ochre, slate blue, and ivory marble. Pieces of a painted trompe l'oeil frame once encircling a portrait survived on the soffit of the stair. Note the rear stair.* (NCDAH)

FIG. 1.36. *Stair hall, Somerville House, ca. 1850, Warrenton. Attributed to Jacob W. Holt. Photograph by JoAnn Sieburg-Baker, 1975.* (NCDAH)

FIG. 1.37. *Jacob W. Holt House, ca. 1855-56, Warrenton. Jacob W. Holt, builder. Photograph ca. 1900.* (NCDAH)

FIG. 1.38. *"A Cottage in the Italian, or Tuscan Style," Andrew Jackson Downing,* Cottage Residences *(1842), fig. 72.* (Courtesy of The Winterthur Library: Printed Book and Periodical Collection)

the convenience of standardization in construction or perhaps Holt's lack of sophistication that restricted his response to new ideas to a traditional framework? Or did the conservatism lie within his clientele? As one specialist puts the question: "Did the ... [craftsman] produce only what pleased himself or did he work to please his neighbors and customers?"[44]

Although the question of the artisan's tastes versus those of his patrons must nearly always remain a mystery, Holt provided a vital clue in the design of his own house in Warrenton, erected in the mid-1850s (fig. 1.37).[45]

Here in a vigorously executed little wooden villa, he demonstrated unmistakably his full comprehension of the meaning of Downing's and Ranlett's volumes. Although for his clients' dwellings he took only a collection of details from these books, for his own house Holt replicated not merely the decoration or even the facade but the boldly three-dimensional massing of Downing's "Cottage in the Italian, or Tuscan Style" (fig. 1.38). Holt's forceful statement of his sophistication as a builder, and presumably of his willingness to venture into the complexities of current pattern books, was far different from his work for his patrons or, for that matter, anything else in the region.[46]

Yet despite its obvious claim to the latest fashion, the little villa remained an anomaly. There is no evidence that Holt's vivid billboard of his abilities whetted the appetites of the community for novel villas or cottages from Downing or any other volume. Nowhere in the region did the builder find a patron venturesome enough to follow his lead, to break free from the box, and to explore the novel offerings of the pattern books' forms and plans.

Community reaction to Holt's villa is suggested by Mrs. Montgomery's recollection: "On the south on the corner Jacob Holt built . . . [an] unusually shaped house for that time, as people knew little else than a square house. This was built for his own use, and he resided there as long as he remained in Warrenton."[47] Her description, together with the dramatic contrast between Holt's own house and his work for his patrons, suggest that perhaps he was more attuned to popular innovations than were those for whom he built. It was, then, not Holt's lack of understanding or appreciation of new ideas that kept his work within a vernacular framework but rather his keen understanding of his clients.

The piedmont plantation gentry were, for all their travels to northern cities and appetites for the latest in fashionable luxuries, at core inherently conservative. Wedded to an entrenched, slave-based agrarian economic system that was threatened by political or ideological change, accustomed to political hegemony, and established among the intricate family connections and elite social position of a provincial aristocracy, the gentry as a class naturally avoided any challenge that might fundamentally change their way of life.

The personal style Holt developed for these patrons in the antebellum period struck a deep and responsive chord, as expressed in their rapid acceptance of his work. Families who needed a new house contracted with him, as did many who wanted to update an older house in his distinctive mode. In Warrentown, construction of the courthouse (see fig. 1.30), drastic remodeling of the modest Episcopal church (fig. 1.39, 1.40), and construction of a new Presbyterian church (see fig. 1.31) placed his stamp on public as well as private structures. Holt's exaggerated trim set off his buildings as unmistakably new, far more "modern" than the conservative, plain architecture that dominated the region; yet the familiar form and plan implied no substantial departure from ingrained custom.

Local understanding of "old" and "new" in the mid-nineteenth century is suggested by contemporary or later descriptions, including Mrs. Montgomery's early-twentieth-century recollections of Warrenton, along with those of her friend Mrs. Pendleton. Consistently they labeled the modest dormered dwellings of the eighteenth and early nineteenth centuries "old fashioned" and in fact remarked that Holt's plainer buildings for modest residents looked "old fashioned" considering their 1840s construction dates. The Greek Revival buildings, on the other hand, they deemed "fine" and "handsome." John White's bold Italianate house of 1850–52 was described by Mrs. Montgomery as late as 1910 as a "large, modern house." In 1870 the *Mecklenburg Herald* praised Holt's outstanding "architectural taste" as well as his "faithfulness to comply with his contracts." And in 1877, Holt's former apprentice declared that his training with Holt had enabled him to build in the "best and most modern styles." Clearly for Holt's patrons his work was "modern" indeed.[48]

Both the design and the repetitiveness of Holt's work enhanced rather than detracted from his appeal. The builder's authorship far more than the personal taste of the owner was apparent in his buildings. Clusters of Holt-built houses indicate that one member of a family or neighborhood after another sought his services. Several contracts even refer to the finish or components of a nearby Holt house to be emulated in the new construction—a stair, for example, to be "like Mr. Williams' rear one" or the finish to be "like Col. W. R. Baskervilles or not inferior."[49] The homogeneity of scale, form, and even detail affirmed the basic unity and shared viewpoint of Holt's clients, with only minor differences suggesting individuality.

For Holt, as for most of his counterparts, conclusions about his design decisions, pattern-book sources, and relations with his patrons come mostly from circumstantial and stylistic evidence. Seldom do documents explicitly state the builder's processes; the buildings remain the principal record. The fullest firsthand confirmation of many aspects of Holt's approach is found in the Baskerville family papers.[50]

The earliest work Holt did for the Mecklenburg County, Virginia, family was the 1855–56 remodeling of a house (now destroyed) for planter William Rust Baskerville. For the alteration of a gabled dwelling of about 1825 into a decorated three-part villa, the builder provided a ground plan to show what was to be done—the sketch is the only carefully detailed ground plan of Holt's known to survive (fig. 1.41). He accompanied it with a contract listing work to be done and materials needed, and together the client and the builder worked out payment in the exchange of provisions and labor for the work.[51]

FIG. 1.39. *Emmanuel Episcopal Church, 1827 and 1854–58, Warrenton. Photograph pre-1906. Remodeling by Jacob W. Holt included the tower, front facade, and probably the side brackets.* (NCDAH)

FIG. 1.40. *"A Village Church," Samuel Sloan,* The Model Architect *(1852). (Courtesy of The Winterthur Library: Printed Book and Periodical Collection)*

FIG. 1.41. *Ground plan for Waverly, Mecklenburg County, Virginia, drawn by Jacob W. Holt. Baskerville Papers, courtesy of William Baskerville. (The Baskerville Papers are now in the Virginia Historical Society, Richmond, Virginia.)*

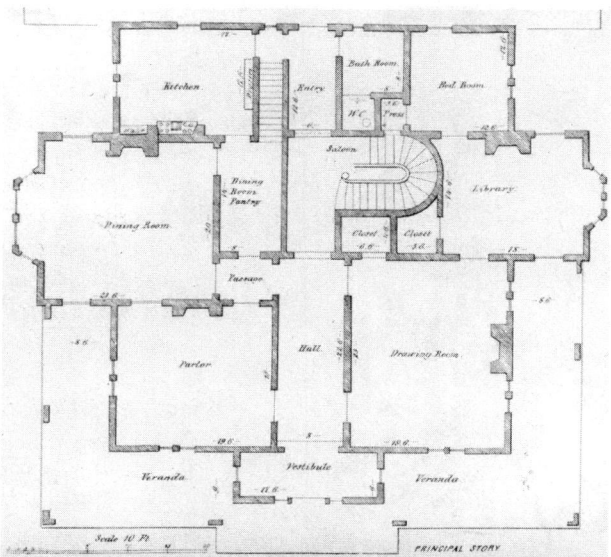

FIG. 1.42. *Ground plan for a villa, design 31, William Ranlett,* The Architect *(1849), vol. 2, pl. 20. (Courtesy of The Winterthur Library: Printed Book and Periodical Collection)*

Baskerville's satisfaction with his newly fashionable house evidently stimulated his son, Dr. Robert D. Baskerville, to engage Holt in 1857 to erect a grand new mansion. Eureka was probably Holt's most elaborate residence, and the documents surviving from its construction provide the most complete accounting of his work. Here he and his wealthy client conferred together to produce a highly original composition.

The initial contract for Eureka set forth clearly the multiplicity of influences that shaped its design and suggested the creative interaction between artisan and patron:

> A Bill for Dweling House to be built [for] Dr. R. D. Baskerville of Mecklenburg County Va. agreeable to the following specifications and to be built by Design 31st plate 19th Volume 2nd Ranlets Architect (Except) in length of Veranda which is to be 40 ft long and not to extend on the ends & to have in the rear of the Building a piazza 8 by 32 feet in place of kitchen Bedrooms &c as described on Ground plan drawn by J. W. Holt.... The style and finish of the work is to be like Col. W. R. Baskervilles or not inferior....

FIG. 1.43. *"Italian Villa," design 31, Ranlett,* The Architect, *vol. 2, pl. 19. (Courtesy of The Winterthur Library: Printed Book and Periodical Collection)*

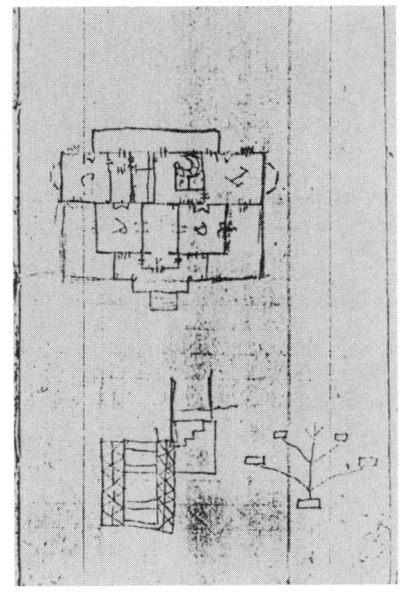

FIG. 1.44. *Sketch of ground plan for Eureka, Baskerville Papers. Drawn by Jacob W. Holt or Robert D. Baskerville in Baskerville's personal notebook. Baskerville Papers, courtesy of William Baskerville. (The Baskerville Papers are now in the Virginia Historical Society, Richmond, Virginia.) The letters refer to rooms as shown in the Ranlett plan (fig. 1.42): parlor, dining or drawing room, library, chamber. The small treelike sketch at lower right shows an arrangement for the house and its outbuildings.*

Jacob W. Holt, An American Builder

J. W. Holt on his part agrees to execute in a good and workmanlike manner the aforesaid Building and defray every expense necessary to completion of the work and to have the building finished by about the 15th of August 1858. Dr. R. D. Baskerville on his part agrees to pay the above mentioned sum of $4885.[52]

The contract cited the pattern-book model but acknowledged functional adjustments to suit the client. The role of the builder in creating the final design and undertaking the entire construction process was clear.

The complex floor plan of Ranlett's "Italian Villa" (fig. 1.42), as much as the elevations (fig. 1.43) and the details, served as model for Eureka. The cross form with grand rear saloon and swirling stair offered a dramatic expansion on the standard central-hall plan. Holt, as the contract specified and his ground plan illustrates, modified the cross plan to a T (fig. 1.44) and altered the rear room arrangement. He placed the kitchen in a separate structure (following standard southern usage) but retained the crucial aspects of Ranlett's plan.

With the "style and finish of the work" like Baskerville's father's house "or not inferior," Eureka's lavishly applied detail epitomizes Holt's repetitive, eclectic vocabulary combined from several of Ranlett's plates (fig. 1.45).[53] The mantels, brackets, windows, stairs (fig. 1.46), and other elements are identical to those in most of Holt's other buildings of this period rather than replications of the relatively simple treatment advocated by Ranlett for the villa.

Baskerville and Holt aggrandized the composition by adding a dominant central tower, perhaps inspired by Holt's own house or, more likely, a plate for an "Italian Villa" (design 6), in Samuel Sloan's *Model Architect*. The result was a spacious villa of original design, far removed from Ranlett's plate cited in the contract.

The initial contract was but the first step in the design of Eureka. Whether at the suggestion of builder or patron, the form of the building continued to evolve. Construction progressed slowly partly because of problems Holt experienced in obtaining manufactured goods. Changes in the design also required additional work. "Extra work on dwelling house" included "Building 2 side piazzas" for $96 each, "Changing roof and building Tower difference" for $45, "Lengthening back piazza from 32 to 49 ft." for $26, and so on, to a total of nearly $1,000.[54] In such ways the design of the house continued to depart from the published model to accommodate the tastes and lifestyle of the client. The resulting building was perhaps Holt's grandest private project, bearing the stamp of his standardized detail but in its dramatic towered form and atypical plan reflecting the productive cooperation of builder and adventuresome client.

FIG. 1.45. *Eureka, 1857–59 or 1860, Mecklenburg County, Virginia. Jacob W. Holt, builder. Photograph by Catherine W. Bishir, 1977.* (NCDAH)

FIG. 1.46. *Rear stair hall or saloon, Eureka. Photograph by Randall Page, 1974.* (NCDAH)

A far less ambitious Holt project for the Baskervilles is even more revealing of the builder's approach. After he completed Eureka, Holt corresponded with the elder Baskerville about remodeling a church:

> Dear sir—Inclosed I send you an estimate for the addition & Alteration to the Church and may seem to you to be too much, but by reference to the Items in the bill you will see that it is not[.] I have put several Items lower than I have been charging for several years, the framing, weatherboarding, sheeting & shingling, Cornice & seats all are lower. The bill is made to have the work done in a manner & style that will suit you, but can be done for less money if done in a plainer manner. I have concluded to put the bill at $1150, you will please let me know whether [you] wish the bill changed to less work & plane. If such a building be entirely new it would be worth about $1900 dollars.[55]

Holt's letter reveals explicitly and unpretentiously the cool confidence, stout practicality, and unerring awareness of his client's taste and purse that undergirded his success. He knew precisely what "manner & style . . . will suit" yet expressed frankly his willingness to accommodate elegance to budget, for he would adjust his work to require "less money if done in a plainer manner."

Holt's contracts, correspondence, and sketches for the Baskerville family confirm the attitudes that permeate all his work. He was a practical builder who established priorities to focus on the needs of his patrons. He erected structures within stipulated budgets using the technology at his command. Like the folk artisans Henry Glassie has described who serve far less self-conscious cultures than Holt's mid-nineteenth-century piedmont planters, Holt and his clients collaborated, "mutually influencing each other's decisions, sharing an unspoken aesthetic, discussing artifacts from the angle of practicality."[56]

Although others of his generation accepted the growing separation of design and construction, Holt continued the integration of the processes well into the 1870s, devising a highly individualized personal style and a system of production that combined standardization and an idiosyncratic version of pattern-book detail.

Because of Holt's identifiable style and the survival of many buildings and documents, his career reveals the outlines of a pattern that informs the work of many other builders across the country. This kind of builder formed a vital bridge between waning traditional culture and the rising challenges of popular culture. Holt was neither the major architect serving the elite nor the unselfconscious artisan of folk dwellings nor even the literal copyist of popular pattern books. Integrating national styles into the framework of the vernacular artisan, he was able to design and build in ways that satisfied his clients' needs for regional and traditional continuity and that also acknowledged the attraction of changing fashions. From such builders' varied and often creative resolutions of these forces springs much of the lively, expressive character of America's architecture.

NOTES

Initial fieldwork behind this article was conducted as part of North Carolina's statewide survey between 1974 and 1976 by the author, assisted by Michael T. Southern and H. McKelden Smith III. In five years of subsequent research, the author depended upon the knowledge and generosity of Thilbert Pearce of Franklin County; Richard Hunter and the late Panthea Twitty of Warren County; Gladys and Mary McKinney of Chase City; Verna P. Bracey of Mecklenburg County; Virginia Redd of Prince Edward County; Frank and Margaret Stephenson of Murfreesboro; J. Marshall Bullock, William Bushong, Keith Morgan, and Thomas Parramore of Raleigh; Holt descendants, especially John Blinn and his wife Felecie of California; many descendants of Holt clients, especially Mrs. William R. Baskerville and William R. Baskerville, Jr.; and, above all, Mary Hinton Kerr and Edgar Thorne of Warren County and John Bishir.

1. See Doug Swaim, "North Carolina Folk Housing," and Michael T. Southern, "The I-House as a Carrier of Style in Three Counties of the Northeastern Piedmont," *Carolina Dwelling: Towards Preservation of Place: In Celebration of the North Carolina Vernacular Landscape*, ed. Doug Swaim (Raleigh: North Carolina State University, 1978), pp. 28–45, 70–83.

2. Herbert W. Bradshaw, *History of Prince Edward County* (Richmond: Dietz Press, 1955).

3. Prince Edward County deeds, wills, estates papers, guardian bonds, Prince Edward County Courthouse, Farmville, Virginia. Howard built courthouses in Lunenburg (1824–27) and Mecklenburg (1838–42), campus buildings at Randolph-Macon College, Boydton, and perhaps others at Hampden-Sydney College. He was often associated with Dabney Cosby, prolific brick contractor in the region who had worked on the University of Virginia under Thomas Jefferson. Holt's possible association with Howard is suggested by the similarity between Holt's early work and the details of the two college campus buildings of the 1830s, the prominence of Howard and his large shop in the 1820s and 1830s, and the fact that Holt named his second son William Howard Kenneth Holt; see Prince Edward, Lunenburg, and Mecklenburg county court records; and Richard Irby, *History of Randolph-Macon College, Virginia* (Richmond: Whittet & Shepperson, 1898), 24.

4. Minutes of Sharon Baptist Church, Prince Edward County, Virginia State Library, Richmond; Prince Edward County marriage bonds, Prince Edward County Courthouse; Aurelia Holt tombstone, Woodland Cemetery.

5. Prince Edward County deeds; Manuscript population schedule, Prince Edward County, Virginia, 6th U.S. Census (1840), microfilm copy, North Carolina Archives. Holt was later a founding member of the Baptist church in Warrenton, North Carolina, and a member of Concord Baptist Church, Mecklenburg County, Virginia; Jacob W. Holt obituary, *Religious Herald* (Richmond, Virginia), October 28, 1880.

6. Built in the Sandy River section of Prince Edward County, Linden, Walnut Hill, and Rotherwood, all ca. 1840, are similar to each other and to later Holt work. Edwin Edmunds, for whom Rotherwood was built, made several entries in his farm accounts that link Holt to the building of Rotherwood; Edwin Edmunds account books, Southern Historical Collection, University of North Carolina, Chapel Hill.

7. Warren County's aggregate personal and real property value per free person in 1860 was by far the highest in the state at $3,092; next highest was Edgecombe County with $2,499; other counties ranged between $200 and $1,800; see Dwight B. Billings, Jr., *Planters and the Making of a "New South"* (Chapel Hill: University of North Carolina Press, 1979), 48. Warren County's planters, with 2,000 to 10,000 or more acres and thirty to eighty slaves—and a few with far more—ranked in the upper one-

half of one percent of population in the state, where average farm size was between 300 and 400 acres, and slightly more than 30,000 out of nearly a million people owned any slaves; see Hugh T. Lefler and Albert Ray Newsome, *The History of a Southern State: North Carolina* (Chapel Hill: University of North Carolina Press, 1973), 391, 420.

8. Lizzie Wilson Montgomery's excellent memoir, *Sketches of Old Warrenton* (Raleigh: Edwards & Broughton, 1924), describes the town's social history and people; it is supplemented by Victoria L. Pendleton's "Reminiscences" (two undated [ca. 1910] ms. notebooks, Warren County Historical Association File, Warren County Memorial Library, Warrenton). See also Manley Wade Wellman, *History of Warren County* (Chapel Hill: University of North Carolina Press, 1959); Manuscript population schedules, Warren County, North Carolina, 6th–9th U.S. Census (1840, 1850, 1860, 1870), Miscellaneous Records, Archives Section, Division of Archives and History, North Carolina Department of Cultural Resources, Raleigh (hereafter North Carolina Archives). See also "The Montmorenci–Prospect Hill School," chapter 7 of this volume.

9. Montgomery, *Sketches*, 196–97. The impact of these builders coming to Warrenton and Warren County and some inkling of why they came are suggested by data recorded in the 1840 census. In 1840, a few years before these craftsmen came to Warren County, the census taker recorded that only thirteen wooden houses and no brick or stone ones were built in the entire town and county. Thirty men worked on the construction of these houses, and the value of the structures was estimated at $5,030. Holt's shop alone exceeded thirty men, and two of his houses would have far exceeded $5,000. By comparison, in Prince Edward County, Virginia, where Holt and his shop were working when the 1840 census was taken, thirty stone or brick houses and fifty-eight wooden ones were built in that year, to a total value of $58,100; the work employed a total of 183 men. *Compendium of the Enumeration of the Inhabitants and Statistics of the United States* (Washington, D.C.: Department of State, 1841), 184–85, 160–61.

10. Bill, M. T. Hawkins to J. W. Holt, 1850. Thomas Pittman Collection, Private Collections, North Carolina Archives.

11. Manuscript population schedule, Warren County, North Carolina, 7th U.S. Census (1850), North Carolina Archives. Carl Lounsbury's survey of builders listed in the 1850 census revealed that Holt's household shop was the state's largest. He hired rather than owned most of the slaves in his workforce.

12. Emmanuel Episcopal Church Records, microfilm copy, North Carolina Archives; county accounts and claims, Courthouse Building Accounts, Warren County Records, North Carolina Archives; addition to contract for building Sylva Sonora, Warren County, North Carolina (1857–58), private collection, photocopy in possession of author.

13. Montgomery, *Sketches*, 197. List of Holt's buildings in possession of author, with author's notes.

14. Manuscript population schedule, Warren County, North Carolina, 8th U.S. Census (1860), North Carolina Archives.

15. After the Civil War, T. J. Holt practiced architecture in Raleigh and in Charlotte, North Carolina. Manuscript population schedule, Wake County, North Carolina, 8th U.S. Census (1860), North Carolina Archives; cornerstone of Raleigh and Gaston Company Shops building (surviving corner of ruin), Raleigh, North Carolina; *Raleigh Register,* October 24, 1860, *Weekly Raleigh Register,* May 2, 1860; *Daily Observer* (Charlotte, North Carolina), October 10, 1869.

16. *North Carolina Standard Weekly* (Raleigh), October 31, 1860; *Proceedings of the Grand Lodge of Ancient York Masons of North Carolina* (Raleigh: Printed by Will C. Daub, 1855), 28; Nora Chaffin, *Trinity College, 1839–1892: The Beginnings of Duke University* (Durham: Duke University Press, 1950), 189–92. On John Berry, see Eva Ingersoll Gatling, "John Berry of Hillsboro, North Carolina," *Journal of the Society of Architectural Historians* 10, no. 1 (March 1951): 18–22.

17. *North Carolina Standard Weekly* (Raleigh), October 31, 1860.

18. Elizabeth C. Waugh, *North Carolina's Capital, Raleigh* (Raleigh: Junior League of Raleigh and North Carolina State University Print Shop, 1967), 107; Chaffin, *Trinity College,* 189–92, 217–20.

19. The county's land, valued at over $3.3 million in 1860, fell to about $1.6 million by 1870, and Warrenton's population dwindled from 1,520 in 1860 to 941 in 1870 (Wellman,

History, 163); *Warren Indicator*, February 14, 1868.

20. Aurelia Holt obituary (*Religious Herald* [October 3, 1895]) states that she moved to Chase City in 1869. See also Douglas Summers Brown, *Chase City and Its Environs, 1765–1975* (Richmond: Whittet & Shepperson, 1975), 103–16. Interview with Gladys McKinney and Mary McKinney, March 1978.

21. *Mecklenburg Herald* (Boydton), December 14, 1870, March 8, 1871. See also Susan L. Bracey, *Life by the Roaring Roanoke: A History of Mecklenburg County, Virginia* (Richmond: Whittet & Shepperson, 1978).

22. *Norfolk Virginian*, April 21, 1875; *Murfreesboro Enquirer*, January 11, 1877.

23. *Chataigne's Petersburg Directory* (1879–80, 1882–83, 1886–87); *J. L. Hill Printing Company's Directory of Petersburg, Virginia* (1905–6, 1907–8, 1909–10, 1911–12, 1913–14, 1915–16, 1917), Petersburg Public Library; *Manufacturer's Record* (Baltimore), July 27, 1884.

24. The volume was published in Philadelphia in 1805 with editions through 1858 and was widely used in North Carolina and Virginia; see Henry-Russell Hitchcock, *American Architectural Books* (Minneapolis: University of Minnesota Press, 1962).

25. Montgomery (*Sketches*, 285) credits Eaton's house to Holt; Jack Quinan, "Asher Benjamin and American Architecture," *Journal of the Society of Architectural Historians* 38, no. 3 (October 1979): 244–56; Hitchcock, *Architectural Books*, 11–12.

26. *The Practice of Architecture* was published in Boston in 1833 and six more editions through 1851. Included was a column and entablature that Benjamin explained in his preface was "selected from the Grecian antiquities and standing, with regard to expense, between the Tuscan and Doric orders."

27. Lafever's first book was published in 1829 and had but one edition. Holt's use of it is not as certain as the other volumes, but certainly Holt's columned door treatment resembles Lafever's plate more than those of Benjamin.

28. See Clay Lancaster, "Adaptations from Greek Revival Builders' Guides in Kentucky," *Art Bulletin* 32, no. 1 (March 1950): 62–70.

29. Ranlett provided designs for the popular periodical, *Godey's Lady's Book,* and two North Carolina houses—Wessington in Edenton and Cooleemee in Davie County—replicated his plates in the 1850s. For Cooleemee, see Thomas T. Waterman and Frances Benjamin Johnston, *The Early Architecture of North Carolina* (Chapel Hill: University of North Carolina Press, 1947), 180, 240–41.

30. See Hitchcock, *Architectural Books*, iii.

31. Henry Glassie, "Folk Art," in *Folklore and Folklife: An Introduction,* ed. Richard M. Dorson (Chicago and London: University of Chicago Press, 1972), 253–80.

32. John T. Kirk, *Early American Furniture* (4th ed.; New York: Alfred A. Knopf, 1977), 81–82.

33. Glassie, "Folk Art," 260, 271.

34. Concerning the long use of the Georgian plan in American vernacular architecture, see also Swaim, "North Carolina Folk Housing"; Henry Glassie, "The Impact of the Georgian Form on American Folk Housing (Abstract)," in *Forms Upon the Frontier: Folklife and Folk Arts in the United States,* ed. Henry Glassie, Austin Fife, and Alta Fife, Utah State University Monograph Series 16, no. 2 (April 1969): 23–25; and Howard W. Marshall, *Folk Architecture in Little Dixie: A Regional Culture in Missouri* (Columbia: University of Missouri Press, 1981), 30–71.

35. Waterman and Johnston, *Early Architecture of North Carolina,* 37–40.

36. Pendleton, "Reminiscences," notebook 1, p. 152. The house was built for Holt and his family about 1849–50 and sold to the Johnson family shortly after. Warren County deed books, vol. 30, p. 98, and vol. 31, p. 71, Warren County Courthouse, Warrenton, North Carolina. Agreement, November 17, 1846, Thomas J. Burrows and J. W. Holt, photocopy provided to the author from private collection, Warren County, courtesy of Richard Hunter.

37. Holt billed John E. Boyd in 1857–58 for "Extra graining in back rooms of house, $25.00" (private collection; photocopy in possession of author). The 1856 contract for Vine Hill, Franklin County, North Carolina, called for some "best style" mantels and some "plain" ones, evidently for principal and secondary rooms, respectively (private collection; photocopy in possession of author).

38. The Vine Hill contract called for "Blind door across passage (four fold) pivot, or stationary slats, $15." Other contracts include similar items. The most extravagant proliferation of doors, porches, stairs, and halls occurred at

Sunnyside, a house described as built by Holt in 1850 for T. W. and Martha Harriss. It stood near Littleton, North Carolina, and burned in 1873. The house had a great front piazza with tall fluted columns. Inside were front, middle, and rear halls, each partitioned by folding (louvered?) doors. More folding doors led from the middle hall to porches on either side and from the rear hall to a porch. Stairs rose from the front and rear halls to the second floor and descended from the middle and rear hall to the basement. (Notes of Annie B. Thorne, Littleton, probably 1930s or 1940s; photocopy in possession of Edgar Thorne, Warren County.)

39. The Vine Hill contract mentions "1 Piazza in the rear 8 ft by 48 Including 2 pantries or closets," and an undated estimate that may be for Cherry Hill refers to "Back porch and closets, $80.00" (unsigned estimate for house for P. G. Alston, Henry G. Williams Collection, Southern Historical Collection, Chapel Hill, North Carolina).

40. For a discussion of this issue, see John D. Morse, ed., *Country Cabinetwork and Simple City Furniture* (Charlottesville: University Press of Virginia, 1969).

41. Holt augmented his work force through the common practice of hiring slaves by the year. He deployed both slave and free workers to his building sites, where often the client paid their board or Holt paid the client for supplying the board.

42. A steam-powered sawmill operated in Warren County by 1860, following earlier water-powered ones, but no sash and blind factory. These mass-production operations were rare in antebellum North Carolina outside a few cities but became prevalent during the industrialization and urbanization of the late nineteenth century; manuscript schedule of industry, Warren County, North Carolina, 8th U.S. Census (1860), North Carolina Archives. The development of building technology in North Carolina is discussed in Carl Lounsbury's 1983 Ph.D. dissertation for George Washington University, "From Craft to Industry: The Building Process in North Carolina in the Nineteenth Century."

43. Montgomery, *Sketches*, 332.

44. See the comments of Edward F. La-Fond, Jr., in "Conclusions," in Morse, *Country Cabinetwork*, 282–83.

45. Montgomery, *Sketches*, 332; Holt leased the property for residence and workshop, Warren County deeds.

46. A. J. Davis designed Blandwood in Greensboro for John Motley Morehead in the 1840s. It was among the few towered villas in North Carolina at this time. Architect William Percival built some florid villas in Raleigh and Tarboro in the late 1850s, but this work postdates Holt's Warrenton villa. See William B. Bushong, "William Percival, an English Architect in the Old North State, 1857–1860," *North Carolina Historical Review* 57, no. 3 (July 1980): 310–39. The only other known extant North Carolina references to this particular Downing plate, which Downing acknowledged as coming from a design by John Notman, are a brick house with Grecian detail, which served for some years as Ravenscroft School in Asheville, and the Hill-Webb House in Hillsborough, North Carolina.

47. Montgomery, *Sketches*, 332.

48. Pendleton, "Reminiscences," notebook 1, pp. 106, 152; Montgomery, *Sketches*, 350; *Mecklenburg Herald* (Boydton), April 20, 1871.

49. Unsigned, undated P. G. Alston contract possibly for Cherry Hill, Warren County, and Baskerville family papers, private collection, photocopies in possession of author. References to another building as an example in Holt's contracts continues an ancient practice among English as well as American builders; H. M. Colvin, *A Biographical Dictionary of English Architects, 1660–1840* (Cambridge, Mass.: Harvard University Press, 1954), 6.

50. William R. Baskervill(e) papers, Baskervill(e) papers, Virginia Historical Society, Richmond (hereafter Baskerville Papers, VHS); Baskervill(e) Family Papers, private collection, photocopies in possession of author (hereafter Baskerville Papers, PC); and William R. Baskervill(e) Papers, Manuscript Collection, Perkins Library, Duke University, Durham (hereafter Baskerville Papers, DU).

51. Baskerville Papers, VHS.
52. Baskerville Papers, PC.
53. Baskerville Papers, PC.
54. Baskerville Papers, PC.
55. Holt to Col. W. R. Baskerville, June 29, 1860, Baskerville Papers, DU.
56. Glassie, "Folk Art," 278.

Two

GOOD AND SUFFICIENT LANGUAGE FOR BUILDING

Most studies of the traditional building process use patterns seen in the buildings themselves as evidence of the thought processes of their makers. Although written evidence of the traditional design process is relatively slim, we can find aspects of it in specifications created by client and artisan to record their intentions about the house, courthouse, church, or barn they planned. Most of us have examined contracts and specifications to learn about the character of buildings themselves; we can also look at such documents as a genre whose patterns of expression suggest the thought processes behind them.

We may begin by envisioning a building from traditional contract specifications. On February 14, 1774, in the little town of Windsor in northeastern North Carolina, carpenters Richard Gill and Benjamin Ward signed a Memorandum of Agreement with the client, Macon Whitfield, for £19 11s.

> To building him a fraimed house sixteen feet square, with a shed 8 feet wide on one side of it, the body of the house to be 10 feet pitch between joints, the shed 8 feet between joints in the Town of Windsor where the said Whitfield shall direct. One pannel door and 30 lights of sash, a pair of stairs, and the other doors to be batten doors, and all to be finished and completed the whole House in a workmanlike manner by the first day of

---

"Good and Sufficient Language for Building" appeared in *Perspectives in Vernacular Architecture IV*, eds. Thomas Carter and Bernard Herman (Columbia: University of Missouri Press, 1991), 44–52, 215–18, and is reprinted by permission of the University of Missouri Press, Columbia, Missouri.

May next. In witness whereof the parties to these presents have hereunto set their hands & seals this February 14, 1774.[1]

For most of us, there are important gaps between what this contract says and what we would have to know to build a building. This contract was signed, sealed, and witnessed. But would you sign it and expect to deliver on it? Most of us would not do so without knowing more than this document states about the intended structure. And of course that is the point. This document, like thousands used for traditional buildings in centuries past, was based on the essential assumption that both parties did know more than it stated.

Before exploring the significance of that assumption, let us attempt to fill in the gaps about the house planned in Windsor. It is not certain whether it still stands, but based on common precedent in the time and place, it is possible to make some educated guesses about its design, materials, and general character.

Although only the basics—the dimensions, the use of frame construction, and a few details about doors and windows—are defined, some of the other elements may be inferred from those in relation to common building techniques of the late-eighteenth-century Upper South. The frame would have been made of mortised and tenoned timbers covered with weatherboards or clapboards. The reference to thirty lights of sash suggests two windows of fifteen panes each—probably six over nine or nine over six panes—though other arrangements are possible. The six-panel door was probably the front door, while the batten doors probably appeared on the side or rear, for paneled doors were considered more formal than doors made of boards. The sixteen-foot-square dimension suggests one main room, possibly a passage, and the mention of the stair indicates an upper chamber.

But there are other essential elements about which nothing at all is stated. There is no information, for example, about the roof. We may suppose from local usage that the roof was probably a gabled one of common rafters covered with wooden shingles. It might, however, have been a gambrel roof, for this form was also used for small houses of the late-eighteenth-century coastal plain. For foundation and chimney, Whitfield probably hired a bricklayer separately, unless he relied on the carpenters to set the house on wooden blocks and erect a wooden chimney, a method that did appear in eastern North Carolina. For such matters as the location of the doors and windows, pitch of the roof, placement of the stair, details of the plan, and most of the finish and quality of the building, nothing is specified at all except that last phrase, "all to be finished and completed the whole House in a workmanlike manner."

Such a contract, with so much apparently left out, seems on the surface like a casual or inadequate approach to building. Perhaps these were simply provincial residents unfamiliar with composing more sophisticated specifications? Actually, such a document is neither a backwater oddity nor inadequate for the job at hand. This agreement for a little frame house presents an archetype of thousands of contracts and specifications executed for hundreds of years. Similar specifications appear frequently in English building practice from the medieval period onward and in America from earliest settlement through the nineteenth century. That two parties would create, sign, and consider legally binding such documents time after time, generation after generation, is one sure evidence of their sufficiency.

They were sufficient not in themselves but, as I suggested earlier, as part of a complex system at work. These documents, like any legally binding agreement, included as much as their makers believed necessary. Those things that went unstated, on the other hand, were those the participants in the contract saw no need to write down. It is into this seeming gap between what was said and what was left unsaid—which is no indication of things done and left undone—that we need to look.

Such brief specifications seem especially sparse in contrast to the long, fully detailed specifications we know from study of high-style and present-day architecture. There, explicitness is required to deal with the many possibilities of complex and diverse technologies, the desire to have the builder replicate closely an architect's design, and the very nature of the triangular relationship of architect, client, and builder. Traditional specifications, however, are part of a different dynamic—the traditional design process.

Several scholars have given us rich analyses of how the vernacular design process works. Henry Glassie's *Folk Housing in Middle Virginia,* Thomas Hubka's "Just Folks Designing," and several works by Dell Upton and John Vlach explain how vernacular designers manipulate concepts of form to create many variations within the narrow context of limited materials, technology, and social expectations.[2] Suffice it to say here that the traditional design process operates in communities where "tradition is the basis for action" and ways of doing things are shared, unstated assumptions. As Hubka observes, the traditional design process operates not through the intentionally original method of the architect, nor through some simple, naive folk spontaneity. Rather, the traditional designer operates within a complex mental system structured by tradition. The individuals who plan each building begin with an understood tradition and a set of rules that defines both a specific vocabulary of forms and techniques and an accepted syntax or structure for combining them. Change is accommodated as the traditional designer solves new design problems through old ways of problem solving. Within this framework, many variations and new possibilities may develop to accommodate individual needs, new elements of technology or style, and other challenges.

Typically, too, the traditional design process involves the direct interaction of two parties: the client and the craftsman. In some cases, the client might deal with a single craftsman who undertakes the entire building project and subcontracts out those elements that he does not perform himself. This approach was especially prevalent in public building projects and became increasingly common in private projects during the nineteenth century. Frequently, however, in private projects, the client made separate agreements with the various craftsmen needed to complete his building— the carpenter, the bricklayer or stonemason, and perhaps others such as a joiner, a plasterer, a painter, or a glazier. In some cases, the client might agree to pay the workman by the day or piece. In others, the two parties signed a contract that involved a single or staged payment for the entire project or the work of a single trade on the project. It was in such agreements that they expressed their mutual expectations in written and more or less detailed terms.[3]

In each case, the client knew, assumed, or hoped that the artisan possessed basic skills that enabled him to apply lessons of experience and example to the job. Both parties assumed that they held, as members of the community, some shared definition of the type of building required, so they needed to define only the particulars. Indeed, often a private traditional building agreement was a verbal one; where much can be assumed both about the thing to be built and the reliability of client and artisan to meet a bargain, a verbal agreement is sufficient. In a traditional community, most interactions are face-to-face and verbal rather than written.[4] Although written agreements were normal for public buildings because of the bidding process and public financial responsibilities, private agreements were very often oral contracts. Berry Davidson, a nineteenth-century millwright in rural North Carolina, proudly recalled, "Looking back over the years, I am safe in saying, I never found a man that asked me to sign a written contract, nor did I have an unsatisfactory settlement." The opposite side of the coin was expressed by a planter who recorded in his diary that Ruben, a mason he had hired, had "agreed to the bargain before Mr. Suter, [but] he seems to be a slippery fellow and I am determined to write out the contract & have it witnessed."[5]

Here we need to raise briefly the myth of the anonymous folk artisan. There is a popular image of the quaint but nameless artisan, wandering around the landscape, a sort of Lone Ranger type: "Who was that guy?" "I don't know. He wouldn't say—anonymous I guess. But look, he left a silver nail!" Ironically, the present anonymity of most traditional artisans stems from a lack of documentation, which springs in turn from their being so well known, so un-anonymous, in their community at the time. If a craftsman did not need to advertise his skills in newspapers to get work or need to sign written agreements with clients, he might leave little or no documentary record of a long and productive career. Ruben, unknown but apparently slippery, gained a written record to pin him down, whereas known craftsmen like Berry Davidson did not.

One approach to understanding the traditional design process, in which artisan and client participated, comes from a definition of linguistic codes provided by sociologist Basil Bernstein and used by Upton and others in analyzing building forms. This code also applies to building documents. Bernstein defines two kinds of codes at work in language and cultural behavior—elaborated codes and restricted codes. Many people use both types as the situation demands.[6]

In an elaborated code, there exist both a large range of forms and a low degree of predictability in both the vocabulary of particular forms and the syntax or grammar of putting forms together in a meaningful structure. In an elaborated code, one may choose from many alternatives in both vocabulary and syntax, which permits and encourages each individual to express himself in unique, original fashion. There are few givens and many possibilities. Hence using or understanding an elaborated code requires detailed and explicit explanations.

A restricted code, by contrast, assumes a high degree of predictability in vocabulary and syntax. Important givens define a narrow range of forms and structures for combining them. The restricted code is learned informally by repeated exposure to example, is understood by most members of the community, and promotes not so much individual originality as group solidarity. Expressions in a restricted code depend on a mutually assumed body of shared knowledge that "allows a few short words or phrases to stand for a whole complex of assumptions" and "removes the necessity of being explicit."[7]

We can see the distinction easily in foodways. In traditional cooking, members of a community share common definitions of traditional dishes—the givens and the possible variations—whether it is bouillabaisse in Marseilles, tamales in Mexico, or barbecue in eastern North Carolina. If preparation of a dish strays far from the norm, it simply is not bouillabaisse or barbecue; yet within that norm every cook has his own method, and members of the community may have strong preferences among subtly different variations. To explain what makes one version better than another, the traditional cook would not restate the obvious but would just note critical variations. Thus in explaining how to bake an especially good apple pie, a traditional American cook could assume many givens and simply say, "I use Winesaps, and a quarter brown sugar." That's a restricted code expression. On the other hand, haute cuisine, including, say, nouvelle cuisine, uses an elaborated code where formal training, spectacularly original creations, and much explicit and erudite discussion are expected.

What are the elements of restricted code expression as seen in traditional building specifications? What are the patterns between what must be said and what is left unsaid? Such patterns are rooted in medieval English building and legal precedents and extend throughout building practice in America from early settlement through the nineteenth century. Although variations in specific elements reflect regional, stylistic, and technological variations with time and place, the consistency among building contracts is marked.

As is true in many types of legal documents such as deeds, wills, and other types of contracts, conventional phrases establish a basic framework. Characteristically, the contract states the parties involved, the date and place, and the financial arrangements. The building expected is usually defined in somewhat conventional fashion. First comes a description of essentials—the dimensions, basic materials, and perhaps the location of the building. Contract form and language take a structure familiar since medieval English building practice and probably earlier. An exemplary late-medieval English contract is one signed in Gloucester, England, in 1483, on June 20 "in the reign of King Edward the Fifth after the Conquest the First." The town stewards and carpenter David Sammesbury agreed that Davy was to "make an house by the Black Freris Gate in Gloucester conteyning in lengthe 47 feet in brede 15 feet, all the tymber sufficant and of oke."[8] Two centuries later, across the Atlantic in England, housewright James Townsend contracted with John Williams to "fframe erect Set up and finish for him the sd Williams upon his Land in Boston in the place where his now dwelling standeth," a house 34 by 20 feet, built of oak with a stone cellar, a good brick chimney, and plastered walls.[9] In 1860 in the mountains of North Carolina, carpenter J. F. Gaddy agreed to build for farmer Thomas Lenoir a log house 16 by 20 feet "this spring in said Lenoir's field at a spot agreed upon."[10]

Then, in the body of the document, aspects of the building are further explained, by reference to community or trade standards, by reference to an existing model, by explicit description, or in more summary fashion. In some cases, a generally understood standard was invoked. Such was the case when Jobe Lane agreed to raise the frame of a house in Boston for Thomas Robinson in 1660. The contract noted, "The frame shall be Euery waye substanshall According to the Judgment of men."[11] In an 1828 contract for a courthouse and jail in Northampton County, North Carolina, the jail of twelve-inch-square heart pine logs was specified in detail, while an adjoining jailer's apartment was simply to be "built in the common way of good framed buildings."[12]

Reference to specific buildings as models is a common and age-old method for defining expectations.[13] A fifteenth-century Nottinghamshire house was to be "in all manner proporcion according as the new howse of John Taverner that William Roodes made."[14] So, too, in 1661 in Marlboro, Massachusetts, a contract for a new minister's dwelling stated that the house was to be built "every way like to ye fframe yt John Ruddocke hath built for himselfe in the afforesd Towne of Marlborough."[15] In Anson County, North Carolina, in 1842, a meetinghouse was planned to have a pulpit to be "after the manner and form of the one in the Methodist church in Wadesboro, but entirely plain and of good hart plank."[16] Jacob W. Holt contracted in 1857 to build Eureka, an elaborate plantation house in Virginia, in "the style and finish . . . like Col. W. R. Baskervilles or not inferior."[17]

Some contracts drew upon more than one example for various components of the building. In Leominster, Massachusetts, Leonard Cozzens contracted in 1849 to build a frame, clapboarded house for Luther Osbourn. It was specified that "the pitch of the roof and the stile of the outside finish to be similar to the house next North of the Methodist meeting house built for their Parsons house." Inside, Osbourn wanted "the casings and Stile of the work to be Similar to that in the house of Mr. Bachellors, built by Mr. E. Robbins."[18] In Wilmington, North Carolina, builders John Coffin Wood and Robert Barclay Wood, brothers involved in brick building and natives of Nantucket, agreed in 1851 to build for Zebulon Latimer an opulent stuccoed masonry residence. They wrote thorough specifications for some components, but they defined the veranda as being "similar to Dr. Dixon's," the piazza as similar to Mr. Kidder's, and the "entire finish" of the interior to be "similar to" that in Dr. A. J. DeRosset's house.[19] Whether for the jettied frame of a seventeenth-century New England house or an Italianate house in a busy antebellum southern port, such references reveal traditional designers' adherence to the familiar, the existing, and the local as important sources for planning new buildings.

Some items in contracts are treated quite explicitly. Materials and their treatment are specified in a manner that reflects established local or regional knowledge. For frame buildings, contracts often specify the type of wood and the size of each element. The fifteenth-century Gloucester building was to be of oak, "the sills a foot square, the posts in height of 18 fete and a foot square, the walplates of thikness 9 and 10 inches." Bostonian John Williams required that James Townsend build his house frame of well-seasoned white oak and black oak. The 1860 North Carolina mountain house was to be of logs hewn 6 inches thick and the sills and the next round to be of chestnut. Luther Osbourn's 1849 house in Leominster, Massachusetts, was to have its roof boarded with hemlock boards and then covered with cedar shingles "to be laid not more than five inches to the weather." Jacob Brewner's contract for the simple framed meetinghouse in Anson County, North Carolina, was typical in its use of heart pine in a southern building and its precise specifications for sizes of components—heart pine bottom sills 12 inches square, 38 sleepers at least 6 inches across the face or top side, the cornerposts of good heart pine 10 inches square hollowed on the inside, door and window posts 4 by 6 inches, and so on. Often, contracts specified precisely the size of nails to be used, the finishing method and exposure of weatherboards, the pane size and number of panes of glass in the windows, the workmanship to be used in such components as window sills or doors, and, increasingly in the mid-nineteenth century, the brands of hardware and other merchandise.

At the same time, however, in many contracts, as in our first example in Windsor, many items are not mentioned at all, or they are required simply to be "sufficient," "necessary," "good," "neat," or, almost universal and still used today, "workmanlike." The house in Gloucester was to have "all manner windows, doors, stairs, beams, rafters," and so on to be "sufficiently and able behoveful to the same worke." The materials for John William's Boston house were all to be "strong substantiall & workemanlike." The mountain log house was to have floors of "good plank," "a good stone chimney," and the whole to be "finished neatly and substantially in a good workmanlike manner." At the meetinghouse in Anson County, "The whole materials of said building [were] to be of a good and substantial kind ... and all the workmanship to be executed in a good and faithful workmanlike manner." Such terms appeared regularly in all kinds of buildings.

The relationship between the explicit and the implicit was far from random. For those matters that gained detailed definition, the participants knew there were significantly different alternatives within their vocabulary of forms, materials, and workmanship. Furthermore, for the project under consideration, it mattered to the participants which of those alternatives was chosen, in terms of quality, durability, status, cost, and difficulty. The superior qualities of a certain type of wood (whether it was oak in New England or heart pine in the South), the sturdiness of a certain size of timber, the permanence or appearance of a certain way of finishing a weatherboard or lapping shingles were known quantities that differed significantly from other available alternatives. When commissioners in Warren County, North Carolina, wrote specifications for a sturdy stone jail 34 by 20 feet (fig. 2.1), they said of the excavation only that it should be "of suitable depth from the surface for a good and solid foundation." Yet they paid close attention to the quality of the stone work, specifying "good, hard, durable & suitable granite"; the stones to be at least 18 inches thick in the first story,

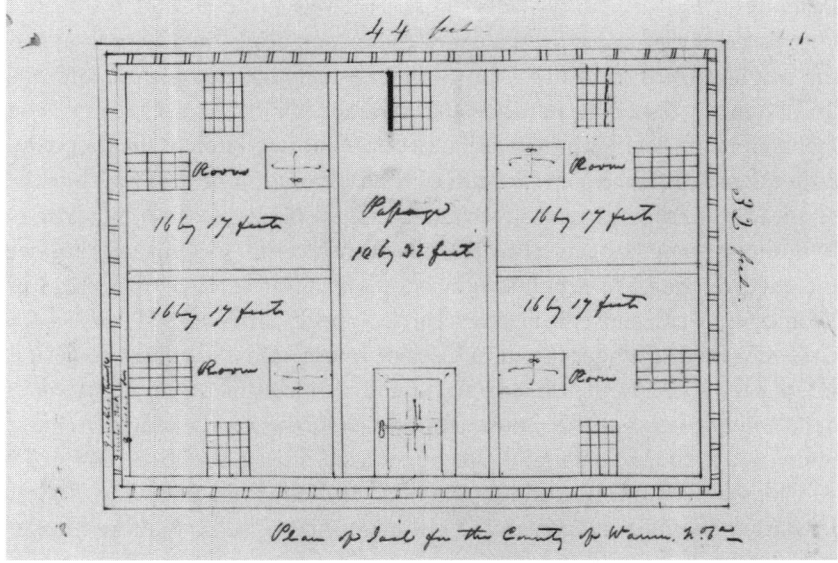

FIG. 2.1. *Plan drawing, 1851, Warren County Jail, Warrenton, North Carolina. Warren County Records,* NCDAH. *Simple drawings such as this one sometimes accompanied building agreements to show the layout, location of doors and windows, and wall thicknesses. (This plan differs from the specifications, indicating different phases in development of the commissioners' deliberations.)* (NCDAH)

12 inches in the second story; and the "kind of work" to be "first class block range rock work, beds and joints *neatly cut,*" and so forth.[20]

Conversely, if a preferred choice was not stated, it is likely that there was a single known standard that was considered sufficient to the task or that any of several known alternatives would do. In some cases, the client and craftsman might have agreed to certain methods verbally. In others, both parties understood that the craftsman was to exercise his judgment within the established norms of his craft. Such was probably the case when Stevens Gray contracted with Gilbert Leigh in 1786 for £115 to build "A house 28 by 18 the Bording to be pland with 6 windows 18 lights, 8 [windows] 15 [lights], 5 doors. The floors to be toung & Groved, the Windows & Door frames with out to be single archives [architraves] & within the lower rooms to be Double with [?] & Chair Boards round the rooms, a Box Cornice outside, a pair stairs, the above articles to be done in a good workmanlike manner what belongs to a carpenter & Joiner."[21]

When builders and clients adapted new elements into their buildings, they often relied on traditional terms and concepts. Unfamiliar elements were often described in some detail, as well as by reference to existing standards. In 1726, joiner Benjamin Porter promised to build a house for David

Good and Sufficient Language for Building | 61

Peabody of Essex County, Massachusetts; it was to have windows "of the bigness as they are generaly made now to housing newly built here abouts in the neighborhood."[22] When John Steele, a widely traveled planter and political figure, planned his new house in piedmont North Carolina in 1799, he included in his detailed specifications a clause for the "pitch of the roof to be rather flatter than the common run of the Buildings in or near Salisbury."[23]

In a few instances, as popular architectural books became increasingly numerous and influential in the nineteenth century, client and builder included reference to a published example in their agreement. In 1848 in Worcester, Massachusetts, builders Burton and Holmes agreed to erect for C. C. Chickering a house "to be a Cottage house with a basement to design III, plates 13 and 14 of Ranletts Architect." The contract then specified in detail the elements of the house from basement to roof, making frequent references to the building being "wrought according to the above design."[24] At Eureka in Virginia, builder Jacob W. Holt and his client Dr. Robert D. Baskerville likewise contracted to build a house "to be built by Design 31st plate 19th Volume 2nd Ranlets Architect"; then they specified a number of deviations from the model to accommodate the family's needs.

Often, however, novel elements were described in familiar terms by reference to existing models. In Salisbury, North Carolina, Andrew Murphy employed Michael Davis in 1853 to build for him a frame house that was to be "finished from foundation to the comb ... in the best manner." For most elements, it was sufficient to specify "the neatest and most fashionable kind." For the unfamiliarly broad eaves of the hip roof, however, it was specified that "the eaves [were] to project over at least two feet or more and to have bracketts and be finished off something like Robert Murphy's house."[25]

*F*inally, we turn again to those broad terms: *necessary, sufficient, good,* and *workmanlike.* On the surface these appear meaningless, almost dismissals of matters of aesthetics, proportion, or workmanship. But, because we are dealing with a restricted code and its use of "short words or phrases to stand for a whole complex of assumptions," these terms are full of meaning. In legal practice today it is common to incorporate by reference. In a legal document a lawyer may state, "The provisions of such and such standards are hereby incorporated by reference and made a part of this agreement as if fully set out herein." Specifications for modern buildings often describe certain elements by reference to sections of a building code or a product manufacturer's published specifications. One can then refer to the cited volume for specifics.

This is what traditional specifications do in their loaded terms—*sufficient, necessary, good,* and *workmanlike.* In some building contracts, this assumption was itself made known: James Townsend's 1678/1679 contract with

Bostonian John Williams stated that Townsend was to "generally do all Carpentry and masons worke whatsoever necessary to the compleating and finishing of so Tenement or building to make it tenantable, although not herein perticularly expres't." More often, such assumptions went without saying. Like any restricted code, these documents incorporate by reference a whole set of community or trade knowledge and assumptions about what these qualities are. Their universal usage in legally signed agreements demonstrates that their meaning was considered enforceable by law.

Such contracts sometimes ended in suits that drew into court artisans and other witnesses to testify whether work met community and trade norms. As it turned out, John Williams insisted that housewright Townsend had not satisfied the terms of their contract for construction of a house. In January 1680, three men testified that they had inspected the house on William's behalf and found several elements improperly done—"Some of the Windows in the house open between the Window frames and the posts," and "The Partition in the Leanto is not done as it should bee by a workeman." Other elements of work they found lacking—"Two jetties not close[d] in the foreside: the one end and the foreside should have been boarded underneath the clapboards wch is not done" and "ffive gable ends to the house and not one of them fil'd," for example. Others defended the craftsman, such as William Dawes, mason, who testified that the work was "done workemanlike according to covenant," that the builder had done "rather more than he was obliged by covenant," and that "it is not usuall to Seel the jetties when the Roomes are not Seeled." Deponent Cornelius White likewise explained that "it is not usuall to fill gable ends where a house jetts." For these participants in the building process as for many others, their understanding of traditional and "usual" norms was the basis of action and judgment.[26]

And so, we can recall our first brief contract for a sixteen-foot-square house in Windsor, to be "finished and completed the whole house in a workmanlike manner"—and from it we can sense not inadequacy or simplicity, but adequacy and complexity. We may not know exactly what kind of building Macon Whitfield and carpenters Gill and Ward intended, but we know they knew—and they knew so well they didn't have to write it down. We can see such a document as a genre within a traditional society's intricate, controlling web of expectations and assumptions. In such a context, such specifications were indeed good and sufficient language for building.

APPENDIX

Three examples of specifications for simple wooden buildings planned in the first half of the nineteenth century in North Carolina illustrate a range of levels of specificity depending on needs and circumstances.

1. A private agreement between owner and artisan, where timing and business arrangements are the principal concerns and the buildings are assumed to be part of established local tradition. Granville County Miscellaneous Land Records, North Carolina State Archives, Raleigh.

Memorandum of an Agreement made and entered into this 9th day of April A D 1845 Between Thomas H. Raney of the first part and Russell Kingsbury of the second part both of the county of Granville & State of North Carolina. Witnesseth that the said Thomas H. Raney agrees with the said R. Kingsbury to do the following carpenters work [inserted: in Oxford], one house thirty six by Eighteen, eighteen feet pitch, with an impediment at one end with thirteen, fifteen light windows, two outside doors, and four inside doors, with a stare case, Wash Board & Chair Board [inserted: Chimney pieces and all other things necessary to complete the woodwork of said building in plain stile]. Also a kitchen of the following description, Eighteen by Twenty, ten feet Pitch, one floor, one door, and two small windows. Also a Smoke House, Twelve feet square, and twelve feet Pitch, a floor & one door. The said Thomas H. Raney agrees to furnish all the wood materials of good & suitable quality and build the above described Houses, in a workman likes manner, for the sum of three Hundred and fifty dollars. And the said Russell Kingsbury on his part agrees to furnish all nails Hinges and all other articles necessary except the wood portion of said buildings as they may be called for by the said Raney and when the said Raney has completed the aforesaid buildings agreeable to the above agreement the said R Kingsbury binds himself and his heirs &c, to pay to the said Raney the above sum of three hundred and fifty dollars. The said Thomas H. Raney binds himself to have said buildings so advanced by the 15th of Sept. next that the masons may do their portion of the work, such as Building chimneys &c, the said Raney is to board himself and hands while doing the work. The parties hereto bind themselves each to the other in the sum of Two Hundred and fifty dollars to stand to perform the foregoing contract and agreement. Witness our hands and seals this day & date above. Thomas H. Raney. Russell Kingsbury. Witness L. A. Paschall.

2. Specifications for a public building, a schoolhouse, to go to contractors by bids, defining requisite elements of quality within a widespread, economical log-building tradition. John L. Clifton Papers, Manuscript Department, Perkins Library, Duke University, Durham, North Carolina.

School House No. 4. The dimensions as follows 18 ft by 24. The logs squared & butted, the sills sleepers plates & joists hewed a good shingle roof, the rafters sheeted with rough edge plank the logs to be hewed inside & out set upon 8 good lightwood blocks a plank floor dressed & laid. The House to be 10 feet high in the body from the sleepers to the joists a good in frame doubbed stickd dirt chimney. For the roof of the House to cover the gable ends to be weather-boarded with square edge plank. Two doors & shutters & hinges four windows & shutters & hinges & hooks 7 staples with six panes of glass & sashes inch. Say a good & complete log house all the materials to be good & new. The cracks to be ceild with dressed plank inside of the house.

NB. If the builder or contractor of sd House finishes the same by the first of December next so the commissioners will receive the same, then they are to have the subscription or such a part as will satisfy the contract for the building of sd House. The commissioner to superintend the work &c.

[Signed] Henry Stevens, Henry J. Darden, J. L. Clifton for Benjm Hargrove, commissioiners. Bid off by Thomas Chestnutt for the sum of Fifty dollars. Abraham Chestnutt, (X) Thomas Chestnutt, Witness, J. W. Clifton.

3. Specifications, 1816, for a courthouse to be built in Jackson, Northampton County. A detailed description for a public building let to a bidder, for a neatly finished building within a frame construction tradition. Northampton County Miscellaneous Records: County Building Records, North Carolina State Archives, Raleigh.

The above plan represents a House forty feet square 14 feet pitch, the wings to be 16 feet Square & 8 feet pitch. The main building to be set three feet from the ground on brick underpining, 18 Inches Thick to be laid with good lime Mortar. The Wings to be 9 Ins. lower than the main building on underpining. The Timbers of the main building to be of the following sises (viz) The sills to be 16 by 12 Inches with a girder of the same sise each way of the House. The cornerposts 12 by 15 Ins; guttered. The Braces 12 by 4 Ins; one directly across the middle of the House, the other two diagonally across the House. The Rafters 6 by 4 Ins. The Roof to be a square Roof with a ridge pole and two supporters, the Joists to be braced in order to support them. The Timber of the Wings to be of the following sises (Viz) The Sills 8 by 12 Ins; the Sleepers 8 by 4 Ins. The Joists to be 6 by 4 Ins; the rafters 4 by 3 Ins; the Posts & Braces 6 by 4 Ins; the corner posts 12 by 8 Ins; Guttered. The Studs 4 by 3 Ins; The inside of the whole building to be Ceiled all that is exposed to view. The Collar beams to be about half way the rafters. The roofs of the Wings to be square Roofs; the Roof of the whole building to be sheated with square jointed Plank. The Timbers that are exposed to View are to be Plained & beaded if required. The Floors are to be laid of plank 2 Ins Thick & 9 Ins. wide, laid with 20 [crossed out] 30 d Nails, Sheating Ceiling to be ¾ Ins. thick to be nailed on with 10 d nails. The Featheredge Plank to be 9 Ins. wide of the usual thickness to raise 6 Inches and nailed on with 20 d Nails. The Shingles to be 18 Ins. long and ¾ Ins. thick to raise 6 Ins. & to be nailed on with 4 d Nails. The top of the whole building is to be painted of Slate Colour & the body white, all in a workmanlike manner. The Doore to the Court House to be a Folding Doore 7 feet wide: the Doores to the Wings to be of a usual Height and Width. There is to be one Chimney in each Wing to be laid of good Brick & lime Mortar. There is to be 14 eighteen lights Windows, glass to be 8 by 10 Ins. to put in the House agreeable to the annexed plan. The Lawyer's bar to run across 14 feet from the back of the House, with an entrance in the Centre; the Jury rooms to be taken off as in the annexed plan, say begining at the Lawyer's bar & describing the figure as laid down or annexed. The seats of the Courts to be four feet from the Floor banistered round. The Clerks Table to be fixed at one end of the Lawyer's Bar; the Floor back of the Lawyers bar to be laid of good tile, the balance of Plank as before described, all the Timber to be of good hart Pine of which this Building and every part thereof is Composed. The inside of the building to be painted brown as high as 8 feet & the balance White. The work of every description &c &c is to be done in a workmanlike manner. To each door of said Building there shall be one 9 inch plate Brass knob Lock.

Based on these specifications and attached plan, builder William Grant took the contract on May 15, 1816, for $2,899. As work proceeded, the commissioners reported after its completion in 1818, "some alterations in the plan of the courthouse was suggsted by the commissioners, such as haveing the roof under a Square, the Ceiling plane instead of being Circular, the floor of plank entirely instread of a part being tile, all of which alterations the commissioners beg leave to say in their opinion would thought would be for the best & that the said William Grant ought to be allowed one hundred dollars in addition to the sum he contracted at to build the Court House."

NOTES

This paper draws on research conducted on North Carolina building practice. See also Catherine W. Bishir, Charlotte V. Brown, Carl R. Lounsbury, and Ernest H. Wood, III, *Architects and Builders in North Carolina: A History of the Practice of Building* (Chapel Hill: University of North Carolina Press, 1990).

The author wishes to acknowledge the assistance of J. Marshall Bullock, Bernard Herman, Carl Lounsbury, Myron Stachiw, and George

Stevenson, who located and provided copies of several documents used in this article.

1. Agreement, Macon Whitfield and Richard Gill and Benjamin Ward, February 14, 1774. Bertie County Land Papers, 1736–1819, Archives and Records Section, North Carolina Division of Archives and History, Raleigh. Courtesy of George Stevenson.

2. See Henry Glassie, *Folk Housing in Middle Virginia: A Structural Analysis of Historic Artifacts* (Knoxville: University of Tennessee Press, 1975), and "The Variation of Concepts within Tradition: Barn Building in Otsego County, New York," in *Man and Cultural Heritage: Papers in Honor of Fred B. Kniffen*, ed. H. J. Walker and W. G. Haag (Baton Rouge: Louisiana State University School of Geoscience, 1974). Thomas Hubka, "Just Folks Designing: Vernacular Designers and the Generation of Form," *Journal of Architectural Education* 32:3 (1979): 27–29; reprinted in *Common Places: Readings in American Vernacular Architecture*, ed. Dell Upton and John Michael Vlach (Athens: University of Georgia Press, 1986), 426–32. Dell Upton, "Toward a Performance Theory of Vernacular Architecture: Early Tidewater Virginia as a Case Study," *Folklore Forum* 12 (1979): 173–98, and "Vernacular Domestic Architecture in Eighteenth Century Virginia," *Winterthur Portfolio* 17 (Summer/Autumn 1982): 95–119. John Michael Vlach, "The Brazilian House in Nigeria: The Emergence of a 20th-Century Vernacular House Type," *Journal of American Folklore* 97:383 (1984): 3–23.

3. For further discussion of such arrangements, see Bishir et al., *Architects and Builders in North Carolina*, 38–41, 60–91. For an analysis of a Delaware carpenter's relations with his clients, see Bernard L. Herman, "Kensey Johns and His Carpenters," in *After Ratification: Material Life in Delaware, 1789–1820*, ed. J. Ritchie Garrison, Bernard L. Herman, and Barbara McLean Ward (Newark: Museum Studies Program, University of Delaware, 1988), 65–77. For a study of a builder's relations with his clients, see "Jacob W. Holt: An American Builder," chapter 1 of this volume.

4. See Louis J. Chiaramonte, *Craftsman-Client Contracts: Interpersonal Relations in a Newfoundland Fishing Community* (St. Johns: Institute of Social and Economic Research, Memorial University of Newfoundland, 1970), for analysis of types of oral contracts between client and craftsman.

5. Berry Davidson, autobiography, undated typescript copy, Alamance County, N.C., Planning Department files, courtesy of Carl Lounsbury. Henry King Burgwyn Diary, March 23, 1841, Archives and Records Section, North Carolina Division of Archives and History.

6. This section draws upon Upton, "Toward a Performance Theory of Vernacular Architecture," 179–86, which includes extensive discussion of Basil Bernstein, *Class, Codes, and Control*, vol. 1, *Theoretical Studies toward a Sociology of Language* (London: Routledge and Kegan Paul, 1971), 122–36.

7. Upton, "Toward a Performance Theory of Vernacular Architecture," 180.

8. 1483, Gloucester, in L. F. Salzman, *Building in England Down to 1540* (Oxford: Clarendon Press, 1952), 542.

9. Boston: House for John Williams, Building contract, January 24, 1678/1679, Suffolk County Court Records, reproduced in Abbott Lowell Cummings, "Massachusetts Bay Building Documents, 1638–1726," in *Architecture in Colonial Massachusetts* (Boston: Colonial Society of Massachusetts, 1979), 204–5.

10. Agreement between J. F. Gaddy and Thomas Lenoir, January 23, 1860. Lenoir Family Papers, Southern Historical Collection, Wilson Library, University of North Carolina, Chapel Hill.

11. Boston: House for Thomas Robinson, Building contract, August 25 (?), 1660, Lane Family papers, privately owned; reproduced in Cummings, "Massachusetts Bay Building Documents," 203.

12. Contract, Frederick Shelton and others, April 28, 1828, Northampton County Miscellaneous Records, Archives and Records Section, North Carolina Division of Archives and History.

13. See H. M. Colvin, *A Biographical Dictionary of English Architects, 1660–1840* (Cambridge: Harvard University Press, 1954), 6, on the frequent use of existing buildings as models among English builders.

14. 1479, Nottingham, in Salzman, *Building in England*, 541.

15. Marlborough: Parsonage, Building contract, April 5, 1661, reproduced in Cummings, "Massachusetts Bay Building Documents," 216.

16. Agreement between Jacob Brewner and James B. Lindsay and others, November 1842. William Alexander Smith Papers, Duke

Manuscript Collection, Perkins Library, Duke University, Durham, N.C.; courtesy of William Erwin.

17. Bill for Dwelling House, 1857, Baskerville Family Papers, Private Collection (see chapter 1, pp. 44–48, this volume). Eureka was built for Robert Baskerville; it was to be built in the same style as the house Holt had recently remodeled and expanded for Robert's father, William.

18. Luther Osbourn and Leonard Cozzens, Agreement, February 7, 1849. Worcester County, Mass., Land Records, 443:468, copy courtesy of Myron Stachiw, Old Sturbridge Village.

19. Specifications of a brick house ... Z. Latimer. Lower Cape Fear Historical Society, Inc., Wilmington, N.C.

20. Warren County Records, North Carolina Division of Archives and History, cited in Carl R. Lounsbury, "The Building Process in Antebellum North Carolina," *North Carolina Historical Review* 60, no. 4 (October 1983): 440.

21. Stevens Gray and Gilbert Leigh, May 1, 1786, Gray Family Papers, Southern Historical Collection, Wilson Library.

22. Boxford: House for David Peabody, Building contract, April 13, 1726, Peabody-Osgood Papers, Essex Institute, reproduced in Cummings, "Massachusetts Bay Building Doc-uments," 207–8, quote from 208. Presumably Peabody had observed that windows had recently become somewhat larger than in the older houses.

23. Agreement, M. Chambers for John Steele with Elem Sharpe, March 28, 1799, John Steele Collection, Southern Historical Collection. See further discussion of this construction project in Bishir et al. *Architects and Builders in North Carolina*, 69–70.

24. Agreement between Burton and Holmes and C. C. Chickering, March 22, 1848, Worcester County, Mass., Land Records, 440:370, courtesy of Myron Stachiw, Old Sturbridge Village. William Ranlett's *The Architect* was a popular architectural book published by William H. Graham in 2 volumes (1847–49).

25. Contract for the house at 229 West Bank St., Salisbury, N.C., copy from files of James Brawley, Salisbury.

26. Cummings, "Massachusetts Bay Building Documents," 204–7. See also the 1680 case of John Bateman of Boston and carpenter Robert Tafft, where Bateman insisted that Tafft had not satisfactorily completed his contract of August 20, 1679, to build the frame of a house, and Bateman defended his actions. Ibid., 197–99. Herman, "Kensey Johns and His Carpenters," 68, cites the detailed specifications (ca. 1790) for the John Dickinson house in New Castle, Del., and the subsequent court case over misunderstandings between builders and client.

Three

BLACK BUILDERS IN ANTEBELLUM NORTH CAROLINA

Willis began to build the great stone chimney for Nicholas Massenburg's plantation house (figs. 3.1, 3.2) at noon on August 13, 1838. By early October the house was nearing completion. The Massenburg yard was filled with artisans and laborers. Stonemason Willis and his assistant Wash had nearly finished the precision task of laying the granite blocks quarried by stonemason Hardy Floyd and other laborers. Willis and Wash would cap the chimney with the elegant band of thin stone that marked the best masonry throughout the region. The craftsmen expected to finish Massenburg's masonry within the month, for they were committed to begin a new project in November.

Inside the house William Jones and his crew of carpenters were completing the work of fitting frames around the doorways and aligning columned mantels around the fire openings, so that Albert, the well-known plasterer from Oxford, and his assistants could begin to install the lathing and apply the plaster. On the road below the house, the driver Cary commanded a team of five horses that pulled a wagon piled with laths from the sawmill. If the Oxford plasterers started soon, and if the weather did not turn cold, the workmen could complete the house by Christmas.[1]

The construction scene at the Massenburg farm near Louisburg in Franklin County typified building projects throughout much of North Carolina. Then, as today, building was accomplished by a mix of black and white

---

"Black Builders in Antebellum North Carolina" appeared in *North Carolina Historical Review* 61, no. 4 (October 1984): 422–61, and is reprinted by permission of the Historical Publications Section, North Carolina Office of Archives and History, Department of Cultural Resources, Raleigh.

FIG. 3.1. *Rear chimney, Nicholas Massenburg House, 1838, Louisburg vicinity, Franklin County, North Carolina. Photograph by Michael T. Southern, 1974.* (NCDAH)

FIG. 3.2. *Massenburg House. Photograph by Larry McBennett, 1987.* (NCDAH)

artisans and laborers working together in a variety of roles and relationships. Stonemason Willis and his helper Wash were the property of planter William Kearney. The Oxford plasterer Albert was the slave of Captain Abraham Spencer, a prominent brick and plaster contractor in Louisburg and Oxford.[2] Cary, the driver, belonged to planter Nicholas Massenburg, as did many of the laborers who hauled materials and assisted the artisans.[3] Hardy Floyd was a free black stonemason in Louisburg.[4] William Jones was a white carpenter from Louisburg, whose crew typically included white, free black, and slave carpenters.[5] Such scenes as this, reenacted throughout the state, must have been in the mind of politician Charles Fisher when he observed in 1828, "What branch of mechanic have we in our country in which we do not find negroes often distinguished for their skill and ingenuity? In every place we see them equalling the best white mechanics."[6]

In North Carolina as in other states, and from early settlement to the present, black craftsmen have played a central role in the creation of the state's architecture. Enslaved artisans provided skills in all the building trades, and they worked in various settings—urban and rural, mobile and stable, highly restricted and relatively independent. At the same time, free black artisans contended with the curious mixture of autonomy and restrictions imposed by antebellum law.[7] It is the purpose of this article to emphasize the importance of black artisans to the state's architectural heritage and, through specific illustrations of workaday experiences, to suggest the diversity and complexity of black artisans' roles in the building industry and in society at large.[8]

Construction in antebellum North Carolina was still predominantly a traditional craft directly dependent upon the skills of artisans. By the 1850s in some parts of the state, to be sure, technological changes had appeared that during the nineteenth century would revolutionize the building industry through mechanized mass production of building parts. In time, these developments would forever alter the role of the artisan; his status would shrink from that of designer and maker to that of assembler of manufactured parts. But most antebellum building still followed traditional patterns. The artisan worked directly with the individual who would use the building. He shaped construction materials by hand, taking most from their natural state and local sources. He made and burned brick from local clay; cut and laid local stone; and cut, sawed, shaped, and smoothed framing timbers, weatherboards, doors, and mantels from local trees. Only a few items such as glass, hardware, and paint were manufactured elsewhere. Rarely did buildings involve the services of a professional architect; rather, the quality of most building was a function of customary forms and craftsmanship and hence of the artisan's taste and skill. Under these age-old conditions, the artisan was the key figure in the building process and in the character of antebellum architecture.[9]

From the earliest years of colonial settlement, many white North Carolinians relied upon enslaved artisans for every kind of craft. Anglican missionary John Urmston observed in 1711 that European settlers had "a bad time" unless they were among those who had "great numbers of slaves who understand most handycrafts," including carpentry, joinery, and other trades. Similarly, John Brickell found around Edenton in the 1730s that there were "several Blacks born here that can Read and Write, others that are bred to Trades, and prove good Artists in most of them."[10] Indeed, so universal was reliance upon black artisans that visitors to the Moravian settlement in the piedmont backwoods in 1773 observed the neat buildings and productive workshops with "wonder and pleasure" and, upon learning that there were only two Negroes in the community, "were the more surprised to find that white people had done so much work."[11]

Enslaved artisans, like free craftsmen, often entered their trades through apprenticeships (fig. 3.3). Some learned their crafts in informal arrangements under a master builder on the plantation, but formally arranged apprenticeships were not uncommon.[12] The slave's owner normally contracted with a master to train the youth for two to four years. Through such an arrangement, the owner could expect to profit by employing the slave's skills on his own building projects, or, more likely, by increasing the slave's value for sale or hire. Planter Benjamin Smith sent slaves out of state for training and hoped to capitalize on this investment when he advertised for hire in Wilmington three carpenters, a shoemaker, and a bricklayer who had "served their apprenticeship in Charleston."[13]

More commonly artisans, slave or free, gained their training locally. In December, 1814, slave owner and banker William Polk of Raleigh advertised that he had for hire six slave carpenters "who will be free from an apprenticeship of four years on the last day of this month." The next summer when Polk offered for sale a mulatto carpenter named Willis, he included a certificate from Raleigh carpenter William Jones, who had trained Willis during a four-year apprenticeship in the carpenter's and joiner's trade. Jones assured prospective buyers that Willis was "capable of doing very good work—he is brisk, active, obedient, and very healthy."[14] It was not unusual for builders to advertise for such youths to be apprenticed to them. In 1810 Raleigh carpenter John J. Briggs sought three or four Negroes as apprentices to the carpenter's trade and assured "Any gentlemen who may think proper to put their boys under my care" that masters "may expect the greatest attention will be paid both to their [slaves'] usage and learning." In such situations, the young slave typically worked and sometimes lived alongside free apprentices, black or white, and gained knowledge from journeymen and master workmen in the shop.[15]

Carpenters were most numerous among artisans in the building trades.[16] Enslaved carpenters ranged the spectrum from the ordinary rough carpenter to the highly skilled house carpenter and joiner. Among the latter were such men as Jacob, a house carpenter from Craven County, who in 1814 was "esteemed to be a most valuable negro, having sold some years since for

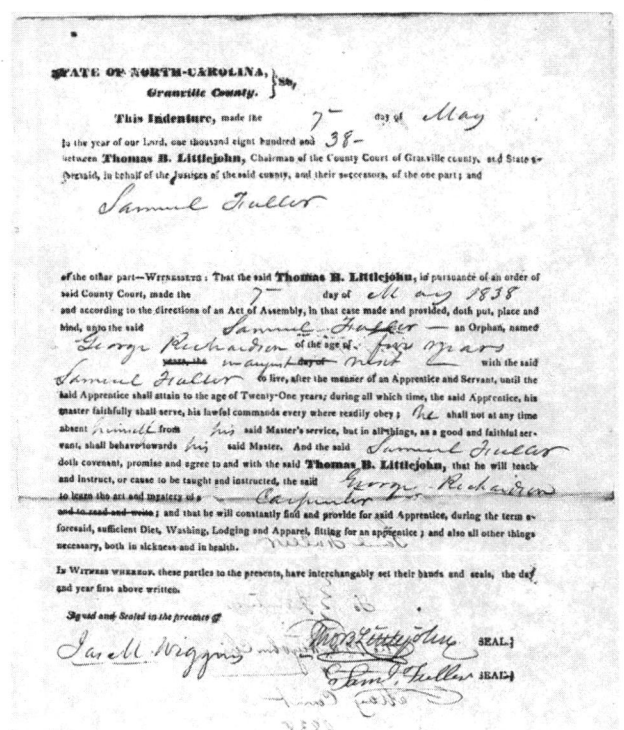

FIG. 3.3. *Apprenticeship bond, Granville County, 1838, George Richardson.* (NCDAH)

800 dollars," and Burklow's Peter, a literate Cumberland County slave carpenter of "much ingenuity."[17] The house carpenter possessed a multitude of skills learned through his apprenticeship and experience: he estimated and ordered the necessary timber for the building he planned; he laid out, cut, marked, and joined the framing that would be pegged together to form the floors, walls, and roof; he took charge of raising the heavy frame; he applied the wood shingle roof, covered the frame with weatherboards, and laid the floors; and he made and installed the doors, moldings, window and door frames, wainscoting, baseboards, mantels, and cornices. For these tasks, the carpenter used a wide variety of tools, including axes, augurs, chisels, hammers, compasses, adzes, saws, and a multitude of planes from the rough rabbit plane to the delicate planes for elegant moldings. The slave artisan might use his master's tools or might be provided with his own set, which often went with him if he were sold or hired to another master.[18]

Slave carpenters, like free men, were often competent in more than one trade. Sam, "originally brought up to the cabinetmakers business," had moved into carpentry,[19] while Stephen, who had belonged to builder Rodham Atkins, was a carpenter who also understood the millwright's business.[20] An especially common combination was shoemaking and car-

FIG. 3.4. *Orange County Courthouse, 1845, Hillsborough. John Berry, builder. Photograph by Tony Rumple, 1970s.* (NCDAH)

pentry. John, who ran away from William P. Little of Warren County in 1817, was a shoemaker and painter as well as a carpenter; and Robin, who worked in the same county, boasted "considerable mechanical knowledge both as a shoemaker and a carpenter."[21] Other slaves combined skill in carpentry with the trade of sawing, as did Ned, a good sawyer, hewer, violin player, and "part of a carpenter," and Diver, a stout, hard-drinking, domineering workman who was not only a good carpenter but also a powerful sawyer and a strong hewer with a broadaxe.[22]

The sawyer was vital to antebellum construction. Although water-powered mills served North Carolina from the early eighteenth century, they were often so far away from building sites as to make hauling lumber to and from the sawmill laborious and unprofitable. Thus, until the establishment of steam-powered mills and the improvement of transportation, sawyers were much in demand to saw planks, weatherboards, and timbers for framing. Further, even where sawmills were convenient and productive, they ordinarily could not handle the largest timbers needed for cornerposts and sills: such massive members were sawed or hewed by hand.[23]

In North Carolina as elsewhere sawyers usually worked in teams (see fig. 6.7, p. 135). Two strong men wielded the great pit saw: one of them—the "top dog"—stood on a platform above, while the other—the "bottom dog"—worked from the pit below, as they pushed and pulled the long saw through the timber.[24] Moses and his partner Stepney and Gilbert and his partner Randall, who belonged to a Virginia master, traveled as teams to take on big sawing jobs in the Albemarle Sound region. In 1814 their master charged for their work at the rate of 5 shillings of "Virginia money" per 100 feet of common plank and scantling, 6 shillings for wide planks. When they headed to Edenton to saw 50,000 feet of lumber for James C. Johnston at Hayes Plantation, they were joined by two more sawyers, Wilson and Anthony, who belonged to Johnston's friend David Clark. Clark wrote to Johnston, "My sawyers are desirous to go with [the others]—I send them—can stay two or three months if they will answer—should they not do their duty without trouble—please send them back—I think they will behave well—they may want papers sometimes—please act to them as your own." Directed by the sawyer Moses, the men averaged about 200 feet of sawing a day. They lost only a few days' labor to rain, sickness, and occasional visits back home. Moses's owner, pleased with reports of their accomplishments, told Johnston, "from the amount sawed they have worked well & will thank you to pay each of them five dollars as an encouragement for further well doing and charge me the amount $20." The other pair also worked so productively that Johnston advised their master that they were "likely to make something handsome for themselves which makes them saw with spirit. I think you ought to keep them at the saw until they are perfect masters of it."[25]

Less numerous than sawyers and carpenters but equally important were brickmakers and bricklayers. Caesar, a slave who had trained and worked in Norfolk before being moved to Greene County,[26] was one of many enslaved workers skilled in the demanding process of brickmaking, which involved digging and refining clay, molding and drying bricks, making, stacking, and firing a kiln, and glazing and rubbing decorative bricks. Brickmakers also had to construct kilns to burn lime from oyster shells or limestone and

FIG. 3.5. *St. Paul's Episcopal Church, 1730s-1770s, restored 1806-9, Edenton. Among the slave artisans involved in the restoration was Joe Welcome, a bricklayer who belonged to church leader Josiah Collins. Welcome also worked at Hayes Plantation and other projects in the Edenton area.* (NCDAH)

mix mortar in the proper proportions of lime and sand. Other slave laborers dug and worked the clay, filled molds, carried bricks, and loaded and unloaded kilns. Slaves also possessed skills as bricklayers, including such men as Nelson of Person County, Dick of Halifax County, and Mack of Granville County, who laid the bricks of chimneys, foundations, and walls in handsome bonding patterns; produced the thin, precise mortar joints between every course; and, in the best work, finished the mortar joint with a fine, inscribed line.[27] Some slaves specialized in the related "trowel trades" of stonemasonry or plastering, such as Ulysses, who trained as a plasterer under New Bern's free black brick builder Donum Montford.[28] A few slaves were even more specialized as, for example, Jerry, "well known" around Raleigh "as an excellent and skillful house painter.";[29] Jim, who was "the most experienced" house mover in New Bern;[30] and Eli, who specialized in bridge building in Edgecombe County.[31]

But such specialization was rare. In North Carolina most slave artisans, like free workmen, were versatile men capable of many tasks. The rural and small-town artisan, whether slave or free, usually could not specialize as narrowly as the city craftsman, for rural opportunities were neither as numerous nor as concentrated. Joe Welcome, a leading mason in the Albemarle Sound area in the early nineteenth century, epitomized the multi-skilled artisan essential to rural building. One of the many slaves owned by planter Josiah Collins, Joe Welcome was evidently a master at his trade, for he earned as much as 12 shillings 6 pence a day (white and black artisans ordinarily earned about 6 to 10 shillings in this period), and he seems to have led crews of slave artisans and laborers in construction projects that included Ebenezer Pettigrew's plantation house Bonarva, James C. Johnston's plantation house Hayes, and renovations of the colonial church St. Paul's (fig. 3.5) at Edenton.[32]

A typical project for the versatile mason Welcome was construction of the Edenton Academy, a frame structure with masonry foundations, brick chimneys, and plastered interiors and porch ceilings. From July, 1800, through the early months of 1801 (see appendix, pp. 97–100), Joe Welcome worked with a crew of men to accomplish a full range of masonry jobs. As the building progressed, he dressed stones, laid the stone foundation, hauled brick to the site by boat, erected the brick chimneys, made lime, lathed walls and ceilings, and applied finish plaster inside and out.[33]

Some historians have suggested that the presence of slave artisans tended to reduce the quality of building by taking away work from free craftsmen—thus implying that slaves' work was of inferior quality.[34] Others suggest that slave artisanry declined during the antebellum years as enslaved craftsmen were "stripped of their crafts."[35] Neither situation seems to have been true of the building trades in antebellum North Carolina. On

FIG. 3.6. *African American carpenter, identified as Haywood Dixon of Greene County. Photograph of mid-nineteenth-century daguerrotype. (Courtesy of William L. Murphy; NCDAH)*

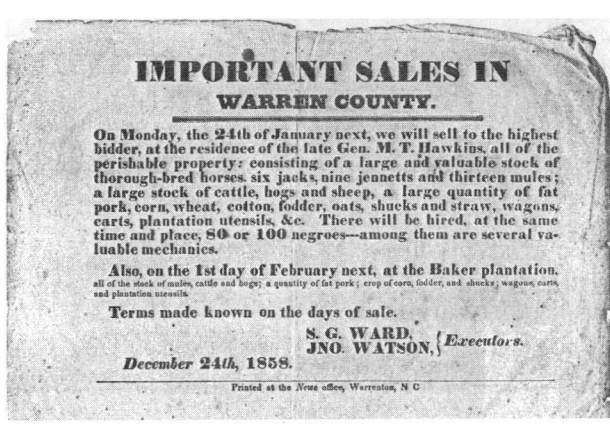

FIG. 3.7. *"Important Sales in Warren County," 1858. (NCDAH)*

the contrary, slave artisans continued to be important to the building industry throughout the antebellum years, and buildings erected by slaves and by combinations of slave and free artisans number among the most ambitious and elaborately executed landmarks in the state.

However vital his skills, the enslaved artisan had little or no choice in the work he undertook: it was his owner, not he, who profited financially from his abilities and who decided where and for whom he would work. The enslaved carpenter or mason found himself assigned to a variety of work situations.

The popular image of the slave builder focuses on his work at his owner's plantation. Certainly this did occur. Planter John Burgwin of New Hanover County apparently intended using his own slaves on his building projects when he advertised in 1798 for free artisans to direct 12 to 18 Negroes in making brick for a year or two and to superintend 6 or 8 Negro carpenters.³⁶ On the Dixon family plantation in Greene County, the slave carpenter Haywood (fig. 3.6) reportedly directed building projects for years in addition to guiding other plantation operations.³⁷

The home plantation, however, was not the only or even the principal setting for the black builder. In contrast to the great self-sufficient estates of colonial Virginia, each with its own bricklayers, shoemakers, carpenters, and blacksmiths, the small or middling North Carolina planter rarely had the means to invest in a full complement of skilled builders.³⁸ Indeed, even the largest of North Carolina's early nineteenth century and antebellum planters—men such as Ebenezer Pettigrew of Tyrrell County, James C. Johnston of Chowan County, Henry K. Burgwyn of Northampton County, and Duncan Cameron of Orange County—hired slave and free artisans for their building projects.³⁹ Accordingly, a slave artisan, far from spending his life building on a single plantation, was likely to be involved in a series of different building projects during his career and to work for many different individuals, even if he was owned by one master throughout his life.

Another widespread image depicts the slave artisan as the property of a free artisan in the same trade with the slave working as part of that artisan's shop. This situation, too, was a common one in the North Carolina building trades. Many of the prominent free carpenters and masons in the eastern part of the state, and some in the piedmont and west, which were less dependent on slave labor, relied consistently upon slave workmen.⁴⁰

In the late antebellum period, as investment in building increased and as builders throughout the state expanded their shops to undertake larger projects, many major contractors assembled their own teams of slave artisans. Brick builder John Berry of Hillsborough owned a self-sufficient and highly competent group of men, including several bricklayers, carpenter Joe Nichols, and tinner Ned Haughawort.⁴¹ The renowned brick builder Dabney Cosby of Raleigh owned with his son upwards of twenty slaves, who enabled the Cosbys to undertake numerous projects throughout the state.⁴² Carpenter Thomas Bragg, who spent a long career in the plantation communities in Warren and Northampton counties, invested heavily in slave workmen as he established himself as a builder in the 1810s and 1820s; he bought Harry for $377 and Kingston for £137 in 1812; John for $900 in 1817; Claiborn for $800 in 1818; Wilson for $700 in 1816; Will for $1,024,50 in 1818; and others.⁴³

However, the black artisans who were owned by other artisans represented but a fraction of the enslaved craftsmen active in North Carolina's antebellum building industry. For builders as for clients, the key to the use of slaves lay as much in hiring as in owning them. The cost of a skilled slave—$600 to $1,200 in 1820—meant that few artisans could afford to buy many slaves. In building as in agriculture and other industries, the hiring of

FIG. 3.8. *State House, 1820-24, Raleigh. William Nichols, architect. Engraving, 1831, by Fenner, Sears and Co., from drawing by William Goodacre. The state hired numerous slaves to work on the remodeling of the State House under architect Nichols.* (NCDAH)

slaves by the day or by the year was a highly effective method of distributing labor as required in the economy. The complex and interlocking patterns of slave ownership and slave hiring enabled free North Carolinians to use slave builders when and where and how they needed them.[44]

The hiring of enslaved artisans for building projects took several different forms. In many cases, the craftsman was hired out by his owner—a planter, a merchant, or a widow—directly to the individual for whom a building was erected. In such situations, the enslaved mason or carpenter worked for the client—a planter, a merchant, or in the case of a public building a building committee or superintendent—and the client paid the artisan's owner for the slave's time. Such was the case when Franklin County masons Willis and Wash built Nicholas Massenburg's chimneys and when planter Ebenezer Pettigrew paid Josiah Collins for Joe Welcome's and Jim Millen's work at Bonarva.[45] Similarly, during the remodeling of the State House in Raleigh (1820–24; fig. 3.8), the state paid several local slave owners for their artisans' work. John Marshall's slave "Peter the carpenter" and John Haywood's slave carpenters Jacob and Mumford were among the many enslaved and free craftsmen who worked under the superintendence of English-born state architect William Nichols.[46]

Occasionally slave owners contributed the time of their artisans to community building projects, especially churches. Trinity Episcopal Church

Black Builders in Antebellum North Carolina | 79

FIG. 3.9. *Market House, Wilmington. Drawing, ca. 1855. Annual slave hirings were held here on or about January 1.* (NCDAH)

near Scotland Neck in Halifax County and Cane Creek Baptist Church in Yancey County were examples in which church members and others donated their workmen's efforts in building.[47] In renovations to the colonial St. John's Church at Williamsboro in 1854, all the work was done by enslaved plasterers, painters, and carpenters who belonged to locally prominent citizens. One of the carpenters, Washington Robards, who built the new pulpit, left penciled inscriptions inside its panels, including his name, a poem, and the notation, "He was the best workman of Granville County."[48]

In many other cases slaves were hired by builders rather than by clients. It was very common for a free builder, even if he already owned a few slaves, to hire additional workmen in order to undertake a large construction project. One practice was for a slave owner to furnish laborers to a builder in exchange for a share of the profits. James Patterson, a Chatham County builder, joined with two local slave owners, Patrick St. Lawrence and George Lucas, to erect the first major structure at the new University of North Carolina in 1793.[49] In a similar arrangement in 1821, Tyrrell County carpenter J. D. Carraway joined with planter Ebenezer Pettigrew to take a contract for building a jail and bridge in Columbia. Pettigrew supplied slaves and materials to a total of $533.61, while Carraway contributed his own work and that of four slaves to the amount of $230.25. The contract had been given for $1,294.90; the men took a profit of over $530 and divided it evenly.[50]

The most common method by which builders expanded their work forces, however, was to hire workmen by the year or the day. Some were free journeymen, but many were slaves. Thus did slave owner and brick builder Dabney Cosby advise his son in 1850,

> You doubt the property [propriety] of Hiring for another year because you have no prospects for imployment. Now I cannot but believe ... sometime shortly some will be turning up that will alter the present state of business, there is to much public improvement going on not to make a stur in other ways and after the regular Hiring time not a hand can be let your wants be what they may—those you can get upon fair terms take.[51]

It was standard practice, as Cosby knew, to employ slaves for a year on or about the "hiring day" of January 1. "The first day of the new year was as usual a noisy day and our streets were thronged with negroes," reported a Salisbury paper in 1859. "On this day servants are hired out and not infrequently sales of large lots of negroes are appointed for the 1st of Jan., so that from these causes New Year's day is one of most importance to negroes of all the days."[52] The carpenter or mason offered for hire might belong to an artisan who did not need him at the moment, but more often he belonged to a planter, a banker, a merchant, a lawyer, a widow, or an orphan who profited from the hire of the slave's time.[53]

Warrenton builder Jacob Holt was one of many who commonly hired slaves as part of his large work force. In 1850 his building shop included not only 18 white journeyman and apprentice carpenters but also 34 male slaves, many if not all of whom probably were hired rather than owned by the builder.[54] Typical of his arrangements with the slaves' owners was an

FIG. 3.10. *Tucker House, 1858, Raleigh. Black artisans helped build the elaborate villa from designs by architect William Percival. Photograph ca. 1953.* (NCDAH)

agreement he signed in 1858: "On or before January 1, 1859, we promise to pay M. K. Williams $150 for hire of negro man Hilliard for the year 1858 and we bind ourselves to furnish said negro with usual summer & winter clothing Hat shoes Blanket & witness our hands and seals 1st of January 1858."[55] Holt also allowed clients to count their slaves' labor as partial payment if the slaves assisted Holt with the building projects.[56] Holt, like other builders, assigned teams of blacks and whites to his various projects.[57] He also participated in the standard practice of expending less for maintaining enslaved workmen than white ones. At one of his building projects, where the planter-client supplied food for the carpenters as part of his payment to the builder, the account noted, "Board of 1 white man from today (August 6) to 22 Decmr ... $36.00; Board one negro same time ... $18.00."[58]

An unusually revealing illustration of how the hiring system worked from the point of view of the owner appears in records kept by New Bern lawyer and slave owner John R. Donnell.[59] Early nineteenth-century New Bern enjoyed a building boom that produced scores of elegant Federal style structures; much of the work was evidently accomplished by slave artisans owned or hired by the town's free black and white carpenters and masons.[60] Donnell, a prominent and wealthy citizen, set up an account for each of his slave artisans, noting his investment in the purchase of the man and man's tools and the income he expected to receive. With each slave Donnell established the amount the slave would earn and what proportion Donnell would take. The New Bern attorney credited the slave for both money handed over ("wages") and for work done for him. If the slave failed to meet Donnell's expectations, then he "owed" his master, and Donnell determined how it would be made up.

Donnell hired out Simon, a carpenter, in 1822 for three months. The employer was to pay Donnell $9 a month and provide Simon's clothing—two shirts, a jacket and trousers, and a pair of shoes. Simon was to work "in the country where his food is found by his employer." Donnell had bought Simon a set of tools for $25.20 at a sale of another carpenter's possessions: the sash planes, ovolo planes, fore planes, molding planes, a tenant saw, rabbit planes, a brace and bits, a handsaw, chisels, a rasp, nippers, gimlets, a hammer, a screw augur, a plow, and other planes constituted the equipment needed for finished carpentry and joinery typical of Federal-era New Bern.

Donnell bought Ben, a carpenter, on July 1, 1823, from John Oliver, a prominent New Bern carpenter, for $615, and also bought a set of tools—an adz, compasses, axes, planes, a square, chisels. He hired Ben in 1824 to a Mr. Stevenson, probably leading carpenter Martin Stevenson. The terms were these:

FIG. 3.11. *Bryan House (left), 1803-5, New Bern. Photograph by Randall Page, 1972. Its builder, Martin Stevenson, regularly employed slave artisans, as did other builders of New Bern's finest Federal period architecture.* (NCDAH)

> He [Stevenson] gives $18 per month of 26 working dayes he to be accountable for the whole time, unless he is sick when I am to have immediate notice—of this I allow him to pay Ben $1.50 per week provided Ben has lost no time & not misbehaved during the week (out of this $1.50 Ben is to board and clothe himself—my object being to reserve $12 per month to myself.

If he netted $12 per month, or $144 a year, Donnell would recoup Ben's purchase price in slightly more than four years and thereafter take a profit on his time.[61]

Some slaves were permitted greater latitude than Donnell's workmen. Described by contemporary observers as "free slaves," they were allowed to hire out their own time without interference from their owners and even to live apart from their owners. This practice was forbidden by state law because it tended to encourage independence and instability among the slave population, but it went on nevertheless with the sanction of the highest officials.[62] In the household of Governor Charles Manly of Raleigh, for example, resided Raleigh stonecutter Allen Lane. Lane's wife and children

FIG. 3.12. *Stewart Ellison (1834-99), who worked as a slave carpenter in Raleigh and after emancipation became a civic and political leader. (Photograph of portrait, courtesy of Elizabeth Reid Murray and Anne Ray Williamson, Ellison's great-granddaughter)*

belonged to Manly, and Lane lived with them, but he hired out his time and gave a portion of his wages to two maiden ladies who owned him.[63]

Whatever the arrangements between the white parties, hiring slaves had risks on both sides: on the one hand, the employer without a long-term investment in the slave's welfare might abuse or neglect him; on the other, the slave might use the opportunity to run away. When Francis Dancy of Tarboro advertised for return of a slave sawyer, Sam, he explained that Sam "had in his possession a pass which I gave him about three weeks past, authorizing any person who wanted sawing done to employ him and his partner, and to account with me for their labour. It is probable he will use this pass as a means of making his escape, by pretending he is in search of employ."[64] Sometimes a slave might be killed during the course of his work for another owner; in such an event, the hirer might willingly or unwillingly reimburse the owner, as occurred after the slave Saul was crushed when John Haywood's house frame collapsed on him.[65] As the observer of a Wilmington slave auction commented, "a negro is capital, put out at a very high interest, but because of elopement and death certainly very unstable."[66] Despite problems inherent in the system, however, slave hiring persisted as a central element in the building industry throughout the antebellum period.

The widespread use of the hiring system, combined with the dispersed nature of the building industry, meant that the enslaved carpenter or bricklayer led a life quite different from the laborer or field hand. He was, as many historians have noted, well acquainted with the white world in a way that the isolated farm worker might never be. An advertisement for runaway slave Dick, a Wilmington bricklayer and plasterer, claimed that the twenty-six-year-old man had "worked in most of the Counties of the State."[67] There is some evidence that artisans were sold from one owner to another more often than the average slave. Such was the case with Park Lawrence, a New Bern carpenter, who had come from Africa as a young adult and was sold to the Lawrence family and then to the Hatch family. Carpenter John Marshall had been owned by three masters before he ran away from Tarboro.[68] Other slaves remained in the same ownership but were sent to distant building projects, as happened to Stewart Ellison (fig. 3.12), a young slave carpenter from Washington, North Carolina, who in 1852 was sent to work in Raleigh on Fayetteville Street commercial buildings and the state's insane asylum.[69]

Some enslaved builders also enjoyed a degree of independence unfamiliar to their brothers who labored in the fields, for many of them were delegated substantial responsibility and autonomy in their work. Jack Dewey, a New Bern carpenter, traveled to Hillsborough in 1834 to execute building projects for planter Paul Cameron. His owner hired him to Cameron at the rate of $100 for a six-month term. Dewey worked on Burnside, Cameron's large frame house at Hillsborough, and on other Cameron family projects in Raleigh. He was given a copy of plans, and he traveled freely from town to town. At one point Cameron reported, "I went over from Person [County] to H'borough to see how Jack and his company had employed themselves. They had not gone on as well as I had expected in laying down

FIG. 3.13. *Old East, 1793-95 and 1844-45, University of North Carolina, Chapel Hill. Photograph ca. 1888. When James Patterson built the first campus building at the state university, he used slave artisans. During the 1844-45 expansion from designs by New York architect Alexander Jackson Davis, contactor Dabney Cosby sent his slave artisans Albert and Osborne to accomplish the plastering.* (NCDAH)

the floors—but said that they had waited until all the flooring plank had been carried up that a selection might be made of the best for the floors of the lower rooms."[70]

Similar autonomy within the limitations of slavery characterized the work of Albert and Osborne, brothers and specialists in plastering. The men belonged to brick builder Dabney Cosby from the late 1820s through the 1840s. Typically, when Cosby had contracted for a project, he would take or send the two men to the job site and leave them to work for long periods on their own.[71] Cosby commented to University of North Carolina president and former governor David L. Swain in 1846, when the men went to work on additions to Old East (fig. 3.13) and Old West on the campus,

> The bearer Albert comes up to help his Bro. do the Plaisterin [sic] in the halls. I have told him to Examine the sand to be used . . . and to procure such as in the Judgment of him and Osborne will make the best work. You may rely on what he tells you, and If I mistake not they will show you firstrate work his plaistering and roughcasting here has preference to any done in this part of the State.[72]

Such was the intimate world of antebellum building relationships that the slave artisans would expect to have direct contact not only with their owner and with other builders but also with the president of the university, who would take an immediate interest in the progress and quality of the buildings under construction.

Harry, a slave carpenter who belonged to the Battle family of Chapel Hill, typified the slave artisan who maintained a modest degree of independence in arranging for his time.[73] Lucy Battle wrote regularly to her husband in Raleigh in the 1840s and 1850s to report on household activities. During 1843 and 1844 Harry had concentrated on remodeling the family house in Chapel Hill, working with a carpenter named Mr. Jenkins. After the house was finished, Harry began work on outbuildings and fences but also found other opportunities for employment. In the spring of 1845 David Swain came to visit. Mrs. Battle reported:

> his object . . . was to know if he could hire Harry, shortly, said he wished him to put up some paling about the Steward's Hall, I told him he could not be spared until he had moved your [Battle's] buildings—I am in hopes, however, that Harry will be ready as soon as the Gov. will . . . I shall be sure to hire Harry out whenever I can I assure you.[74]

Later that year the carpenter Jenkins sought to hire Harry to help build another house but haggled over the terms. Jenkins, wrote Mrs. Battle, "does not seem to like to give $15 a month unless I bord [sic] him [Harry] which I don't like to do as I am going on the last side [of meat]." Harry himself entered into the negotiations to clarify his own terms of employment: "Harry says he has always received $15 a month and that the person who hires him boards him—he wishes to know what you say."[75] A few years later Mrs. Battle observed that she had hopes of erecting an arbor and reported, "Harry says he can do it, as soon as he gets the timber—he is now working on the Presbyterian Church but says he can stop long enough to do my job."[76]

Not every slave artisan, of course, lived on such seemingly harmonious and secure terms as did Harry with the Battle family. Some slaves were mistreated by their owners or employers: a slave cabinetmaker's descendant remembered, "If he made one [a piece of furniture], and it didn't suit the man he would beat him and kick him around."[77] Similarly, slave carpenter William McIntire's daughter recalled, "dey worked from light till dark, and pap said dey beat him so bad he run away a lot o'times."[78] Further, whatever the ease or difficulty of daily life, the slave possessed the grim knowledge that his status as property might result in his being sold if an owner died or fell into financial difficulties. Reminders of this condition appeared regularly when slave buyers came into communities, such as one Ansley Davis of Petersburg, Virginia, who advertised his plans for "a long stay" at the Carolina Hotel in Wilmington. Davis hoped to purchase "a large number of negroes aged 14 to 30," including not only laborers but also carpenters and bricklayers, "for which I will pay the highest cash market prices."[79]

It was not surprising that enslaved carpenters and masons sometimes sought to escape their bondage and pass as free men. Artisans, because they were practiced in dealing with white society, were among the slaves who found it easiest to take on new identities as free men.[80] Further, slave builders worked alongside men of equal skills who were free, they were accustomed to operating independently, and they often heard of opportunities in distant places where they might disappear in a busy work force. Slave carpenter Allen's master supposed he would "make for some of the northern cities, and attempt to pass himself for a free man."[81] When Moses Camden, a carpenter from Maryland, escaped his Rockingham County, North Carolina, owner, the master predicted he would "attempt to pass for a free man."[82] In 1815 and 1816 several Halifax County artisans ran away to Petersburg, Virginia, so their owners surmised, in hope of finding work amid "the high wages given there in consequence of the destructive fire."[83]

A few black artisans were not slaves but free men. Some had obtained their freedom by manumission or by buying their own liberty, while others had inherited free status.[84] Free black artisans were heavily represented in North Carolina's antebellum building trades, and although they worked primarily as carpenters—257 of them in 1860—they also included 120 masons, 25 plasterers, 66 painters, and a small number of stonecutters, brickmakers, and mechanics.[85] In contrast to some service trades such as barbering, which were often considered especially the purview of Negroes, free black builders worked in parallel situations and often in close proximity to whites and slaves operating in the same trades.[86]

Free blacks' prominence in the building trades arose in part because of the emphasis upon free black children in apprenticeship laws. From the colonial era onward, free black children were singled out for court-ordered indentures, and the conditions of their indentures were differentiated from white children. Among males, carpentry was the most common trade besides farming to which apprentices were bound.[87] The masters of free black apprentices might be either black or white men, and it was not unusual for a white artisan to have both black and white apprentices, as did Chowan County carpenter William Bentley in September, 1784, when he apprenticed James Bentley, age seventeen and probably a relative, and William Lane, a six-year-old mulatto, to the house carpenter's trade.[88]

Some free black youths entered building trades not through court-ordered indentures but through apprenticeships arranged by their parents who wanted them trained for a livelihood or who sought to assure their welfare after the parents' death. Thus, New Hanover County planter Edmund Corbin, who had evidently fathered two children by a slave woman, Nelly, urged the executors of his will to buy her freedom and that of "the child she is big with" and to have Nelly's son, Lewis LeGrand, manumitted and "schooled and qualified for a Carpenter & . . . kept as much from Negroes as they can." Corbin further wished to have "all the Negroe boys I have left placed out to the Carpenters trade as soon as they are old enough" so that when Lewis arrived at the age of twenty-one he would have his own trained work force.[89]

To avoid being mistaken for a slave, the free black apprentice often carried documentation of his status, particularly when leaving his home community. When one young "free boy of colour" was apprenticed by the Cumberland County court in 1832 to learn the trade of a bricklayer, he took with him a note signed by several leading citizens of his hometown of New Bern in Craven County, which was attached to his indenture.

> The bearer of this Cicero or Cicero Richardson, a mulatto boy about 13 or 14 years of age was born of a free mother in this town. He is about leaving here as we understand for Fayetteville, and this certificate is given as testimony of his freedom. His grandmother is a well known huckster or cake woman by the name of Caty Webber.
> If any difficulty should occur Cicero can hand this paper to Louis D. Henry Esq. who is acquainted with the signers.[90]

The free black adult also needed to carry a pass that documented his free status. One carpenter carried a copy of his former owner's will manumitting him, while another retained a court order terminating his apprenticeship and stating that he had been "ordered to be liberated and set free."[91]

Free black artisans suffered from increasingly harsh laws in North Carolina as in other states, which affected their economic capabilities as well as their political rights.[92] In contrast to some other southern states, North Carolina did not threaten the property rights of black artisans or their ability to work independently of whites, but in 1861 the legislature passed a law that would have placed severe restrictions on free black builders: it forbade free blacks to buy, hire for any length of time, bind as apprentice, or "in any other wise … have the control, management or services of any slave or slaves."[93] This measure would have essentially destroyed the operations of the leading free black builders, for they, like their white counterparts, owned slaves and took apprentices on a large scale. The law had little effect, for it did not alter existing ownership or indentures, and within a few years of its enactment, slavery had been abolished.

There were other attempts to limit the economic opportunities of free blacks, especially artisans, as white mechanics lodged complaints against the competition they presented. One such episode occurred in the early 1850s when an organized series of rallies across the state brought together white mechanics who sought to control black competition.[94] Petitions to the legislature originated not only in such eastern counties as Beaufort, Craven, and Cumberland, where many free blacks worked, but also in the piedmont where free black mechanics were few but antiblack feeling was nevertheless intense.

A typical petition was forwarded from mechanics who met in Salisbury, Rowan County, on December 14, 1850. The white mechanics asserted that the mechanical arts were "greatly depressed in North Carolina by an undue competition arising, First from free negro mechanicks, and Second from mechanicks both white and black in the non-slaveholding States." The petitioners made no suggestions for dealing with northern competitors but rather focused on the free Negroes as "a degraded class of men," who, "never governed in fixing the prices for their labour by consideration of a fair compensation for the services rendered," could underprice white artisans and thus take away trade. The whites insisted that all free Negro mechanics be bound as permanent apprentices to whites—essentially become enslaved—and that the black artisans be permitted to work at their trades only "under the direction and control of the master to whom they are bound." The whites further demanded that manumission be declared illegal and that funds be increased to aid free Negroes to leave the state.[95] The petitions did not gain the status of law, but their language exposed deeply

FIG. 3.14. *Union Tavern, ca. 1818, Milton. From 1848 to 1859 this was the residence and workshop of cabinetmaker Thomas Day. Photograph ca. 1972.* (NCDAH)

FIG. 3.15. *Stair, Bartlett Yancey House, 1856, Yanceyville vicinity, Caswell County. Attributed to Thomas Day. Photograph by Tony P. Wrenn, 1972.* (NCDAH)

bitter attitudes. Though such feelings were not universal, inevitably they shaped the climate in which the free black artisan worked.

Despite the problems they faced, however, several free black artisans achieved success in the building trades and prominence in their white-dominated communities. The best known was Thomas Day of Milton. A slave-owning, well-educated resident of Caswell County, Day operated a workshop that produced not only some of the most sophisticated Empire style furniture made in North Carolina but also elegant interior woodwork. Mantels attributed to Thomas Day exhibit robust interpretations of then current neoclassical motifs, while stairs credited to his shop feature opulently curved, stylized newel posts (fig. 3.15). His work was concentrated in Caswell County, but it appeared in the homes of elite citizens of nearby counties as well. Day occupied a position of considerable status in his community, the quality of his work won him commissions over white competitors, and his correspondence with members of his family suggests a sophistication beyond that of many of his planter and merchant clientele.[96]

The town of New Bern included many free black as well as slave artisans.[97] Donum Montford, one of the town's principal brick builders, owned or hired a large slave and free black work force, which gained him a reputation as a fast and efficient contractor for big projects. Notwithstanding his inability to read and write, Montford took a leading role in the community's building business, including such duties as serving on a committee of three builders to judge a white builder's work. Montford clearly enjoyed an economic position equivalent to the white middle class in his community, and his household possessions at his death suggest a genteel style of living: his personal estate included such goods as mahogany furniture, pictures of Napoleon and Christ, a dining table and a secretary, a family Bible, silver spoons and oyster dishes, as well as workaday furniture, utensils, and tools.[98] Also prominent among New Bern's free black citizens was John C. Stanly, who, although apparently not himself an artisan, was an important figure in New Bern's building industry. He was often entrusted with the care of free black and slave children, many of whom he apprenticed to the building trades in New Bern. Under his guardianship, slave children were taught a trade and often manumitted; many free black children were bound by the court to Stanly, and he in turn probably assigned them to a local artisan, slave or free, for training.[99]

Similar concern for the training of young black builders characterized the career of Wilmington carpenter James Sampson. He is said to have been "the son and slave of a rich planter in Sampson County." According to family tradition, "in 1819, when James was about eighteen years of age, his father carried him to Wilmington, North Carolina, found him a suitable location, set him up as a carpenter (James had been well-trained in this work) and liberated him." Within a short time, the family recalled, his father "brought him several slave boys to be trained and instructed by James whom he told, 'Do for them what I have done for you.'" Sampson therefore trained many young black artisans, slave and free, and, though forbidden by law, he enabled many of the slave youths to learn to read and write. Through his father's backing and his own efforts, Sampson was among the few builders in the state, black or white, who accumulated property valued as high as $20,000. He spent a productive career in Wilmington, and his children and protégés were prominent in its building trades and community life through much of the century.[100]

These successful builders, however, were no more typical of the free black artisan than were prosperous white contractors characteristic of the white artisan class. Representative of many builders of the period was Thomas Sheridan of Bladen County, a free black carpenter who served a rural community and achieved modest prosperity during a career that extended from the 1810s through the 1850s. Sheridan, who was connected through his kinsman Louis Sheridan with the community's white establishment, is chiefly remembered as the builder of Brown Marsh Presbyterian Church (fig. 3.16). At his death in 1863 he owned a small farm, household goods, his carpentry tools, and enough lumber in his shop for his coffin.[101]

The career of James Boon illustrates the difficulties experienced by the ordinary free black builder. Boon, trained by Franklin County carpenter William Jones, completed his indenture in 1829. At first Boon operated as an independent rural artisan, building for planters in Franklin and nearby Halifax County; there he gained a good name as "an orderly and well behaved man" whose work, one client stated, was "executed better and with more taste than any persons within my knowledge in this section of the country."[102]

In the late 1840s Boon left these familiar environs for new urban opportunities: he joined his brother in Wilmington in 1848 and then went to Raleigh in 1849, where he worked under contractor Dabney Cosby on construction of the Yarborough House hotel. Despite many patterns in common with white artisans, as a free black Boon suffered from the restrictions placed on his class. He remained illiterate, for in accordance with state law his master had not taught him to read. Further, wherever he went he had to find white backers and to carry letters from white employers to identify him as a free man. Thus, his brother advised him before he traveled to Wilmington in search of work: "Yo will Pleas es Mr. Duke harrison and get him write Mr. Jeffrey and get him to be there protector as my Protectr dont appear as he wants to be bothered with them. I offered to pay him but he wont act." William Jeffreys provided Boon with the requisite endorsement

FIG. 3.16. *Brown Marsh Presbyterian Church, 1828, Elizabethtown vicinity, Bladen County. Thomas Sheridan, builder. Photograph by Ruth Little-Stokes, 1974.* (NCDAH)

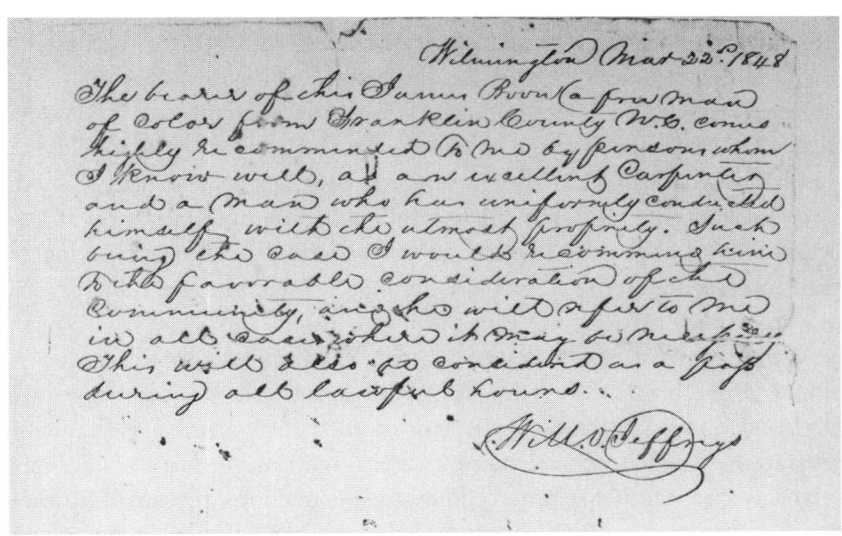

FIG. 3.17. *Pass, Wilmington, 1848, for James Boon.* (*James Boon Papers*, NCDAH)

that recommended him as an employee and that served "as a pass during all lawful hours" (fig. 3.17) while the carpenter lived in Wilmington.[103] Occupying a curious middle rank in the society, Boon, like many other free black artisans, possessed only limited freedoms, though he could employ his time as he saw fit. Like the enslaved artisan, he was constantly at risk unless he adhered to the restrictions whites placed upon him.

Black Builders in Antebellum North Carolina | 93

Blacks were important to the building industry in every eastern North Carolina town, but probably nowhere did they enjoy such success or face such problems as in Wilmington. The city was the largest in the state, and about half its population was black: in 1850 there were 3,570 whites, 2,873 slaves, and 657 free blacks.[104] Wilmington artisans included a diverse, mobile, and ever-changing population of whites, including many specialists from northern cities drawn by the railroad-induced building boom; a substantial group of free blacks; and an unknown number of enslaved artisans.[105]

The large number of slaves, the commitment of the white power structure to the slavery system, and, ironically, the latitude permitted the slave population meant that the free black occupied a position of some delicacy in Wilmington.[106] Passes for free blacks were policed closely, and whites sought to restrict contact between free blacks and the large slave population: James Sampson's efforts to teach slaves to read met with hostility from white leaders,[107] and one former slave whose family belonged to a wealthy white resident of Wilmington recalled, "We had a lot of these malatto negroes round here ... they was free issue and part Indian. The leader of 'em was James Sampson. We child'en was told to play in our own yard and not have nothin' to do with free issue child'en or the common chil'en 'cross the street, white or colored, because they was'nt fitten to 'sociate with us."[108] Yet, as elsewhere, black builders did succeed in the city. In addition to several members of the Sampson family, other prominent free black builders included carpenter Solomon Nash and members of the Artis and Howe families, who remained important in the city for several generations. There were also many free black carpenters, masons, and mechanics who, if less prominent or successful materially, were nevertheless earning a living at their trades: of 97 free residents of Wilmington listed in the building trades in 1850, 34 were blacks.[109]

Wilmington's slave artisans, by contrast, enjoyed freedoms unusual even among urban blacks. Since the eighteenth century slaveholders who usually resided on plantations had permitted their slave artisans to maintain separate living quarters and hire out their own time in North Carolina's towns. A 1777 statute to prevent "domestic insurrections" forbade this practice, but the law went largely unenforced. A new law in 1785 allowed slaves in Wilmington (as well as those in Fayetteville, Washington, and Edenton) to hire their own time if their masters registered them with town authorities, paid certain taxes, and affixed to the slaves' clothing "a leaden or pewter badge." The badge signified that slaves could "lawfully" hire themselves out without a master's direct supervision.[110] In 1846 the situation was much the same. The Providence, Rhode Island, *Journal* observed, "There is probably no place in the world where slaves are treated with more lenity and indulgence than in Wilmington."[111] As a former slave recalled:

FIG. 3.18. *Bellamy Mansion, 1859–60, Wilmington. James F. Post, the architect-contractor, and Rufus Bunnell, assistant architect, were white men, but most of the artisans who built the house were African Americans, including carpentry contractor Jim Artis, a free man, and George Price, William H. Gould, and Henry Taylor, who were slaves. (Photograph by U. C. Ellis, ca. 1900, courtesy of the Bellamy Mansion Museum)*

> We had a lot of them artisans 'mongst our folks. They all lived on our place with they famlies. They hired theyselves where they pleased. They colle[c]ted they pay, an' the onliest thing the owner took was enough to support they fam'lies. They all lived in our yard, it was a great big place, an' they wimmen cooked for 'em and raised they chilluns.[112]

Wilmington's opulent pre–Civil War buildings were in large part the work of slave and free black carpenters, masons, and plasterers. The grandest of the residences that rose in the late antebellum boom years, the Bellamy Mansion (fig. 3.18), was supervised by a white builder, James F. Post, but as Post's son recalled, it was in fact "built by colored workmen."[113] John D. Bellamy, son of the first owner of the house, explained further, "all the carpentry work was performed by negroes, chiefly free negroes. The masonry and plaster work, the cornices and other ornamental work on the walls was also done by negroes. As a matter of fact, in ante-bellum days, white men generally refused to ply the trade of carpenters and masons, thinking it beneath their dignity. So the employment of the negro carpenters and masons was not a matter of choice but one of necessity."[114] In other cases, black and white, northerner and southerner, worked literally elbow to elbow.

When the scaffolding fell from a building in 1846, three white workmen, two slaves, and a free black carpenter tumbled to the walk below.[115] Thus, the social and racial mix in Wilmington's building trades was a productive but complex one in which Yankees from Nantucket found themselves hiring slaves or competing with them for contracts, and Scots-born artisans worked alongside slave and free carpenters from the low country.

A startling incident one hot summer midnight brought to a boil the tensions that simmered in the community. In early August, 1857, the *Wilmington Herald* reported, a party of about fifteen men "by agreement endeavored to tear down or injure the frame work of a building" under construction, and they left a placard stating that "a similar course would be pursued, in all cases against all buildings to be erected by Negro contractors or carpenters." According to one rumor, this nocturnal demonstration was the work of an "organized association" of 250 or more workmen angered by "what they considered a grievance in the matter of negro competition with white labor."[116] The white mechanics objected to competition from slaves, not free blacks. They asserted that they were "unable to compete with negro mechanics, from the fact that the latter were cared for by their master's, were at trifling expense for living, and were thereby enabled to underbid them in contracts." The whites further insisted that "contracts made by slaves were contrary to law; and that it was an evasion of the law and against good policy for masters to take these contracts and pass them over to their slaves." They complained that this practice "cheapened labor to such a degree that they the white mechanics could not live, and would be compelled to abandon their occupations or to leave the place."

Public "outrage" at "the act of endeavoring to destroy the property of a citizen by an illegal combination" brought about a public meeting. The *Wilmington Herald* sardonically observed: "It is hardly necessary to say that there was excitement manifested." The meeting revealed sharp divisions between the white mechanics and the "gentlemen" of the city. One Eli Hall, Esq., speaking for the latter group, "deprecated the arraying of one class of the community against another" and suggested that

> if under the present situation of things as regards slave competition in labor, the mechanics felt aggrieved, the proper mode of redress was not to right a wrong by committing a wrong, but by appealing to the laws—that if the present business did not justify them in remaining here, they were at liberty to leave the place and seek a living elsewhere.[117]

The white mechanics had directed their wrath at slave builders, but their complaint went higher, as Hall's statement about class conflict acknowledged. The free black artisan when attacked by white mechanics had little

FIG. 3.19. *City Hall, or Thalian Hall, 1855-58, Wilmington. John M. Trimble, architect, James F. Post, superintending architect, Robert B. Wood and G. W. Rose, contractors. Photograph early twentieth century. Among the black artisans involved were plasterers George Price and Robert and William Finney.* (NCDAH)

defense, but the slave artisan was part of a social and economic system well guarded by the slave-owning elite.

Building in Wilmington continued to depend on black artisans, slave and free. Former slave John H. Jackson, recalling the construction of the ambitious and elegantly finished City Hall (fig. 3.19) at the end of the 1850s, declared:

> I remember all the bricklayers, they was all colored. The man that plastered the City Hall was named George Price, he plastered it inside. The men that plastered the City Hall outside and put those colum's up in the front, their names was Robert Finey and William Finey, they both was colored. Jim Artis now was a contractor an' builder. He done a lot of work 'round Wilmington. Yes'm, they was slaves, mos' all the fine work 'round Wilmin'ton was done by slaves. They called 'em artisans. None of 'em could read, but give 'em any plan an' they could foller it to the las' line.[118]

In the city or in the countryside the black artisan's career was filled with paradoxes as he plied his trade in a world ruled by whites. Whatever his condition of servitude or freedom, however, the black craftsman was crucial to all aspects of antebellum building. So vital were his skills that any exploration of North Carolina's architectural heritage must take into account the contributions of the black artisan. The observer of today's building industry sees at nearly every building site a mix of black and white workmen handling steel, pouring concrete, installing plumbing and wiring, and laying bricks. Such scenes represent strong continuities with an architectural history that from its beginnings has depended upon black labor and skill.

APPENDIX

Josiah Collins's Notes on the Construction of Edenton Academy

The following extracts from Josiah Collins's notes titled "Account of Work done by Sundries on the Academy" in the Cupola House Papers (microfilm copy), Southern Historical Collection, University of North Carolina Library at Chapel Hill, provide an unusually detailed account of a team of workers at a building site. Although records of many building projects exist, seldom do they illuminate so precisely the changing daily tasks of individual workmen. The author has summarized some entries.

> July 18, 1800. Joe Welcome[119] dressing stones. Andrew, Coper, Lewis digging foundation.
>
> 19. Old Welcome[120] laying foundation & dressing Stones. Joe Welcome dressing Stone. Jeffrey, Andrew dressing stone, digging foundation. Lewis dressing Shingles.
>
> 21. Old Welcome laying foundation. Jim[121] do [ditto]. Andrew assisting. Joe Welcome, Jeffrey dressing Stones. Old Ben Sawyer making Mortar. Old Lewis dressing Shingles.
>
> 22. Old Welcome, Joe Welcome & Jim laying foundation. Jeffrey & Ben Dressing Stones. Andrew & Dick[122] making Mortar & attending. Old Lewis dressing Shingles. Joe Bartlett dressing Stone.
>
> 23. Joe Welcome & Jim, Old Welcome laying foundation. Andrew & Dick making mortar & tending Masons. Jeffrey and Ben dressing Stones. Coper, Lewis dressing Shingles.
>
> 24. Welcome, Joe Welcome & Jim laying foundation. Old Ben, Jeffrey, Andrew & Dick raising the frame. Old Lewis dressing shingles.
>
> 25. Dick and Andrew raising house.

With the stone foundation thus laid in a week's time, the laborers helped the carpenters (unnamed in this account, and possibly free men hired for the job) raise the frame. Collins's account stops for several weeks, during which time the carpenters would have completed framing and weatherboarding and roofing the building. The masons began again in September, with Welcome making up putty and Andrew and Jerry painting the roof and the weatherboards. In early October the men began to build the chimneys, which were made of bricks floated to the site by water.

October 7. Joe Welcome, Silvester, Dick & Marshall & 2 Flatts & Canoe—getting [illegible] Bricks from Wilders Mill.

October 8. Joe Welcome, Silvester, Dick & Marshall & 2 flatts & canoe do. do. Andrew & Old Lewis carting do. [bricks] from McDonald's wharf to Acady.

9. Ditto. Joe Welcome, Old Welcome & Jim building chimney. Old Ben Sawyer and Silvester digging foundation for do.

10. Joe Welcome and Jim Building chimney. Ben Sawyer, Silvester & Lewis making mortar and attending.

11. Joe Welcome & Jim Building Chimney. Ben Sawyer, Silvester & Lewis attending. Andrew casting [carting?] Dirt for Mortar.

13. Old Welcome, Joe Welcome & Jim building Chimney. Ben Sawyer & Silvester attending do. Andrew casting dirt. Jeffrey, Marshall, Joe Bartlett, Dick, Old Lewis & Welcome Getting Bricks from Wilders with 2 flatts & Canoe.

14. Old Welcome, Joe Welcome & Jim, building Chimney. Old Ben Sawyer & Silvester attending do. Andrew [illegible] and Lewis carting brick from McDonalds whf.

15. Dick casting dirt for Mortar. Joe Welcome, Old Welcome & Jim building. Ben Sawyer & Silvester attending do.

16. do. do. do. Old Welcome, Joe Welcome & Jim building Chimney. Joe Bartlett, Jeffery, Welcome, Dick & Marshall getting Bricks from Wilders.

Through much of October, the men continued bringing bricks—a total of 25,000—to the wharf by boat and hauling them to the building site where the masons were erecting the chimneys. Then, while some of the workmen began to build the fence around the academy, Welcome and his crew turned to the final work of lathing, making lime, and plastering the interior walls and ceilings and the porch ceilings of the building.

October 29. Joe Welcome underpinning Piazza, Silvester and [?] attending.

30. do. lathing, do. attending.

31. do. do. Silvester attending.

November 1. Joe Welcome lathing & Silvester attending. (Hector worked from 9th October to the 28th about the chimneys 16 days.)

3. Joe Welcome lathing & Hector cutting lime wood. Hector about fence & Silvester sawing lathes.

4. Joe Welcome lathing, & Silvester carting lime wood.

5. Joe Welcome Lathing & Hector about fence.

6. Ditto do do do

7. Joe Welcome Lathing & Silvester attending do. Andrew & Cart Carting Lime Wood. Ben Sawyer Cutting do. Hector about Fence.

8. Joe Welcome Lathing & Silvester attending do. Ben Sawyer making Lime kill &c. Andrew Carting Lime Wood. Hector about Fence.

10. Joe Welcome lathing & Silvester attending do. Ben Sawyer slacking Lime. Hector about Bricks at Collector Office.

11. Do. Silvester do. do. Joe Welcome lathing. Ben Sawyer sifting Lime. Andrew carting.

In November the men worked on a smaller house at the site for a time, then returned to the academy building itself.

17. Joe Welcome underpinning Back Piazza, Silvester attending do. Ben Sawyer & Hector making Mortar.

18. Joe Welcome underpinning back Piazza & Silvester do., Ben Sawyer & Hector making Mortar.

19. Joe Welcome underpinning Piazza, Silvester & Hector attending do. Ben Sawyer making Mortar. Andrew & Jerry painting.

20. Joe Welcome plastering piazzas, Silvester & Hector attending, Ben Sawyer making mortar. Andrew and Jerry painting.

Welcome continued plastering the piazza ceilings through November and began plastering the interior of the building. Other workers continued making plaster, erecting fence, and attending. This work, plus masonry work at the Little House, continued through December and into January, 1801. Early in the new year, the men completed their work on the buildings. Collins's account indicated they had spent a total of 326 work days on the project.

NOTES

Much of the research for this article was conducted for Catherine W. Bishir, Charlotte V. Brown, Carl R. Lounsbury, and Ernest V. Wood III, *Architects and Builders in North Carolina: A History of the Practice of Building* (Chapel Hill: University of North Carolina Press, 1990). The author acknowledges with gratitude J. Marshall Bullock, who as research assistant located much essential material used in this article. In addition, the author wishes to thank Dr. Lounsbury, William Reaves of Wilmington, Elizabeth Reid Murray of Raleigh, the late James Brawley of Salisbury, William L. Murphy of Wendell, and Elizabeth Vann Moore of Edenton for sharing their research files, and Peter H. Wood, Sydney Nathans, and John Bishir for critical readings. Finally, the author acknowledges with thanks the groundwork research in two collections compiled from newspapers, apprentice bonds, and other sources, which have facilitated this study and many others: James H. Craig, *The Arts and Crafts in North Carolina, 1699–1840* (Winston-Salem: Museum of Early Southern Decorative Arts, 1965) and the Museum of Early Southern Decorative Arts, Winston-Salem, hereinafter cited as MESDA.

1. The scene is reconstructed from the Nicholas B. Massenburg Plantation Journal, Nicholas B. Massenburg Papers, Southern Historical Collection, University of North Carolina Library at Chapel Hill, hereinafter cited as Massenburg Journal. Thilbert H. Pearce of Franklin County brought the journal to the author's attention. The March–December, 1838, project was an expansion of a one-story house into a two-story T-shaped one. Observations about Franklin County architecture are based on the survey conducted by the author, Pearce, and Michael T. Southern. See T. H. Pearce, *Early Architecture of Franklin County* (Franklinton, N.C.: Privately printed by the author, 1977).

2. Massenburg Journal.

3. Massenburg Journal.

4. Hardy Floyd was one of a cadre of artisans in Louisburg, where in 1850 the building trades included two black stonemasons, a free black stonecutter, two free black carpenters, two white carpenters, and a white brickmason. George-Anne Willard (ed.), *Franklin County Sketchbook* (Louisburg: Franklin County–Louisburg Bicentenary Committee, 1982), 81.

5. William Jones (ca. 1785?–1851) appeared in Franklin County about 1817. He may have been the same William Jones who was active earlier in Wake County, where he took slave apprentices and hired or owned slave artisans. Wake County Tax Lists, 1809–15, Archives, Division of Archives and History, Raleigh; *Raleigh Register*, May 21, 1816. Jones also trained free black carpenter James Boon. John Hope Franklin has observed: "It was men like William Jones ... who did much toward making life bearable for free Negroes." John Hope Franklin, "James Boon, Free Negro Artisan," *Journal of Negro History*, 30 (April, 1945), 175.

6. *American Farmer* (Baltimore), 9 (January, 1828), 353. Charles Fisher (1789–1849), a noted proslavery spokesman, made his comments in the North Carolina House of Commons. A native of Rowan County, Fisher was elected to the state senate in 1818 before serving in the U.S. Congress, 1819–21. He was a member of the House of Commons, 1821–36, and served as speaker in 1831 and 1832. Fisher, a Democrat, served one more term in Congress, 1839–41. *Biographical Directory of the American Congress, 1774–1971* ... (Washington: United States Government Printing Office, 1971), 889.

7. Several studies of slavery and free blacks deal with black artisans' experience in building. See Peter H. Wood, "Whetting, Setting, and Laying Timbers: Black Builders in the Early South," *Southern Exposure*, VIII (Spring, 1980), 3–8; Mary Allison Carll, "The Roles of the Black Artisan in the Building Trades and the Decorative Arts in South Carolina's Charleston District, 1760–1800" (unpublished doctoral dissertation, University of Tennessee, Knoxville, 1982); John Michael Vlach, "'Us Quarters Fixed Fine': Finding Black Builders in the South," unpublished typescript, copy in the possession of the author; Leonard Stavisky, "The Origins of Negro Craftsmanship in Colonial America," *Journal of Negro History*, 32 (July, 1947), 417–29, and "Negro Craftsmanship in Early America," *American Historical Review*, 25 (January, 1920), 315–25, both reprinted in James E. Newton and Ronald L. Lewis (eds.), *The Other Slaves: Mechanics, Artisans, and Craftsmen* (Boston: G. K. Hall and Company, 1978); Gregory S. Peniston, "The Slave Builder-Artisan," *Western Journal of Black Studies*, II (Winter, 1978), 284–95; Gerald W. Mullin, *Flight and Rebellion: Slave Resistance in Eighteenth-Century Virginia* (New York: Oxford University Press, 1972); Eugene D. Genovese, *Roll, Jordan, Roll: The World the Slaves Made* (New York: Pantheon Books, 1974); Richard C. Wade, *Slavery in the Cities: The South, 1820–1860* (New York: Oxford University Press, 1964); and Ira Berlin, *Slaves without Masters: The Free Negro in the Antebellum South* (New York: Pantheon Books, 1974).

Studies on slaves and free blacks in North Carolina include Guion Griffis Johnson, *Ante-Bellum North Carolina: A Social History* (Chapel Hill: University of North Carolina Press, 1937); John Hope Franklin, *The Free Negro in North Carolina, 1790–1860* (Chapel Hill: University of North Carolina Press, 1943); James H. Boykin, *The Negro in North Carolina prior to 1861* (New York: Pageant Press, 1958); Jeffrey J. Crow, *The Black Experience in Revolutionary North Carolina* (Raleigh: Division of Archives and History, Department of Cultural Resources, 1977); and Gale J. Farlow, "Black Craftsmen in North Carolina before 1850" (unpublished master's thesis, University of North Carolina at Greensboro, 1979).

8. It is beyond the scope of this article to explore possible African or other specific aesthetic or formal contributions made by blacks to American building. That important subject merits ongoing consideration. For preliminary discussion of such topics, see Wood,

"Whetting, Setting, and Laying Timbers"; Genovese, *Roll, Jordan, Roll,* 394–98; Vlach, "Black Builders in the South"; and John Michael Vlach, *The Afro-American Tradition in Decorative Arts* (Cleveland, Ohio: Cleveland Museum of Art, 1978).

9. These observations are based on the author's research for the period 1730–1860 in Bishir et al., *Architects and Builders in North Carolina.*

10. John Urmston to the Society for the Propagation of the Gospel, July 7, 1711, William L. Saunders (ed.), *The Colonial Records of North Carolina* (Raleigh: State of North Carolina, 10 volumes, 1886–90), I, 764; John Brickell, *The Natural History of North-Carolina* . . . (Dublin: Printed by James Carson, 1737; Murfreesboro, N.C.: Johnson Publishing Co., 1968), 275.

11. Extracts from the Bethabara Diary, 1773, in Adelaide L. Fries, Douglas LeTell Rights, Minnie J. Smith, and Kenneth G. Hamilton (eds.), *Records of the Moravians in North Carolina* (Raleigh: North Carolina Historical Commission, 11 volumes, 1922–1969), II, 780. In contrast to most North Carolina towns, the Moravians in Salem specifically prohibited slaves from learning or working at trades well into the nineteenth century. Fries et al., *Records of the Moravians,* 7:3447, 3545; 9: 4485, 4821–4823.

12. Johnson, *Ante-Bellum North Carolina,* 476–77; Carll, "The Black Artisan in the Charleston District," 37–48; and Mullin, *Flight and Rebellion,* 86–87.

13. *Wilmington Centinel and General Advertiser,* July 9, 1788. Benjamin Smith (1755–1826) was a Brunswick County planter who served as governor, 1810–11. Samuel A. Ashe et al. (eds.), *Biographical History of North Carolina: From Colonial Times to the Present* (Greensboro: Charles L. Van Noppen, 8 volumes, 1905–17), 2: 401–5. Equally brief terms of indenture were common among free apprentices, except among orphans and illegitimate children where care as well as training was involved.

14. *Raleigh Minerva,* December 16, 1814; also *North Carolina Star* (Raleigh), September 2, 1814, MESDA, hereinafter cited as *North Carolina Star.* William Polk (1758–1834) was a Revolutionary War officer; he represented Davidson County in the North Carolina House of Commons (1785, 1786) and Mecklenburg County (1787, 1790). He moved to Raleigh about 1800 and served as president of the State Bank, 1811–19, Alice Barnwell Keith, William H. Masterson, and David T. Morgan (eds.), *The John Gray Blount Papers* (Raleigh: Division of Archives and History, Department of Cultural Resources, 4 volumes, 1952–82), 4: 611n. Polk seems to have trained, hired, and sold slaves often. One authority believes he was a slave trader. Farlow, "Black Craftsmen," 150. See also *Raleigh Register,* August 4, 1815; *North Carolina Star,* July 28, 1815; *Raleigh Minerva,* July 28, 1815, MESDA.

15. *North Carolina Star,* December 6, 1810. John J. Briggs, for example, also took white apprentices. Craig, *Arts and Crafts,* 321. In another example, Greene County carpenter Murfree Dixon is remembered as having white and slave apprentices in his shop, all of whom lived in the same room in his house. "Myrtle Lawn," recollections (ca. 1890) of Martha Sugg Dixon (1829–1904), Dixon Family Papers, in the possession of William L. Murphy, Wendell, N.C.

16. For comparative numbers of slaves in various trades see, for example, Mullin, *Flight and Rebellion,* 94–95.

17. *Norfolk* (Virginia) *Herald,* July 1, 1814, MESDA; *Fayetteville American,* September 26, 1816; Craig, *Arts and Crafts,* 339.

18. See, for example, E. T. Read to David L. Swain, November 25, 1846, in which a slave's tools were considered "part of his appurtenances" if he were purchased. Private Collections, David L. Swain Papers, PC 84, State Archives. See also note 60 below.

19. *Wilmington Centinel and General Advertiser,* February 26, 1789.

20. *Raleigh Minerva,* March 24, 1801, files of Elizabeth Reid Murray.

21. *Petersburg* (Virginia) *Republican,* April 1, 1817; *Raleigh Register,* September 15, 1815, MESDA; Farlow, "Black Craftsmen," 136, 144; Mullin, *Flight and Rebellion,* 94.

22. *Virginia Gazette* (Williamsburg), November 3, 1768, cited in Lathan A. Windley (comp.), *Runaway Slave Advertisements: A Documentary History from the 1730s to 1790* (Westport, Connecticut: Greenwood Press, 4 volumes, 1983), I, 65–66; and *Edenton Gazette,* June 16, 1808, MESDA.

23. See Carl R. Lounsbury, "The Wild Melody of Steam," in *Architects and Builders in North Carolina,* 195–201.

24. Wood, "Whetting, Setting, and Laying Timbers," 4.

25. W. W. Wilkins to James C. Johnston, April 10, 1814, and note of David Clark to

Johnston; Johnston to Wilkins, August 27, 1814; Wilkins to Johnston, September 6, 1814; Johnston to Clark, June 2, 1814, Hayes Collection, Southern Historical Collection. The "papers" were probably passes to permit the slaves to travel home.

James Cathcart Johnston (1782–1865) was the son of former governor, United States senator, and Revolutionary patriot Samuel Johnston (1733–1816). David Clark was a merchant with commercial interests in Plymouth and Edenton. Keith et al., *Blount Papers*, 4: 22, 75, 355. For another reference to sawyers working in pairs, see the will of Arland Parker of Northampton County, citing "two negroes by the name of Peter & Ben my Noted sawyers." Will of Arland Parker, January 19, 1803, Northampton County Wills, State Archives, courtesy of George Stevenson.

26. *American Beacon and Commercial Diary* (Norfolk), March 9, 1818, MESDA. Caesar, who belonged to one William Rowe, deceased, had been "bred to the Brickmaking business" and was "well known in the Borough of Norfolk" before being sold away from his wife and native region to Greene County, North Carolina.

27. Nelson, a stonemason and bricklayer, about twenty-two years of age, took with him two brick trowels and a stone hammer when he ran away. *American Beacon and Norfolk and Portsmouth Daily Advertiser*, July 29, 1819, and *Raleigh Register*, July 23, 1819, MESDA. Dick, "proud and fond of dress, and very fond of waiting about a house," was by trade a bricklayer. *Petersburg Intelligencer*, October 4, 1816, MESDA. Mack was about thirty or thirty-five, "very sensible and well behaved." *Virginia Gazette and Petersburg Intelligencer*, June 3, 1796, MESDA.

28. *Norfolk and Portsmouth Herald*, February 2, 1818, MESDA. Ulysses, who could read and write, worked as a plasterer in Hyde County before escaping.

29. *Raleigh Register*, February 15, 1851.

30. John Daves to John Haywood, January 21, 1800, Ernest Haywood Collection, Southern Historical Collection, hereinafter cited as Haywood Collection. Regarding Daves see Lynda Vestal Herzog, "The Early Architecture of New Bern, North Carolina, 1750–1850" (unpublished doctoral dissertation, University of California, Berkeley, 1977), 300–301.

31. *Southerner* (Tarboro), January 1, 1854; he belonged to planter J. J. W. Powell.

32. Handwritten transcripts of "Statement of Restoration Expenses, St. Paul's Church, Edenton, December 12, 1805–January 6, 1807," and of Josiah Collins's memorandum book of restoration expenses, June 15, 1806–February 3, 1808, supplied to the author by Elizabeth Vann Moore, Edenton. The Collins family owned several slaves named Welcome during the antebellum decades. Probably the Joe Welcome who was working in the period 1800–1806 was the man later known as "Old Joe Welcome" (1774–1859). His sons were Gilbert (b. 1799) and Bill Beasley (b. 1801). Another Joe Welcome, born about 1846, seems to have been his great-grandson. The man called "Old Welcome" in 1805 has not been identified. Welcome family data were supplied to the author by Elizabeth Fenn and Peter Wood, who researched the Josiah Collins Papers, State Archives. See also Hayes Collection, 1814–18; Bennett Harrison Wall, "Ebenezer Pettigrew: An Economic Study of an Ante-Bellum Planter" (unpublished doctoral dissertation, University of North Carolina at Chapel Hill, 1946), 167; and receipt, Ebenezer Pettigrew to Josiah Collins, October 4, 1816, Pettigrew Papers, State Archives, hereinafter cited as Pettigrew Papers.

The Collins family had extensive agricultural, commercial, and land interests, particularly in Chowan, Tyrrell, and Washington counties. Josiah Collins I (1735–1819) emigrated from England in 1773. His descendants included Josiah II (1763–1833), Josiah III (1808–63), and Josiah IV (1830–90). Ebenezer Pettigrew (1783–1848) owned plantations in Tyrrell and Washington counties. He served one term as a state senator (1809–10) and one term as a Whig congressman (1835–37).

33. Josiah Collins; Edenton Academy Sundries, 1800, Cupola House Papers (microfilm copy), Southern Historical Collection. McDonald's Wharf, at the mouth of Queen Anne's Creek in Edenton, facilitated the transport of bricks by boat. Elizabeth Vann Moore to the author, May 28, 1981, in the possession of the author.

34. Carl Bridenbaugh, *The Colonial Craftsman* (Chicago: University of Chicago Press, 1961), 31, 120, 138, 140, passim. Why black or slave artisanry is considered less refined or expert than white or free craftsmen's work is puzzling. One possible explanation might be the widespread complaints by individuals who objected to competition from blacks. Such racial tensions are discussed below.

35. Ira Berlin and Herbert G. Gutman, "Natives and Immigrants, Free Men and Slaves: Urban Workingmen in the Antebellum American South," *American Historical Review,* 88 (December, 1983), 1192. Berlin and Gutman base this statement in part on an estimate of the numbers of slaves owned by artisans. As the discussion of slave hiring below indicates, this method would not be a reliable basis for estimating numbers of artisans in the building trades, nor, by extension, for assuming that slave participation in trades diminished in this period. Similarly, Genovese argues that skills among slaves declined during the nineteenth century because of the effects of increasing dependence on northern manufactures, growing devotion of slave labor to agriculture, as well as exclusionist policies of hostile white labor in towns (*Roll, Jordan, Roll,* 389).

Whatever the situation in other crafts, North Carolina's building industry continued to rely heavily on black artisans throughout the antebellum period. The main changes seem to have reflected economic modernization, with the decline of the individual rural artisan (slave or free) and the rise of major builders who employed large numbers of men to meet contracts. This shift paralleled similar patterns in other aspects of labor. Peniston also distinguishes between a general decline in slave craftsmanship and its continuation in building ("Slave Builder-Artisan," 291).

36. *North-Carolina Journal* (Halifax), October 1, 1798. Regarding the slave carpenter Abram/Abraham, who escaped from Burgwin, see the *Wilmington Chronicle,* August 17, 1795, and *Wilmington Gazette,* December 17, 1795, and January 20, 1803; Farlow, "Black Craftsmen," 122. See also Wall, "Ebenezer Pettigrew," 160. John Burgwin (1731–1803) migrated from England to the Carolinas in the 1750s and established a major plantation on the Cape Fear River and lucrative mercantile operations in Wilmington, Charleston, and Fayetteville. He was thought by some to be a Tory during the Revolution. William S. Powell (ed.), *Dictionary of North Carolina Biography* (Chapel Hill: University of North Carolina Press, 1979), 1: 274–75, hereinafter cited as Powell, DNCB.

37. "Myrtle Lawn." See also the employment of Cuningham slave artisans—Burwell, Robinson, and Anderson—in building a plantation kitchen in 1845. Cited in Jane Turner Censer, *North Carolina Planters and Their Children, 1800–1860* (Baton Rouge: Louisiana State University Press, 1984), 102.

38. See Genovese, *Roll, Jordan, Roll,* 389–90, and Mullin, *Flight and Rebellion,* 3–33. A North Carolina example of a small farmer hiring enslaved artisans was Silas M. Stone's construction of farm buildings in the 1860s, for which he hired slaves at $1.25 per day. Silas M. Stone Papers, Duke Manuscript Department, Duke University Library, Durham, from the files of Carl R. Lounsbury.

39. See Wall, "Ebenezer Pettigrew," 151–70, 306–15, and Pettigrew Papers; Hayes Collection, 1814–18; Henry K. Burgwyn Diaries, 1840–42, 1844–48, State Archives; Jean Anderson, unpublished reports on Stagville and Fairntosh plantations, typescripts in the possession of the Historic Sites Section, Division of Archives and History, Raleigh; and Cameron Family Papers, 1810–20, Southern Historical Collection, hereinafter cited as Cameron Papers. Henry King Burgwyn, Sr. (1813–77), was the father of two noted Confederate officers: Henry, Jr. (1841–63), killed at Gettysburg; and William Hyslop Sumner Burgwyn (1845–1913), lawyer and banker. Powell, DNCB, 1: 276–77, 278–79. Duncan Cameron (1777–1853) was a planter, judge, politician, and banker. Powell, DNCB, 1: 311.

40. See, for example, the runaway notice for a slave of Wake County carpenter Rodham Atkins (note 21 above); John Oliver, a New Bern carpenter who sold black carpenters, *Carolina Centinel* (New Bern), June 2, 1821, cited in Herzog, "Early Architecture of New Bern," 325; New Bern carpenter Hardy B. Lane file, Craven County Estates Records, State Archives; and Tyrrell County carpenter Jesse Carraway's receipt for his work and that of his slaves, May 31, 1817, Pettigrew Papers, cited in Wall, "Ebenezer Pettigrew," 153.

41. Powell, DNCB, 1: 146–47; Mary Claire Engstrom, typescript entries "John Berry," "Joe Nichols," and "Ned Haughawort" for "Architects and Builders in North Carolina."

42. J. Marshall Bullock, "The Enterprising Contractor, Mr. Cosby" (unpublished master's thesis, University of North Carolina at Chapel Hill, 1982), 14–17. Bullock analyzes the builder's use of slave workmen and lists the numbers of slaves in the Cosby family's workshop from 1840 to 1860. In 1850, for example, the elder Cosby owned 18 slaves, including 8 males over fourteen years of age, while his son owned 16 slaves of whom 10 were males of working age.

43. The author wishes to acknowledge use of the deed summaries cited below from the files of Mary Hinton Kerr, Warrenton, N.C. Warren County Deeds, Office of the Register of Deeds, Warren County Courthouse, Warrenton, Book 19, pp. 16, 18, 164, 205; Book 20, pp. 178, 265, 266; Book 22, p. 38; Book 27, pp. 185–87, 401–4, 432; Thomas Bragg file, Northampton County Estates Records, State Archives. Thomas Bragg (1778–1851) the carpenter was the father of Thomas Bragg the governor as well as of military figure Braxton Bragg, attorney John Bragg, and Alabama builder Alexander Bragg. Powell, *DNCB*, 1: 209.

44. Concerning slave hiring practices, see Genovese, *Roll, Jordan, Roll,* 390–92; Carll, "The Black Artisan in the Charleston District," 67–72; and Wade, *Slavery in the Cities,* 28–54. Wade states that hiring and urban slavery were "never very satisfactory," but David R. Goldfield suggests that hiring was an effective, profitable, and flexible system. David R. Goldfield, "Pursuing the American Dream: Cities in the Old South," in Blaine A. Brownell and David R. Goldfield (eds.), *The City in Southern History* (Port Washington, N.Y.: National University Publications, 1977), 65–67. Sarah S. Hughes asserts that hiring was "the key to the survival of slavery" because it permitted the adjustment of labor supply to demands. Sarah S. Hughes, "Slaves for Hire: The Allocation of Black Labor in Elizabeth City County, Virginia, 1782 to 1810," *William and Mary Quarterly,* 35 (April, 1978), 260–86.

45. Receipt, Ebenezer Pettigrew to Josiah Collins, October 4, 1816; Day Book of E. Pettigrew, 1816–25, Pettigrew Papers; Wall, "Ebenezer Pettigrew," 167.

46. Capitol Buildings, Treasurer's and Comptroller's Papers, State Archives.

47. National Register of Historic Places nomination, Trinity Church, Survey and Planning Branch, Archaeology and Historic Preservation Section, Division of Archives and History, Raleigh; and John C. Inscoe, "Mountain Masters: Slaveholding in Western North Carolina," *North Carolina Historical Review,* 61 (April, 1984), 166.

48. Slave artisans included carpenters Washington and Damon, "servants" of Dr. H. J. Robards; carpenters Willis and Moses, owned by the Reverend W. H. Jordan; painters Aleck, owned by W. B. Hamilton, and Albert, owned by Colonel S. S. Royster; and plasterers Lafayette, servant of Mrs. Mary Williams, and Cambridge, who belonged to Dr. P. B. Hawkins. Transcription from panel inscriptions provided to the author by Charles H. Brewer, Jr., Oxford, N.C., January 15, 1983.

49. J. Marshall Bullock, "James Patterson," unpublished typescript for "Architects and Builders in North Carolina," and contract for building, July 19, 1793, University Papers, University Archives, University of North Carolina Library at Chapel Hill, hereinafter cited as University Papers. Samuel Hopkins, a competing bidder, complained that George Lucas employed a low-paid "parcel of awkward negroes" to win contracts cheaply. Samuel Hopkins to John Haywood, January 1, 1794, University Papers.

50. Day Book of E. Pettigrew, 1816–25, p. 44, Pettigrew Papers.

51. Dabney Cosby to Dabney Cosby, Jr., November 28, 1850, Dabney Cosby Papers, Southern Historical Collection.

52. *Carolina Watchman* (Salisbury), January 4, 1859, hereinafter cited as *Carolina Watchman*. The paper noted that the hiring rates were lower and sales prices drastically higher than in previous years. Concerning hiring rates around Wilmington, see Thomas Wright to John H. Bryan, January 4, 1854, John Herritage Bryan Collection, State Archives.

53. See, for example, William Williams file, Warren County Estates Records, State Archives; Abraham Spencer file, Granville County Estates Records, State Archives. After the 1846 death of Wilmington free black builder Solomon Nash, administrators of his estate offered for hire his slaves—two carpenters, a woman, and two children—for the balance of the year. *Wilmington Chronicle,* September 23, 1846, files of William Reaves. The actual ownership of enslaved artisans was so thoroughly distributed among the slaveholding population—merchants, bankers, planters, attorneys, physicians, ministers, widows, and orphans—that no estimate of their numbers seems possible based on owners' occupations.

54. Seventh Census of the United States, 1850: Warren County, North Carolina, Population Schedule, 26, and Slave Schedule, 19, microfilm of National Archives manuscript copy, State Archives, hereinafter cited as Seventh Census, 1850, with appropriate schedule, county, and page number. Warrenton tax lists of the 1850s show Holt with six or fewer black

polls. Warren County Tax Lists, State Archives. See also "Jacob W. Holt: An American Builder," chapter 1 of this volume.

55. J. W. Holt to M. K. (probably Mrs. Mary K.) Williams, February 1, 1858, Lucy Williams Polk Papers, State Archives.

56. Panthea Twitty to author, June 17, 1974, in the possession of the author. Twitty's grandfather, J. E. Boyd, supplied workmen and timber to Holt.

57. "J. W. Holt in a/c with WRB" (William Rust Baskervill), 1855–56, Baskervill(e) Family Papers, Virginia Historical Society, Richmond, Va., hereinafter cited as Baskervill(e) Papers. See also Lucy Martin Battle to William Horn Battle, October 14, 1851, noting, "Capt. [John] Berry has at length commenced our work . . . there are two white & two colored ones engaged—the Capt. stays with them a good part of the time." Battle Family Papers, Southern Historical Collection, hereinafter cited as Battle Papers.

58. "J.W. Holt in a/c with WRB," 1855–56, Baskervill(e) Papers. See also Johann Schoepf, *Travels in the Confederation, 1783–1784*, translated and edited by Alfred J. Morrison (Philadelphia: W. J. Campbell, 2 volumes, 1911; New York: Burt Franklin, 1968), 2: 147–48.

59. John R. Donnell Account Book, Bryan Family Papers, Southern Historical Collection, hereinafter cited as Donnell Account Book. Donnell (1791–1864) graduated from the University of North Carolina in 1815; he was a judge on the state superior court, 1819–36. Keith et al. *Blount Papers,* 4: 372n.

60. See, for example, brickmason Joshua Mitchell's receipts for construction of the Craven County jail, 1821–22, and receipts for work by carpenter Martin Stevenson, 1820s, records of Craven County Treasurer of Public Buildings, State Archives; New Bern carpenter John Dewey's advertisements for Negroes for sale, *Carolina Federal Republican* (New Bern), February 23, 1809; various artisans taking free black apprentices in New Bern, Craig, *Arts and Crafts,* passim; files of carpenters Frederick and Hardy B. Lane and brickmason Donum Montford, Craven County Estates Records, State Archives.

61. Donnell Account Book; for information on Oliver and Stevenson, see Herzog, "Early Architecture of New Bern," 324–25, 333–35.

62. See James Howard Brewer, "Legislation Designed to Control Slavery in Wilmington and Fayetteville," *North Carolina Historical Review,* 30 (April, 1953), 155–66; Wade, *Slavery in the Cities,* 40–43, 48–54; Crow, *Black Experience,* 28–29; and Genovese, *Roll, Jordan, Roll,* 392.

63. George P. Rawick (ed.), *The American Slave: A Composite Autobiography* (Westport, Connecticut: Greenwood Press, 1972–1977), Series 2, Volume 15, 329. Lane belonged to Susan and Emma White, daughters and heirs of William White, secretary of state for North Carolina. Elizabeth Culbertson Waugh, *North Carolina's Capital, Raleigh* (Chapel Hill: University of North Carolina Press, 1967), 29.

64. *Norfolk and Portsmouth Herald,* October 11, 1816, MESDA. Daniel, a carpenter "of Indian extraction" who belonged to a South Carolina attorney, escaped while working in Morganton, was caught in Wilkes County, then escaped again with a pass in hand. *Raleigh Register,* March 3, 1808, MESDA. See also *Norfolk Herald,* July 1, 1814, MESDA; Crow, *Black Experience,* 34–46; and Windley, *Runaway Slave Advertisements,* passim.

65. Statement, John Haywood et al., to Wake County Court of Pleas and Quarter Sessions, June 16, 1800, and Statement, Nathaniel Jones et al., June 26, 1800, Haywood Collection.

66. Schoepf, *Travels in the Confederation,* 2: 148.

67. *Wilmington Advertiser,* June 30, 1837, files of William Reaves.

68. *New Bern Times,* August 1, 1871; *Carolina Federal Republican* (New Bern), August 2, 1817, MESDA. See also Mullin, *Flight and Rebellion,* 83–98.

69. *Raleigh Daily Examiner,* newspaper clipping, February 15, 19, 1874, Charles N. Hunter Papers, Scrapbook, 1875–1924, Duke Manuscript Department, courtesy of Elizabeth Reid Murray. Ellison (1834–99) was born in Washington, Beaufort County. He was apprenticed to carpenter Marrs Newton, a black mechanic, and worked in Raleigh from 1852 to 1854. Ellison returned to Raleigh in 1862 and after the Civil War began taking contracts for building projects, which included work sponsored by the Freedmen's Bureau. He rose to a position of leadership as a builder and political figure and was elected to several public offices, including city commissioner and state legislator. See Elizabeth Reid Murray, "Stewart Ellison," Powell, DNCB, 2: 152–53.

70. J. Marshall Bullock, "Jack Dewey," un-

published typescript for "Architects and Builders in North Carolina"; receipt of C. Dewey, May 15, 1835, and Paul C. Cameron to Duncan Cameron, November, 1834, Cameron Papers.

71. Bullock, "Cosby," 14–17.

72. Dabney Cosby to David L. Swain, May 11, 1846, University Papers.

73. J. Marshall Bullock, "Harry," unpublished typescript for "Architects and Builders in North Carolina"; Lucy Martin Battle to William Horn Battle, March 29, September 27, 1845, Battle Papers.

74. Lucy Martin Battle to William Horn Battle, March 6, 1845, Battle Papers.

75. Lucy Martin Battle to William Horn Battle, October 11, 1845, Battle Papers.

76. Lucy Martin Battle to William Horn Battle, March 31, 1848, Battle Papers.

77. Rawick, *The American Slave: A Composite Autobiography*, 14: 260.

78. Ibid., 67.

79. *Wilmington Chronicle*, May 5, 1847, files of William Reaves. Regarding advertisements to buy and sell enslaved mechanics, carpenters, and masons, see Boykin, *Negro in North Carolina*, 36. See also Censer, *North Carolina Planters and Their Children*, 137, concerning sale of Jack, a carpenter owned by Elizabeth Ellis Pearson.

80. Mullin says competence in English, spoken and written, was a measure of assimilation common among escaped artisans (*Flight and Rebellion*, 89–92). North Carolina examples include John Brown, a carpenter who escaped from James Kelley of Beaufort in 1817. Brown could read, write, and speak French and some English. *Norfolk and Portsmouth Herald*, June 18, 1817, cited in Farlow, "Black Craftsmen," 125. Charleston carpenters George and Isaac were captured in Fayetteville; George could read and write, and Isaac talked "sensibly." *Fayetteville Gazette*, July 2, 1792.

81. *American Beacon and Commercial Diary* (Norfolk), March 17, 1818, MESDA. See also Sam, New Bern carpenter and seaman, expected by his owner to "go to some of the Northern seaports." *Carolina Centinel* (New Bern), June 3, 1820, MESDA.

82. *Petersburg Republican*, June 17, 1817.

83. *Petersburg Intelligencer*, October 4, 1816.

84. See Franklin, *Free Negro*, especially pp. 14–57; Boykin, *Negro in North Carolina*, 37–40; and Johnson, *Ante-Bellum North Carolina*, 582–612.

85. Franklin, *Free Negro*, 122–30, and table 5, "Occupations of Free Negroes in North Carolina in 1860," 134–35; Boykin, *Negro in North Carolina*, 17–23. See also Berlin, *Slaves without Masters*, 237.

86. Berlin cites several such "stigmatized" occupations. Some of the patterns he suggests do not appear to have been prevalent in North Carolina building trades. In addition to such services as barbering and drayage, he also identifies carpentry, plastering, and bricklaying as being so-called black occupations. In North Carolina thousands of whites as well as free blacks and slaves worked at these trades. Berlin notes characteristics present in Richmond and other cities, including the exclusion of free blacks from the stonemason's trade and the refusal of white artisans to hire free black artisans or work alongside them, that are not borne out in North Carolina examples (*Slaves without Masters*, 234–38).

87. Franklin, *Free Negro*, 122–30; Craig, *Arts and Crafts*, 279, 281, 302, passim.

88. Craig, *Arts and Crafts*, 286.

89. Will of Edmund Corbin, January 30, 1781, New Hanover County Wills, State Archives; courtesy of Bruce Cheeseman. In North Carolina as in other states, the status of a child of a free parent and a slave parent was determined by that of the mother. Johnson, *Ante-Bellum North Carolina*, 607–8.

90. Cumberland County Apprentice Bonds, State Archives. Louis D. Henry, a native of New Jersey, practiced law in New Bern, then in Fayetteville; he served in the House of Commons in the 1820s and 1830s; in 1842, as the Democratic candidate for governor, he was defeated by John Motley Morehead. Ashe, *Biographical History*, 2: 163–65.

91. *Raleigh Register*, January 6, 1815; *North Carolina Star*, January 6, 1815, MESDA; Franklin, "James Boon," 154; James Boon Papers, State Archives, hereinafter cited as Boon Papers.

92. Boykin, *Negro in North Carolina*, 37–45; Franklin, *Free Negro*, 58–120, 156–57; and Johnson, *Ante-Bellum North Carolina*, 597–606.

93. *Public Laws of North Carolina, 1860–1861*, c. 36; Franklin, *Free Negro*, 156–57.

94. Franklin, *Free Negro*, 137–39; Boykin, *Negro in North Carolina*, 26.

95. *Carolina Watchman*, December 19, 1850. The mechanics also urged that "all children of free negroes over 3 years of age" be indentured to white persons. The Salisbury group "con-

curred with similar resolutions" adopted in Fayetteville. Courtesy of the late James Brawley, Salisbury.

96. Michael Smith, *North Carolina Furniture* (Raleigh: North Carolina Museum of History, 1977), 47–48, 52, 54; Ruth Little-Stokes, *An Inventory of Historic Architecture: Caswell County, North Carolina* (Yanceyville: Caswell County Historical Association, 1979), 35–38; Rodney Barfield, *Thomas Day, Cabinetmaker* (Raleigh: North Carolina Museum of History, 1975); and W. A. Robinson et al., "Thomas Day and His Family," *Negro History Bulletin*, 13 (March, 1950), 123–26, 140.

97. Among the free black residents of New Bern in the building trades in the 1850 census were William Handcock, a carpenter owning four slaves, who had trained under white carpenter Uriah Sandy (Craig, *Arts and Crafts*, 341); carpenter James Green; house joiner Israel Braddock; house joiner Rigdon Green; carpenter Robert Hazle, who had trained under Green; plasterer Isaac Rem; house joiner Lewis Sawyer; and brickmasons William Allen and George Stringer. Seventh Census, 1850: Craven County, Population Schedule, various pages.

98. The name is variously spelled Montford, Montfort, Mumford. See Stephen Miller, "Recollections of Newbern Fifty Years Ago," *Our Living and Our Dead*, 1 (November, 1874–February, 1875), 461; Catherine W. Bishir, "Donum Montfort," unpublished typescript for "Architects and Builders in North Carolina"; Herzog, "Early Architecture in New Bern," 342; Calvin D. Wilson, "Negroes Who Owned Slaves," *Popular Science Monthly*, 81 (November, 1912), 486; Donum Montfort file, Craven County Estates Records, State Archives.

99. John Carruthers Stanly was a free black barber who accrued considerable property in land and slaves. Although Herzog's dissertation and the MESDA files have identified him as a builder because of his signing many indentures for young black apprentices to the carpentry and building trades, this writer believes that he was taking responsibility for black youths, free and slave, and placing them with artisans for training. See L. C. Vass, *History of the Presbyterian Church in New Bern* . . . (Richmond: Whittet & Shepperson, 1886); wills of Elizabeth Henry, February 26, 1819, and Mary Marshall, January 16, 1823, Craven County Wills, State Archives; Franklin, *Free Negro*, 31; and Johnson, *Ante-Bellum North Carolina*, 608.

100. James B. Browning, "James D. Sampson," *Negro History Bulletin*, 3 (January, 1940), 56. Browning's account evidently came from interviews with Sampson descendants. See also James Sampson file, New Hanover County Estates Records, State Archives. He owned over $21,000 worth of real and personal property.

101. Will of Thomas Sheridan, April 29, 1863, Bladen County Wills, Book I, 317; will of J. R. Gautier, August 4, 1800, Bladen County Wills, Book I, 352 (microfilm copy), State Archives. Joseph R. Gautier, a prominent Elizabethtown political figure, left his plantation, household and plantation utensils, and five slaves to Nancy Sheridan, "my emancipated black woman"; three slaves to "her child" Louis Sheridan; and $500 to Thomas Sheridan. Louis Sheridan became a prominent free black merchant in Bladen County and emigrated to Liberia in 1837. Franklin, *Free Negro*, 144–45. A Thomas Sheridan, who was either Louis's brother or another relation, remained in Bladen County as a carpenter and later a farmer until his death in 1863 at the age of about seventy-six. Seventh Census, 1850: Bladen County, Population Schedule, 98; Eighth Census of the United States, 1860: Bladen County, North Carolina, Population Schedule, 489, microfilm of National Archives manuscript copy, State Archives, hereinafter cited as Eighth Census, 1860, with appropriate schedule, county, and page number.

102. R. H. Mosby to Jesse Faulcon, February 22, 1842, Boon Papers.

103. Carter Evans to James Boon, January 20, 1848, and letter of William Jeffreys, March 22, 1848, Boon Papers; see also Franklin, "James Boon," 164–65, and Bullock, "Cosby," 82–83.

104. *Wilmington Chronicle*, August 28, 1850. In 1840, by contrast, there had been 1,920 whites, 356 free blacks, and 1,992 slaves in the city. This and following Wilmington newspaper citations below are from the files of William Reaves.

105. In 1850 Wilmington's building trades included 97 free men. Of these, 34 were black or mulatto (one from South Carolina, the others from North Carolina). Five of the artisans were whites from Europe or Canada, 20 were whites from other states, and 38 were white North Carolinians. By 1860, 161 free men were working in building trades in the port city. These included 41 black or mulatto craftsmen (all North Carolinians), 10 Europeans, 22 out-of-state whites, and 88 white North Carolin-

ians. No figures are available on the number of slave artisans. Only 12 of the men engaged in building trades in Wilmington in 1850 were still practicing their craft there by 1860. Seventh Census, 1850: New Hanover County, Population Schedule, 394–447; Eighth Census, 1860: New Hanover County, Population Schedule, 1–147.

106. Franklin, *Free Negro*, 59.

107. Browning, "James Sampson," 56.

108. Rawick, *The American Slave: A Composite Autobiography*, 15:3.

109. Seventh and Eighth Censuses, 1850 and 1860: New Hanover County, Population Schedules, various pages.

110. Walter Clark (ed.), *The State Records of North Carolina* (Winston and Goldsboro: State of North Carolina, 16 volumes, numbered 11–26, 1895–1906), 24:15, 726–27; Brewer, "Legislation to Control Slavery," 164–65.

111. *Wilmington Chronicle*, August 26, 1846.

112. Rawick, *The American Slave: A Composite Autobiography*, 15:3.

113. Thomas R. Post, "The Architect, James F. Post" (1941), 12, unpublished typescript memoir, Avery Architectural Library, Columbia University, New York.

114. John D. Bellamy, *Memoirs of an Octogenarian* (Charlotte: Observer Printing House, 1942), 8.

115. *Wilmington Chronicle*, July 1, 1846. The slaves were Ben Berry and Ephraim Bettencourt and the free black the prominent carpenter Solomon Nash. Nash, who died as a result of the fall, was identified as a "respectable man of his class" who "carried on a large business on his own account." He owned a number of slaves. He is probably the same Solomon W. Nash active in New Hanover County in 1828, in Cumberland County in 1832 and 1834, and in New Hanover County in 1838 and 1840. Nash also accepted black apprentices for the carpenter's and house carpenter's trade (Craig, *Arts and Crafts*, 355, 360, 362, 365, 368). In 1835 when in Fayetteville, Nash petitioned for the manumission of his children by his slave wife, who had died (Brewer, "Legislation to Control Slavery," 159) See also note 53 above.

116. *Wilmington Herald*, August 6, 1857.

117. Ibid.

118. Rawick, *The American Slave: A Composite Autobiography*, 15:2. George Price became a leading plasterer and political figure in postwar Wilmington. *Wilmington Star*, July 26, 1871. Because he did not appear in the 1850 or 1860 censuses among free artisans, he may have been a slave. So too with Robert Finney, a carpenter in postwar Wilmington, and William Finney, a brickmason; both appeared in *Smaw's Wilmington Directory* (Wilmington: Published by Frank D. Smaw, Jr., 1867), 208. See also Isabel M. Williams, "Thalian Hall," unpublished typescript in files of the Research Branch, Archaeology and Historic Preservation Section, Division of Archives and History, Raleigh.

119. On Joe Welcome, see note 32.

120. On Old Welcome, see note 32.

121. Jim is probably Jim Millen, who worked with Joe Welcome on several other projects; see note 32.

122. Dick may be Dick Hoskins or Horniblow's Dick, both mentioned in Collins's summary of work done on the project. The other individuals have not been identified further.

PART II

Local, Regional, National
Paths of Influence

with J. Marshall Bullock

Four

Mr. Jones Goes to Richmond

A Note on the Influence of Alexander Parris's Wickham House

Early in the summer of 1814 General Calvin Jones took time off from the pressures of war against the British to visit the newly completed Wickham House in Richmond. The mansion, considered "the best house in Richmond,"[1] owed its elegant design to the collaboration of New England architect Alexander Parris and his mentor Benjamin Henry Latrobe.[2] The observant General Jones strode through the spacious chambers, sizing up the stylish decorations, admiring the soaring skylit stair, and exploring the novel floor plan. Within a few days, he had convinced leaders in his adopted hometown of Raleigh, North Carolina, to model the new Governor's Palace after the Wickham House plan. The story of the Governor's Palace illuminates the process by which high-style architecture influences provincial buildings; in particular it highlights the role of the layman, as contrasted with the architect or artisan, as a carrier of stylistic ideas.[3]

The relationship between the Wickham House (1811–12) and the Governor's Palace (1814–16) is best understood in the context of the times. Early nineteenth-century North Carolina suffered from such poverty and insularity that it was scornfully nick-named the "Rip Van Winkle state" and the "Ireland of America." Its economic and cultural life was shackled by conservative leaders unwilling to tax or pay for the internal improvements, education, and transportation the state needed. The tight public purse also assured that the young state's first public buildings of the 1790s were un-

---

"Mr. Jones Goes to Richmond: A Note on the Influence of Alexander Parris's Wickham House" appeared in *Journal of the Society of Architectural Historians* 43, no. 1 (March 1984): 71–74, and is reprinted by permission of the Society of Architectural Historians, Chicago.

pretentious and old-fashioned structures. In the wake of the War of 1812, however, North Carolina shared in the national upsurge of patriotism and confidence, and the proponents of change and improvement enjoyed unprecedented success. The legislature authorized new public investment in internal improvements, public buildings, and even the arts, commissioning a statue of George Washington by Antonio Canova and portraits of him by Thomas Sully. Embarrassed by the old State House and governor's residence, the state focused its attention on erecting a new house for the governor and revamping the State House (1819–21) in Grecian style to accommodate Washington's statue.[4]

Construction of the Governor's Palace, as it was often called, began in the midst of the war years. In May 1814 state lands were sold to raise money and commissioners were authorized to contract for a building. The building committee drafted a plan and advertised for contractors, hoping to settle on a contract on June 15. But three days later they announced that they were dissatisfied with the prospects before them and had decided to extend the deadline until July 1 to give "architects at a distance ... another opportunity of putting in their terms."[5] It was at this point that Calvin Jones entered the picture to propose a model for the building.

Jones (1775–1846) was not a member of the committee, but he was one of the state's most active proponents of improvement in all fields of public life, the ideal of the energetic northern immigrant eager to rouse the Rip Van Winkle state. A Massachusetts-born physician, Jones had come to North Carolina at age 20 and quickly assumed a role of leadership in public and private undertakings as a militia officer, legislator, and an organizer of the North Carolina Medical Society. After moving in 1803 to Raleigh, the new capital city, Jones added to his successful medical career the roles of legislator, mayor, justice of the peace, Masonic officer, and trustee of the Raleigh Academy and the University of North Carolina. A leading figure in grand internal improvement schemes, he also founded Raleigh's third newspaper, *The Star*, and was North Carolina's adjutant general during the War of 1812.[6]

Jones's thinking about architecture corresponded with his views about other aspects of community life. In the course of his travels, he recorded his impressions of important new buildings. He decried North Carolina's reliance on old methods and styles of buildings, and advocated a more sophisticated and up-to-date architecture as an antidote to the aura of backwardness and poverty. Jones's multifaceted public life enabled him to put his views into effect. Thus in 1810 his newspaper, *The Star*, described a building under construction for the Raleigh Academy, of which he was trustee, as "a handsome specimen of the chaste, elegant and correct style of building

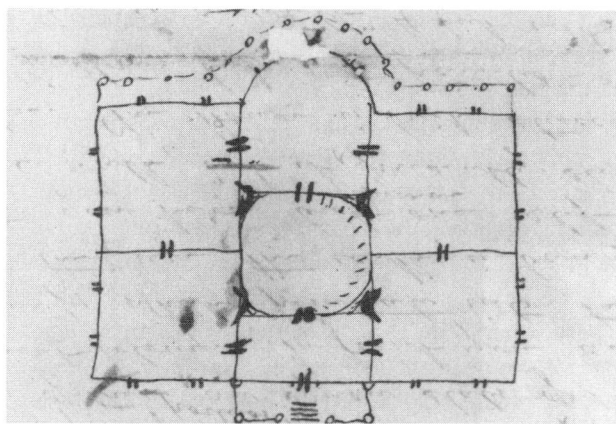

FIG. 4.1. *Ground plan, Wickham House, 1811–12, Richmond, Virginia. Drawing by Calvin Jones. (Calvin Jones Papers; Courtesy of the Southern Historical Collection, Wilson Library, University of North Carolina at Chapel Hill)*

[that should] contribute somewhat to eradicate the vandalism that so generally pervades our architecture."[7]

Dissatisfied with the community's traditional norms and the capabilities of its vernacular building process, Jones sought models elsewhere.[8] At one point, he sought advice from a friend in Petersburg, Virginia, whose response was hardly encouraging: "We are as much at a loss here, as you can be south of us for models and improved plans in Architecture." The Virginian urged Jones to send a description of his needs to his congressman in Washington, "where the best craftsmen are to be found." The Washington builders could provide a model of a building "upon the most modern improved plans; the present taste in the erection of Public Buildings seems to be a strict attention to neatness strenth [*sic*] and plainness with a minute attention to the quality of the materials."[9]

Thus it was entirely in character for Jones to involve himself in the design of the new Governor's Palace, even in the midst of his wartime activities. On a visit to Richmond. Jones chanced to visit the newly completed Wickham House. He was so struck by its quality that he fired off a letter to John Haywood, state treasurer and member of the building committee, sending along a sketch plan (fig. 4.1) and detailed description:

> Understanding that the Governors House is not to be let untill other plans shall be submitted I have thought it might be useful to the commissioners to have before them a plan and description of a very handsome & I think convenient house in this city which belongs to Mr. Wickham and that if they did not adopt it in its full extent they might notwithstanding derive some hints from it to improve such plan as they may have in view.

Though I recollect tolerably well the ground plan and arrangements of the house I will not pretend to know its dimensions—nor is this material as it does not affect the plan.

The House is 60 or 70 feet long & 45 or 50 feet deep not including the projection about 14 feet between joists. The front is a portico supported by large pillars a walk at the top. in the rear is a long collonade the whole length of the building supporting at the top (the height of the first story) a flat top which is another walk the floors of the porticos are square slabs of Marble of different colours. In front you ascend 6 or 8 steps which penetrate into the portico but in the rear the earth is banked up so that you have but one step down upon the gravel walk, it however presently slopes into a garden. The House is brick stuccoed over to resemble stone but not painted—On the top there is a walk 4 feet wide all round. The roof is covered with slate. At the entrance is a room 12 or 14 by 16 or 18 feet square. Then you enter a rotunda (lighted from the top) in which is an elegant circular stair case, from this you go into the drawing room.

The upper pannels in the drawing room were painted with scenes from the Illiad—the dining room with unmeaning figures in the Egyptian style. I saw no other rooms. The Chimneys I think (see the plan) are well arranged for inside convenience and outside appearance. I will anex a plan drawn without any scale or measurement to come in aid of my imperfect description. I perceive in my coarse draught the proportions are not well observed. You will understand the marks intended to represent doors, windows, fire places, pillars &c without specific explanation. I could wish your funds would enable you to build such a house as this, with such offices as are anexed to it for this is considered ... the best house in Richmond. But if you can derive one useful hint from this to improve in any way the plan of yours my purpose will be answered.[10]

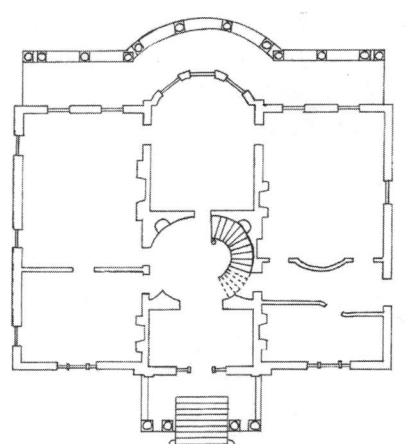

FIG. 4.2. *Ground plan, Wickham House, 1811–12, Richmond. Alexander Parris, architect. Drawing by Edward F. Zimmer. (Courtesy of Edward F. Zimmer)*

And indeed Jones's purpose was "answered" with remarkable alacrity. He wrote his letter on June 29; by mid-July the committee had awarded the contract to an out-of-town builder; and in mid-August *The Star* observed that the governor's house was to be "somewhat similar in plan (tho' not in decorations) to Mr. Wickham's superb house in Richmond."[11] The committee cut out such details as the scenes from the Iliad and the "unmeaning figures in the Egyptian style" that graced Wickham's house. But the plan (fig. 4.2)—the very feature that made the Wickham House so remarkable[12]—was strikingly similar:

> The front 78 feet—depth 50 feet, and two stories high, beside the basement story. In front is a portico by which you enter the anti-chamber; from this you pass into the rotunda in the centre of the building, which is lighted by a lantern window in the roof. In this is a circular staircase. Beyond this is the saloon, and on one hand the drawing, and on the other the dining room. The library and parlour are the front rooms. The upper story has similar divisions and for appropriate family uses. Running around the top of the building next the parapet wall is a walk of six feet in width. The building is to be of brick.[13]

The exterior of the completed palace with its red brick walls and simple fenestration bore little resemblance to Parris's sophisticated design of the Wickham mansion (figs. 4.3, 4.4). It was widely admired, however, and the unusual Parris-inspired plan and skylit stair gained special attention.[14] Its position at the south terminus of Raleigh's main street, Fayetteville Street, made it a prominent landmark. Within a decade the State House at the street's north end was remodeled in elegant Grecian style, thereby encouraging a growing taste for architectural elegance. Other public and private buildings soon followed suit.[15]

Calvin Jones's efforts had been successful in more ways than one. He had presented the palace building committee with a scheme that appealed to their desire for an impressive and fashionable building, one that could be adapted to the available budget and workmen. Moreover, the Governor's Palace was the first building in the young capital that explicitly emulated national architectural modes. As such, the palace departed from the precedents of the state's first building projects and set the tone for future generations of the capital's public architecture.

Neither the Governor's Palace nor the State House survived the century. The State House burned in 1831, taking with it the statue of Washington by Canova. A Greek Revival Capitol of fireproof granite construction took its place in 1833–40, designed by Ithiel Town and A. J. Davis upon a floor plan by William Nichols, Jr., with details executed by Scots architect David

FIG. 4.3. *Governor's Palace, 1814–16, Raleigh, North Carolina. Photograph ca. 1885.* (NCDAH)

FIG. 4.4. *Wickham House. Photograph ca. 1940.* (*Courtesy of The Valentine Museum, Richmond, Virginia, and Edward F. Zimmer*)

Paton. Not until 1970 was a copy of Canova's statue installed in the Capitol, carved from a surviving Canova model. The Governor's Palace was occupied by Union troops at the end of the Civil War, used as a school, and razed in 1885. Only the Sully portrait of Washington, which hangs in the Capitol, survives to recall the state's early nineteenth-century investment in public art and architecture.[16]

NOTES

Jones's letters were found by J. Marshall Bullock during his research for *Architects and Builders in North Carolina: A History of the Practice of Building*. The authors wish to thank Elizabeth Reid Murray, Raleigh historian, for making her research files available before publication of her Wake County history (see note 4).

1. Calvin Jones to John Haywood, 29 June 1814, Calvin Jones Papers, Southern Historical Collection, University of North Carolina, Chapel Hill.

2. Edward F. Zimmer and Pamela J. Scott, "Alexander Parris, B. Henry Latrobe, and the John Wickham House in Richmond, Virginia," *JSAH*, 41 (3), 1982, 202–11.

3. Abbott Lowell Cummings in "The Beginnings of Provincial Renaissance Architecture in Boston, 1690–1725," *JSAH*, 42 (1), 1983, 43–53, explores the role of artisans as "'carriers' of stylistic ideas." C. Ford Peatross, *William Nichols, Architect* (Tuscaloosa, 1979), shows a North Carolina example of the architect as agent of change in the 1810s and 1820s.

4. Hugh Talmage Lefler and Albert Ray Newsome, *The History of a Southern State: North Carolina* (Chapel Hill, 1973), 272–326, and Elizabeth Reid Murray, *Wake: Capital County of North Carolina* (Raleigh, 1983), 74–91, 128–160. The State House (1792–94) was designed by the building committee to accommodate the legislative limit of £10,000; the plain, late-Georgian-style building gained almost universal condemnation for its lack of elegance. Murray, *Wake*, 87–89. A governor's residence of uncertain date was by 1811 considered "unfit." *The (Raleigh) Star*, 26 July 1811.

5. *The Star*, 20 May and 27 May 1814; *Raleigh Register*, 10 June 1814; *The Star*, 18 June 1814. These and other newspaper references were found in the Museum of Early Southern Decorative Arts, Winston-Salem. North Carolina, and through Murray's research files.

6. Born in Great Barrington, Massachusetts, Jones was licensed to practice medicine at age 17, and moved to Smithfield, North Carolina, in 1795, three years later. He was also involved in collecting scientific and historical materials for a botanical garden, a museum of natural history, and a museum of history. He moved in 1803 to Raleigh, a town established only 11 years earlier, where he immediately took on a variety of civic duties: Raleigh's "intendant of police" (the de facto office of mayor) and state legislator in 1807, and adjutant general of the militia (1808–13). Jones was also involved in the Neuse River Navigation Company's ambitious if unsuccessful scheme to make the Neuse River navigable from the seaport town of New Bern to Raleigh. A successful and innovative physician, he is said to have been an early proponent of vaccination rather than inoculation against smallpox. Jones's prominence grew during the War of 1812 when he effectively led the defense of the Carolina coast and frequently consulted with military leadership in Washington, D.C., and Virginia. His role in the war effort gained him such celebrity that a march was composed in his honor. About 1820 Jones moved to a plantation in the Wake Forest section of the county, became first postmaster of Wake Forest, and established a school there. In 1832 he joined the throngs of Carolinians leaving the state for westward prospects and established a plantation near Bolivar, Tennessee, selling his Wake Forest property to the North Carolina Baptist State Convention as a site for Wake Forest Institute, the forerunner of today's Wake Forest University. Jones died in Tennessee in 1846. See Dumas Malone, ed., *Dictionary of American Biography* (New York, 1933), 162, and Elizabeth Reid Murray, *Wake*, passim. The "General Calvin Jones Grand March" music was found by

Sarah M. Lemmon and subsequently recorded for insertion in *North Carolina and The War of 1812* (Raleigh, 1971).

7. *The Star*, 31 May 1810. Jones's sketches and notes on buildings in Virginia and South Carolina appear in his papers (Southern Historical Collection).

8. See Amos Rapoport, *House Form and Culture* (Englewood Cliffs, NJ, 1969), 7, on the modern society's characteristic dissatisfaction with traditional forms and the eradication of the vernacular building process. For private building, vernacular architecture remained vital in North Carolina, but increasingly, public building committees sought more stylish models and out-of-state architects.

9. Robert Bolling to Calvin Jones, 1 April 1816, Calvin Jones Papers, Southern Historical Collection, University of North Carolina, Chapel Hill. At this time, Latrobe and scores of workmen were rebuilding the Capitol after the burning of Washington by the British in August 1814. Jones's inquiry may have concerned the First Presbyterian Church in Raleigh (1816–18); Jones was not a communicant but was one of the three trustees of "The Church Society," a stock company that owned the church property. ("Church History," undated manuscript, Records of First Presbyterian Church, Raleigh, microfilm, North Carolina Archives, Raleigh.) The imposing brick church displayed considerable novelty with its recessed blind arches and lancet windows; its designer and any Washington connection remain unknown. Ill. in Murray, *Wake*, 178.

10. Calvin Jones to John Haywood, 29 June 1814, Calvin Jones Papers, Southern Historical Collection. Spelling, punctuation, and capitalization are reproduced as written.

11. *Raleigh Register*, 15 July 1814; *The Star*, 19 August 1814. It is uncertain to what degree *The Star*'s account reflected only Jones's hopes for the unbuilt palace, and how literally the actual building embodied this scheme. See note 14. The contract went to one James Calder, who claimed to be an "Architect and practical builder" originally from Boston and with experience in Washington and North Carolina.

Raleigh Register, 15 July 1814. However, Calder is not found in Boston directories of the period. He moved on to Fayetteville, North Carolina, then disappeared. The fact that Jones, Calder, and Parris all claimed New England connections illustrates an active exchange between the coastal South and New England.

12. Zimmer and Scott, "Wickham House," focus principally on the development of the plan. The plan of the Governor's Palace may also have been influenced by that of Tryon's Palace (1767–70), which though it burned in 1798 still wielded an influence on North Carolina's public architecture. The plans of the two governor's palaces are similar, though the skylit stair hall in the earlier building was rectangular, not circular. See Frances Benjamin Johnston and Thomas Tileston Waterman, *The Early Architecture of North Carolina* (Chapel Hill, 1941, 1947), 82–83, for John Hawks's ground plan of Tryon's Palace.

13. *The Star*, 19 August 1814.

14. Murray, *Wake*, 207, quotes a description from memory in 1913: "There was a hall with pillars on each side, these marking the entrances into reception rooms right and left. A special staircase, of an odd form, led to the upper floor, and to a cupolo [sic] on the roof in which there were seats giving room enough for several persons" (Fred Olds, *The Raleigh Times*, 27 March 1913).

15. The State House was remodeled by architect William Nichols in an unusually early application of Grecian motifs. Peatross, *Nichols*, 11–12, and "William Nichols" in Adolf Placzek, ed., *Macmillan Encyclopedia of Architects*, 4 vols. (New York, 1982), 3: 299–300. Peatross (*Nichols, Architect*, 12) suggests that the Ionic portico of the Governor's Palace may have been added by Nichols in the 1820s. Other notable Federal, Greek Revival, and even Gothic Revival style buildings were erected in Raleigh in the late 1810s and early 1820s, including banks, stores, houses, churches (see note 9), and a Masonic building.

16. Murray, *Wake*, 230–55, and Elizabeth C. Waugh, *North Carolina's Capital, Raleigh* (Chapel Hill, 1967), 43–45.

Five

PHILADELPHIA BRICKS AND THE NEW BERN JAIL

Historians usually counter tales of "brick brought from England" with accounts of local brickyards as sources of the brick used in eighteenth- and nineteenth-century American buildings. In New Bern, North Carolina, however, despite the presence of a local brickyard and kiln, bricks were shipped by the thousands into the port town for the construction of an 1821–25 jail—not from England, but from Philadelphia. Surviving public building accounts document the shipment of Philadelphia brick along with stonework, stone ballast, nails, lead, and other materials from New York. The budgetary restrictions on a public building and the functional character of the jail suggest that such importation of bricks was probably not unique to this building, and this project thus raises the possibility that many if not most of New Bern's better brick buildings of the period also used imported bricks. The questions raised and information provided by the records of the construction of the jail add to the picture of early nineteenth-century construction along the eastern seaboard.

New Bern, the most centrally located of North Carolina's ports and long the colonial capital, had a brickyard and kiln as early as the 1760s, which supplied brick for the construction of the splendid palace of colonial governor William Tryon. C. J. Sauthier's map of 1769 shows the kiln on the edge of town.

In the period ca. 1795–1825, New Bern, no longer the capital, was a mercantile center on the triangular trade route between the Carolinas, the West

---

"Philadelphia Bricks and the New Bern Jail" appeared in *APT Bulletin* 10, no. 4 (Spring 1977): 62–66, and is reprinted by permission of the Association for Preservation Technology.

Indies, and the northeast. The waterfront bustled with ships carrying naval stores and forest products out and manufactured goods in. Construction boomed as the cosmopolitan tastes of New Bern's prosperous merchants found expression in elegant Federal style town houses, banks, churches, stores, a Masonic lodge and an academy—many of them brick buildings.

Little is known of the source of brick for New Bern's fine Federal period buildings, though it has been assumed that the local brickworks were adequate to meet the needs of the construction boom.

Investigation of the "Publick Building Accounts" for the construction of a new jail in the period 1821–25 reveals that a major expense was the purchase and shipment of bricks from Philadelphia. As usual for public buildings, a committee was appointed for the project. In 1821 its members—Francis Hawks (son of John Hawks, English architect of Tryon Palace in the 1760s), Elijah Clark, Asa Jones, and a Dr. Hatch—reported that they had "adopted a plan for the Jail the best they could devise within the means at their disposal for security and comfort." The building was to be 53 by 55 feet and two stories high, with walls of solid masonry and the door and window sills and lintels of stone. The committee reported that they had already purchased many of the materials and hired the best workmen. No mention was made of an architect or master builder.

Elijah Clark, a merchant, and treasurer of the committee, kept detailed accounts, including a great sheaf of receipts. His records show that three local craftsmen—Joshua Mitchell, mason, Donum Montford, plasterer, and John M. Oliver, carpenter—were chiefly involved in the construction and were paid at intervals for both labor and materials. Much of the material needed for the building was obtained from these and other local workmen and merchants, including quantities of lumber, lime, nails, lathing, and the like. Over 300,000 bricks were bought for a total of $1,500 from Montford and a local merchant named Stephen B. Forbes. Whether these suppliers obtained them from a local kiln is not known, but it seems probable.

In addition, Clark's account with the Philadelphia firm of Snowden and Wagner demonstrates that considerable money and effort were expended in acquiring additional brick—perhaps of a finer quality suitable for facing the building—to be carried from Philadelphia to New Bern by ship. A portion of the accounts for the year 1821 is as follows:

Mr Elijah Clark in acct with Snowden & Wagner C^r

1821 15	To Postage	.27
March 24	To advertising for vessels to carry Bricks	$3.00
May 28	" Cash paid Draft favor of H B & Burdett	92.50
Apl 20	" Postage	.27
June 23^d	" 101,000 Bricks @6$ per M [thousand]	606.00

June 23^d	" 582 water table [bricks @] 65cts per doz^n		31.52
June 23^d	" Commissions on $637.52 @ 2½ pr ct		15.93
		Supra C^r	$749.49
April 14	By Sales	× $92.50	
April 23	" Cash in NC Notes	$670	
April 23	" less 3½ pr ct disct	23.45 646.55	739.05
	E. E. Phil^a Jany 1 1822		10.44
	Snowden & Wagner		

Elijah Clark Esq
Newbern N.C. Dr Sir
      Be pleased to pay to Captn Wm Phillips order Ten $^{44}/_{100}$ Dollars balance of Accts & oblige your obt servts

                            Snowden & Wagner
                            Phila^d Jany 23rd 1822

The advertisements, presumably placed in Philadelphia papers by Snowden and Wagner, for ships to carry 101,000 bricks to New Bern were successful. Clark's receipts include seven for the period April 28 to August 7, 1821, presumably from ship captains, for seven loads of brick ranging from 7,475 to 25,000 bricks per load. Freight rate was $3 per thousand bricks, and the total was exactly 101,000 bricks. If the Philadelphia bricks originally cost $6 per thousand as Snowden and Wagner's account indicates, plus another $3 per thousand to ship, the total of $9 per thousand for 101,000 brick, $909, is almost twice the price locally paid for the other 300,000 bricks (at $5 per thousand). The water table brick, probably molded ones, were even more costly at 65¢ a dozen. It is interesting to speculate why the committee felt that such an expense was justified and what sort of brick these were.

Tons of stone also arrived on the ships sailing into New Bern's busy waterfront. Because eastern North Carolina lacks good building stone, any stone trim had to be obtained from distant quarries. On May 11 and 16, 1821, Elijah Clark was given receipts for "a quantity of stone ballast say about 40 tons," and again, "stone ballast," this time along with four kegs of nails. No mention is made of the port of origin of the ballast. Also of interest is the finished stone obtained at New York through the firm of Hyer Bremner and Burdett. On June 13, Clark's account with the firm listed,

2 Tool'd Lintles .... 8 ftt 6 in 3/ D^{rs}	3.19
1 Circular Arch Polished .. 5 ftt 4 in 6/	4.--
1 Pair inposts [sic] pr piece 8 /	2.--
1 Key Stone	1.50

FIG. 5.1. *New Bern Jail, 1821-25, New Bern, North Carolina. Photograph 1864. (Courtesy of the North Carolina Collection, University of North Carolina Library at Chapel Hill)*

To this was added 2½ percent commission and 5 percent exchange in New York. An earlier payment to the same firm had included several rolls of sheet lead, 22 lintels, 22 window sills, and three pieces of stone. The lead was used for such purposes as gutters and flashing, for in February, 1822, Kevan and Lorimer, unidentified slaters, were paid for "leading of gutters" as well as for "slating the Gaol."

As was typical, Clark acquired nails, iron, and other goods from northern merchants as well as local ones. Although quantities of lime were obtained locally, probably burned from coastal oyster shells which were also acquired in great quantities, lime was also shipped in—such as the 24 casks of lime on the Sloop *Fame*, for which Clark paid freight of $12 on October 31, 1821.

The lime, brick, and stone, assembled from near and far, were used within the year. In November, 1821, Joshua Mitchell was paid $498.12½ for "laying 399,500 bricks"—nearly all of the 300,000 obtained locally and the 101,000 shipped from Philadelphia. Work on the building continued through 1824, and the final accounts were examined by the building committee in May, 1825, indicating a completion date.

Within a few years, however, additional work of a specially skilled nature was required, and again the officials turned to the northeast. In the summer of 1832, two workmen came to New Bern by ship to work on the jail—Thomas Turner, slater, and William A. Baker, coppersmith, "as agreed with Messrs. Ransom and Spelman of New York"—and stayed from mid-June to the end of July. Whether any other imported craftsmen were involved in building or repairing the jail is not known.

The jail, though razed in the late nineteenth century, is shown in a Civil War era photograph (fig. 5.1). It was a handsome and substantial building, resembling a town house more than a jail. The photograph shows a nearly square structure whose brickwork is essential to its character. The stone sills and lintels are clearly visible, as is the semicircular arch over the entrance.

New Bern's early-nineteenth-century jail, prominently placed near the center of town, was far from a crude or unsightly prison. With its Philadelphia brick and New York stonework, it was a suitably dignified expression of the small but cosmopolitan port town at the apex of its prosperity. Elijah Clark's records and receipts give an insight into not only the mercantile wealth that produced New Bern's brilliant boom era, but also the source of many of the materials used in the construction of its fine buildings and the dependency upon sea trade with northeastern port cities.

FURTHER READING

On New Bern and the jail: Public Building Accounts, Craven County Records, Archives and Records Section, Division of Archives and History, Raleigh, North Carolina; National Register of Historic Places nominations for New Bern Historic District and several individual New Bern buildings, copies in Survey and Planning Branch, Division of Archives and History; Stephen B. Miller, "Recollections of Newbern Fifty Years Ago," 1873 typescript in Archives and Records Section, Division of Archives and History; Alonzo T. Dill, *Governor Tryon and His Palace* (Chapel Hill: University of North Carolina Press, 1955).

On bricks: Harley J. McKee, *Introduction to Early American Masonry, Stone, Brick, Mortar, and Plaster* (National Trust for Historic Preservation and Columbia University, 1973); Calder Loth, "Notes on the Evolution of Virginia Brickwork from the Seventeenth Century to the Late Nineteenth Century," *APT Bulletin,* 6, no. 2 (1974); A. Lawrence Kocher, "Early Building with Brick," *Antiques,* July 1957.

Six

"Severe Survitude to House Building"

THE CONSTRUCTION OF HAYES PLANTATION HOUSE, 1814–1817

The character of the neoclassical mansion at Hayes plantation near Edenton sprang from a unique blend of old and new architectural concepts, from established regional traditions and from emerging national and international trends. Similarly, the story of Hayes's construction reveals changing building practices, for in its creation as in its design Hayes embodied familiar and unfamiliar patterns. It grew out of the interaction between an adventurous English-trained architect and a strong-minded client and from a combination of local workmanship—much of it by slave artisans—and New York–purchased finishing elements. The situation was novel in that architect-builder William Nichols planned and superintended the work, thereby operating in a professional role still new in most of America. However, in time-honored fashion James C. Johnston, planter and client, served as his own contractor and managed many aspects of the project. Because Johnston's papers document the range of individuals, influences, and processes involved, the construction history of Hayes provides insights into American building in a transitional era.[1]

When James Cathcart Johnston (1782–1865) set out in 1814 to build Hayes, he was well prepared for the task. His father, Samuel Johnston (1733–1816), had provided him with much that he needed. Samuel, a Scotsman, came to North Carolina as a child in 1736, studied at Yale College, and became a

---

"'Severe Survitude to House Building': The Construction of Hayes Plantation House, 1814–1817" appeared in *North Carolina Historical Review* 68, no. 4 (October 1991): 373–408, and is reprinted by permission of the Historical Publications Section, North Carolina Office of Archives and History, Department of Cultural Resources, Raleigh.

successful attorney and planter. Considered one of the most intelligent and best-educated North Carolinians of his time, Samuel became a leader in the Revolution, governor of the new state (1787–89), and its first member of the United States Senate (1790–93). He married Frances Cathcart in 1770, and throughout most of his public career, except for a period in New York and Philadelphia during his tenure as senator, Samuel and Frances Johnston and their family resided at Hayes. After Johnston completed his term in the Senate, the family moved from Hayes to his Hermitage plantation in Martin County, where they occupied a newly completed house. Frances died in 1801, and Samuel remained there with his children until his death in 1816.[2]

Near the end of his life, Samuel Johnston made provisions for a new residence for his adult children. In December, 1814, he gave his Hayes plantation to his son, James, by deed of gift. After years of neglect, however, the house and outbuildings there were "out of repair and uninhabitable." Thus in his will of November, 1814, Samuel stipulated that James should "reimburse to himself all such sums of money as he may actually disburse and expend in erecting & furnishing a dwelling House & offices for the

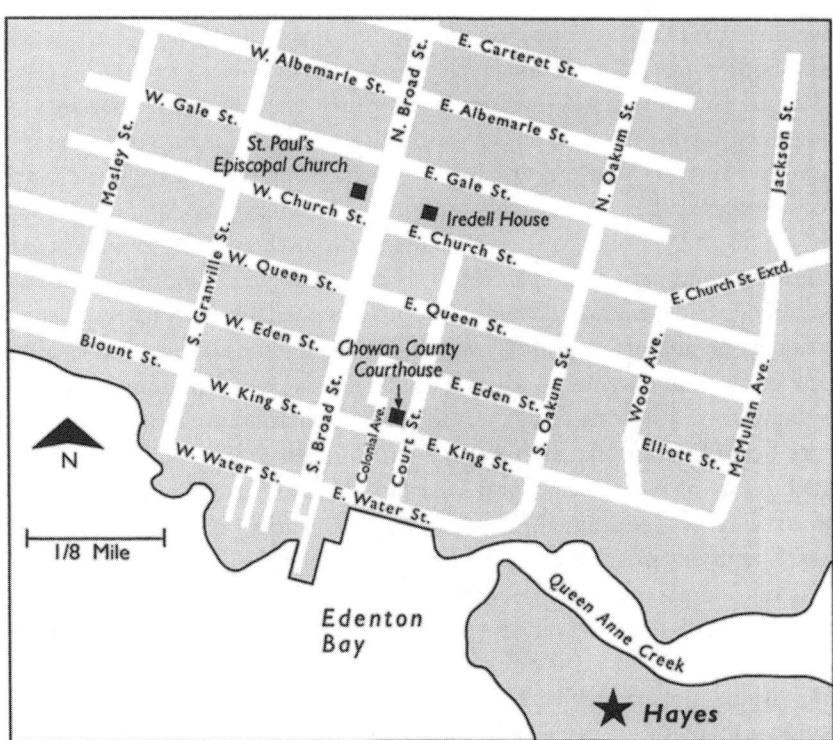

FIG. 6.1. *Edenton, Chowan County, North Carolina, showing Hayes and related sites. Map by Michael T. Southern, 2004.*

FIG. 6.2. *James Cathcart Johnston.* (NCDAH)

residence of himself and sisters on my Plantation called Hayes out of the profits of my estate." James's sisters, all residing at home, were Penelope Swann (1771–1820), a widow, and Frances (1785–1837) and Helen (1787–1842), who both remained unmarried.[3]

James C. Johnston, by this time aged thirty-two, had never married; he described his frequent travels as a "substitute for the pleasure of domestic life." Nor did he follow his father into a political career. Rather, he devoted his energies to personal management of his plantations, expanding upon the holdings he inherited from his father and distinguishing himself as an innovative and productive planter; he became known as "an intelligent and cultured, if eccentric, gentleman who had improved upon his inheritance to become one of North Carolina's wealthiest men." James had received a classical education; he entered a Long Island school when the family moved to New York while his father served in the Senate, studied at the Woodbury School near Philadelphia (1792–96), and was graduated in 1799 from the College of New Jersey (later Princeton University). Upon returning to North Carolina, he studied French at the University of North Carolina and read law under his father before turning to his chief interest, agriculture. Like his father, James was part of the small, interconnected North Carolina elite who took part both in the intimate local culture of their immediate community and in a variety of supralocal associations. Through family ties, friendships, political affiliations, and business connections they joined in regional, state, and national spheres of influence, taste, trade, and ideas.[4]

James also received from his father an interest in building and sage advice on the topic. After settling at his Hermitage plantation near Williamston in 1793, Samuel had written of his hopes of spending "the remainder of my days in improving this little spot and adding every year something either of beauty or convenience to it." He observed, "I have an opinion that nothing in life gives a man more satisfaction than improvement planned and executed by himself, therefore the more rude and [illegible] a situation is the greater scope there is for the imagination to plan schemes of improvement which in all probability will never be fully carried into effect, and they answer the purpose well by keeping the mind in action and perhaps better than if they were completed."[5] On the other hand, Samuel warned James in 1814 that his funds were too limited to "admit of profusion or any great degree of elegance in your establishment." He urged James always to "prefer a plain and simple stile of living to a gaudy and tinsel appearance, a passion to which there are no bounds and which too often leads to the want of solid comforts and a wretched state of dependence."[6]

James took his father's advice as well as his gifts, for although Hayes was a grand mansion compared to most residences in North Carolina, it was nevertheless a frame house of moderate scale, modest in cost compared to the elaborate brick and stone edifices erected by planters and merchants to the north and the south. In furnishings, too, James recalled his father's advice. Ordering furniture for Hayes from New York City, he advised a friend who was selecting items for him, "It is unnecessary for me to say that I wish them of the plainest and neatest kind and not in the extreme of the fashion but what would suit a moderate liver in New York. A man by appearing very different from his neighbors is more apt to excite their ridicule and perhaps envy than their esteem & respect—you know very well what will suit the meridian of Carolina and I dont wish to be to much out of the latitude—I trust altogether to your judgmt only I wished you to have and [*sic*] eye to the latitude & longitude of the place for which they are intended."[7]

Nonetheless, in building his new house at Hayes Johnston embarked on a project that marked a bold innovation in the architecture of the early-nineteenth-century Albemarle. Not only was the house exceptionally large and stylish, but his handling of the project was unusual in that he chose to employ an architect and to pay him a salary of $60.00 a month solely to superintend the project—in addition to the usual costs of workmen and materials. In eighteenth- and early-nineteenth-century North Carolina, most building projects involved a direct relationship between client and artisans; architects were few and far between, for the architectural profession was still in its infancy nationwide. Employment of architects was restricted to the most ambitious undertakings, chiefly elaborate public buildings, and was rare in private residential projects. William Nichols, then residing in Edenton, became an early and influential exponent of the architectural profession in North Carolina and the larger South. At Hayes, Johnston provided Nichols with a private commission that offered new opportunities to display his abilities and promote his blossoming career.⁸

Nichols (ca. 1780–1853) was just two years older than Johnston and, like Johnston, combined familiarity with local circumstances with a keen interest in the broader world and fashionable taste. Trained in Bath, England, he came to North Carolina about 1800 and worked for a time in New Bern as engineer, surveyor, architect, and carpenter; no New Bern buildings, however, have been documented as his work. Nichols's first documented work is in Edenton: he went there from New Bern as "Architect, and House Joiner" to plan and execute extensive repairs and renovations to St. Paul's Church (1806–9). Although limited by financial constraints and the character of the old colonial church, Nichols proposed an elaborate neoclassical interior renovation and a spire adorned with neoclassical urns. When the vestry sought a more economical scheme, the ambitious young architect objected to any "abridgement of the work," which, he believed, "would procure me no credit which is an object with me." Within a few years, Nichols moved into prominence as his talent, his ambitions, and well-placed friends led to important commissions in Fayetteville, Raleigh, and beyond. All this lay in the future, however, when the two young men, Nichols and Johnston, began to plan the construction of Hayes.⁹

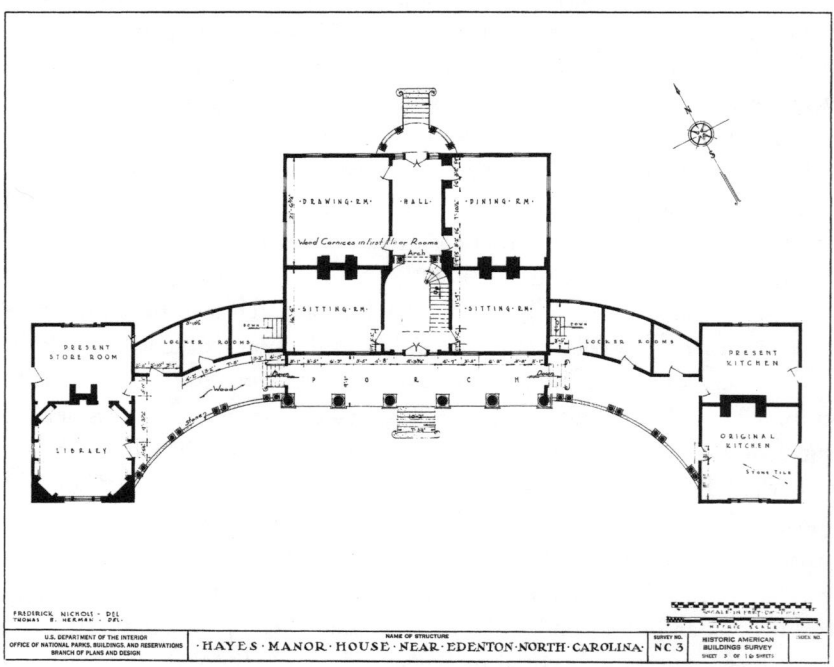

FIG. 6.3. *Ground plan of Hayes, Frederick Nichols and Thomas B. Herman, delineators.* (*Historic American Buildings Survey, Library of Congress*)

Johnston provided Nichols with the opportunity to design a house of extraordinary individuality. The basic layout (fig. 6.3) recalls long-standing planning principles: a central block, curved hyphens, and projecting smaller wings outlining a forecourt. Located on the Albemarle Sound, the house has a dual orientation, with quite different facades presented to the drive on the landside and the waterfront overlooking the sound. The antecedents of the tripartite arrangement extend from the *Four Books of Architecture* by the Italian Renaissance architect Andrea Palladio to British houses and books influenced by Palladio and to American houses such as Mount Airy in Virginia and Tryon Palace in New Bern. The palace, designed by English architect John Hawks for royal governor William Tryon in 1767, burned in 1798, but James Johnston may have seen it in his youth, and its influence in New Bern was still strong when William Nichols arrived there in 1800. Furthermore, in the early national period Palladian tripartite schemes were still fashionable; one such design, published in Boston architect Asher Benjamin's *Country Builder's Assistant* of 1798, has enough similarities to that of Hayes to be considered as a possible source for Nichols and Johnston's planning.[10]

At Hayes, Nichols combined this familiar and formal layout with a remarkable variety of other elements to create a unique ensemble. Regional adaptations to the climate include the double, louvered blinds and the big cupola with its own louvered blinds, providing shade and ventilation. Distinctive touches of the Adam style then current in American architecture appear in such prominent features as the fanlit entrance facing the land (fig. 6.4), its delicate, geometric half-round portico, and most of the interior trim. Nichols incorporated still more advanced stylistic features in the Grecian style, both in the recurrent Greek key motif in interior details and, most prominently, in the towering double porch of the water facade (fig. 6.5). Here he adapted the order of the tall columns from James Stuart and Nicholas Revett's *Antiquities of Athens,* published in England in the eighteenth century. In the 1820s and 1830s, Stuart and Revett's book became the bible for American architects working in the Greek Revival style, but in 1815–17 Nichols's use of such models was quite progressive. Nichols installed a highly functional kitchen in one of the wings, while in the other he placed an elegant octagonal library (fig. 6.6) in yet another novel style—the Gothic Revival. Presented occasionally in eighteenth-century books—such as Horace Walpole's *Encyclopedia* (part of the library at Hayes)—and in a few neoclassical buildings as an accent or counterpoint to classicism, the Gothic Revival had just begun to appear in American architecture. The use of the associative, picturesque Gothic style was considered particularly appropriate for a library.[11]

Johnston and Nichols began to plan the project as early as 1814. An un-

FIG. 6.4. *Land facade, Hayes, 1814-17, Edenton, North Carolina. Photograph by Frances Benjamin Johnston, 1930s. (Courtesy of the North Carolina Collection, University of North Carolina Library at Chapel Hill)*

FIG. 6.5. *Water facade, Hayes. Photograph by Frances Benjamin Johnston, 1930s. (Courtesy of the North Carolina Collection, University of North Carolina Library at Chapel Hill)*

dated letter from Nichols to Johnston, believed to have been written late in 1814, indicates their early negotiations:

> Sir: I take the opportunity by your Boys to inform you that what time could be spared from the attention required by a very sick family has been entirely taken up by the business of my shop, the only [th]ing I have to depend on for subsisten[ce]. Your plans have consequently been [neglected?] if however Sir I can be of service to you after the first day of January you may command me—having arranged my business in such a manner as to be able to attend to you. Yr. obdt and hbl servt, Wm Nichols.[12]

It is impossible to know how far planning of the house had advanced before illness delayed Nichols's preparation of drawings. At a minimum, the two men would have reached an understanding of the essential elements—the basic size and construction materials of the house and perhaps the outbuildings—which permitted Johnston to proceed in obtaining materials.

FIG. 6.6. *Library, Hayes. Photograph by Frances Benjamin Johnston, 1930s. (Courtesy of the North Carolina Collection, University of North Carolina Library at Chapel Hill)*

"Severe Survitude to House Building"

This was a standard method of operating. It was also standard practice to produce working drawings as necessary, as construction progressed. During 1815, Nichols presumably devoted time to drawing plans, while Johnston proceeded with the preparation of materials and the hiring of workmen. It was not until the first of October, 1815, that Johnston recorded in his memorandum book, "Nichols engaged to superintend my building at $60 pr month commence 3rd of Oct. 1815."[13]

For more than a year Johnston had been busy. He took principal responsibility for managing the project financially and logistically, locating and contracting for materials, arranging to have materials worked from their raw state into finished building components, recruiting and hiring and paying workmen, keeping track of costs, and making frequent visits to the site. In December, 1815, when planter Ebenezer Pettigrew visited Edenton from across the Albemarle Sound, he wrote to his wife, "Mr. Johnston is here and stays with me in the house we occupied when here. . . . have been several times with him over the Creek where he is building a large house."[14] Such direct involvement was normal in private building projects. Although in public works such as courthouses and town halls building committees often awarded a lump-sum contract to a single contractor, in private undertakings it remained common for the client to retain control and responsibility for the cost, quality, and progress of the work. Many farmers, planters, and merchants had at least a rudimentary understanding of building types, materials, and techniques and were accustomed to dealing with suppliers and workmen. Whether serving as members of building committees or managing their own projects, leading citizens were used to taking a direct role in the building process of their communities and to looking to one another for advice and assistance.[15] Accordingly, Johnston drew upon his network of acquaintances throughout the region to obtain the materials and workmen he needed.

Once the general plan of the building was conceived, the first requirement was timber. Johnston alone or Johnston and Nichols would have made out the bill of timber, a standard construction document that listed all the sizes and quantities of timber needed. This included the scantling (large and small timbers measured in three dimensions, such as plates 12 by 5 inches and 54 feet long, rafters 4 by 4 inches and 28 feet long) and the plank (boards measured in standard thicknesses such as 1, 1½, or 2 inches and then in width and length). Timber had to be found and cut in time to dry before construction began. Thus, in the spring of 1814, months before he was formally deeded the plantation, Johnston located a source of standing timber. William Darlet of nearby Windsor, who owned a tract of woodlands, responded to Johnston's request to purchase "a considerable quantity of pine timber" and informed him on April 19 that he could "commence

FIG. 6.7. *Sawyers, pictured working in a pair at a pit saw, in* The Book of Trades *(1837). (Courtesy of The Winterthur Library: Printed Book and Periodical Collection)*

geting it as soon as you please. I shall be over on your side of the river shortly and we can then agree on a price for the timber."[16]

Johnston also needed to have the timber cut and then sawed into framing, flooring, weatherboards, and other elements. There were water-powered sawmills in the Albemarle region by the late eighteenth century (and by 1814 New Bern and Wilmington boasted steam-powered sawmills), but Johnston chose instead to have his timber sawed by teams of sawyers, pairs of men who were skilled in handling the heavy pit saws[17] (fig. 6.7).

The sawyers he hired were slaves who belonged to other residents of the region. In 1814 Johnston contracted with a Virginia man, W. W. Wilkins, to employ two teams of sawyers: Moses and his partner Stepney, and Gilbert and his partner Randall. Because of the unusually large quantity of sawing involved, Wilkins offered Johnston a bargain rate of 4 shillings 6 pence per hundred feet of sawing for his slaves' work—lower than his usual charge of 5 shillings a hundred feet. Another team of sawyers also joined in: Wilson and Anthony, who belonged to merchant David Clark. Clark, who had served as intermediary between Johnston and Wilkins, told Johnston that his two workmen were "desirous to go" with the other men to Edenton. Clark also advised Johnston that from time to time they might want papers or passes to return home, and he urged Johnston to "act to them as your own," and "should they not do their duty without trouble—please send them back."[18]

The sawyers began work for Johnston on April 20, 1814. Evidently Johnston already had some timber, perhaps from his own land, in addition to that he obtained from Darlet's land. In each team, one man stood as "top dog" upon the sawhorses, while the other worked as "bottom dog" in the sawpit below, pulling and pushing the heavy saw to cut the lumber to the sizes required. In June, 1814, Johnston reported to David Clark that Wilson and Anthony "have got under a good way of sawing & laying off their stocks and are likely to make something handsome for themselves which makes them saw with spirit. I think you ought to keep them at the saw until they are perfect masters of it." He wrote at the same time to Moses and Gilbert's owner, W. W. Wilkins, that he was "much pleased with them" and expected to have even more work for them than anticipated.[19]

As the sawing got under way, Johnston queried Wilkins about another matter: "They inform me that give them a task and that all they saw over they have—you will please to say what is their task and whether I may pay them for all they cut over." In the task system, slaves were assigned a certain amount of work to do and thereafter could stop work for the day or do additional work and receive pay for themselves; this provided more opportunity for initiative and a degree of autonomy among slaves. The politics of the system could be delicate, as is evident in Wilkins's response to Johnston: "I make it a rule to give my sawers all they get over their task but I settle with them myself for it and I do not wish any gentleman to pay them. I am glad to hear that they please you, they have done pretty well and I will thank you to pay each sawer two dollars in all $6 and which they have sawed over their task and charge me with the same." With that matter settled, work proceeded. In August, 1814, Johnston reported to Wilkins on the sawyers' accomplishments—over 25,000 feet of timber sawed—and Wilkins responded that "from the amount sawed they have worked well & will thank you to pay each of them five dollars as an encouragement for further well doing and charge me the amount $20." And again in March, 1815, Wilkins informed Johnston that Moses and Stepney had sawed 1,300 feet "over task, for which I will thank you to pay them."[20]

And so the sawing continued, month after month, through 1814 and 1815 and even into 1816, as the teams cut the seemingly endless feet of timber the big frame house and its outbuildings required. A receipt covering work from November, 1814, to August, 1815, showed that one team had sawed featheredged weatherboards; rafters, sleepers, and plates; 34 doors; and many feet of black walnut planks. In December, 1815, Johnston found it necessary to purchase new sawing equipment from New York: two 7-foot-long, cast steel pit saws at 84 shillings apiece and a 6½-foot-long German steel saw for 3 pounds 12 shillings.[21]

The other principal building material Johnston needed was brick, to underpin his house and to build the chimneys. He ordered 100,000 bricks at $5 per thousand from local brickmaker James Cunningham. Cunningham had operated his brick manufacturing business in Edenton for several years. In 1806–9 he supplied bricks for restoration of St. Paul's Church. And in 1810 he had advertised 130,000 bricks for sale, along with his willingness to undertake construction of a brick house; he had at that time a "man from Philadelphia" assisting him, who was "well acquainted with making, burning and laying of Bricks, and was regularly brought up to the business," meaning that he had been fully trained in a formal apprenticeship. For Johnston's project, Cunningham delivered the first batch, approximately half the total, in March, 1815, and promised the remainder soon. And in September, 1816, Johnston paid Cunningham for an additional $95 worth of bricks.[22]

For other essential materials such as glass, hardware, and paint, Johnston drew upon distant suppliers. Most of those items, along with other manufactured goods, he ordered from his New York factors, Treadwell and Thorne. One bill, dated December 16, 1815, recorded costs for 1,000 feet of glass in panes of 12 by 16 inches, 8 kegs of ground white lead paint, 16 jugs of linseed oil (to mix with the pigment to make liquid paint), 110 pounds of steel, and other goods to a total of over £200 (pounds as well as dollars being used in transactions at the time). Throughout the project, Johnston ordered other manufactured goods at intervals.[23]

In his reliance on northern manufacturers, Johnston followed a pattern common among wealthy citizens who were enmeshed in the coastwise trading network. Although local blacksmiths and foundries produced nails, hinges, and simple hardware, for some of those same products and for specialty hardware, glass, paint, and many other goods, southerners depended heavily on northern, English, and European manufacturers. When Johnston acquired items from northern suppliers, the original costs were compounded by the commission fee he paid his factor and the cost of shipping. Such expenses meant that most North Carolinians built in ways that involved a minimum of manufactured goods. It was chiefly the coastal and mercantile elite, already immersed in an interregional commercial system, who could afford and had access to such materials.[24]

In addition to acquiring materials, Johnston's other principal concern was recruiting and managing workmen to erect and finish his buildings. A great deal of the work involved laborers who carried or hauled heavy materials, lifted timbers or bricks, and undertook the multitude of unskilled tasks involved in preparing materials and erecting a building. Doubtless

FIG. 6.8. *Water facade showing brick arcade, Hayes. Photograph by Frances Benjamin Johnston, 1930s. (Courtesy of the North Carolina Collection, University of North Carolina Library at Chapel Hill)*

Johnston diverted some of his own laborers for those duties. At the same time, however, he hired other men who were artisans, including carpenters, bricklayers, and plasterers. As he had not contracted with a single workman to build his house for a lump sum, Johnston employed a series of individual artisans, each to do the work of his trade. There was a chronic shortage of skilled workmen in rural North Carolina, and the negotiating and timing of bargains between clients and artisans to accommodate multiple schedules and far-flung construction sites made for a complicated process.

Late in 1814 Johnston began to look for bricklayers. He had contacted a team of masons named Parker, and in December an Albemarle resident, R. H. Smith of Fairfield, who had previously employed the Parkers, wrote to Johnston on their behalf. Smith reported that they were "sober sturdy men" and "as Industrious as can be wished for," and he invited Johnston to "ride over and see a specimen" of their work at his house. Smith also said that given the "considerable job" Johnston had, the Parkers were eager to hear from him because they "wish to hier several labourers by the year Provided that they are likely to get sufficient work to authorize it." December was an important time for builders to make commitments, for January 1 was traditional hiring day, on which owners hired out their slaves for the year to come, and builders had to estimate the number of workmen they expected to employ during the next year and hire accordingly.²⁵ Evidently Johnston established contact with the Parkers, and they agreed to do his brickwork when the time came.

By the following summer, Johnston was ready for the bricklayers to begin. In August, 1815, he wrote to the Parkers that he would soon need their services. On September 1, Marshall Parker responded that he himself could not come at the present, as he was building a customhouse in Norfolk, but his brother could come. Though workmen were very scarce, "If you want your brickwork done this fall I have force enough to complete it in three weeks from the commencement."²⁶ But then, on October 5, Parker wrote to Johnston that the Norfolk project had been slowed by gales and was to be built a story higher than expected, so that he (and presumably his workers) would be in Norfolk throughout October and could not come immediately to Edenton. Then he advised Johnston, "if your Frame is ready to put up I am afraid it would not be advisable to wait until next Month, but we may have very good weather in November for Brickwork, you will have very little outside work as I suppose you will build all your Chimneys inside." Parker offered to come to Edenton if Johnston could wait until November.²⁷

Johnston, however, chose not to wait and hired other artisans to lay the brick underpinnings immediately. Among them was the well-known slave artisan Joe Welcome, who belonged to merchant-planter Josiah Collins, Jr., of Edenton. Welcome was already acquainted with Nichols, for he had worked previously on the restoration of St. Paul's Episcopal Church in 1806–9. Welcome possessed the versatility characteristic of many rural and small-town artisans, particularly in the "trowel trades"; for example, in another project, the 1800 construction of the Edenton Academy, Welcome headed a team of workers who executed the bricklaying, stonework, and plastering. Johnston's accounts record a long series of payments to him and other men who underpinned the dwelling, built the interior chimneys, and probably helped to plaster the interior. Payments for Joe Welcome's work appear at intervals from October, 1815—"Welcome for himself and boys"—through 1816. Another skilled bricklayer and plasterer, Jim Millen, appeared prominently in Johnston's payments from 1816 through 1817. Millen likewise belonged to Josiah Collins. Johnston's accounts with Collins included payment for Welcome's and Millen's work, for which he paid Collins at the rate of $1 a day, but Johnston also made payments to Welcome and Millen separately, which probably reflects work done beyond their tasks.²⁸

Once the workmen assembled in October, 1815, the building site teemed with activity. The bricklayers were preparing the foundations, while carpenters under William Nichols's direction were readying the house frame from the timbers the sawyers had sawn. Johnston's memorandum book noted payments in October to "Mr. Nichols" and to several "Workmen at Hayes," including Jim O'Mally, Bill Blount, Miles Badham, and others listed only by first names, evidently slaves, including Merrick, Andrew, Wilson and boys, Dave, and Perry. Finally, on the last day of October, 1815, Johnston could write, "I have commenced building and go on very well I expect to raise next week underpinning all done."[29]

"Raising" was the most dramatic step in the construction process. Johnston's statement meant that Nichols and the carpenters had completed and laid out the big, weighty timber frame, with its heavy sills, cornerposts, secondary posts, and plates, its joists, rafters, and other members, cut in a fashion to assemble with mortise-and-tenon joints secured with pegs. The raising of a large house frame involved many workers, who gathered to pull the walls up into place and join them together in a skeletal structure rising two full stories above the foundation. That complex and dangerous task proceeded under the direction of the master carpenter, Nichols.

With the frame up, the carpenters continued their work. Nichols probably executed some of the carpentry along with superintending the project. Day by day, month by month, the carpenters applied the weatherboards, put on the roof, built partitions, laid floors, and made and installed doors, mantels, and trim. Not all the carpenters are identified with certainty. Cato was a carpenter, evidently owned by Johnston, who in June, 1815, bought "a chest of tools for Cato" worth more than $40. Occasional notations showed Cato and Elijah making doors and Dave and Jim laying floors.[30]

Typically artisans, whether slave or free, came to a work site with their kits of tools in hand. But for Hayes the ordinary run of tools seems not to have been adequate. In addition to obtaining new saws, in the fall of 1815 Johnston ordered from New York an elaborate collection of fine tools necessary to complete the building in the latest fashion. The bill of over £31 included a variety of files, chisels, saws, and planes of all sorts and sizes. Planes, fitted with blades of various profiles, shaped moldings to finish the baseboards, doors, mantels, and so forth and thus defined a subtle aspect of the workmanship and style of the house. Among the molding planes in Johnston's 1815 order were two "cornish" or cornice planes and one bed mold, ovolo planes of several different widths, ogee planes of various sizes, a cove-and-bead plane, and a double-sash plane.[31]

From the fall of 1815 through 1816 and 1817 Johnston's account books recorded the continuing outlay of payments to workmen. He paid Nichols's salary month by month and other men by wages or small cash payments at various intervals. Tasks were begun and completed and artisans and laborers came and went as building proceeded. Prominent among the workmen, in addition to Joe Welcome and Jim Millen and Cato, were Harry, Elijah,

FIG. 6.9. *Kitchen wing, Hayes. Photograph by Frances Benjamin Johnston, 1930s. (Courtesy of the North Carolina Collection, University of North Carolina Library at Chapel Hill)*

Dave, Merrick, Perry, Jim, Aaron, Jack, Miles Badham, Dave Dickinson (Dickerson), and John Walker. Johnston's accounts, however, do not state what their trades were nor always which men were slaves and which were free.[32]

By the spring of 1817 the house was ready for plastering and final finish items. In April, a ship arrived from New York bringing both the plaster and a finish plasterer, Benjamin French. Johnston's bill included 50 casks of lime at $2.50 per cask and "the passage of Mr. French." Subsequent shipments brought additional lime. From the first of May through early July, Benjamin French worked at the plastering at Hayes; payments to Harry, Aaron, Cato, Dave, Miles, and Elijah, as well as William Nichols, suggest the makeup of the work force during that time. On July 10 Johnston paid Benjamin French $250 against "his account for plaistering," which included 1,425 yards of plastering in the house and "offices," flagging laid and brick hearths installed in the kitchen (fig. 6.9), stone curbing set under the colonnade, hearths plastered, marble set around fireplaces, and hard-finished plaster applied in the drawing room.[33]

Meanwhile, in late April Johnston dispatched Nichols to New York to acquire specialty items: stone steps, iron railings, fanlights, marble mantels, a mahogany handrail, and such decorations as sculpture and draperies. Nichols obviously prided himself on his stylish taste, and he relished the

FIG. 6.10. *Land portico and stone steps, Hayes. Photograph by Frances Benjamin Johnston, 1930s. (Courtesy of the North Carolina Collection, University of North Carolina Library at Chapel Hill)*

opportunity to make rounds in the city and assess the offerings of New York's manufacturers and suppliers.

Nichols first ordered stone for the steps (fig. 6.10). He reported to Johnston, "Your letter to Mr. Lenox procured me a very gracious recognition, notwithstanding his opinion that we were blockheads to come here after stone, while there was good pitch pine in Carolina, which though not verbally expressed—yet by various shrugs and contortions was as legible on his phiz, as if it had been scratched on a piece of rough granite with a rugged flint." Nichols continued, "for these three days I have been continually in pursuit of the articles required—the steps are in hand of an excellent stone [illegible] and will be ready in all next week—the [iron] railing for Steps and Balcony is undertaken by a very good workman and I believe will give satisfaction—to be finished next week and also the fanlight." At this time, wealthy residents of New Bern were likewise obtaining steps, ironwork, and fanlights from New York. Some manufacturers supplied standardized items for purchase in various models and sizes, but it appears from Nichols's account that he had the components for Hayes custom made, perhaps from drawings he supplied.[34]

Nichols was less successful in obtaining adornments for the interior. "I am not so well satisfied as to the marble work. There are only two mantels finished for sale—of inferior marble and devoid of tastes for which they have the impudence to ask $300—so that I have struck that article from the list being satisfied that with the assistance of a few composition ornaments I can make one of wood that will answer the purpose much better—marble or stone carving appears to be done away and cast iron [illegible] and backs substitute—in all the best houses—this will make a material reduction in the marble bill." He also observed that "mahogany hand rails are made perfectly round and have a very simple and pleasing effect—I find no difficulty in getting one made from the plan."[35]

Nichols also found that "there taste in finishing the interior of the Houses in New York is greatly improved, particularly in plaster cornices—how much I regret that we did not get a plasterer from hence—be pleased Sir to inform me if your workman will undertake plain cornices as I have an opportunity of getting any kind of molds—if he is incapable which I am very much unwilling to believe—I can procure some compasses which will make tolerable ones—for cornices are indispensible in two best rooms & the passage." Finally, Nichols reported, "Busts of Washington & Hamilton, only, are to be obtained. Window curtains are made in a beautiful style. I have enclosed an estimate given by an upholsterer who would no doubt take much less. I have drawn a rough sketch on the back of the estimate, which by no means does justice to the effect they produce."[36]

Nichols was keenly attuned to the shift in taste then taking place in urban areas and among advanced clients in rural and small-town settings. The delicate, Adam-influenced neoclassical mode had appeared in a few extremely stylish houses in America before the Revolution, but it became widely popular in the 1790s and early 1800s. Further, by the time Nichols went to New York in 1817, another influence, the chastely simple Greek Revival style, had begun to appear in a few buildings. In 1816 a Virginian wrote to a friend in Raleigh, North Carolina, that in Washington, D.C., "the present taste in the erection of Public Buildings seems to be a strict attention to neatness strenth and plainness with a minute attention to the quality of the materials."[37] Evaluating the newest trends in New York, Nichols confidently adapted them to the nearly completed Johnston residence, providing Hayes with the sheen of the latest urban fashion.

Nichols's finds were soon shipped back to Hayes—the elegant stone steps with their curved curtail step and molded nosings, the delicate iron railings of front and rear porticoes, and the broad, intricately leaded fanlight of the landside entrance (fig. 6.11). The mahogany stair rail in the central passage (fig. 6.12) exemplifies the shift from the heavily molded handrails characteristic of Georgian-style woodwork both before and after the Revolution

FIG. 6.11. *Land-side entrance from inside, Hayes. Photograph by Frances Benjamin Johnston, 1930s. (Courtesy of the North Carolina Collection, University of North Carolina Library at Chapel Hill)*

to the slim, rounded railings emblematic of the Federal style. The mantels follow a variety of models; the drawing room features a simple, Greek Revival–inspired mantel (fig. 6.13). As to the plaster moldings, Nichols had his way: the plaster ceiling cornices in the passage feature decorations in a floral and classical design characteristic of the early Greek Revival, including several motifs that appeared in Asher Benjamin's *American Builder's Companion* of 1806.[38]

By the early summer of 1817, as work neared completion, Johnston began living at Hayes a good bit of the time, though not until September did he move his sisters there. Some construction work continued into the fall of 1817. Several workmen—Dave Dickinson, Jim Millen, and John Walker—continued to draw payments into October. On October 14, Johnston paid Nichols "in full" $200.

Meanwhile, Johnston set out to obtain from New York furniture and decorations to complement the stylish architectural elements Nichols had selected and installed. Despite Johnston's insistence on simplicity and avoidance of "the extreme of the fashion," the furnishings were costly and

FIG. 6.12. *Stair hall, Hayes. Photograph by Frances Benjamin Johnston, 1930s. (Courtesy of the North Carolina Collection, University of North Carolina Library at Chapel Hill)*

FIG. 6.13. *Mantel in drawing room, Hayes. Photograph by Frances Benjamin Johnston, 1930s. (Courtesy of the North Carolina Collection, University of North Carolina Library at Chapel Hill)*

"Severe Survitude to House Building"

fashionable. In July, 1817, Johnston wrote to businessman Joseph Blount in New York for help in obtaining various articles in the city. He wanted a carpet for the drawing room made "agreeable to the plan of the room enclosed," an oil floorcloth for the dining room, likewise agreeable to the plan, another oil floorcloth for the passage (10 feet 9 inches long), and another for the vestibule (19 feet 10 inches by 9 feet 5 inches). Also from his plan, Johnston asked Blount to order fenders to fit the hearths in the drawing room and dining room, to accompany iron shovels and tongs for those rooms, as well as additional fireplace fittings for the back parlor and six chambers. He wanted twelve pairs of window curtains, similarly made "to fit the windows as laid down in the plan." Finally, he wanted two pier glasses for the drawing room and another for the dining room.[39]

Although Johnston possessed a good supply of furniture already, he needed a few items to equip the new mansion for large-scale hospitality. For the drawing room, he wanted a dozen fancy chairs—large numbers of chairs were common in that sociable age—as well as a "settee or sopha." He also wanted a dozen common Windsor chairs and a dozen fancy chairs for the dining room. Also for the dining room, he sought a sideboard not to exceed 6 feet in length to fit within the niche Nichols had built for the purpose—a common architectural feature in dining rooms of the period (fig. 6.14). Johnston evidently already had a dining room table, but he ordered a new set of table china, castors, a salt cellar, a bread basket, a dozen decanters and stands, three dozen wine glasses, two dozen tumblers, two dozen knives and forks, two dozen dessert knives and forks, and a set of waiters.[40]

FIG. 6.14. *Mantel and niches in dining room, Hayes. Photograph by Frances Benjamin Johnston, 1930s.* (Courtesy of the North Carolina Collection, University of North Carolina Library at Chapel Hill)

Joseph Blount, like Nichols a few months earlier, made the rounds of the city's suppliers and met with mixed success. After two months' time, he reported, most of the items were in hand, but the oilcloth was not yet finished and the sideboard presented problems: he had ordered one made at the 6-foot size specified, but on completion it was $8\frac{1}{2}$ inches too long, and of those available in the market, "all that was good enough for you were too long." Nor had he been able to find a suitable sofa. He shipped the other articles from New York on the schooner *Louisa Childs*, including three dozen chairs (drawing room, Windsor, and curly maple fancy chairs), lamps, looking glasses, Brussels carpeting and borders, curtains, a hearth rug, two doormats, fireplace equipment, a dining set of Liverpool ware, ivory-handled knives and forks, and other tableware.[41]

As Johnston and his sisters unpacked the boxes and crates of household goods, they were "much pleased." Family and guests, he reported to Blount on November 9, greatly admired the new furnishings "not only for the style and elegance but for the suitableness of the articles to the rooms." The problem of the sideboard was quickly solved, for Johnston had sent a mistaken measurement; the recess measured 7 feet, 6 inches, not 6 feet as he had stated. He still wanted a sofa, he advised, and hoped to obtain some patriotic prints as well. Nichols, he remembered, had seen in New York "a very large and elegant print of the Battle of Waterloo," which Johnston rather fancied. "I have the Battle of Bunker Hill and Death of General Montgomery by Trumble—and should like to have his Declaration of Independence if it is in Print on a large scale." Soon Blount obtained a sideboard to fit the 7½-foot niche, as well as a "Grecian Sopha" and various curtains, ornaments, and fixtures. But he reported that the print of the Battle of Waterloo was "not to be had," and "Trumbull's Declaration of Independence has not yet been published." Finally, by the end of 1817, Johnston and his sisters were established at Hayes, surrounded by old and new furniture and adornments in the latest New York fashion.[42]

During a four-year campaign James C. Johnston had completed construction of a major house, a project that demanded much of his time, thought, and money. His experience, while atypical in the wealth he had available and the use of an architect as superintendent, was also representative of that of scores of planters, merchants, and others directly involved in construction projects. They put to use management skills developed in other aspects of their lives, and they called upon networks of friends and acquaintances to recruit workmen. They combined local and distant goods to produce buildings that embodied their own tastes and needs and also the "latitude & longitude of the place for which they are intended."

Doubtless Johnston, like many of his fellows, viewed his completed building with satisfaction and relief. The shared experience of building was

FIG. 6.15. *Drawing of Hayes, undated. Hayes Papers.* (*Courtesy of the Southern Historical Collection, Wilson Library, University of North Carolina at Chapel Hill*)

expressed by Ebenezer Pettigrew, who managed construction projects on his Bonarva plantation across the Albemarle Sound, including a residence built in 1815. The two often commiserated in wry terms over their problems and ventures. In May, 1817, Pettigrew wrote to Johnston, "I am satisfied you have had severe survitude to house building but am glad to know your labours are nearly at an end. I pray God you may live to enjoy the fruit of your industry as long as you can say there is any pleasure in it." Sending compliments to "our friends in Edenton," he teased Johnston, "tell them we should be glad to see them if we are not too much out of the fashion."[43]

For William Nichols, success at Hayes served as an important springboard. The house itself presented his abilities in no uncertain terms. And by satisfying Johnston, he had gained a generous and influential patron. In December, 1816, several months before the house was finished, Johnston was looking out for Nichols's future. He wrote to his cousin James Iredell, Jr., an Edenton lawyer then serving in the North Carolina General Assembly in Raleigh, "I observed a long report of the Committee on the Penitentiary[.] Should the Legislature do any thing on that subject I must beg the favor of you to remember Nichols—if anything can be done for him in his line—I know of no man so well qualified to superintend a public building of that kind and I think you might venture to recommend him in that way." Johnston added, "It would be of infinite advantage to the public to have such a man to superintend their buildings instead of trusting the business to a committee as is usual who know nothing about it." His comment, which doubtless echoed Nichols's own ideas, embodied new views that asserted the superiority of the professional mode of building over the traditional way, in which the public or private client dealt directly with the artisans.[44]

Probably through Iredell's and Johnston's influence, Nichols gained a foothold. The penitentiary committee reported that it had obtained information on model penitentiaries in other states and had also "been furnished with an elegant plan drawn by Wm. Nicholls, a professional architect of Edenton, together with some remarks and explanations, and an offer of his services, should the measure be adopted." The penitentiary bill ultimately failed, but a year later, with Hayes completed, Iredell reported to Johnston: "Nichols has got into employment at Fayetteville—Mr. [John] Winslow, member from Fayetteville, took Nichols there about a week ago and procured for him an engagement to superintend the building of the State Bank Branch and Cape Fear Branch Bank at Fayetteville at 90 dollars a month—His plans have been very much admired." Before another year had passed, Nichols fulfilled Johnston's earlier suggestion to Iredell and obtained an official position as architect in charge of state building projects. After remodeling the North Carolina State House and completing several prominent public and private projects, he left North Carolina in 1827 for an illustrious career in Alabama and Mississippi.[45]

Johnston, on the other hand, remained at Hayes. His pleasure in building and improvement, which he had learned from his father's example, did not abate. Even before the house was finished, Johnston had begun a windmill project in which Nichols had taken a hand during the summer of 1817. After some false starts, the undertaking proceeded in 1818. For Johnston it provided an antidote to a bout of "melancholy," of which Johnston's friend Pettigrew wrote, "A multiplicity of business provided it proceeds to ones expectation will generally relieve that disease." To build the windmill, Johnston hired a New York mechanic, Adam Brody; Pettigrew assured his friend, "Your workman being so clever a fellow and so competent to his undertaking will greatly relieve your mind from an anxiety regarding sucess and the fear of being much crippled by your attack of a wind mill. For my part I have no doubt but you will reign triumphant over the conqueror of that famous knight, Don Quixot de La Mancha. However both Wind & Water Mills have conquered many a clever and ingenious Knight since Don Quixot's day."[46]

In November, 1818, following a visit to Pettigrew's plantation, where he studied his friend's extensive improvements, Johnston wrote, "My visit to your house has *added* imposed another year or two of bondage on me—My head has been full of machinery, mills & canals ever since I saw you I believe I should build a water mill cut canal where there was no water if nature had not place[d] in my hands that element." Describing his plan

FIG. 6.16. *Land side, Hayes. Photograph by Cyrus P. Wharton, late nineteenth century. (Courtesy of the North Carolina Collection, University of North Carolina Library at Chapel Hill)*

to build a mill to combine a saw, cotton gin, threshing machine, and corn crusher, Johnston observed, "it will only add as I said before one or two more years of bondage—My Wind mill is now nearly off the stocks and I shall want something else to plague me." He commented to his happily married friend, "People must have something in this world to give them trouble and when I can find nothing else I may perhaps get married which will keep me in supply of that article during life. You and Mrs. Pettigrew will not admit to that Proposition but I can find others that will—but I shall be reduced to this alternation [*sic*] only in the last extremety that is when there is no repairs wanting on wind mills & water mills when ditches are sufficiently large and draw well and when I have no more land to clear & improve &c."[47] But such an eventuality never came. Johnston remained single throughout a long life at Hayes, which kept him in "bondage" enough.

At his death in 1865, his sisters having predeceased him, James C. Johnston left his cherished Hayes to his friend Edward Wood, "to keep my property from being scattered and divided and dilapidated." Wood's descendants have maintained the plantation—its landscape, its many farm buildings, the great house and its contents—with careful stewardship to the present day.[48]

NOTES

Thanks to Elizabeth V. Moore, Catherine Hutchins, and Damie Stillman for their assistance in the preparation of this article; John Sanders and C. Ford Peatross for sharing material on William Nichols; and John Gilliam and Annette Wood for their generous assistance and hospitality.

1. The principal source for this article is Johnston family papers contained in the Hayes Collection, Southern Historical Collection, University of North Carolina Library at Chapel Hill, hereinafter cited as Hayes Collection. Students of North Carolina architecture have focused much attention on the planta-

tion house at Hayes, and for many years it was believed to have been built in 1801 for Samuel Johnston. (See, for example, Frances Benjamin Johnston and Thomas Tileston Waterman, *The Early Architecture of North Carolina* [Chapel Hill: University of North Carolina Press, 1941], 42–43, Federal Writers' Project, *North Carolina: A Guide to the Old North State* [Chapel Hill: University of North Carolina Press, 1939], 280; and Blackwell P. Robinson [ed.], *The North Carolina Guide* [Chapel Hill: University of North Carolina Press, 1955], 186.) However, research in the 1970s by Elizabeth V. Moore and further study by John G. Zehmer, Jr., and C. Ford Peatross established its construction in the 1810s and revealed the hand of William Nichols in the project. See John G. Zehmer, Jr., "Hayes: An Architectural Analysis," typescript of paper presented at the Edenton Symposium, April, 1974, copy in Survey and Planning Branch, Division of Archives and History, Raleigh. The donation of the Hayes papers by John Gilliam Wood to the Southern Historical Collection and the completion in 1979 of restoration, arrangement, and description of the papers and in 1980 of a microfilm edition of the papers permit closer examination of records of the building project. In addition to correspondence, James C. Johnston's small personal and plantation memorandum books establish William Nichols's ongoing superintendence of the construction of Hayes. The context of building practices and roles in the state is discussed in Catherine W. Bishir, Charlotte V. Brown, Carl R. Lounsbury, and Ernest H. Wood III, *Architects and Builders in North Carolina: A History of the Practice of Building* (Chapel Hill: University of North Carolina Press, 1990). On North Carolina architecture, including Hayes, see Johnston and Waterman, *Early Architecture of North Carolina*; Mills Lane, *Architecture of the Old South: North Carolina* (Savannah: Beehive Press, 1985) and Catherine W. Bishir, *North Carolina Architecture* (Chapel Hill: University of North Carolina Press, 1990).

2. Samuel married Frances Cathcart (1751–1801) in 1770, and the couple had nine children. Four died before reaching the age of two; one son, Gabriel, was retarded and died when he was about twenty-five; and James and his three sisters survived their parents. Samuel Johnston owned acreage in Pasquotank, Currituck, Tyrrell, and Bertie counties and had three large plantations—the Hermitage in Martin County, Caledonia in Halifax County, and Hayes in Chowan County. He bought Hayes in 1765 from David Rieusetts, whose brother John had bought it from William and Harding Jones; in 1765 Hayes included 543 acres, and Samuel and, later, James expanded the acreage. From William Cathcart, his father-in-law, Samuel received 1,500 acres of Roanoke Island and about 3,000 acres of Caledonia plantation in Halifax County. Cathcart had acquired the property after the death of his wife, Penelope Maule, daughter of William Maule, a large landowner in early North Carolina. William S. Powell (ed.), *Dictionary of North Carolina Biography* (Chapel Hill: University of North Carolina Press, multivolume series, 1979–96), 3:306–8, hereinafter cited as Powell, DNCB; *Guide to the Microfilm Edition of the Hayes Collection, 1694–1928* (Chapel Hill: Southern Historical Collection, 1980), 3–5.

3. Deed of gift from Samuel Johnston to James C. Johnston, December 29, 1814; will of Samuel Johnston [November 9, 1814], both in Hayes Collection. In that year, tax lists stated that the 665-acre plantation near Edenton "called Hayes" had a dwelling house "out of repair and uninhabitable," as well as small framed buildings, two barns, some log cabins, and log fish houses—all ruinous or out of repair and unused. Tax lists, 1814, 1815, Hayes Collection. Samuel Johnston's property as listed for tax purposes in May, 1815, also included a plantation of 2,375 acres on the Roanoke River and Connecanary Creek, with a frame house 30 by 16 feet, one story, and three barns, and Margaret McKenzie's property, 2,031 acres on the Roanoke River, with a log dwelling house and two barns and slaves. According to his 1814 property listing, Samuel Johnston's Hermitage plantation near Williamston included 567 acres with a one-story house 40 by 20 feet "in body," with a 13-foot shed, two wings measuring 18 by 16 feet, and a 9-foot piazza. There were a kitchen, smokehouse, carriage house, barns, a sawed log stable, a log house, 6 "negro cabbins," and a dairy—the usual assortment of domestic and agricultural buildings. (The reference to log buildings is indicative of the presence of log farm buildings and dwellings in eastern North Carolina in the eighteenth and early nineteenth centuries, a situation that contrasts to the paucity of such structures at the present time. See Bishir, *North Carolina Architecture*, 3–7, and Carl R. Lounsbury, "The Building Process in

Antebellum North Carolina," *North Carolina Historical Review,* 60 [October, 1983], 437–38.) On the Johnston family see Powell, DNCB, 3: 302–4, and Max R. Williams, "The Johnston Will Case: A Clash of Titans," *North Carolina Historical Review,* 67, part 1 (April, 1990), 193–221, especially page 196. It is not clear why the family decided to move back to Hayes rather than remaining at the Hermitage; possibly James and his sisters wanted to be nearer Edenton or to return to the plantation where they had lived as small children. As far as is demonstrated by the records he kept, James C. Johnston took the principal role in planning the new residence; if his father or his sisters took a hand in planning the arrangement, finishing, and furnishing of the household, their roles are not recorded in his correspondence and accounts.

4. Williams, "Johnston Will Case," 193 (quote), 196; Powell, DNCB, 3: 302–4.

5. Samuel Johnston to Hannah Iredell, May 9, 1793, Private Collections, Charles E. Johnson Collection, PC 67, Archives, Division of Archives and History, Raleigh, hereinafter cited as Johnson Collection, PC 67.

6. Samuel Johnston to James C. Johnston, November 14, 1814, Hayes Collection. Fatherly cautions of this kind seem to have run in the family: Samuel's uncle, Gabriel Johnston (1698–1752), colonial governor of North Carolina who brought Samuel's family to the colony, instructed that his daughter Penelope be brought up to "confin[e] her desires to things Plain, Neat and Elegant ... not aspiring after the Gayety, Splendour and Extravagance and Especially to take care to keep within the Bounds of her Income and by no Means to Run in Debt." Quoted in Powell, DNCB, 3: 301.

7. James C. Johnston to Joseph Blount, July 15[?], 1817, Hayes Collection. In the same letter, Johnston asked Mrs. Joseph Blount to purchase for his sisters bonnets "or whatever is most worn in New York suitable to their different ages and habilement they are still in mourning as plain as possible," Johnston's bills with the local tailor included costs of "making fashionable coat with sewed lapel" and "fashionable buttons." Receipts, Joseph Manning to Johnston, March 21, 1816, March 21, 1817, Hayes Collection.

8. On the early development of the architectural profession in North Carolina see Bishir et al. *Architects and Builders in North Carolina,* 120–28. John Hawks, English-trained architect of Tryon Palace in New Bern, was the first professional architect in North Carolina and one of the first, if not the first, in the colonies. Although there were several professional engineers and surveyors working in Federal-period North Carolina, Nichols was the only professional architect in the Federal era. Not until the antebellum period did architects become more numerous in the nation and in the state.

9. Josiah Collins to William Nichols, January 18, 1806; Nichols to Collins, February 29, 1806; Collins to Nichols, April 4, 1806; restoration committee to Nichols, May 12, 1806; and Nichols to Collins, May 28, 1806, all in St. Paul's Church Records, Edenton, transcribed by Elizabeth V. Moore and provided to the author. On Nichols see C. Ford Peatross, *William Nichols, Architect* (Tuscaloosa: University of Alabama Art Gallery, 1979) and Powell, DNCB, 4: 369–71. See also Bishir et al. *Architects and Builders in North Carolina,* 126–28, and Bishir, *North Carolina Architecture,* 78–81, 96–101.

10. Both Tryon Palace and Hayes have waterfront locations, but their orientations differ: the palace has the forecourt toward the town and land, while Hayes has the forecourt toward the water. On the stylistic antecedents and influences on Hayes see particularly Peatross, *William Nichols,* 10–11, and Zehmer, "Hayes: An Architectural Analysis." On similarities of Hayes with plate 31 in Asher Benjamin's *Country Builder's Assistant* (Boston, 1798), see Lynda Vestal Herzog, "The Early Architecture of New Bern, North Carolina, 1750–1850" (unpublished doctoral dissertation, University of California, Los Angeles, 1977), 107. Herzog and others have noted similarities between details of Hayes and various buildings in New Bern, including the flush-paneled lower panels of the landside door, a type frequent in New Bern, and the paired modillion blocks and half-round portico, as at the New Bern Academy. Although it seems quite likely that Nichols was involved in those and other New Bern buildings, no documentation has been found. Another interesting question is whether Hawks might have supplied Samuel Johnston with house plans; a letter of 1773 from Hawks to Joseph Hewes in Edenton has a postscript requesting Hewes to deliver an enclosure (unexplained) to Johnston. John Hawks to Joseph Hewes, September 29, 1773, John Hawks Papers, Southern Historical Collection. Whether Hawks influenced anything built at Hayes or at the Hermitage is not known. Another question concerns the disposi-

tion of the old house at Hayes that was "out of repair" and "uninhabitable" in 1814 when James Johnston began his undertaking. It is not known whether any elements of that house were reused, or whether its form and plan might have influenced the new house. Mills Lane points out that a sketch on an 1812 map of Hayes shows a three-part house there, which he suggests might have been incorporated into the present house (*Architecture of the Old South*, 147–48).

11. See Louise Hall's eloquent commentary on Hayes in Robinson, *North Carolina Guide*, 119, in which she notes the Palladian influence and observes, "At that point the pedigree of Hayes gallops off in all directions." Praising the "enviable verve" of the house, she states that "Could one house only be seen" in North Carolina from its period, she believes it should be Hayes. See Peatross, *William Nichols*, 10–11, and Zehmer, "Hayes: An Architectural Analysis." Peatross suggests that Nichols's use of the small, curved portico design of the New Bern Academy, which he attributes to Nichols, was influenced by George Richardson's *New Vitruvius Britannicus* (London, 1802), 1: plate 56. A similar design is used at Hayes on the land front. The Greek key motif appears at Hayes on the rear entrance and inside the passage. A similar motif appears at the Joseph Blount Skinner Law Office in Edenton, ca. 1815, which Peatross also attributes to Nichols (*William Nichols*, 5, 7). The tall columns of the waterfront portico of Hayes, while inspired by the Temple of Apollo at Delos (James Stuart and Nicholas Revett, *Antiquities of Athens* [London, 1794], 2: plate 1, as cited in Peatross, *William Nichols*, 14), also have characteristics more akin to earlier phases of neoclassicism, including their attenuated height and Roman-type bases.

12. William Nichols to James C. Johnston, [1814], Hayes Collection. Archivists have assigned 1814 to the undated letter based on circumstantial evidence; it is possible that it dates from late 1813.

13. Personal and plantation expense memorandum book, 1815–16, Hayes Collection.

14. Ebenezer Pettigrew to Ann Shepard Pettigrew, December 2, 1815, Sarah McCulloh Lemmon (ed.), *The Pettigrew Papers* (Raleigh: Division of Archives and History, Department of Cultural Resources, projected 3 volumes, 1971–), 1:500.

15. Bishir et al., *Architects and Builders in North Carolina*, 60–91.

16. William Darlet to James C. Johnston, April 19, 1814, Hayes Collection.

17. On sawmills see Bishir et al., *Architects and Builders in North Carolina*, 196–97. and Carl R. Lounsbury, "From Craft to Industry: The Building Process in North Carolina in the Nineteenth Century" (unpublished doctoral dissertation, George Washington University, 1983), 156–66.

18. W. W. Wilkins to James C. Johnston, April 10, 1814; David Clark to Johnston (accompanying note), Hayes Collection. In early June some of the men returned to their owners briefly to help with harvesting and then returned to Johnston's employ. Johnston to David Clark, June 2, 1814, Hayes Collection. Hiring slave artisans for construction was common practice. Few planters, even those who had many slaves, owned enough skilled artisans to complete a major building project. Nor did free artisans such as Nichols typically own more than a few slaves themselves. Hence in building, as in farming and industry, many slaves were hired out by their owners for the job, the day, or, often, the year. In some cases slaves were given considerable latitude in hiring out their time, as in Wilmington and Fayetteville, where slave artisans ran their own affairs to an extent that offered serious competition to free artisans. Ordinarily, however, bargains were made between the owner and the hirer for a certain sum to be paid the owner for the slave's work. See "Black Builders in Antebellum North Carolina," chapter 3 of this volume.

19. James C. Johnston to David Clark, June 2, 1814; Johnston to W. W. Wilkins, June 14, 1814, both in Hayes Collection.

20. James C. Johnston to W. W. Wilkins, June 14, 1814; Wilkins to Johnston, June 19, September 6, 1814; Johnston to Wilkins, August 27, 1814; Wilkins to Johnston, March 6, 1815, all in Hayes Collection. In August, 1814, Johnston still had 30,000 to 40,000 feet left to saw and asked if Wilkins had any other hands available: "they are to work under Moses and to be subject to his control."

For analysis of the task system in an agricultural setting see, for example, John Scott Strickland, "Traditional Culture and Moral Economy: Social and Economic Change in the South Carolina Low Country, 1865–1910," in Steven Hahn and Jonathan Prude (eds.), *The Countryside in the Age of Capitalist Transformation: Essays in the Social History of Rural America*

(Chapel Hill: University of North Carolina Press, 1985), 144–48, and Philip D. Morgan, "Work and Culture: The Task System and the World of Lowcountry Blacks, 1700–1880," *William and Mary Quarterly,* 39 (October, 1982), 563–99, reprinted in Robert Blair St. George (ed.), *Material Life in America, 1600–1860* (Boston: Northeastern University Press, 1988), 203–32. The system was also in effect in North Carolina. Guion Griffis Johnson, *Ante-Bellum North Carolina* (Chapel Hill: University of North Carolina Press, 1937), 476–79, 487–88, indicates that the task system was widespread in North Carolina agriculture, especially on turpentine and rice plantations in the southeastern part of the state; on the latter, the "task was usually a quarter of an acre." Johnson notes that "on plantations where the task system was used, the slave had the rest of the day to spend as he pleased when he finished the task assigned him. This meant that he sometimes had three or four hours of his own before dusk. When slaves worked in gangs on a given job, work usually stopped at 'first dusk.'" She reports that generally work stopped at noon Saturday and did not commence again until Monday morning, usually at daybreak. Overtime work, she states, was usually rewarded with a "money wage." James C. Johnston's memorandum books included payments to slaves for amounts of corn that they raised on their own time and sold for themselves; this suggests an agricultural task system at work at least in Chowan County. See also *Guide to Microfilm Edition of Hayes Collection,* 6.

21. Bill from Treadwell and Thorne, New York, to James C. Johnston, December 26, 1815; receipts, Johnston to W. W. Wilkins, 1815–16, all in Hayes Collection.

22. Receipt for James Cunningham, April 12, 1815; personal and plantation expense memorandum book, 1816–18, both in Hayes Collection. Johnston's choice of local brick for foundations and chimneys was a thrifty and convenient one. If he had been building a fine brick structure, however, he might well have decided to use Philadelphia brick at least for outer facing. In North Carolina port towns, traffic in brick from Philadelphia was commonplace. Philadelphia bricks were considered to be superior in quality, and as early as the 1780s Philadelphia bricks arrived at the Edenton wharves by ship. Contemporary brick construction in New Bern, whence William Nichols had recently come, also employed Philadelphia face brick. Bishir et al., *Architects and Builders in North Carolina,* 74–79; Catherine W. Bishir, "Philadelphia Bricks and the New Bern Jail," chapter 5 in this volume.

23. Receipt, Treadwell and Thorne, December 16, 1815, and other receipts, Hayes Collection.

24. See Bishir et al., *Architects and Builders in North Carolina,* passim, on problems and sources of manufactured materials.

25. R. H. Smith to James C. Johnston, December 13, 1814, Hayes Collection. On slave hiring days, see "Black Builders," chapter 3 of this volume.

26. Marshall Parker to James C. Johnston, September 1, 1815, Hayes Collection.

27. Marshall Parker to James C. Johnston, September 1, October 5, 1815; Johnston to David Clark, October 31, 1815, both in Hayes Collection.

28. At St. Paul's, Welcome and Millen had been assisted by Dick Blount, Dick Hoskins, Hector, and Jim Frog. St. Paul's Church Records, Edenton, transcript notes by Elizabeth V. Moore provided to the author. At the Edenton Academy, Welcome was assisted by Andrew, Jeffrey, Old Welcome, Lewis, Dick, and others. Josiah Collins's notes on "Account of Work done by Sundries on the Academy," Cupola House Papers (microfilm copy), Southern Historical Collection, reproduced in part in chapter 3, pp. 97–100, this volume. See data on Joe Welcome (1774–1859), provided by Elizabeth Fenn and Peter Wood, cited in chapter 3, p. 103 n. 32, this volume. Joe Welcome and others, including Dick Blount, also identified as a shoemaker, are mentioned prominently in Dorothy Spruill Redford, *Somerset Homecoming: Recovering a Lost Heritage* (New York: Doubleday, Anchor Books, 1989), 153, though there is some confusion concerning Welcome's role, which was not in the original construction of St. Paul's (1730s–1760s) but in its "restoration" in 1806–9. Personal and plantation expense memorandum books, 1815–16, 1816–18; account with Josiah Collins, Jr., May 10, 1817, all in Hayes Collection.

29. Personal and plantation expense memorandum books, 1815–16, 1816–18; James C. Johnston to David Clark, October 31, 1815, all in Hayes Collection.

30. Receipt from Malachi Etheridge, June 26, 1815; personal and plantation expense memorandum book, 1816–18, both in Hayes Collec-

tion. Nichols may also have brought his own apprentices or hired workmen to the job. Notes from Chowan County deeds, apprentice bonds, and court minutes (Chowan County Records, State Archives) referring to William Nichols and provided to the author by Elizabeth V. Moore show that Nichols took as apprentices to the house carpenter's trade Benjamin Boulton in 1807; Cornelius Leary, orphan of John Leary, in 1810; and James Read, free mulatto, in 1810. The latter two might have been in Nichols's employ during construction of Hayes.

31. Bill from Treadwell and Thorne to David Clark "for Mr. Johnston," October 14, 1815, Hayes Collection.

32. It is not entirely clear which individuals were free workmen, which were hired slaves, and which were Johnston's own slaves. Payments to the latter may have been for extra work. Johnston paid Miles Badham wages, according to his records, but Badham was a Johnston slave, at least in later life. The same was true of Aaron. Jack and Merrick were hired from E. Hoskins; E. Wood was paid $6.50 when Jack—another or the same—painted the house; Dover was "Mr. Treadwell's man"; Dick was hired from Dr. James Norcom; Elijah and Bob were hired from Nathaniel Bond. Regular wages were paid to one John Walker, who signed his receipts with an *X*; his identity is not known, nor whether his work for Johnston was connected with Hayes. Dave Dickinson and Aaron were also paid "wages." Several men were identified as "Negroes": Harry, Jim, Cato, Elijah, and Dave (who may be the same as Dave Dickinson or another Dave). Only once, in 1815, were men specifically listed as being "workmen at Hayes." Very rarely were specific tasks noted: Cato for making doors, Dave for laying floors, Elijah for making doors, Daniel for lathes, Jim for laying floors, Merrick for ditching, Peter for ditching, and Old David for lathes early in 1817. Once Henry Chaves was paid $5 for "Sunday work." Personal and plantation expense memorandum books, 1815–16, 1816–18; receipts to Josiah Collins, Jr., and John Walker, 1815–17, all in Hayes Collection. In his will of 1863, Johnston made special provisions for his slaves Aaron, Davy Blount, Osborne, and Miles Badham, as described in Williams, "Johnston Will Case," 217–18.

33. Account with Benjamin French [1817]; James C. Johnston to B. Fuller, April 9, April 23, April 29, 1817; personal and plantation expense memorandum book, 1816–18, all in Hayes Collection.

34. William Nichols to James C. Johnston, May 1, 1817, Hayes Collection. Robert Lenox was a prominent New York businessman with whom Johnston had continuous dealings. The "pitch pine" Nichols mentioned was doubtless the hard, insect- and rot-resistant lightwood pine often used for foundation blocks in humbler buildings; it was scarcely suitable for the steps of an elegant residence.

35. William Nichols to James C. Johnston, May 1, 1817, Hayes Collection.

36. Ibid. The comment on the plasterer is confusing, given that French came on the ship from New York.

37. Robert Bolling to Calvin Jones, April 1, 1816, Calvin Jones Papers, Southern Historical Collection, quoted on p. 115 of "Mr. Jones Goes to Richmond: A Note on the Influence of Alexander Parris's Wickham House," chapter 4 of this volume.

38. Whether Nichols copied these from the Benjamin plates or whether both Nichols and Benjamin were inspired by a common, possibly New York, source is not certain. Other motifs at Hayes, including the Greek key or fret pattern on doors, also resemble plates in Benjamin's *American Builder's Companion*. As Zehmer, "Hayes: An Architectural Analysis," points out, additional motifs from the same volume appear elsewhere in Edenton domestic architecture of the period—in details at the Skinner Law Office and the porch cornice of an addition to the James Iredell House. Those elements, combined with circumstantial evidence, suggest Nichols's hand in the projects.

39. James C. Johnston to Joseph Blount, July 15, 1817, Hayes Collection. The drawing room at Hayes was graced with a spectacular set of fittings that included tall, eagle-topped pier glasses between pairs of windows surmounted by large arrow valances draped with swags; this scheme, in keeping with the national symbolism of the Federal era, may date from the period of original decoration of the house.

40. James C. Johnston to Joseph Blount, July 15, 1817, Hayes Collection.

41. James C. Johnston to Joseph Blount, July 15, 1817; Blount to Johnston, October 22, 1817, both in Hayes Collection.

42. James C. Johnston to Joseph Blount, November 9, 1817; receipt, schooner *Louisa*

Childs, 1817; receipt to James C. Johnston, November 29, 1817; Blount to Johnston, December 2, 1817, all in Hayes Collection.

43. Ebenezer Pettigrew to James C. Johnston, May 19, 1817, Lemmon, *Pettigrew Papers,* 1: 567–68. On Pettigrew's house construction see Ebenezer Pettigrew to Ann Shepard Pettigrew, November 21, 1815, Lemmon, *Pettigrew Papers,* 1: 497–98.

44. James C. Johnston to James Iredell, December 10, 1816, Johnson Collection, PC 67. On the development of the architectural profession at this time in North Carolina, see Bishir et al. *Architects and Builders in North Carolina,* 120–28.

45. "Report on the Penitentiary," *Star* (Raleigh), November 29, 1816, courtesy of C. Ford Peatross; James Iredell to James C. Johnston, December 11, 1817, Hayes Collection. As late as 1818 Johnston and Nichols stayed in touch; in November of that year, for example, Johnston noted in his memorandum book that he had lent or sent William Nichols $70.00. Personal and plantation expense memorandum book, 1816–18, Hayes Collection. On the proposal for the penitentiary by Archibald D. Murphey and Frederick Nash of Hillsborough, one of various reforms proposed in the mid-1810s, see Johnson, *Ante-Bellum North Carolina,* 661–73, especially 668. Disagreement over the location of the proposed institution resulted in defeat of the penitentiary bill. The penitentiary committee's survey of criminal offenses in various counties appears in the General Assembly Session Records, State Archives, but the author has not located Nichols's "elegant plans" or his explanations and offer of services for the project. Over the years the penitentiary issue reappeared at intervals, but not until after the Civil War was a state penitentiary constructed, in Raleigh.

After leaving Johnston's employ, Nichols designed the State Bank and Cape Fear Bank in Fayetteville in 1817 and the Fayetteville waterworks in 1820. As state architect from 1819 to 1825, he accomplished the impressive neoclassical renovation of the State House in Raleigh and extensive projects at the University of North Carolina. His private practice included, in the 1820s, the Mordecai House and the first Christ Church in Raleigh, St. Matthew's Church and probably Eagle Lodge in Hillsborough, courthouses in Guilford and Davidson counties, and other houses built and renovated. After he left North Carolina to pursue his fortune in Alabama and Mississippi, Nichols provided, in association with his son, William, Jr., the initial design for the North Carolina State Capitol, from which plan the New York firm of Ithiel Town and Alexander Jackson Davis developed the present building. Nichols's productivity and prominence continued in the southwestern states, where he designed and built capitols and great plantation houses that dominated the emerging architecture of the region. See Peatross, *William Nichols,* and Powell, DNCB, 4: 369–71.

46. Ebenezer Pettigrew to James C. Johnston, June 6, 1818, Lemmon, *Pettigrew Papers,* 1: 621; Adam Brody to William Nichols, in care of James C. Johnston, July 12, 1817; Joseph Blount to Johnston, September 20, 1817; Adam Brody to Mr. Jackson [December, 1817]; Blount to Johnston, December 2, 1817, all in Hayes Collection. Johnston had been thinking about windmill building for quite some time; in 1815 Thomas Trotter, a multitalented Scots-born mechanic active in the Albemarle region, had provided Johnston with specifications for an octagonal windmill. Thomas Trotter to James C. Johnston, June 8, 1815, Hayes Collection. On Trotter see Lemmon, *Pettigrew Papers,* 1: 91n.

47. James C. Johnston to Ebenezer Pettigrew, November 15, 1818, Lemmon, *Pettigrew Papers,* 1: 648.

48. Johnston left his other plantations to trusted overseers, made arrangements for several slaves (freedmen by the time of his death), and left cash bequests to various family members and others. He was buried at the family graveyard at Hayes. His will was challenged by relatives, but in the end Johnston's wishes were confirmed. See Williams, "Johnston Will Case." For a brief account of the subsequent history of Hayes see *Guide to Microfilm Edition of Hayes Collection,* 7–9. In 1989 a reproduction of the library room at Hayes was installed at the North Carolina Collection in Louis Round Wilson Library at the University of North Carolina at Chapel Hill, and the contents of the Johnston-Wood library were placed there. Hayes plantation continues as a working farm.

PART III

Constructing Group Identity
Architectural Landscapes, Community, and Power

Seven

THE MONTMORENCI–PROSPECT HILL SCHOOL

A STUDY OF HIGH-STYLE VERNACULAR ARCHITECTURE IN THE ROANOKE VALLEY

The energy and variety of nineteenth-century American vernacular architecture are expressed not only in the unpretentious, astylistic structures of indigenous and ethnic cultures, but also in the more ambitious buildings of the increasingly sophisticated but still provincial planters and merchants who grew in wealth and numbers in the early years of the century. The interaction of a regional clientele, local craftsmen, and traditional technology with current architectural fashions produced a high-style vernacular architecture of lively individuality intensely expressive of the culture that produced it.

In the period following the Revolution, American architectural fashion still followed British models. Classicism was still predominant, but the decorative innovations of the brothers Robert and James Adam had introduced a new lightness and delicacy and a greater variety of motifs, derived from discoveries in newly dug Roman ruins. Garlands, swags, sunbursts, flowers, urns, and wreaths applied in sprightly abundance, plus a general flattening and attenuation of forms, changed the aspect of British and hence American classicism. The Adamesque mode was dominant during the Federal period in America (ca. 1780s–1820s) and hence often carries the name Federal.

"The Montmorenci–Prospect Hill School: A Study of High-Style Vernacular Architecture in the Roanoke Valley" appeared in *Carolina Dwelling: Towards Preservation of Place: In Celebration of the North Carolina Vernacular Landscape,* ed. Doug Swaim (Raleigh: North Carolina State University School of Design Student Publication 26, 1978: 84–103), and is reprinted by permission of the College of Design, North Carolina State University, Raleigh.

FIG. 7.1. *Mantel design by Robert and James Adam.*

In urban trade centers like Philadelphia, Boston, Charleston, and New York, the Federal style caught on quickly and was executed expertly. Pattern books were published by the brothers Adam and by other British and American architects and designers, which communicated new fashions to builders and clients (fig. 7.1).

In rural areas and provincial towns, new styles found expression less quickly, and were usually interpreted to suit the tastes and resources of the locality. Pattern books were a major source of inspiration, but many local craftsmen produced their own versions of academic motifs. Departing from bookish Adamesque examples, these regional craftsmen created identifiable localized pockets of architecture that are as vernacular as they are Federal.

Outstanding among the examples of high-style vernacular architecture in North Carolina is a group of late Federal-style plantation houses located in a small area of Warren and Halifax counties. This group of houses, while sharing many of the characteristics common to vernacular Federal architecture, is distinguished by certain highly personalized and unusually elaborate detail. Mantels, doorways, windows, stairs, and other elements are treated in a distinctive fashion whose individuality sets off these houses as an identifiable entity unique in the state.

The catalyst for their construction was evidently a single great seminal house, Montmorenci[1] (figs. 7.2, 7.5–7.8). Probably the most ambitious house of the region, Montmorenci was a spectacular blend of vernacular energy and Philadelphia elegance. It was built, probably about 1820, for William Williams, a Warren County planter of unusual wealth and urbanity. His house, grand and novel, was at once representative of the plantation culture of the region and foreign to it, bringing both a stimulus for change and an affirmation of the society.

The body of architecture associated with Montmorenci is expressive of a broader culture, that of the prosperous plantation society of the Roanoke Valley; an understanding of this regional culture is vital to the study of the architecture it produced. Located in the northeastern Piedmont, the present counties of Warren and Halifax were settled chiefly from Virginia in the mid-eighteenth century. By the post-Revolutionary era the region was dominated by large planters, in marked contrast to most of North Carolina (fig. 7.3). By the early nineteenth century, ownership of two thousand acres or more, and more than fifty slaves, was not unusual for the planters of the Roanoke. In 1790 Warren County was the only county in the state with more slaves than free citizens, and as time passed and agricultural technology changed, planters accrued more acres and more slaves to till them. Socially and economically the region was oriented toward Virginia. Cash crops, not subsistence farming, was the basis of the economy, and tobacco was sold by the planters in Virginia markets, usually Petersburg. With wealth and established family came political power; in the late eighteenth and early nineteenth century the Roanoke planters provided the state with many of its most powerful political leaders.[2]

Prosperous as the region was, it was nevertheless shackled by the bonds that made North Carolina in the early nineteenth century the "Rip Van Winkle State" and the "Ireland of America." The Roanoke Valley was ac-

FIG. 7.2. *Montmorenci, 1810s, Warren County, North Carolina. Photograph ca. 1930s. This and the following photographs of Montmorenci show elements* in situ, *before the interiors were removed to the Winterthur Museum. (Courtesy of The Winterthur Library: Printed Book and Periodical Collection)*

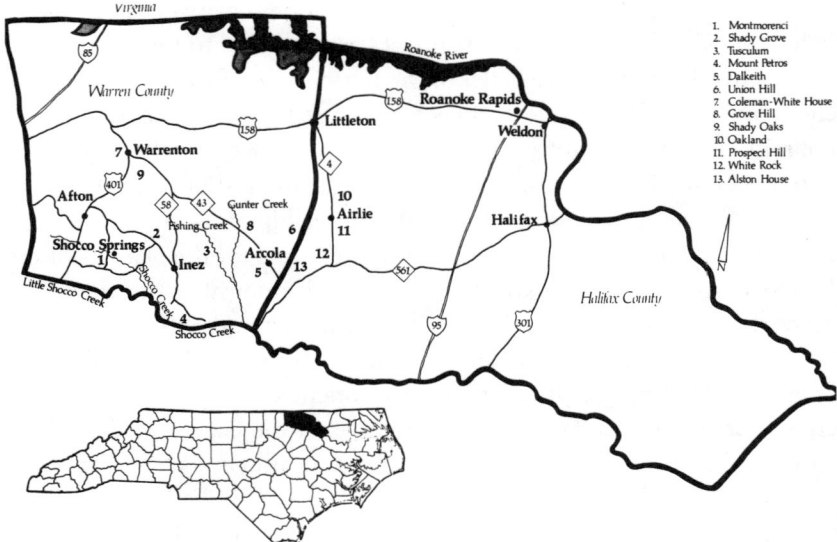

FIG. 7.3. *Map showing locations of the Montmorenci–Prospect Hill school in the Roanoke Valley.*

cessible only by miserable roads and inadequate waterways, so that contact with other areas was difficult. There were no large cities, for the profits of agriculture went not to local towns like Halifax and Warrenton, but out of state to Petersburg and Norfolk. The economy of the region was agrarian, with nearly every person engaged in some aspect of agriculture or related trade. There was little cross-fertilization of population: with few exceptions people came from families long established in the region, living near where they were born.[3] Marriage for the upper classes and the less affluent alike was usually with folk of similar standing within the region. For the proportionately small planter gentry, marriages were within a small population from the immediate vicinity or from compatible families from nearby areas. This pattern reinforced the sense of intimacy and insularity (fig. 7.4).

Within the isolated rural context, the planters of the early nineteenth century Roanoke Valley achieved a level of prosperity and sophistication seldom rivaled in the state, a lifestyle described as the "most refined type to be found in rural North Carolina."[4] Building on the plantations and fortunes established by their grandparents' pioneer generation, these planters had the money and the desire to seek learning, pleasure, and fashion beyond that found in most of rural North Carolina.

The planters' wealth enabled them to provide their children with the classical education their cultural aspiration deemed necessary. Families sent children north to be educated, hired private tutors, or formed private classical academies. Warrenton, the county seat of Warren, was noted

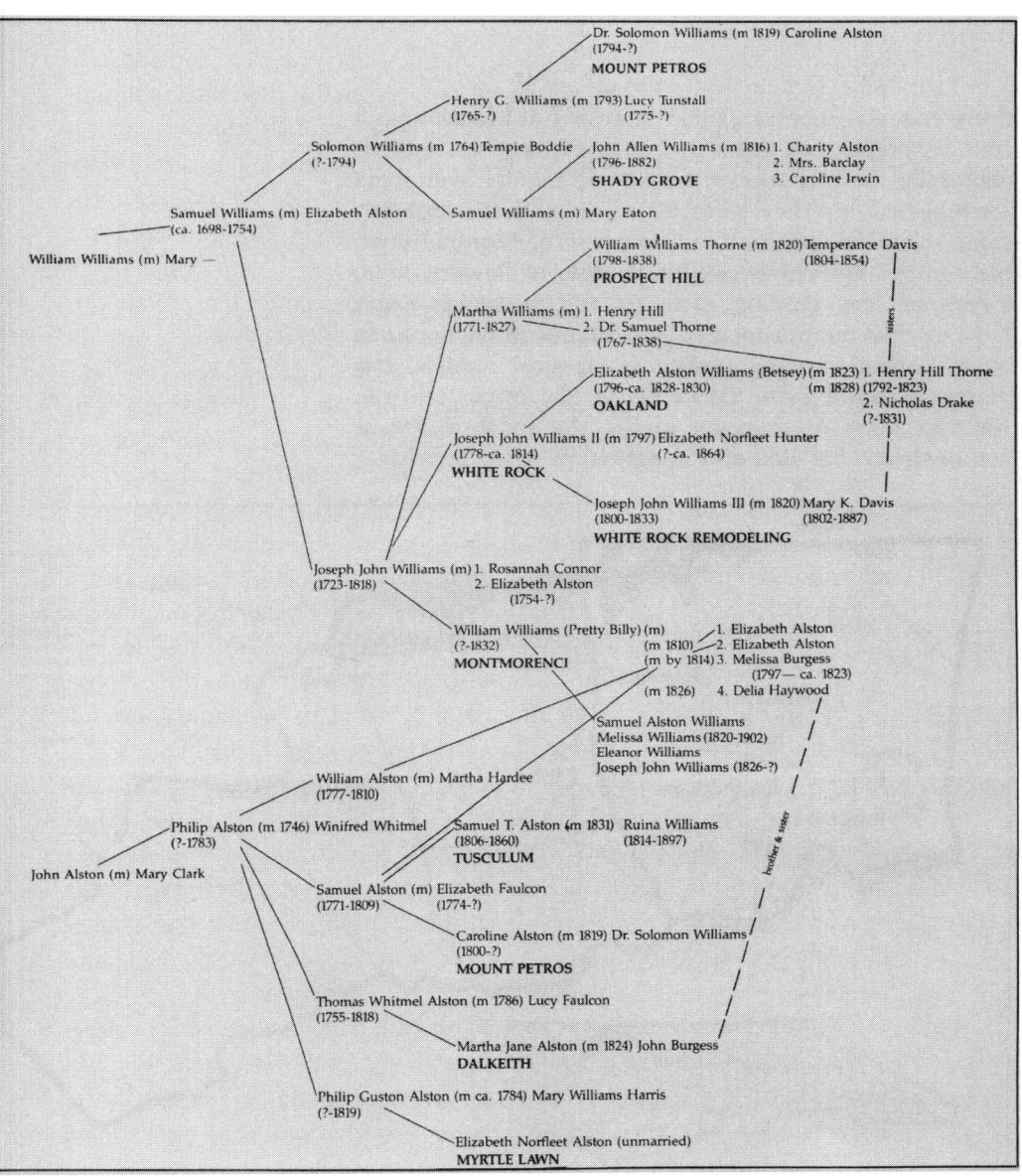

FIG. 7.4. *Genealogical chart relating houses of Montmorenci–Prospect Hill school built for members of Alston-Williams family. Extracted from "Unwieldy Chart, showing identity of houses in the Alston-Williams family," prepared by Edgar Thorne, 1976. Family members not associated with cited houses are generally omitted from this chart.*

for its fine academies, one established as early as 1788 headed by an Irish scholar. Teachers from the north or from Europe provided instruction in Latin, Greek, composition, mathematics, and English literature, with music, painting, and the like added for girls. Many planters attended colleges and universities, with the University of North Carolina, William and Mary, and Princeton being favored. The result of this education was evident in the gracefully written letters containing frequent classical allusions and in the richly stocked libraries of the planter families.[5]

Despite bad roads, travel was a vital part of the planter life, private carriages providing some compensation for miserable roadways. Visits for weeks to plantations or town homes of friends and relatives were common. Planters seasonally met their fellows and their factors on business trips to the markets at Petersburg, Norfolk, and beyond. Occasional journeys were made to the great northeastern commercial and cultural centers—Baltimore, Boston, Philadelphia, and New York. Here at the fountainhead of culture one could find fashionable goods, manufactured items, a fine education, and sparkling society, all of a quality impossible in rural North Carolina. The influence of these cities, particularly Philadelphia, upon the plantation culture of the Roanoke Valley is inestimable. Wrote one descendant, "There is no question that for antebellum Warrenton, the omphalos was in Philadelphia. Even after the war, with [the plantation] lost, my Grandmother somehow managed to make the trek to Philadelphia."[6]

Newspapers of the day in the Roanoke Valley demonstrate the attitudes about these cities as well. Advertisements of hotels, bookshops, and manufacturers from Philadelphia, Baltimore, and Norfolk appear regularly; beside them run the advertisements of local tradesmen who declare that their own local goods are as fine and as fashionable as those of northern cities. One Warrenton cabinetmaker advertised in 1811 that his locally made furniture was "executed a la mode New York or Philadelphia."[7]

The breeding and racing of thoroughbred horses was the focus of community social and recreational life. Many planters expended much time and money in maintaining fine stables which rivaled those of Virginia in the early nineteenth century. Seasonal races, cockfights, and card games were, along with taverns and hotels, among the entertainments of Warrenton and Halifax.

The social life of the region was widely known for occasioning elaborate balls and sumptuous dinners. Adding spice to this social life were the mineral springs resorts of Warren County, such as Jones's Springs and Shocco Springs, which were established in the early nineteenth century and attracted throngs of the fashionable as well as the fevered each season. At resort and ball alike, fashion was perhaps as important as social intercourse: "At a dance or on a visiting party the dress of the gentry conformed to the dictates of fashion from Charleston, Petersburg, Philadelphia, and New York.... The leaders of society ... always had definite ideas as to what was the style and what old fashioned."[8]

As is always true, the character of the culture was expressed in the buildings it created. Most of the planters of the Roanoke Valley who came to maturity in the period 1810–30 had grown up in the traditional Tidewater-type houses long characteristic of the region—well-proportioned, handsomely crafted, but by the early nineteenth century old fashioned in a culture increasingly conscious of current fashion. Modishness was to be found in the Adamesque style which was gradually making itself felt in piedmont North Carolina. Aware of the fine mercantile mansions of Philadelphia and Boston, yet far removed from the sophisticated designers and materials of these urban centers, the Roanoke planters of the early nineteenth century created an architecture that expressed with precision the character of their "opulent rural culture."

William Williams, for whom Montmorenci was built, seems to epitomize this opulent planter culture. He was the quintessential representative of his class, typical yet larger than life. As a member of the Alston-Williams family, a family of planters long rooted in the region, with connections entwined through the culture, he was very much the product of the provincial area. Yet, wealthy and well-traveled, he was able to make the journey to urban areas and enjoy the fruits of urbanity there and at home, bringing to his plantation the latest and finest fashions.

William, the son of Joseph John Williams II and Elizabeth Alston, was a colonel, then general, in the militia and was state senator from Warren County in 1814. Married to two women named Elizabeth Alston and twice widowed before 1814, he married Melissa Jane Burgess, daughter of a Halifax planter, and in 1820 the couple had a daughter, also Melissa. Widowed again, he married Delia Haywood of Raleigh in 1826 and fathered two children before his death in 1832.[9]

"Pretty Billy," as General William Williams was known, either for his beauty or for his lack of it, possessed a fortune in land and slaves exceeded by few men in the prosperous Roanoke region. Much of his estate was inherited before 1820. Warren County tax lists of the 1820s show him with nearly 6,000 acres in that county (valued at $32,545 in 1828) and as many as sixty-six slaves. At his death in 1832 William Williams owned five far-flung plantations: the home plantation (Montmorenci) of 1,600 to 1,700 acres on Shocco Creek, the Gunter Creek plantation, the Union Hill plantation, and another plantation, all in Warren County, plus his father's plantation in Halifax County. More than ninety slaves, among them several craftsmen including a carpenter named Wiley, were also to be divided among his heirs.[10]

Williams's broad acres and scores of slaves supported a lifestyle that mirrored his milieu but on a grander scale. Hints of the way of life at the Shocco plantation (Montmorenci) are provided by the household goods Williams owned at his death. His "horse and carriage and chamber furniture" were left to his wife Delia, and the inventory of goods to be sold included quantities of furniture and a wide range of kitchen and farming equipment, stock, provisions (including nine hundred pounds of pork and many bushels of wheat), lot after lot of books, much silver, demijohns of wine and whiskey, and dozens of wineglasses and accompanying decanters. More personal possessions included a backgammon box, a writing desk, a spy glass, and "one old peacock." Two objects of special significance vividly define Williams's lifestyle as expressed at Montmorenci: the volume of Lafayette's Travels and, bequeathed in his will to his nephew and executor Joseph John Williams, the latter's "sister Betsey's portrait which was presented to me by her."[11]

The Lafayette volume recalls an event singled out in family memory, the visit to Montmorenci in February, 1825, of "the Nation's Guest," the Marquis de Lafayette, savior of the American Revolution and the ultimate embodiment of aristocratic elegance.[12]

The portrait of William's niece Betsey, so carefully bequeathed in his will, is especially eloquent of Williams's lifestyle, for it is an icon not only of close family connections but also of the fine and fashionable goods Williams obtained during his visits to Philadelphia. Frequently in the city on business, Williams was well acquainted with its fashions, its shops, its craftsmen, its grand houses, and its prominent people. On a visit in 1822 he commissioned the portrait of Betsey to be painted by Charles Willson Peale, the eminent painter whose subjects had included George Washington, Benjamin Franklin, and many others of the young nation's social and political leaders. On other visits, Williams ordered fashionable gowns for his wife Melissa and other novelties of dress, and commissioned a gleaming yellow custom-made coach.[13]

William Williams's most impressive Philadelphia purchases, however, were no doubt those for his new plantation house which rose on an imposing site on the Shocco Creek plantation near the Shocco Springs resort. It is not known whether Williams employed a Philadelphia craftsman or designer for the planning and construction of Montmorenci, or whether (as seems likely) he used ideas gathered from grand houses he had seen, plus decorative elements obtained in Philadelphia, and worked with a local builder to create a mansion with all the grandeur local resources could muster.[14]

A Philadelphia origin for the elegant, academic composition ornament is generally accepted. One study has suggested as a source Robert Wellford's

FIG. 7.5. *Drawing room, Montmorenci.* (NCDAH)

FIG. 7.6. *Drawing room mantel, Montmorenci.* (*Courtesy of The Winterthur Library: Printed Book and Periodical Collection*)

firm in Philadelphia, which produced such ornament during the early nineteenth century. Comparison of Wellford's known work seems to confirm this.[15]

Surprisingly little is known with certainty of the date of construction of Montmorenci or of its local builder. The presence of a mantel decorated with a composition scene of the Battle of Lake Erie, which took place in 1814, suggests the earliest limit (figs. 7.5, 7.6). Enduring family tradition holds that Williams's daughter Melissa (1820–1902) was the first child born at Montmorenci and so indicates a later limit.[16] Correspondence between Williams and his wife Melissa in 1814 and 1819 is to and from their home at the Union Hill plantation, implying that Montmorenci was not yet their home.[17] Thus the years 1819–20 seem to be the most likely for the construction of Montmorenci.

Tradition identifies a Mr. Burgess of Virginia as the builder of Montmorenci.[18] Existing documentation, while not solidly confirming the tradition, is in harmony with this attribution. A James Burgess took an apprentice to the house carpenter's trade in 1824, and otherwise appears in Warren County records in the 1820s.[19] More telling are notes taken from a ledger recording the construction of Prospect Hill, a stylistically related house (see below). These notes, made by a descendant of William Williams Thorne (keeper of the ledger and first owner of Prospect Hill) state that "the architect for the house Prospect Hill was a Mr. Burgess and his fee according to the ledger was $1800."[20] In addition, local tradition as recorded by a memoir written in the early twentieth century cites a connection between a Mr. Burgess and yet another house in the stylistically related group—the Coleman-White House (see below).[21] No further clues have been found to identify the role of Mr. Burgess or any other craftsman in the many houses whose connections with Montmorenci and Prospect Hill suggest his inventive hand. As is so often true, the vernacular builder remains a mystery, the buildings themselves the chief document.

Montmorenci, faded as it was on the eve of its demolition, was an imposing mansion of late Adamesque grandeur evocative of the graciousness and aspirations of its owner and the culture from which it sprang. The facade of the T-plan frame structure was dominated by a full-height portico with slim columns carrying a garlanded entablature. The glory of the interior and no doubt the wonder of the county was a magnificent free-standing spiral stair.

At Montmorenci was found a lively counterpoint between the suave academic decoration and the lively vernacular woodwork. The Philadelphia elements, formally treated mantels, and door and window frames, are beautifully encrusted with graceful composition swags, garlands, rosettes, acanthus, urns, and classical scenes of academic propriety, and ceilings are enriched with an abundance of fine plaster ornament (fig. 7.7). In the local work, Adamesque motifs are the basis for a delightful series of inventions, reeded, gouged, and carved, which complement the imported elements.

The stair seems most succinctly to express the contradictory character of the house (fig. 7.8). Such a splendid free-standing spiral stair was found in only the finest houses of the seaboard states, and that William Williams should insist on having one is indicative of his ambitions for his house. Yet the grand sweep of the stair was produced not by an expert designer confident of his engineering but rather by the local technology which gathered its best powers of improvisation and rose to the occasion. This "not inconsiderable" structural feat was the product of "trial and error, as during demolition it could be seen that the carriages had been reinforced again and again, until the stair became steady." Thus was the soaring elegance of a

FIG. 7.7. *Medallion at top of stair, Montmorenci. (Courtesy of J. Myrick Howard; NCDAH)*

FIG. 7.8. *Stair, Montmorenci. (Courtesy of The Winterthur Library: Printed Book and Periodical Collection)*

spiral stair brought to reality at Shocco Creek. The trim of the stair, apparently unique to the region, is beautifully responsive to the curving form: the treads are treated with "single, concave scrolls, edged with a series of tiny, reeded scallops,"[22] punctuated with rosettes.

This distinctive stair decoration, plus several other clearly identifiable and seemingly original motifs, occur in their earliest form at Montmorenci. These, not the imported Philadelphia elements, were to be the hallmarks of the high-style vernacular oeuvre that rose in Montmorenci's wake. It is interesting to note that, unlike most of the state's fine vernacular Federal architecture, where simple, traditional exteriors give little hint of the full-blown interior treatments, much of the distinctive character of the Montmorenci school is exterior. The modishness and individuality of the house is thus readily apparent to all, not hidden within—an expenditure of detail more than coincidentally expressive of the clientele.

Four very particularized exterior motifs are repeated again and again. Each derives from the standard classical vocabulary, but is here reinterpreted with a unique accent. A Palladian entrance is changed slightly in proportion, with sidelights shortened by the very deep entablatures carried on pilasters or colonnettes, and elements are outlined by a curious band of highly unusual turned molding resembling a fat bead and reed or string of spools, augmented with gouged and molded decoration. The Palladian motif is given another form in the flanking triple windows with their "curious, baroque entablature supporting fanlights, [which] though they had leaded radii and concentric lines, were false, and were glazed with glass painted black."[23] An archless version of the window appeared at the second level. A motif which cannot be made out in photographs of the original house but seems to have existed is the variation on the spool molding which occurs on the long pilasters at the corners of the house. Also not visible in photographs but occurring in the Winterthur installation (see note 1) is a sprightly reinterpretation of the classic Doric entablature: in an otherwise sober treatment, the standard guttae at the lower edge of the triglyph are replaced by an inverted, fluted fan.

Within, the decoration of the stair is complemented by the woodwork throughout, where formally proportioned mantels, chair rails, door and window frames are richly worked with reeding, gougework swags and scallops, rosettes, and the like, all following identifiable patterns.

These motifs—seen first at Montmorenci and found nowhere else in North Carolina outside this regional school—were the hallmarks of a highly personalized style popular in the immediate cultural area for about a decade. Perhaps craftsman Burgess himself—if tradition is correct in recalling him as builder—and perhaps a wider group of craftsmen influenced by Montmorenci and Prospect Hill (see below) found these motifs flexible enough to be applied with grace to a variety of houses and to accommodate the first hints of the coming Greek Revival style in the early 1830s. Exterior details repeat the motifs introduced at Montmorenci rather literally. The interiors of the related houses, however, show great individual variation. At Montmorenci vernacular Adamesque motifs were handled with restraint as background to a collection of expensive imported elements, but in the region's related houses the vernacular themes played so subtly at Montmorenci find far bolder and more inventive expression. Formal, classically-derived door, window, and mantel treatments are repeated, but they are enriched not with the sophisticated, classical composition ornament of Montmorenci, but instead with an unacademic array of flowers, fans, swags, rosettes, reeding, garlands, and guilloches. Eager to be modish but unshackled by academic restrictions of a more bookish understanding of classical models, the planter clientele gave the carpenter the opportunity to develop from Adamesque motifs the most inventive compositions his skill and imagination could provide.

A half dozen major houses bespeak Montmorenci connections clearly and abundantly; as many more houses employ some of the same motifs. All are within thirty miles of Montmorenci (see fig. 7.3) and many have close family connections (see fig. 7.4). Technology and form remain traditional. All are of heavy, timber-frame construction of medieval origins using hand labor (probably slaves). Foundations of most are of great cut blocks of local stone, and chimneys are exterior brick stacks skillfully laid in Flemish bond. With slight exceptions, house forms and floor plans are of the types usual in the Virginia–North Carolina area. Only in their decoration are these houses extraordinary.

Perhaps the most intimately related to Montmorenci in some respects yet most antithetical in others is Prospect Hill, located near Airlie in Halifax County (fig. 7.9). It was built for William Williams Thorne, a young nephew of William Williams. Thorne married Temperance Davis in 1820. Thorne's ledger of 1825–28 documents the construction of the house, recording a total cost including materials, labor, and architect, of $3,545.30. The exterior of Prospect Hill has a sense of proportion and unity perhaps exceeding that of Montmorenci[24], with a small, graceful entrance portico and a dramatic rear loggia. Harmoniously incorporated into the whole, the characteristic Palladian entrance, spool moldings, fan-edged cornice, and elaborate window treatment here occur in their fullest combination of the entire group (fig. 7.10); if documented as the work of builder Burgess, they give Prospect Hill a central place among all of his creations.

Within, however, with the exception of a quiet and lovely curving stair (fig. 7.11), grace is overwhelmed in the welter of intensely vernacular ornament that is applied with almost obsessive extravagance to every possible

FIG. 7.9. *Rear view of Prospect Hill, ca. 1820, Halifax County, North Carolina. Photograph by Frances Benjamin Johnston, 1930s.* (*Courtesy of the North Carolina Collection, University of North Carolina Library at Chapel Hill*)

FIG. 7.10. *Front entrance and window, Prospect Hill. Photograph by Frances Benjamin Johnston, 1930s.* (*Courtesy of the North Carolina Collection, University of North Carolina Library at Chapel Hill*)

FIG. 7.11. *Stair, Prospect Hill. Photograph by Frances Benjamin Johnston, 1930s. (Courtesy of the North Carolina Collection, University of North Carolina Library at Chapel Hill)*

FIG. 7.12. *Mantel, Prospect Hill. Photograph by Frances Benjamin Johnston, 1930s. (Courtesy of the North Carolina Collection, University of North Carolina Library at Chapel Hill)*

surface (fig. 7.12). Here, it seems, perhaps no longer playing second fiddle to imported elements, or to compensate in sheer quantity for their absence, the craftsman attacked the task with more gusto than taste. Yet, though lacking in the suavity that is the spirit of the Adamesque, the work at Prospect Hill has a vibrant energy and passion that defies condescension.

Suave restraint is serenely present, however, at the Coleman-White House in Warrenton—the only surviving house of the three known to have had the curious Palladian-derived windows (figs. 7.13, 7.14). Not related to the others by family ties, it was built for Dr. Littleton H. Coleman between 1821 and his death in 1825,[25] and is thus probably among the earliest in the group. The exterior, though lacking the rear loggia, is similar to Prospect Hill, and the characteristic Palladian doorway is enhanced by delicate tracery. Missing, however, is the fanciful fan entablature and spool corner molding. The center-hall plan interior seems almost severe in its simplicity, with ornament reduced to graceful incised swags and quiet reeding. Somewhat more elaborate is the fine plaster work of the ceilings. The stair is a simple one with no reference to the grandeur of Prospect Hill and Montmorenci.

In two other houses of the group, however, the detail if not the soaring grace of those stairs is recalled. The only house known to be remodeled in the Montmorenci mode was, appropriately enough, White Rock, longtime plantation seat of the Williams family.[26] It is believed to have been modernized for Pretty Billy's nephew Joseph John Williams III about the time of his marriage to Mary K. Davis in 1820, the year William Williams Thorne of Prospect Hill married her sister (William Williams may have owned the plantation at this time).[27] Young Joseph John Williams's estate inventory of 1833 expressed a typical planter lifestyle, with two carriage houses, one riding horse, seventy-six slaves, ample supplies of provisions and stock, mahogany and walnut furniture, and a library of more than one hundred thirty volumes: Wesley's works, a prayer book and bibles, *Roman History*, Aristotle and *Natural Philosophy*, *Pilgrims Progress* and *Paradise Lost*, *History of America*, one volume of *American Revolution* and a five-volume *Life of Washington*, *Advice to Young Ladies* and *The Female Spectator*, and Gibson on horses and Mills on cattle—these were but a sampling of the subjects of interest to a family of this milieu.[28]

At White Rock a traditional Georgian house was updated with modish elements: the vertical proportions of Adam-derived mantels are stretched to accommodate a broad early fire opening, and the three short, utilitarian flights of the stair are adorned with the graceful scalloped scroll and guilloche band (fig. 7.15).

A similar treatment to the initial flight of an enclosed stair was executed at Mount Petros (since demolished) located near Inez in Warren County, and probably built for Dr. Soloman Williams and Caroline Alston, who married in 1819. At this house, the entrance motif and the overdoors and mantels were handled with restraint and feature intricate geometric moldings—without the usual rather feminine flowers, swags, and garlands.

Mount Petros was one of several Montmorenci-related houses that follow the formal, Virginia-influenced, pedimented-front house form. The

FIG. 7.13. *Coleman-White House, 1820s, Warrenton, Warren County. Photograph by Catherine W. Bishir, 1974.* (NCDAH)

FIG. 7.14. *Windows, Coleman-White House. Photograph by Catherine W. Bishir, 1974.* (NCDAH)

FIG. 7.15. *Stair, White Rock, ca. 1820, Halifax vicinity, Halifax County. Photograph by Catherine W. Bishir, 1974.* (NCDAH)

FIG. 7.16. *Oakland, 1820s, Halifax County. Photograph by Randall Page, 1972.* (NCDAH)

FIG. 7.17. *Dalkeith, 1820s, Warren County. Photograph by Greer Suttlemyre, 1972.* (NCDAH)

reorientation of the gable end to the front of the house creates an arrangement suggestive of the temple form (the plan of this temple-form house being essentially a reorientation of the side-hall plan, with a front cross-hall and two rear rooms[29]). With the addition of wings or side porches a three-part Palladian composition develops. The distinctive Montmorenci–Prospect Hill decoration was gracefully adaptable to this stylish house. In addition to Mount Petros, four other pedimented-front houses in the region relate to Montmorenci and Prospect Hill: Oakland, Dalkeith, Shady Grove, and Elgin. Three of the four were built for young couples of the Alston-Williams family, relatives of William Williams.

The history of Oakland, located within a few miles of Prospect Hill and White Rock, illustrates the complexity of family connections (figs. 7.16, 7.22). It was probably built for William Williams's niece Elizabeth (Betsey), perhaps at the time of her marriage to her cousin Henry Hill Thorne in 1823. Thorne was the brother of William Williams Thorne of Prospect Hill. Since Henry Hill Thorne died the year of their marriage, it is also possible that Oakland was built for Elizabeth and her second husband Nicholas Drake after their marriage in 1828. She soon died as well, and Oakland was Drake's residence at the time of his death in 1831. Oakland then passed to Betsey's brother, Joseph John Williams, and at his death in 1833 it went to his wife Mary K. Williams. She in turn sold Oakland and bought Montmorenci.[30]

Dalkeith (fig. 7.17), part of the land in the estate of Samuel Alston, was near William Williams's Gunter Creek plantation. The house, possibly begun by Warren County builder Thomas Bragg, was completed for newlyweds John Burgess and Martha Jane Alston; Burgess was the brother of Melissa Burgess Williams of Montmorenci (no known relationship to the builder Burgess). The couple bought the plantation in 1825, and the house is believed to date from that time.[31] Shady Grove is believed to have been built for John A. Williams, who married Charity Alston in 1816. It is not certain when the house, located near Dalkeith and Montmorenci, was built.

Elgin, though perhaps the most representative of the pedimented group and most closely related to Montmorenci and Prospect Hill, was not connected with them by family ties (figs. 7.18–7.21, 7.23–7.25). Located near Warrenton, Elgin was built during the years 1827–32 for Elizabeth Person and Peter Mitchel. Elizabeth was the daughter of old-school planter William Person, who typified the proud Roanoke gentleman. Family tradition recalls that he had denied his daughter's hand in marriage to an earlier suiter, saying, "My daughter is for no damned poor Virginian. I have quite other plans." The prosperous Scots merchant, Peter Mitchel, several years her senior, evidently suited Person's requirements, and the couple married

FIG. 7.18. *Elgin, 1827-32, Warren County. Photograph by Randall Page, 1978.* (NCDAH)

FIG. 7.19. *Rear-side view, Elgin. Photograph by Catherine W. Bishir, 1972. The dormered rear ell follows a traditional eighteenth-century house form but was added as a wing to the formal front section soon after the front section was completed.* (NCDAH)

FIG. 7.20. *Detail of portico and facade, Elgin. Photograph by Catherine W. Bishir, 1972.* (NCDAH)

FIG. 7.21. *Detail of entrance and portico, Elgin. Photograph by Catherine W. Bishir, 1972.* (NCDAH)

FIG. 7.22. *Detail of entrance with blind arch, Oakland, 1820s. Photograph by Randall Page, 1972.* (NCDAH)

in 1824. Person settled upon the couple a rich tract near Warrenton, which became part of their extensive plantation of two thousand acres. Her husband's long illness and death in 1846 left to the well-read, intelligent Elizabeth the role of managing the vast plantation.[32]

All four houses share the distinctive Burgess-type fan-edged cornice and spool-lined corner pilasters, some having fans atop the pilasters as well. Only at Elgin, however, is the beautiful Palladian doorway repeated (fig. 7.21); at Oakland a broad blind lunette occurs over the entry (fig. 7.22). Dalkeith's pedimented five-bay front leaves little room for the Palladian entrance treatment, which is replaced by a simple entablature. Within, all but one of these houses follow a similar plan, with a front lateral hall and two main rooms to the rear.

The familiar motifs enrich the formally handled doors, windows, mantels, and wainscots, but in each house the distinctive elements are selected and varied in a quite different way, providing great individuality of character within overall unity. Dalkeith, recalling Mount Petros, has a masculine directness stemming from the introduction of some Greek Revival motifs and the absence of flowers and swags. At Oakland, a restrained elegance is combined with almost playful inventiveness in the handling of reeding, gouged scallops, and cables. The fine parlor mantels in particular possess much of the finesse of the simpler mantels of Montmorenci, as do the swags and flowers of the chair rail. Elgin's interior, on the other hand, achieves a satisfying blend of Oakland's restraint with a discreet spicing of the flowers, sunbursts, rosettes, and abundant reeding of Prospect Hill (figs. 7.23–7.25). For none of these houses is a builder known, though the Burgess attribution is appealing.

Still more houses testify to the pervasiveness of the Montmorenci–Prospect Hill influence, combining the oeuvre's distinctive elements with other details typical of later styles of the period around 1830, or incorporating isolated but identifiable "Burgess" elements into an otherwise traditional house. Here, of course, the question of authorship and influence becomes still less clear.

FIG. 7.23. *Stair hall, Elgin.* Photograph by JoAnn Sieburg-Baker, 1978. (NCDAH)

FIG. 7.24. *Mantel, left-hand parlor, Elgin. Photograph by Randall Page, 1978.* (NCDAH)

FIG. 7.25. *Mantel, right-hand parlor, Elgin. Photograph by Randall Page, 1978.* (NCDAH)

Tusculum (fig. 7.26) near Arcola was built for Samuel T. Alston and Ruina Williams, who married in 1831. The Palladian entrance, entablature, windows, and spool moldings occur on a house of severe dignity on land Alston inherited from his father Samuel's great Gunter Creek plantation. The interior, featuring a handsomely treated stair (fig. 7.27) is a late expression of the mode with strong suggestions of the coming Greek Revival.

The distant Woodlawn in Halifax County, known as the 1833 home of political leader Mason Wiggins, is an intriguing late adaptation of many of the familiar motifs, highly personalized by the subtle and inventive use of a lifelike acorn motif, handled in a way reminiscent of the earlier fan motif.

The fan-edged cornice, spool-edged corner post, and a limited assortment of interior decoration are applied to an Alston House in Halifax County and the house called Grove Hill in Warren (figs. 7.28, 7.29)—both

FIG. 7.26. *Tusculum, early 1830s, Warren County. Photograph by Randall Page, 1972.* (NCDAH)

FIG. 7.27. *Detail of stair, Tusculum. Photograph by Randall Page, 1972.* (NCDAH)

otherwise restrained traditional houses which received a soupçon of high style by association. An especially vivid motif found among the extravagances of Prospect Hill—a florid mantel with pilasters featuring a guilloche naturalized into an entwining vine pattern—crops up in more than one house in the region. At the Shady Oaks south of Warrenton, the vine mantel is part of an elaborate decorative program for the chief room of an intriguing tripartite house, rivaled only by the demonstration of the wood carver's invention on the stair. The mantel decoration is employed also on a Franklin County house on the main road from Warrenton to Raleigh.

Great in itself, yet perhaps greater in its role as catalyst for a free-wheeling, highly creative body of related houses, Montmorenci combined vernacular invention with high-style sophistication in a way peculiarly appropriate to the larger-than-life man who built it. Wealthy beyond his compatriots, accustomed visitor to Philadelphia—the source of urbanity and culture—and host to Lafayette, "Pretty Billy" Williams brought to the rolling fields of the remote rural plantation region a house of grandeur and panache never seen there before. Here, in peculiarly satisfactory form, Philadelphia classical propriety joined with the inventions of local craftsman in a house that captured the imaginations of a generation and thus stimulated a craftsman's more inventive potential.

In these houses the contradictions of the aspiring but provincial planter

FIG. 7.28. *Grove Hill, 1820s, Warren County. Photograph by Catherine W. Bishir, 1974.* (NCDAH)

FIG. 7.29. *Detail of cornice and pilaster, Grove Hill. Photograph by Catherine W. Bishir, 1974.* (NCDAH)

The Montmorenci–Prospect Hill School | 183

elite were embodied in an unselfconscious expression of ethnic domain that transcends the very self-consciousness with which these houses were so carefully built. It was a culture where earthiness and gusto still underlay careful decorum and classical education, where an entrenched economy and traditional technology was the background for an increasingly leisured, fun-loving, and fashion-conscious lifestyle, and where satisfactions of the bottle, cockfight, and racecourse were esteemed along with those of a well-stocked library, polished manners, and well-ordered plantation.

This culture was forcefully expressed in vernacular architecture, in which slave labor and local materials and expertise could produce buildings whose modishness was announced in every lavish detail. Fashionable, classical motifs were admired and copied, not slavishly or literally, but with a joy in inventiveness that took none too seriously the dictates of classical propriety. Antithetical in every detail to the present world, here was a tightly unified and traditional agricultural community with a powerful sense of family and place whose aspiring expression of ethnic domain created an oeuvre at once unified and bursting with exuberant individuality.

AFTERWORD

Not the Civil War but the changes it brought have destroyed most of this world and many of its monuments. Irony abounds. The region remains agricultural within an industrializing state, and population figures, black and white, remain little changed. Figures for poverty and outmigration of the young and talented whisper of the Rip Van Winkle years the region once escaped. The great mansions are carried off to be installed not far from the northeastern cities that inspired them. Descendants of the slaves who made the culture possible are tenants in many of the great houses, but leave when the places fall further into decay, to be replaced by stores of the other great resource that built these houses—tobacco.

Too slowly, nearly too late, and for far too few, realization is dawning that in this small region there survive vivid vestiges of a material culture unique in the world, which gives to a region now struggling for a positive identity a potential that can be gained in no other way.

NOTES

1. Montmorenci was owned after Williams's death by a relative, Mary K. Williams, who evidently gave it that name. She moved to Warrenton in the late 1850s but retained ownership of Montmorenci. Falling into disrepair in the twentieth century, Montmorenci was held by a series of owners in the 1920s. In 1935 its interiors and elements of its exterior were removed for installation in the Henry duPont Winterthur Museum, Winterthur, Delaware, and elsewhere. The installation was directed by Thomas T. Waterman. A replica of the stair is

a prominent feature of the museum. Reports of the installation vary: recollections by men who worked at the museum include one account of its being the wrong size to use in the museum and one account of the stair having fallen off the truck and broken into pieces on the way to Delaware. Winterthur maintains a file on Montmorenci in the Joseph Downs Manuscript Collection, and much information on the history of the house has been gained with the assistance of this collection. After the interiors were removed, Montmorenci served as a tenant house for a time but was taken down by 1940.

2. The social and political history of the region is obtained from several secondary and primary sources. Particularly useful books are: Manly Wade Wellman, *The County of Warren, North Carolina, 1586–1917* (Chapel Hill: University of North Carolina Press, 1959) and *The Life and Times of Sir Archie: The Story of America's Greatest Thoroughbred, 1805–1833* (Chapel Hill: University of North Carolina Press, 1958); and Lizzie Wilson Montgomery, *Sketches of Old Warrenton* (Raleigh: Edwards and Broughton Printing Company, 1924), a personal memoir. Unpublished documents include the memoir of Warrenton school teacher Victoria Louise Pendleton, in possession of Warren County Historical Society; the "History of Hastings," by Ellen Mordecai, reproduced in part in *Sketches of Old Warrenton;* and "The Roanoke Valley: A Report for the Historic Halifax State Historic Site," by Elizabeth Wilborn, Jerry L. Cross, and Boyd D. Cathey (1974).

3. Census records, tax records, estates papers, North Carolina Division of Archives and History. Many of the descendants of these families remain in the region to the present, and the continuity of family memory and traditional history is an invaluable and demonstrably reliable source of local history. Access to this lode has been made possible by Warren County's unfailingly generous historians, Mary Hinton Kerr, Pantheo Twitty, and for this project by a special mentor, Edgar Thorne.

4. Guion Griffis Johnson, *Ante-Bellum North Carolina* (Chapel Hill: University of North Carolina Press, 1937), 81.

5. Montgomery, Wellman, Alumni Records of the University of North Carolina, private estates papers and guardian papers, N.C. Archives.

6. Edgar Thorne to author, November 27, 1976.

7. *North Carolina Star,* April 12, 1811.

8. Johnson, *Ante-Bellum North Carolina,* 87. See "History of Hastings," for accounts of dances and dinners and other events in early-nineteenth-century Warren County.

9. Genealogical material from Edgar Thorne and Mary Hinton Kerr, and see chart. Also marriage bonds (Warren County), wills, estates papers.

10. Warren County Tax Records, 1824–28, N.C. Archives. No Halifax County tax records for the period are available to show Williams's holdings in that county. William Williams's will (Warren County Will Book 33, p. 443) and estates papers (N.C. Archives), plus an advertisement of a sale of his property in the (Halifax) *Roanoke Advocate* of November 1, 1832 (provided by Henry Lewis of Chapel Hill to Edgar Thorne and thence to author in 1976), identify Williams's real estate. William Williams's real estate in 1828 in Warren County was second in value only to that of William Eaton, whose 7,750 acres were valued at $44,665, and who owned ninety-four slaves. These were the only two persons in the county at this time with land valued at more than $20,000. Few households, even in the planter class, held land valued at more than $10,000 or $12,000 and thirty to fifty slaves. The wealth of the Roanoke planters, however, seems never to have been in the same league as the great eighteenth-century estates of Virginia or the antebellum spreads of the cotton planters of the Old Southwest.

11. William Williams's will (Warren County Will Book 33, p. 443).

12. Family and local tradition state that General William Williams escorted Lafayette during his North Carolina tour and took him to Montmorenci to spend the night before escorting him to Raleigh. Though the visit to Montmorenci is not documented, known facts of the tour are not inconsistent with such a visit. General Williams was among those offering toasts at the elaborate dinner at Halifax held February 27, 1825 after Lafayette arrived in North Carolina; Williams toasted "The rising generation—may they follow the examples of Washington and Lafayette." When the Nation's Guest and his party departed Halifax, they proceeded to Raleigh, spending one night on the road. Since the road from Halifax to Raleigh passed within a very few miles of Williams's grand and luxurious new house, a stay there, invited by a member of the escort group, seems

most credible. "The Roanoke Valley," an account of "General Lafayette visits Halifax."

13. Melissa Williams to William Williams at Philadelphia, June 8, 1819, "If Mowhare Caps are worne Mary wishes you to bring her one.... there is two small tapes with a hook and eye sowed in the back of the Frock you carried, rip them off as they would not meet and probably they will guess at my size by that if you have a dress made." (Courtesy, Joseph Downs Manuscript Collection, Henry Francis duPont Winterthur Museum). E. A. (Betsey) Williams to Melissa, from Philadelphia to Warren County, April 13, 1819. Polk Family Papers, N.C. Archives. Charles Coleman Sellers (Peale biographer) to author, August 5, 1977. Charles Peale letters of June 9, 14, and 25, 1822, concerning portrait commissioned by Williams of Betsey, American Philosophical Society Library, Philadelphia.

14. Peggy Burke, "The Montmorenci Stairway: A Cultural Study," September 1, 1972, unpublished term paper for Winterthur Summer Institute, copy at Winterthur Museum. In this excellent study of the house and cultural background, Ms. Burke surmises that Williams, "having seen such elaborate staircases in sophisticated urban areas and desiring one for his soon-to-be-constructed fashionable residence, commissioned a local Warrenton area craftsman, who relied upon a builders' guide as his primary source for construction details" (8).

15. Wellford is suggested as a source by Burke (6). Further investigation and comparison with a known Wellford mantel seem to support this. A Wellford mantel in the Metropolitan Museum of Art indicates strong similarities to work at Montmorenci, with both featuring a scene from the Battle of Lake Erie (1814). Robert Wellford sold plaster or composition ornament which was to be attached to mantels and other elements. Further study of Wellford and his impact in North Carolina is needed.

16. Letter from Henry Lewis, Chapel Hill, to Edgar Thorne (1976), and information obtained from Heath Long Beckwith, descendant of Melissa Williams, by Mary Hinton Kerr.

17. William Williams (Raleigh) to Melissa Williams (Warren County), December 2, 1814, and Melissa to William, December 1, 1814, and June 8, 1819; the name Union Hill is consistently used to refer to the couple's home.

18. Frances Benjamin Johnston and Thomas T. Waterman, *The Early Architecture of North Carolina* (Chapel Hill: University of North Carolina Press, 1941, 1947), 40–41, offers a discussion of these houses. Waterman notes in his account that "these houses" are attributed to "Burgess, a builder of Boydton, Virginia," but it is not certain if "these" include Montmorenci or only Prospect Hill and related houses. Waterman suggests possible Virginia work by Burgess as well. Waterman also notes at Montmorenci the "strange combination of urban and rustic detail." The Burgess connection with Montmorenci is somewhat tenuous, perhaps inferred from similarities of Montmorenci to Prospect Hill, where the Burgess tradition is strong. Edgar Thorne notes the ironic fact that "whatever propelled Montmorenci to its exceptional position in the Burgess *oeuvre* may also make it the least essentially Burgess of all the houses"; Thorne to author, November 30, 1976.

19. James Craig, *The Arts and Crafts of North Carolina, 1699–1840* (Winston-Salem: Old Salem, Inc., Museum of Early Southern Decorative Arts, 1965), 349. A James Burgess obtained marriage licenses in Warren County in 1822 and 1832, and some deeds involve him. No will or estates papers were found for him in Warren or Halifax county records.

20. William Williams Thorne's ledger of the 1820s is owned by a descendant, and has not been accessible to this author. Several years ago, notes were made from the ledger by Annie B. Thorne of Littleton, and a transcription of these notes was supplied to the author by Edgar Thorne. When T. T. Waterman recorded Prospect Hill for the Historic American Buildings Survey in the 1930s, he too made notes on the ledger records; there is a variation between the two sets of notes, for Waterman gives dates for entries and adds information about plaster decoration. Both sources cite Burgess as builder, but it is not clear if this is actually in the ledger. Other pages from Thorne's ledger (not mentioning construction of the house) include entries under the name James Burgess and have been copied from the original ledger and provided to the author by the owner of the ledger. The woodwork at Prospect Hill was removed to Connecticut and the house taken down.

21. Victoria Pendleton's unpublished memoir (written in the early twentieth century to record her recollections of antebellum Warrenton) states that "this house was built by a Mr. Burges, a contractor, and he lived there for

some time himself. The next time I can find out anything about it, this house was owned by Dr. Coleman." Documentation indicates that the house was built for Coleman between 1821 and 1825, but the traditional Burgess association is of interest.

22. Johnson and Waterman, *The Early Architecture of North Carolina*, 40.

23. Ibid., 39.

24. Edgar Thorne to author, November 30, 1976.

25. Coleman-White House, National Register of Historic Places nomination, copy in Survey and Planning Branch files, N.C. Archives (as are copies of all other National Register nominations hereinafter cited); research by Charles Blume.

26. Histories of houses are from Edgar Thorne unless otherwise noted, augmented by research from estates papers, wills, marriage bonds, deeds, etc. Contemporary accounts, correspondence, estates papers, wills, etc., indicate that the names White Rock, Union Hill, Prospect Hill, and Oakland were used as early as the 1820s and 1830s. Tusculum and Dalkeith are also believed to be early names. Montmorenci was possibly so called by Williams, but the first known use of the name is during Mary K. Williams's residency there in the early 1840s. In no case is the name of the plantation a recent glamorization.

27. Joseph John Williams will, proved 1818, Halifax County Will Book 2, p. 615.

28. Joseph John Williams estates papers, 1833, Halifax County Estates Papers, N. C. Archives.

29. See Carl Lounsbury, "The Development of Domestic Architecture in the Albemarle Region," in *Carolina Dwelling: Towards Preservation of Place: In Celebration of the North Carolina Vernacular Landscape*, ed. Doug Swaim (Raleigh: North Carolina State University School of Design Student Publication 26, 1978: 46–61), for documentation of the appearance of this house type in an adjacent area of the state.

30. Oakland, National Register nomination, research by author; Edgar Thorne, William Thorne, letters to author; Nicholas Drake estates papers, 1831, Halifax County Estates Papers, N.C. Archives; Joseph John Williams will, 1833, Halifax County Will Book 4, p. 94; Polk Family Papers (N.C. Archives), etc.

31. Dalkeith, National Register nomination, reasearch by author; information supplied by Lula Hunter Skillman, Dalkeith.

32. Elgin, National Register nomination, research by author.

Eight

The "Unpainted Aristocracy"

The Beach Cottages of Old Nags Head

Fashion and frolic hold revel as though that remorseless leveler, old ocean, did not daily threaten a revolution.

—HARPER'S NEW MONTHLY MAGAZINE, MAY 1860

Facing the Atlantic Ocean across a narrow strip of beach like a line of great hulking turtles in the sand stands a mile-long row of somber gray-brown beach cottages. Dubbed by editor Jonathan Daniels the "unpainted aristocracy,"[1] the oceanfront beach cottages of Nags Head, North Carolina, were built during the years between the Civil War and World War II for merchants, planters, and professional men and their families from northeastern North Carolina—primarily the Albermarle region—and from Virginia. Descendants of those families still summer there as regularly as in the halcyon days of the time between the wars. The cottages, starkly handsome, functional, and resilient, express a healthy respect for the power of the ocean they overlook.

The history and character of Nags Head were directly produced by its location on the Outer Banks, that long, narrow chain of islands that shields the North Carolina mainland from the force of the ocean—but which also prevents direct passage of ships to mainland ports. The banks were explored

---

"The 'Unpainted Aristocracy': The Beach Cottages of Old Nags Head" appeared in *North Carolina Historical Review* 54, no. 4 (October 1977): 3–28 (republished as an offprint booklet by the North Carolina Department of Cultural Resources in 1978), and is reprinted by permission of the Historical Publications Section, North Carolina Office of Archives and History, Department of Cultural Resources, Raleigh.

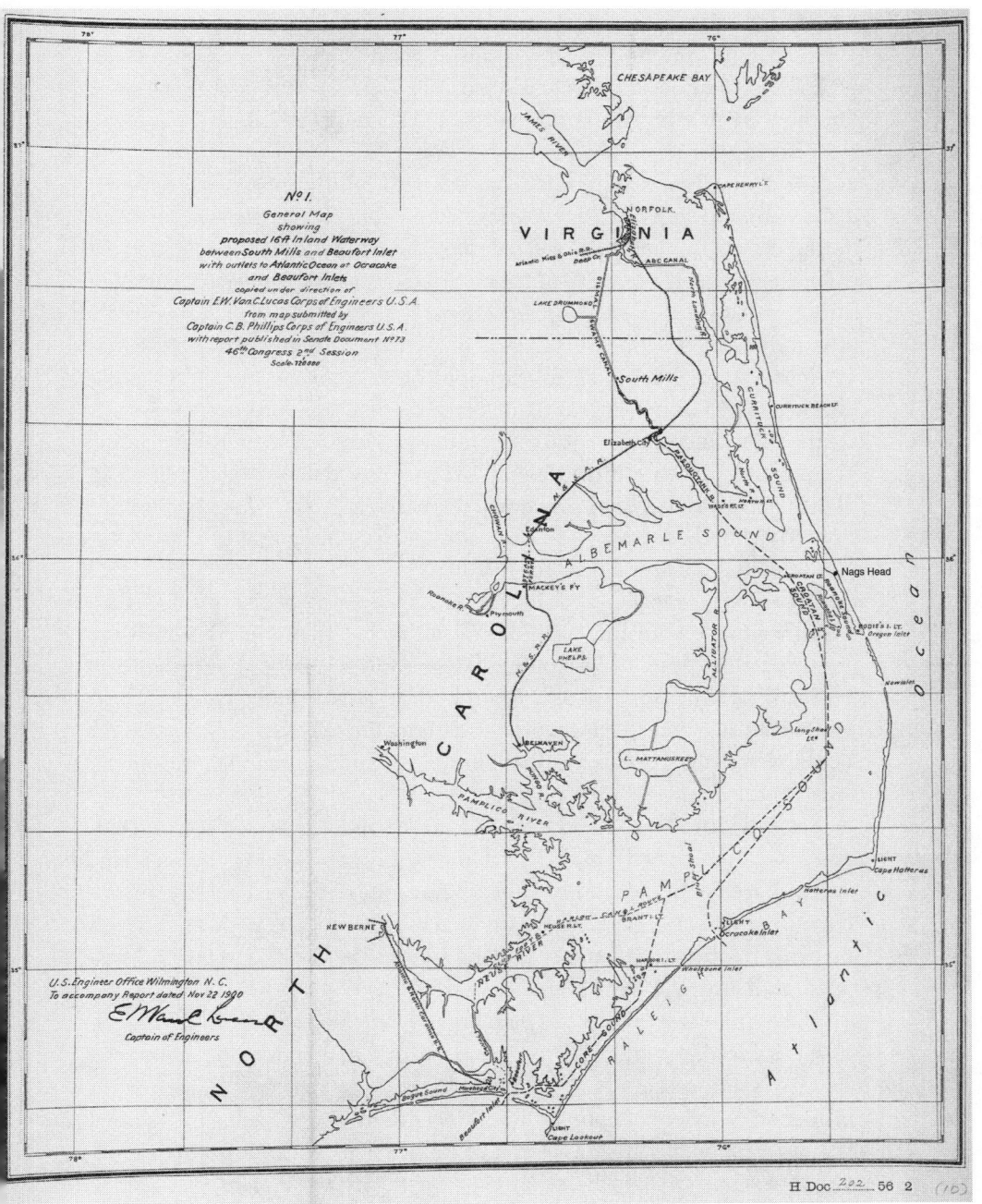

FIG. 8.1. *Coast of northeastern North Carolina and southeastern Virginia. Portion of "[Map] No. 1, General Map showing proposed 16 ft Inland Waterway between South Mills and Beaufort Inlet..." Extracted from U. S. Congress 56:2, House Document 202 [Washington: Government Printing Office], 1900; M.C. 325-N, NCDAH.*

in the early sixteenth century and have perhaps existed for eons, but their form changes constantly at the whim of nature, being subject on the east to the forces of ocean tides and winds, the Gulf Stream, and storms; and on the west to terrestrial winds and mainland rivers which empty into the sounds[2] (fig. 8.1).

The Outer Banks were settled in the eighteenth century by herdsmen, fishermen, and ship salvagers, many of them from England. With no bridge to the mainland, the small, isolated population, long called "bankers,"[3] developed a distinctive pattern of habit, life, and speech—a salty, cockney-like twang that gained these people the nickname "hoi toiders." Surviving for generations on the limited resources of the narrow, sandy banks, the bankers found ship salvaging an erratic but lucrative source of income. One traditional origin of the curious name Nags Head is the story, current as early as the mid-nineteenth century when it was recorded by a visiting writer for *Harper's*, of "an old device employed to lure vessels to destruction. A Banks pony was driven up and down the beach at night, with a lantern tied around his neck. The up-and-down motion resembling that of a vessel, the unsuspecting tar would steer for it."[4]

Beaufort, Ocracoke, and Portsmouth had been acclaimed for their healthy situations in the eighteenth century, but by the early nineteenth century Nags Head had become established as a widely popular summer resort. It was the isolation and healthy clime of the Outer Banks that attracted mainlanders to resort there. Breathing the salt air and bathing in the ocean were believed to exempt the bankers from the mainland's summer curse of malaria.

Settlement in Nags Head focused in three distinct areas: the sound side and dunes, where early resort development occurred, facing the mainland across Roanoke Sound and Roanoke Island (site of Sir Walter Raleigh's ill-fated Lost Colony); the "flats," a wooded mid-island area populated chiefly by bankers who farmed there; and the ocean side, left essentially undeveloped until after the Civil War.[5]

The small summer trickle of planters and merchants from the Albemarle to Nags Head, a trend said to have been initiated about 1830 by planter Francis Nixon of Perquimans County,[6] soon increased to a freshet of the fashionable, and development along the sound grew apace. The summer visitors were chiefly from North Carolina, but many came from Virginia, and some from the Northeast. By 1838 a large hotel, complete with a grand ballroom and said to have accommodated 200 guests, had been built near the sound. In 1849 a visitor from Norfolk reported seeing at the hotel

> A company that would have done credit to any of the popular watering places in the country. I venture nothing in saying that the ladies were

as pretty, and as tastefully dressed, as if they had just returned from the venders of fashion in Paris.⁷

Gentlemen and their families went to Nags Head not only for short visits to the hotel but more often for summer-long stays at their own cottages. A fictionalized account of a sojourn there was published in 1850—*Nags Head: or Two Months among "The Bankers." A Story of Sea-Shore Life and Manners*, by Gregory Seaworthy—identified by Richard Walser as the work of George Higby Throop (1818–96). The novel and another Throop book are described by Walser as being "the first North Carolina novels of 'local color,' . . . and thus . . . highly significant in the literature of the State."⁸ The book presents a vivid picture of the summer lifestyle that continued without drastic change well into the twentieth century.

The novel opens "on the afternoon of a pleasant day in July," on the banks of the Perquimans River at Hertford, where a schooner is being loaded with the necessities for the household's stay at the Banks—"baskets, axes, beds and bedding, cart-wheels and bodies ruthlessly divorced, parasols, a venerable umbrella, and a bottle of Sand's sarsaparilla," plus ducks, hens, and various livestock. At the beach the household is "a little world of itself," composed of a cow, three horses, two dogs, and twenty people, a third of them Negro servants. Chartered packets run twice weekly between the plantations and the Banks to provision the planter and his family

FIG. 8.2. *"Grand Trunk Railway," Nags Head, from E. C. Bruce, "Loungings in the Footprints of the Pioneers,"* Harper's New Monthly Magazine, *vol. 20, May 1860. Families arrived by boat at Nags Head with many furnishings and goods for their household's use for the summer, which were hauled to their cottages by carts.*

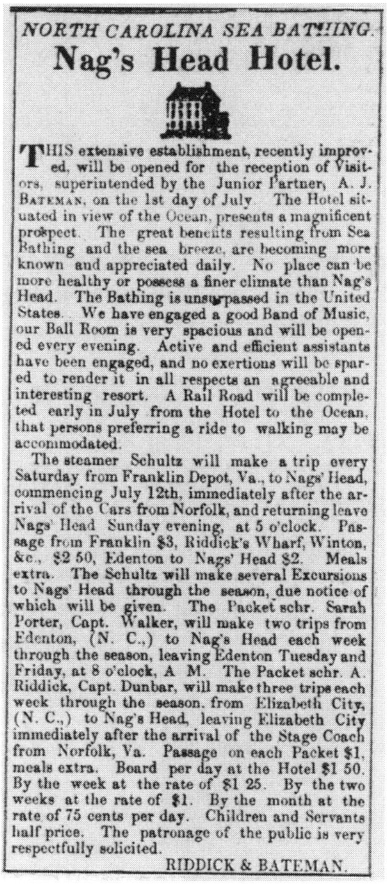

NORTH CAROLINA SEA BATHING.

Nag's Head Hotel.

THIS extensive establishment, recently improved, will be opened for the reception of Visitors, superintended by the Junior Partner, A. J. BATEMAN, on the 1st day of July. The Hotel situated in view of the Ocean, presents a magnificent prospect. The great benefits resulting from Sea Bathing and the sea breeze, are becoming more known and appreciated daily. No place can be more healthy or possess a finer climate than Nag's Head. The Bathing is unsurpassed in the United States. We have engaged a good Band of Music, our Ball Room is very spacious and will be opened every evening. Active and efficient assistants have been engaged, and no exertions will be spared to render it in all respects an agreeable and interesting resort. A Rail Road will be completed early in July from the Hotel to the Ocean, that persons preferring a ride to walking may be accommodated.

The steamer Schultz will make a trip every Saturday from Franklin Depot, Va., to Nags' Head, commencing July 12th, immediately after the arrival of the Cars from Norfolk, and returning leave Nags' Head Sunday evening, at 5 o'clock. Passage from Franklin $3, Riddick's Wharf, Winton, &c., $2 50, Edenton to Nags' Head $2. Meals extra. The Schultz will make several Excursions to Nags' Head through the season, due notice of which will be given. The Packet schr. Sarah Porter, Capt. Walker, will make two trips from Edenton, (N. C.,) to Nag's Head each week through the season, leaving Edenton Tuesday and Friday, at 8 o'clock, A. M. The Packet schr. A. Riddick, Capt. Dunbar, will make three trips each week through the season, from Elizabeth City, (N. C.,) to Nag's Head, leaving Elizabeth City immediately after the arrival of the Stage Coach from Norfolk, Va. Passage on each Packet $1, meals extra. Board per day at the Hotel $1 50. By the week at the rate of $1 25. By the two weeks at the rate of $1. By the month at the rate of 75 cents per day. Children and Servants half price. The patronage of the public is very respectfully solicited.

RIDDICK & BATEMAN.

FIG. 8.3. *Advertisement for Nags Head Hotel,* North State Whig, *June 11, 1851.*

with fresh vegetables. "One of these *plies* between Elizabeth City and Nags Head. Another comes from Hertford, another from Edenton, and another from Salmon River, or Merry Hill; the latter being owned and employed by a wealthy gentleman for the convenience of his family and friends."

Upon arriving at the Banks, Throop reported, the schooner anchors half a mile offshore, in the sound, for there is no pier, and sends passengers and provisions to land in smaller boats. A walk through the sand leads the visitor to a small "story-and-a-half cottage, shingled and weatherboarded, but destitute of lath and plaster," and "surrounded by a dwarfish growth of live-oak." On its "eastern side, it has a comfortable piazza, where the family gather of an evening for a social chat, and for the enjoyment of the sea-breeze." The author, perhaps accustomed to resorts of a more transient clientele, was struck by "the fact that a very large proportion of the visitors are actual residents in private dwellings" owned by them, the "Planters, merchants, and professional men."

During the summer's stay, as Throop recorded, visitors would bathe in the ocean before breakfast, go to the bowling alley or riding or fishing, dine and then take a siesta in the afternoon, swim again, and in the evening, go to the hotel. There "the musician makes his appearance," and "it is not long before the ladies make their appearance; the sets are formed, and the long-drawn *'Balance, all!'* gives the glow of pleasure to every face." The dance goes on for hours, until you "are afraid to look at the clock, and then you dig your way ... through the dry, yielding, cringing, shrinking, nerve-depressing sand, homeward."[9]

The hotel, center of social evenings, flourished in the antebellum years. During the 1850s its owners advertised (fig. 8.3) that they had improved access to Nags Head by arranging for the steamer *A. H. Schultz* to come regularly from Virginia; had begun construction of a horse-drawn railroad one mile long from the hotel clear through its property to the ocean side; had built "a substantial Wharf ... from the landing on the Sound shore, to an anchorage, a distance of half a mile"; and had constructed plank walks "from the Sound to the Hotel, and from the Hotel to the Ocean."[10]

The hotel was the center of a growing cluster of cottages, whose residents regularly attended the social occasions there. When the editor of the *American Beacon* of Norfolk, Virginia, visited Nags Head in the summer of 1851, he described it as having

> picturesque dwellings on the hills occupied by the intelligent and wealthy Carolinians, who for twenty years have regularly congregated at Nags Head about the first of July, to pass in refined social intercourse, surrounded by the health reviving breezes of old Ocean, the season of the year that would expose them to sickness on their plantations.

The cottages were

> of considerable size, ... built in the fashion of regular homesteads with spacious porches and balconies and convenient out houses as if for permanent occupancy. They are generally situated on high hills with beautiful wooded sides commanding a magnificent prospect of the ocean and sound, and separated in many instances by most romantic vallies thickly covered with stunted pine and oak and luxuriant grape vines.[11]

The visits to Nags Head became a regular summer event for many eastern North Carolinians and had a lasting impact on the social fabric of the region. In 1900 the editor of the Elizabeth City *Economist* recalled the pleasant antebellum days at Nags Head. The resort was, he said, one of the most valuable institutions of the Albemarle country.... At one time it was ... patronized by most all the citizens of Albemarle, Tar River, and Pamlico sections.... Up to the Civil War it brought us together and made us one people. It intertwined our children in the happy days of childhood.... It established new and dear social relations. [The children] grew up together and ma[r]ital relations followed. It became the summer resort of wealthy Carolinians, who built cottages, originated new business enterprises, revived old memories, gossiped on current events, and enjoyed the happiness of their families and were lavish in their hospitalities.[12]

By the mid-1850s Nags Head had become one of the noted resorts of the eastern seaboard. The popular recreation area attracted a writer for *Harper's New Monthly Magazine,* visiting the South on the eve of the Civil War, who wrote of his travels in "Loungings in the Footprints of the Pioneers" (fig. 8.4):

> As we steered obliquely across to the Banks a group of twenty or thirty houses, all of the same model, scattered over the sand-hills, with a long wooden pier in the foreground, bespoke Nag's Head.... Bright white cabins among dark masses of foliage, relieved strongly against the evening sky, with some scores of people on the landing, attracted by the great event of their day, made up quite a lively and pleasant scene. No building that could be taken or mistaken for a hotel was in sight. But its representatives, in the shape of a dozen Africans and an ox-car that moved on rails along the delapidated pier, were as conspicuous as possible. The hotel came forward piecemeal as we mounted the shore. First a row of attic windows, then the second, and then the first story of a long, low building that threw out its arms, right and left, as if to welcome the wayfarer, told of mine inn. A queer nest in the sand has the wind shaped for it. East and west, toward the sea and the sound, ridges of blown sand conceal it till you come within a few yards. On either flank high hills of the same shifting material look down on it. The elements obviously grudge it the narrow resting-place it occupies.... Were it razed, a single winter, or mayhap a single storm, would obliterate all traces of its existence, and pile upon the spot a tumulus worthy more noble remains....
>
> Meanwhile the establishment literally dances over its grave. Fashion and frolic hold revel as though that remorseless leveler, old ocean, did not daily threaten a revolution. We found the celebrated band in full squeak, and a few couples threading the mazy under the influence of the same.... [A]mong the two or three hundred guests was a full share of female loveliness.[13]

FIG. 8.4. *"The Beach," Nags Head,* from E. C. Bruce, *"Loungings in the Footprints of the Pioneers,"* Harper's New Monthly Magazine, vol. 20, May 1860.

The regular pilgrimages of the fashionable were interrupted by the outbreak of the Civil War. The strategic character of the Outer Banks attracted military action, and by January, 1862, Confederate troops encamped at Nags Head, where the hotel served as the headquarters of Gen. Henry A. Wise. When Union troops captured the island in February the retreating Wise and his staff set fire to the hotel to prevent its being used by the enemy.[14] Another casualty of the war was the Episcopal church, which had been a feature of the resort community for well over a decade, having been established by the summer people and consecrated by Bishop Levi Silliman Ives in 1849 as All Saints Church. In 1865 the building was "torn down by the Federal troops under General Burnside and the material was used to build shelter for the runaway slaves who sought refuge on Roanoke Island."[15]

During the Civil War not only were the hotel and church destroyed but the fortunes of many of the planters who had formerly patronized Nags Head were reduced as well. Yet some of them were able to hold on to their summer places and, soon after the war ended, returned as regularly as before. There on the island, perhaps, the old order was resumed, in contrast to the changes sweeping the state during Reconstruction. The *Norfolk Journal* reported in August, 1867, that Nags Head "has never been patronized more than during the past season."[16]

After the war a new hotel and new cottages were built along the sound, where the boats still anchored; also, for the first time cottages were constructed on the ocean side. Some families built new cottages; others put the old ones on rollers and moved them from the sound across the flats to the beach. (Moving these houses built on sand was a common feature of Nags Head life, sometimes to accommodate the whim of an owner, more often as the only means of saving a cottage threatened by sand or sea. With foundations only of pilings, and without chimneys or utility connections, the cottages were relatively easy to detach and move.)[17]

According to local historian Edward G. Outlaw, Jr., who began to summer at Nags Head as a boy in 1884, the first to build a house on the Atlantic beach was Dr. W. G. Pool[18] of Elizabeth City:

> Dr. Pool decided to build on the ocean front. Over there by themselves, his family was very lonely. So he acquired all the property north of the hotel property as far up as the Samuel Tillett line, and commenced to donate to his friends' wives, building lots which were about 130 feet wide with a 40-foot street between each lot, running from west to east to the ocean.[19]

Dr. Pool's efforts at popularizing the ocean front were successful, for in the postwar years thirteen beach cottages sprang up along the Atlantic. Outlaw recalled that the structures were "strung along the edge of the surf, above high water within 300 feet of the line of breakers, a single row of buildings with generous spacing between the cottages, and next door neighbors were not within 'speaking distance.'"[20]

These cottages were devoid of the trappings of architectural vogue—a sharp contrast with the grand, fashionable town and country houses of their owners, who numbered among the wealthiest families in northeastern North Carolina. The dwellings were built simply, even casually, of readily available materials, including used lumber from Elizabeth City or other Albemarle origins, and wood salvaged from shipwrecks. Destruction by storms was thus no great loss, and additions and expansions were made almost continuously, as were necessary repairs nearly every season. Despite storms and occasional fires, nine of those original thirteen are believed to survive now as the cores of extant beach cottages. Most have been expanded radically from their original one-story, two- or three-room size.[21]

The dictates of survival and convenience on the weather-battered Outer Banks, not the whims of fashion, dictated the form and detail of the cottages built at Nags Head. Functional characteristics established during the early years, proving themselves serviceable, have shaped Nags Head construction to the present, giving the area a distinctive style of building all its own (figs. 8.5, 8.6). The cottages stand high on their timber pilings, well above low waves that lap along the beach. Between the pilings is often stretched a latticework screen—originally to keep out the wandering pig and cow population, attended by fleas and flies, which found shady refuge beneath the cottages. The walls of the buildings are covered with unpainted siding or wooden shingles, weathered to a rich gray-brown in the salt air. Protection from sun in summer and from storms in other seasons is provided by wood batten shutters, hinged at the top and, to capture the languid winds, held open with a prop stick. During the season the repetition of the diagonals of the shutters copies in miniature the angles of roof and porch; in winter, with their windows battened tight, the cottages have a stern aloofness—like a gathering of "haughty old ladies." Expanding the interiors of the cottages are the broad porches, skirting two, three, or even four sides of the houses. Ubiquitous benches emerge from simple wooden porch railings and slant out over thin air to catch the ocean breezes and to enlarge the usable area of the porch. To the rear of the cottages, expanding still further, are separate kitchens, linked by breezeways and often separate wings for the servants who spent the summer with the family.

In the postwar era access to Nags Head was by boat. Freighters came to the island, and there was also a sailboat, the *Lew Willis*, that "called twice a

FIG. 8.5. *Beach cottage, Nags Head. Photograph by Catherine W. Bishir and Janet K. Seapker, 1975.* (NCDAH)

FIG. 8.6. *Beach cottage, with porch detail showing typical "lean out" benches. Photograph by Catherine W. Bishir and Janet K. Seapker, 1975.* (NCDAH)

The "Unpainted Aristocracy" | 197

week," running from Elizabeth City to Manteo[22] and Nags Head. In 1874 the editor of the Elizabeth City *North Carolinian* observed:

> A number of citizens are making preparations to spend the summer at Nag's Head. Some go to worship at the Shrine of Hyge[i]a, others that of Cupid and Terpsichore, and still others, we fear will "worship and fall down" at the feet of Bacchus. Health to the first! pleasure to the second! and to the third the mildest of head-aches in the morning.[23]

Once at Nags Head, many of the families accustomed to town life and the plenty of plantations reveled in the uncomplicated isolation and primitive conditions of the Banks. Horse carts (fig. 8.7) conveyed baggage and people from place to place—two-wheelers, mostly, with room for a driver and a crowded load of people or possessions. Sailboats furnished access to Manteo for provisions not available from Hollowell's sound-side store or local farmers and year-round residents like Tilghman Tillett,[24] who brought fresh produce around in his cart. Life was casual, but with a degree of elegance: "In those days, finery was a prerequisite to a summer at Nag's Head. There was lots of dressing done by the few visitors who went to Nag's Head."[25] A young woman, presumably a student at St. Mary's school in Raleigh, wrote in the *St. Mary's Muse* of November, 1883, of her visit to Nags Head:

> At the house we find the usual throng of summer boarders, engaged in the summer boarder's usual occupations; lounging or promenading on the piazzas; here a party starting for a drive, there a crowd of excursionists landing from a sloop which has just stopped at the pier. We wander over the long, rambling hotel, and finally come out on one of the upper verandas. Across the sands appears a broad expanse of blue with fringes of white; a familiar, longed-for voice calls to us, and in obedience to the summons, we are soon on our way to the ocean. Along the beach extends

FIG. 8.7. *Horse cart at Nags Head beach. Photograph ca. 1930. (Courtesy of Fred L. Fearing; NCDAH)*

FIG. 8.8. *Hotel, sound side, Nags Head. Photograph late nineteenth century. (Courtesy of Fred L. Fearing; NCDAH)*

a row of houses grown old and gray under the suns and rains of many summers; they seem to look with an air of superior wisdom on the pert new cottages scattered here and there among them.[26]

Adding variety to the day were occasional drives to the Fresh Ponds, located amid the wooded hilly land of the central part of the island. Wrote the young lady from St. Mary's:

> in the depths of a green wilderness where wooded hill and valley combine to shut out the sight and thought of the glaring sands ... we come to an open space where, at the foot of green hills, lie the Fresh Ponds.... The largest lies near the centre of the open space ... and has a regular tide. The others are nearer the surrounding hills. All are fresh and teem with fish of various kinds; consequently they are a favorite resort for fishing parties. In strange contrast to the wastes of sand around are these oases of green hills, cool, deep woodland, and quiet waters beautiful with white lilies.[27]

During this period the resort's popularity continued to grow, and the managers and owners of hotels continued to improve their operations; though the hotels were on the sound side (fig. 8.8), they accommodated visitors to the ocean side as well. A. E. Jacobs, owner and manager of the Nags Head hotel, called the Alexina, advertised in the July 13, 1886, issue of the Elizabeth City *Economist*:

> This long established and favorite seaside summer resort of Eastern North Carolina will be open for the season, June 21, 1886, with several new attractions [including] a railroad from the pier to Ocean Beach, with a comfortable pavilion on the "Sea Beach" ... [and] three restaurants on the Sound Side. There will be an abundance of cistern water for drinking.[28]

At the same time, families expanded or built new beach houses. On June 12, 1883, the editor of the *Economist* observed that "We hear of several new houses going up at Nag's Head. This is as it should be. Let Nag's Head be the nursery of the Albemarle. Put bells on the children and turn them loose on the sand hills and all will be well."

Sometimes storms, fires, and wars interrupted the serene rhythm of summer life. Outlaw recalled that during the Spanish-American War the hotel did not open, and very few families went to Nags Head. In 1899, the year after the war, he remembered, "a terrific hurricane roared up the coast, ... striking Nag's Head with a northeast gale registering at the Nag's Head life saving station 85 miles an hour. Then the windgauge blew away."[29] When "the ocean swept across the sandy strand from sea to Sound," an inlet was cut across, and "cottagers on the beach made their way to the hotel on the Sound side by using lifelines to which each person was tied." Others were rescued by boat, and all gathered at the hotel, where, after the "provisions and liquor ran out," only salt herring and biscuits were left to eat.[30]

The hotel, a haven in the storm and center of social activity, was subject to less sudden destruction by moving sands. Jacobs's hotel closed after having been "sanded," which necessitated the construction of a new hotel on the sound side of Nags Head.[31] The new hotel, managed by John Z. Lowe of Norfolk, soon suffered from encroaching sands as well. One longtime visitor recalled that in the summer of 1893 "the sand came up so high to the windows that a sedge hen got into the hall one day and I chased her down the hall and out a window to finally capture her in the sand."[32]

It was not sand, however, but fire that destroyed Lowe's hotel. The three-story building, containing a hundred rooms and 150 guests, caught fire late in the afternoon on a Sunday in July, 1903. The building burned quickly—within 45 minutes—and caused the death of Mrs. John Z. Lowe. Only the old barroom and tenpin alley were left standing.[33] The guests boarded the *Guide*, which also took the body of Mrs. Lowe, to Elizabeth City. A contemporary report predicted that "the disastrous fire ... will almost break up that place as a resort for this season."[34]

Not only was the center of social life destroyed, but the steamer chartered by the hotel stopped as well. "After the hotel burned ... the only transportation to Nag's Head was a sail boat about three trips a week. Then finally engines were put in the Hattie Creef [a sailboat], and Martin Johnson [its skipper] ran daily trips."[35]

The burning of the hotel, which had restricted steamer access to the only large pier at Nags Head, opened a new era of steamers (fig. 8.9); soon a colorful crowd of them began to arrive. Sunday excursions on the *Guide* and *Tourist*—popular with businessmen visiting their summering families—found heavy competition in the North River Line's *Virginia*, which

Spend Your Vacation at Nags Head and Roanoke Island
SEASHORE BATHING, BOATING and FISHING

GET really acquainted with this remarkable section of your own state, with its enchanting waters, its rich history, its hospitable and interesting people. Only 45 miles from Elizabeth City, in the heart of the wildfowl and fishing country where ocean breezes blow. Bathing, boating, and fishing for drumfish and ocean trout, that weigh 20 to 60 pounds apiece. See its picturesque and historical scenery, where the first English colonists landed nearly 400 years ago, and built the cradle of American history. Visit the lighthouses, the Coast Guard Stations, and the towering sand hills where the first airplane was made. Take your car down. Nowhere can you have so good a time for so little money. Nowhere, will you find less noise, confusion and hustle that takes away the joy of vacations in other places. Reduced rates in effect on railroads and steamers.

These Comfortable Steamers Will Take You There:

Steamer ANNIE L. VAN SCIVER
Of the North River Line

Excursions every Sunday until September 12 inclusive, to Nags Head direct. Large Swift and Comfortable vessel. Leaves Elizabeth City 8 a. m. Returning leaves Nags Head at 5 p. m. arriving at 9:30 p. m. Low round trip fares. For further information address:

C. H. BROCK, Supt.
Elizabeth City, N. C.

Str. TRENTON
of Eastern Carolina Transportation Company

Capt. Martin Johnson, Master

Operating daily between Elizabeth City, Nags Head and Manteo. Leaves Eliz. City at 1:30 p. m. daily except Sunday, for Nags Head and Manteo. Returning leaves Manteo at 5 a. m. and Nags Head at 5:30 a. m. Meals on Boat and Automobile Accommodations.

Wanchese Line
Operating the Steamers:
HATTIE CREEF, POMPANO and O. T. & LLOYD, JR.

To Wanchese on Roanoke Island, Manns Harbor; Stumpy Point except Saturday. Steamers leave Elizabeth City at 12:30 daily. Automobile accommodations, at reduced round trip rates. For further information address

R. E. BLACK, Agt.
Elizabeth City, N. C.

FIG. 8.9. *Advertisement*, Elizabeth City Independent, *July 2, 1926.*

burned and was replaced with the long-lived *Annie L. Vansciver.* Plying the waters to Nags Head along with the *Hattie Creef* (which transported the Wright brothers to the Banks) was the *E. R. Daniels.*

The *Trenton*, operated for decades by Martin Johnson, was the mainstay, running six days a week; the *Haven Bell* and the *Vansciver* made excursion

FIG. 8.10. *Beach cottage, Nags Head, with vacationers lounging on the porch. Photograph early twentieth century. (Courtesy of James Hathaway; NCDAH)*

FIG. 8.11. *Nags Head Lifesaving (Coast Guard) Station, built 1874. Photograph early twentieth century. (Courtesy of James Hathaway; NCDAH)*

FIG. 8.12. *Bathhouse, beach, Nags Head. Photograph early twentieth century. (Courtesy of James Hathaway; NCDAH)*

trips, leaving Elizabeth City in the morning and returning at night.[36] On the *Vansciver* Flat's Band of local black musicians played the bones, bass fiddle, and kazoo as the boat full of vacationers in their leg-of-mutton-sleeve dresses and flat, boater hats, steamed its way to Nags Head. Two rival steamers would push their engines to the limit as they approached the island, racing full steam ahead, bands playing to tempo, to try to arrive first at the pier crowded with summer people and natives alike.

As soon as the boat tied up, visitors for the day would "head out for the ocean side as hard as they could," and when the day ended and the boat blew its whistle to signal departure, from all over Nags Head "people would streak back to the boat." The black musicians, too, went ashore to visit and play popular selections at various cottages, passing a hat for contributions.[37]

Not long after the hotel burned, Elizabeth City physician Dr. C. W. Sawyer, in good Nags Head salvage tradition, purchased the remaining bar building of the hotel, moved it to his property, and set up a boardinghouse, the Albemarle, which stood out over the sound on piers. In front of it, on the sand, he built a pavilion which soon replaced the hotel as the center of evening social life.[38]

The early twentieth century at Nags Head is an era well remembered by people who have spent their summers there. The recollections of these doctors, architects, matrons, and ministers in their fifties, sixties, seventies, and eighties have without exception an aura of sunlit clarity—their memories of those long, lovely barefoot summers distilled a heady blend of adventurous, glorious freedom and an underlying certainty of familiar faces, accustomed places, and unchanging patterns.

As had been true for generations in this isolated world, the day was spent "either swimming . . . or lounging around in the hammocks on the cottage porch; possibly interspersed with a visit either across to [Roanoke] island or across the beach to the Coast Guard Station. No more diversion than this was to be had, and idleness in its purest and most pleasant form prevailed"[39] (figs. 8.10, 8.11). The focus of daytime activity was the bathhouse near the ocean:

> At 11 o'clock in the morning everybody on the ocean side would gather up at the bathhouse because they had a life line . . . that went out in a V, and everybody wanted to be inside that V to go bathing. . . . On the sound side, Miss Allie Grice (Mrs. Charles Grice) had a flag that she'd run up, about 10:15 or 10:20 . . . to notify all the people on the sound side it was time to go to the ocean side. They'd all meet and come over in a group, and get over there about 11 o'clock. . . . The sound side people and the ocean side people all went to the ocean together, which brought about a friendliness as well as contributing to . . . safety.[40]

At the bathhouse (fig. 8.12) there was not only a lifeline but also the only refreshments sold on the beach—"soft drinks, Coca Cola, a few snacks . . . zu zus (an old fashioned kind of gingersnaps), lemon snaps, animal crackers, vienna sausage, a can of beans, that was about it."[41]

In the evening

> there was always a diversity of activity; some canoeing in the sound as the waters were always calm and perfect for such a pastime; ... while many chose to mount the summit of Engagement Hill, to sit and enjoy the quiet moonlight reflections and to sing their favorite sentimental songs usually accompanied by a guitar.[42]

The center of evening social life was the pavilion, which was, remembered one regular visitor,

> not a thing in the world but lanterns hanging around and an old scratchy victrola; it was my job to keep the victrola cranked. That's how I could stay there all summer. I slept in a little room back there and I kept the dance hall swept out and kept the sand off the records. They just had open windows, that's all.[43]

Bands, too, played at the pavilion: "Mr. Perry had a piano, had a fellow there that played square dance music. Mr. John Culpepper played accordian for square dancing.... For ballroom dancing, a fellow named Howard Weaver had a little orchestra, piano, violin, accordian."[44]

Besides the pavilion and the bathhouse, new hotels and boardinghouses were constructed. The Albemarle, of course, was connected with the pavilion. There was the LeRoy Hotel, sound-side predecessor to the ocean-side LeRoy Seaside Inn (now the First Colony Hotel). Also well known was Hollowell's Hotel; like many Nags Head buildings, it was moved at one time, and local residents recall that "Miss Ethel Hollowell never stopped cooking while Old Man Twine moved it."[45] The Arlington, originally located on the sound side, was moved to the ocean side and was recently destroyed by storms. Miss Cassie Morrissette of the Arlington had a wooden walkway built across the flats from the sound side to her hotel, so that people could traverse the distance over the sand instead of through it. The hotels provided food, some of it locally caught fish. Recalled one man of his young days there:

> John Moore [a local banker boy, later a colorful character of the Banks] would come knock on the floor boards under my room early in the morning, and we'd go out and catch soft-shell crabs. We'd sell them for twelve or fifteen cents a dozen to Mrs. LeRoy's hotel or if we would carry them to the ocean side, to Miss Cassie at the old Arlington, we could get three or four cents more a dozen.[46]

FIG. 8.13. *Ziegler Cottage, overturned in 1918 storm. Photograph 1918. (Courtesy of James Hathaway).*

Punctuating the leisurely tempo was the daily arrival of the steamer at the pier, with mail, supplies, and visitors:

> The boat came in about 5 o'clock, and we would leave home about 4 o'clock to meet the boat and see who was coming to Nags Head. . . . We waited for the mail to be put up, went back to the ocean side, had supper, and after supper, we went back to the pavilion for the entertainment, and walked back home again that night. But we were young, and we didn't mind it. Nobody minded it. It was always done in groups, a whole crowd together . . . there was no danger anyhow because everybody down there knew each other. No strangers could come in except on that boat, and if they did, you'd see them. Nobody was afraid . . . you never thought about locking a door.[47]

Storms continued to plague Nags Head, with the worst occurring in two consecutive years, 1917 and 1918. As in 1899, again "the ocean met the sound," and water poured across the island. Along the beach in 1917 cottagers moved their houses back from the ocean, only to find them after a storm the following year "with their steps hanging in the water"[48] (fig. 8.13).

Despite the ravages of storms and the threats of World War I along the coast, the years before and after 1920 were prime ones for Nags Head's beach, which experienced steady growth, with the old cottages being expanded for growing families and new cottages filling in the beachscape (fig. 8.14). Hints of modernity began to appear—automobiles were brought over from the mainland, but few enough to continue to be a novelty; the coast

The "Unpainted Aristocracy"

FIG. 8.14. *Beach cottages, Nags Head. Postcard, ca. 1926. (Courtesy of Janet K. Seapker; NCDAH)*

guard station got a telephone; some Delco electric generators were installed for electric lights—but most of the Nags Head regulars held tenaciously to the unique characteristics that distinguished the place from other resorts along the coast. The Raleigh *News and Observer* reported in 1929:

> The fascination of Nags Head is its absolute lack of any pretense to formality. Its beauty is its very primitiveness which has not been touched by the hand of man.
>
> There are those who are lured to Nags Head by the enthusiasm of Nags Headers, and leave in high disdain because of mosquitoes, of oil lamps, which make the mosquitoes worse, no running water, no board walks, "and you positively ruin every pair of shoes and every piece of clothes you take down there." And that is just the point—one doesn't take good clothes to Nags Head, nor wear the best, or even the second best shoes, unless one just wants to do it.
>
> It is not unusual to see folks change shoes and clothing before leaving the good ship Trenton at the pier, and if one goes down in the car, after leaving Point Harbor on the ferry, the feeling grows that here is the place where appearances don't count for so much.[49]

The increased development of the beach side after about 1915 coincided with the blossoming of a genius responsible for much of the character of Nags Head as it currently appears—builder S. J. Twine of Elizabeth City[50] (fig. 8.15). From the early teens of the century through the 1940s most of the moving, remodeling, and expansion of old cottages, and construction of new ones, was the careful handiwork of Twine. He produced in his long career not only a collection of sturdy, superbly functional and handsome cottages but also a reputation as a man of irreproachable honesty: "If he gave you a price for a job but lost money on it, he would give you a good job just the same." Twine, with his "little glasses pinched up on his nose," was "a little shrimp of a fellow, but he knew his work."[51]

Twine's early training is uncertain—"Old Man String just grew up building houses, I reckon"—but he was "in full swing by about 1915," the year he constructed the simple Gothic Revival Episcopal church, St. Andrew's-by-the-Sea.[52] There were other builders at Nags Head, including such local people as Hal Wood Culpepper and Marshall Field Tillett, but Twine was preeminent: "Nobody could build nothing down there if Mr. Twine didn't do it."[53] After a big storm had altered the landscape, pushing the beach westward yet again, Twine would put the storm-battered cottages on rollers and move them back along the beach to a distance which seemed safe from the sea for a time. As a family grew, he would construct additions, in a nearly continuous process for some: "We added on to that cottage every time we turned around."[54] He busied himself during the winter in Elizabeth City with odd jobs, went down to Nags Head in March before the season began to get houses into repair, and remained after the season ended to secure them against winter storms. Year after year, Nags Head depended upon Twine's comfortable, sturdy, flexible houses, which regularly withstood the fierce weather: "You never heard of a cottage Twine built being blown down in a storm."[55]

Taking his cue from the traditional, functional house forms long established at Nags Head, Twine introduced a more massive and dramatic

FIG. 8.15. *S. J. Twine. Photograph ca. 1930s. (Courtesy of Frederick Drane; NCDAH)*

form dominated by broad dormers and sweeping rooflines (reflecting then-current bungalow and shingle styles), to produce a magnificent series of cottages. Their robust forms, rich organic colors, and varied angles seem a natural outgrowth of the slope of the beach and the changing colors of the sky and sea.

The cottages are large one-and-one-half-story structures, with full dormers carrying across the front and rear slopes of the gable roof. The acute angle of the roofline slopes into the shallower angle of the porch roofs that fan out around the house. Within, the simply furnished interiors follow a rather standard floor plan, with two front rooms and, to the rear, a hall separating two more rooms. Additional bedrooms were provided on the second floor. Still used are the ubiquitous angled shutters and lean-out benches. In some cases new construction and in others an expansion of smaller older cottages, all the Twine houses bear the imprint of his vigorous pragmatic genius.

S. J. Twine's long career at Nags Head spanned a period of change for the summer village, change of a more lasting nature than the resort had ever seen before: the construction of a bridge to the mainland. Led by County Commissioner Wash L. Baum, the citizenry of Dare County sought modernity and an end to its isolation, greeting progress with enthusiasm.[56] But progress was eyed warily by the summer people. In 1929, as the pilings for the Currituck Sound bridge were driven, the *News and Observer* reported:

> the folks outside of Dare County who have been going down to Nags Head summer after summer look askance on the coming of a road. Will it ring the death knell of the Nags Head that has been so pleasant a place in which to spend the summer weeks ... where Nature reigns supreme and man still lives in primitive simplicity? ... The Nags Header loves Nags Head for the very things it lacks, and feels some regret at the promise of civilization.[57]

The bridge and the paved road that followed along the Atlantic beach did bring "civilization"—and change. Twentieth-century conveniences and fashions made themselves felt, and automobile traffic across the bridge soon put the steamers out of business. Development grew up along the road:

> Dancing places and cafes have been built all along the road ever since paving.... Brack and Bill Dawson promoted and had erected The Nag's Header and Beach Club opposite the A.B.C. store.... Mr. and Mrs. J. H. LeRoy built the First Colony Inn.... Graham Hollowell moved his store and hotel on the road side just west of the Pruden cottage on the ocean

side. Moncie Daniels of Manteo built The Casino, a dancing-bowling hall.[58]

The new beach road, and serious damage to the sound-side cottages by storms in the 1930s, reinforced the shift in development away from the sound to the ocean. The lifestyle at Nags Head began to reflect these changes.[59] By 1938, less than a decade after the bridge had been completed, the *Nags Tale*, a short-lived local newspaper, reported:

> Times were when the favorite pastimes at Nags Head were climbing sand-dunes and sitting around bon-fires on the beach. They've been replaced in the last few seasons with running over to Manteo for a movie, or just going to ride along the beach. Can it be that Nags Head's going modern?[60]

The *Nags Tale* writer recalled the days when "they held square dances at the old dance hall on the sound side" and noted among the coming attractions at the Nags Head Beach Club a series of well-known dance bands, with plans for "a change of bands every one and two weeks." The Nags Head Casino advertised dancing on Saturday night "to the music of Clarke Godfrey and His 11 Piece Swing Orchestra Featuring Miss Honey Lane, Vocalist." Dance-step fads changed nearly as often as the bands: by late August 1938 the *Nags Tale* noted that at the Beach Club "The Big Apple is gone, the Cotton Club Jump takes its place." Along with the dance halls came filling stations (fig. 8.16), grocery stores, and—perhaps a latter-day competitor for hungry bathers at the old bathhouse—a restaurant called "Joe College and Betty Co-Ed, The Brightest Spot on the Beach, where all the crowd meets."[61]

FIG. 8.16. *Modlin service station, Nags Head. Photograph probably 1930s. (Courtesy of Fred L. Fearing; NCDAH)*

The *"Unpainted Aristocracy"*

FIG. 8.17. *Beach cottages. Photograph by Catherine W. Bishir and Janet K. Seapker, 1975.* (NCDAH)

Amid the rapid growth and the frenetic novelties of resort development, Nags Headers continued their perennial summer-long visits, holding tenaciously to many of the traditional aspects of summer life among increasing numbers of tourists. Perhaps most important was the retention of the sense that despite the changes old Nags Head was a special place, not to be swallowed up by the numerous motels that proliferated along the beach. In 1952 Tazewell H. Lamb, a transplanted Nags Header, wrote from California:

> Nag's Head has changed—but not completely: the sun still comes up out of the sea and goes down in the Sound. In calm weather, the little waves wash gently on the beach; March and September Northeasters drive ashore with sound and fury. And there is the old music of the salt sea wind in the pines and the booming surf in the distance, if the juke boxes and traffic noises are not too loud.[62]

In the last quarter century development has surrounded what was once a tiny, isolated summer community—only the view across the Atlantic remains unchanged. The Ash Wednesday storm of 1962 ripped across the beach, demanding yet another move back from the sea toward the road, repeating the moves of 1917, 1918, and the 1930s. Thus far, though, the sense of continuity and love of families for Nags Head have prevailed against fierce storms and development alike. The mile-long row of cottages (fig. 8.17), weathered dark and rich with summer memories, survives, embracing the little colony of pioneer beach cottages and the grand, sweeping cottages of S. J. Twine.

NOTES

Material concerning the early-twentieth-century history of Nags Head was gathered through a series of interviews with people who summered there and have shared their memories and documentary photographs. Information was provided by Mrs. Betty Wales Silver of Raleigh; the Reverend Dr. Frederick B. Drane and Mrs. Drane of Edenton; Mrs. Lloyd Horton of Hertford; W. C. Dawson, Frank Benton, and James Hathaway of Elizabeth City; and Carolista Baum of Chapel Hill and Nags Head. Special assistance was given by Fred L. Fearing of Elizabeth City, who arranged several interviews and was consistently generous with his extensive collection of materials on Nags Head.

1. Jonathan Daniels, editor emeritus of the *News and Observer* (Raleigh) to the author, October 1, 1976: "Yes, I guess I am guilty of the 'unpainted aristocracy' line. Those were charming old beach houses even if you could sometimes look through the floor and see the sand fiddlers." Postcard in the Survey and Planning Branch files, Division of Archives and History. This newspaper will be hereinafter cited as the *News and Observer*.

2. The best history of the Outer Banks is David Stick, *The Outer Banks of North Carolina, 1584–1958* (Chapel Hill: University of North Carolina Press, 1958). For a discussion of the recent physical changes on the Outer Banks see the first chapter, "Sands, Sounds, and Inlets," 1–10. A list of twenty-four Banks inlets, their locations, dates of origin, and status will be found on page 9.

3. Stick (*The Outer Banks,* 22–43, 72–74) deals specifically with the "bankers," people of primarily English descent with a sprinkling of Italian, Danish, Greek, French, and even perhaps Arabic derivation. Roughly a thousand people were living on the Banks and the nearby islands as early as 1783, making a living from farming, fishing, and stock raising.

4. E. C. Bruce, "Loungings in the Footprints of the Pioneers," *Harper's New Monthly Magazine,* 20 (May, 1860), 733.

5. The landscape has changed greatly over the decades, even since Nags Head was established as a resort. In the early years of its popularity much of Bodie Island, on which Nags Head is located, was heavily vegetated, and the bankers had farms and gardens. By the latter part of the nineteenth century, however, a major problem was the movement of sand, which increased in the twentieth century. Stick (*The Outer Banks,* 3–4) describes the process by which the sand bars that form the Outer Banks became fertile and vegetated so that by the time "white men first viewed the Banks, a lush growth of cedar, pine, and live oak, mingled with dense grape vines, cover[ed] much of what was once a bare sand beach." Human use of the land, cutting forests and permitting stock to graze, destroyed much of the stabilizing vegetation, allowing sand to blow to create sand waves, which became moving dunes that covered forests and man-made structures alike in their relentless path.

In 1931 Capt. W. J. Tate interviewed several residents of the Outer Banks and recorded their recollections. Two brothers remembered that "during their boyhood their home was in the Nags Head woods and that they cultivated, under their father's direction, several acres of corn, potatoes, and garden vegetables at a point which is now underneath of Jockey's Ridge." Tate also cited the Nags Head Hotel which, according to local residents, "was enveloped and destroyed by a drifting sand dune and a new one had to be built," plus at least one cottage at Nags Head which had often been "moved out further towards the water to escape the desire of a drifting sand dune to demolish everything in its path." "Capt. Tate Says Frank Stick 'A Good Man Gone Wrong, Theoretically,'" newspaper clipping dated February, 1931, in the collection of Fred L. Fearing, Elizabeth City, hereinafter cited as Fearing Collection.

6. Edward R. Outlaw, Jr., *Old Nag's Head* (Norfolk, Va.: Privately printed, 1952; second edition, with revisions and additions by Louise Greenleaf Outlaw, 1956), 18. This informal memoir is the best source of personal recollections of late-nineteenth-century Nags Head.

7. Quoted in Stick, *The Outer Banks,* 97–98.

8. Richard Walser, "The Mysterious Case of

George Higby Throop (1818–1896) . . . ," *North Carolina Historical Review*, 33 (January, 1956), 13.

9. Excerpts from *Nags Head: or Two Months among "The Bankers,"* in Walser, "George Higby Throop," 17–20.

10. Stick, *The Outer Banks*, 103.

11. *American Beacon* (Norfolk, Va.), August 25, 1851, quoted in Stick, *The Outer Banks*, 102.

12. *Economist* (Elizabeth City), July 6, 1900, hereinafter cited as *Economist*.

13. Bruce, "Loungings," 728–29.

14. Stick, *The Outer Banks*, 102.

15. [Frederick B. Drane], "St. Andrews-by-the-Sea at Nags Head," in Outlaw, *Old Nag's Head*, 8.

16. *Norfolk Journal*, August, 1867, quoted in Stick, *The Outer Banks*, 106.

17. Outlaw, *Old Nag's Head*, passim.

18. William Gaskins Pool (1829–87), son of Solomon Pool, Sr., and Martha Gaskins Pool, was born near Elizabeth City. He received A.B. and M.A. degrees at the University of North Carolina, Chapel Hill, and attended medical colleges in New York, Philadelphia, and Cincinnati. Among his six siblings were congressman Walter F. Pool, circuit judge C. C. Pool, U.S. senator John Pool, and Solomon Pool, who served as president of the University of North Carolina during Reconstruction (1869–75). Daniel Lindsey Grant (compiler), *Alumni History of the University of North Carolina* (Chapel Hill: [General Alumni Association], second edition, 1924), 499; *Cyclopedia of Eminent and Representative Men of the Carolinas of the Nineteenth Century* (Madison, Wis.: Brant & Fuller, 2 volumes, 1892), 2: 401. Bettie Freshwater Pool, *Literature in the Albemarle* (Baltimore: Baltimore City Printing and Binding Co., 1915), 247–49.

Dr. Pool is connected with one of the Outer Bank's most intriguing and romantic mysteries; it was he who discovered the identity of the portrait believed by many to be that of Aaron Burr's daughter, Theodosia Burr Alston. In the summer of 1869, so the story goes, Dr. Pool was called to the side of an old banker woman, and she insisted on paying him for his services with the gift of a portrait she said had been salvaged many years earlier from a mysteriously empty grounded vessel. The doctor took the portrait home and later detected the resemblance of its subject to Theodosia; this was confirmed by descendants of the Burr family, and the story attracted much attention. Theodosia had indeed been lost at sea in January, 1813, off the Outer Banks, aboard a ship which had disappeared while en route from South Carolina to New York, where Aaron Burr awaited his daughter. See Outlaw, *Old Nags Head*, 23–27; David Stick, *Graveyard of the Atlantic: Shipwrecks of the North Carolina Coast* (Chapel Hill: University of North Carolina Press, 1952), 5–8; Catherine Albertson, *Legends of the Dunes of Dare* (Raleigh: Privately printed, 1936), 13–14.

19. Outlaw, *Old Nag's Head*, 21–23. On September 14, 1866, William G. Pool bought from members of the Midgett family for $30 fifty acres "at or near Nags Head," bordering on the Atlantic Ocean. The following November 6 Pool sold to Kate Overman for $1 a lot near the ocean at Nags Head and stated in the deed his desire for R. F. Overman and his wife Kate of Elizabeth City "to build on my land at Nags Head and reside there during the summer months." Similar deeds were executed between Pool and Florence L. Grandy and between Pool and Henrietta Fearing. Currituck County Deeds, Book 30, pp. 19, 108, 112, 444, microfilm copy, Archives, Division of Archives and History, Raleigh. These deeds confirm Outlaw's account of the first beach development at Nags Head. Outlaw, as a boy and young man, participated in the late-nineteenth-century history of Nags Head, and his memories and secondhand accounts of this period are generally accurate. A photograph owned by Dr. and Mrs. Frederick B. Drane of Edenton shows the beach with the scattered baker's dozen cottages of the late-nineteenth-century era.

20. Outlaw, *Old Nag's Head*, 21.

21. Comparison of Outlaw's description of the original (pre-1910) cottages with traditional and firsthand recollections of longtime visitors to Nags Head indicates that the nine survivors are these: (1) The Sumner Cottage, dated by Outlaw as 1868, is said to be that now owned by the Gaither family of Elizabeth City. (2) The E. F. Lamb Cottage, described by Outlaw as moved from the sound side, is said to be part of the present Patterson Cottage. (3) The present Wales Cottage is said by Outlaw to be the original 1869 Henrietta Fearing Cottage, but the present owner believes it was built ca. 1875 and was bought by her grandfather in 1880. (4) The W. W. Griffin Cottage, described by Outlaw as being owned by Mrs. Duncan Winston and Mrs. Wales, is believed to be the core

of the cottage now owned by Mrs. Frederick Drane. The early portion contains hand-hewn timbers said to have come from a church in Elizabeth City. (5) The George Pool Cottage (owned by Dr. W. G. Pool's brother), dated by Outlaw as 1866, is said to be the Turner Cottage now owned by the MacMullen family. (6) The cottage built for Florence Grandy at Dr. Pool's behest, said by Outlaw to be that sold to Tom Nixon in 1908, is thus probably the core of the cottage still owned by the Nixon family of Hertford. (7) The home built about the same time for Kate Overman on land sold to her by Dr. Pool is described as the house moved back of the highway, now the Whedbee Cottage. (8) The Gurkin Cottage, undated, is thought to be the present Martha Wood Cottage. (9) The Edward Outlaw, Sr., Cottage, built in 1885 for his father, according to Outlaw, is described by him as being "fabricated" near the family homeplace in Bertie County and carried by boat to Nags Head where it was erected. This was a smaller cottage and is thought to be the core of the present large two-story cottage, which does include a notable amount of early building fabric. It is now a Worthington cottage.

These statements are based on Outlaw, *Old Nag's Head,* passim, and several interviews: Catherine W. Bishir, interview with Betty Wales Silver, Raleigh, March 12, 1976, hereinafter cited as Silver interview; Bishir and Fred L. Fearing, interview with Frank Benton, Elizabeth City, April 29, 1976, hereinafter cited as Benton interview; Bishir and Fearing, interview with Dr. James Hathaway, April 29, 1976, hereinafter cited as Hathaway interview; Fred L. Fearing, interview in May, 1976, with W. C. Dawson, Elizabeth City, hereinafter cited as Dawson interview; Catherine W. Bishir, interview with Dr. and Mrs. Frederick B. Drane, Edenton, April 29, 1976, hereinafter cited as Drane interview. [Author's note, 2006: Many of these cottages have changed ownership since 1976.]

22. Manteo, founded on Roanoke Island in 1865, is the county seat of Dare County. Nags Head was a part of Currituck County until Dare County was established in 1870. William S. Powell, *The North Carolina Gazetteer* (Chapel Hill: University of North Carolina Press, 1968), 134, 311.

23. *North Carolinian* (Elizabeth City), July 8, 1874.

24. Among the family names of bankers prominent in the late 1790s was Tillit near Kitty Hawk (Stick, *The Outer Banks,* 73). Tilletts lived in the area in the late nineteenth and early twentieth century and frequently provided goods and services to the summer people. One longtime summer visitor recalled: "We got fresh vegetables and occasionally we got beef from a Mr. Tillett, who lived up in Nags Head woods. Had a farm up in there, and he'd raise vegetables and come by in a horse and cart and sell them to you. About every Friday he'd butcher a calf or a cow, and he'd come by with that meat in his cart, flies all over it. He had a piece of mosquito netting over it, but there were flies on the mosquito netting. He'd cut off whatever you wanted to buy, and that's the way you got your meat ... about as tough as you ever tried to eat." Dawson interview.

25. Outlaw, *Old Nag's Head,* 43.

26. *St. Mary's Muse,* 6 (November, 1883), 10, copies in the St. Mary's College Library, Raleigh, and in the North Carolina Collection, University of North Carolina Library, Chapel Hill, hereinafter cited as *St. Mary's Muse.* The table of contents, which gives authorship credit, is missing on this particular issue.

27. *St. Mary's Muse,* 11. These fresh ponds seem to have existed when the first settlers came to the Banks; a grant in 1716 refers to the "great fresh pond," as does another in 1737. Stick, *The Outer Banks,* 269–70.

28. *Economist,* July 13, 1886. According to an article written in 1933, the hotel Jacobs owned was the chief hotel in Nags Head in the 1870s and 1880s. It was named Alexina for one of Jacobs's children and was built out over the sound, as were many of the sound-side cottages. "Finally the encroaching sand made it necessary to abandon the Alexina, and another hotel was built further out into the sound." "First Nags Head Cottages ... ," *Daily Advance* (Elizabeth City), July 19, 1933, clipping in the Fearing Collection. The newspaper will be hereinafter cited as the *Advance.*

29. Outlaw, *Old Nag's Head,* 29.

30. Ibid., 29–30.

31. "Guide Is at the Dock," *Advance,* July 19, 1933, clipping in the Fearing Collection. In this article Graham Hollowell, longtime postmaster at Nags Head, is quoted as identifying the site of the hotel that burned and also the nearby site of the hotel that preceded it. "The older hotel," Mr. Hollowell said, "was torn down in sections as the new one over the sound was being built.

Before all the timbers could be moved, they collapsed under the weight of the sand that pressed upon them and they were submerged, lost to view for many years. Recently, however, the sands are blowing off the old site, revealing jagged edges of old timbers."

32. "Guide Is at the Dock."

33. Outlaw, *Old Nag's Head,* 45; "Guide Is at the Dock"; "Destructive Blaze at Nags Head," *Economist,* July 31, 1903. Outlaw (28) says this occurred in 1900, but 1903 is the correct date.

34. "Destructive Blaze at Nags Head."

35. Outlaw, *Old Nag's Head,* 41–42.

36. Hathaway interview.

37. Ibid.

38. Benton interview.

39. Arch B. Brown, *Historic Sands of Eastern Carolina* (Washington, D.C.?: Privately printed, 1937), 26.

40. Dawson interview.

41. Ibid.

42. Brown, *Sands of Eastern Carolina,* 26.

43. Benton interview.

44. Dawson interview.

45. Ibid.

46. Hathaway interview.

47. Dawson interview.

48. Silver interview.

49. Carolyn L. Reynolds, "A Lost Frontier Joins Civilization," *News and Observer,* September 8, 1929.

50. S. J. Twine was born on January 6, 1874, in Perquimans County but lived most of his long life in Elizabeth City. At the time of his death on September 3, 1973, he was described as a "retired carpenter." Information supplied by Fred L. Fearing; obituary in *Advance,* September 4, 1973.

51. Silver and Drane interviews.

52. Drane interview. Construction of the church was financed by money collected and saved over the years, increased by funds finally provided by Congress as restitution for the destruction of the Episcopal church by Union soldiers years earlier. [Drane], "St. Andrew's-by-the-Sea at Nags Head," in Outlaw, *Old Nag's Head,* 8. It was moved to its present site in 1937.

53. Hathaway interview.

54. Catherine W. Bishir, telephone interview with Mrs. Lloyd Horton, Hertford, summer, 1976.

55. Hathaway interview.

56. See Stick, *The Outer Banks,* 242–49, for an account of the coming of bridges and roads to this section of the Outer Banks and the effect on tourism and the economy of the area.

57. Reynolds, "A Lost Frontier Joins Civilization."

58. Outlaw, *Old Nag's Head,* 58–59.

59. Also in the 1930s came federally sponsored projects on the Outer Banks (including construction of the Wright Brothers National Memorial in 1932), and reconstruction of Fort Raleigh on Roanoke Island was initiated in 1941. On Roanoke Island the commemorative "symphonic drama" *The Lost Colony,* by Paul Green, was first performed in the new amphitheater in 1937 and soon became a popular tourist attraction. During the first season Pres. Franklin D. Roosevelt came to attend the dedication of the Waterside Theater. Silver and Drane interviews.

Long before reconstruction of the fort, visits to the site of Fort Raleigh on Roanoke Island had been an annual event of a summer at Nags Head. Dr. Drane, minister of the Episcopal church in Edenton and at Nags Head, would hold an annual memorial service on or about August 18, and the whole group would go over to Roanoke for the event. There "we'd get full of red bugs, so when we got back, we'd go right into the ocean to get rid of them." Hathaway interview.

60. *Nags Tale,* July 16, 1938.

61. *Nags Tale,* July–August, 1938, passim.

62. Tazewell H. Lamb, foreword to Outlaw, *Old Nag's Head,* 11.

Nine

"A STRONG FORCE OF LADIES"

WOMEN, POLITICS, AND CONFEDERATE MEMORIAL ASSOCIATIONS IN NINETEENTH-CENTURY RALEIGH

On a fine day in May 1895, at the State Capitol in Raleigh, North Carolina, Nancy Haywood Blount Branch surveyed the scene around her. Wearing her customary black, and seated on a grandstand among other dignitaries, the seventy-seven-year-old widow gazed across a crowd of thousands that extended as far as the eye could see. Confederate flags, some bright and new, others faded to pale pink and blue, fluttered throughout the gathering of men and women, young and old. Line after line of aging veterans stood in wait for the occasion—the unveiling of the state's Confederate monument (fig. 9.1). Near Mrs. Gen. Lawrence O'B. Branch, as she was known, sat a few other women including her daughter, Nancy Branch Jones, and two other Confederate widows, Mrs. Gen. D. H. Hill and Mrs. Gen. "Stonewall" Jackson. Julia Jackson Christian, Jackson's seven-year-old granddaughter, clad in white organdy and with pink ribbons in her golden hair, sat in readiness to unveil the seventy-five-foot granite monument.[1]

For Nancy Branch, as for many others, the occasion evoked memories that reached back three decades. In May 1866 she had moved into a position of new leadership as founding president of Raleigh's first organization to assure the proper burial and commemoration of the Confederate dead.

"'A Strong Force of Ladies': Women, Politics, and Confederate Memorial Associations in Nineteenth-Century Raleigh" appeared in *North Carolina Historical Review* 77, no. 4 (October 2000): 455–91, and is reprinted by permission of the Historical Publications Section, North Carolina Office of Archives and History, Department of Cultural Resources, Raleigh.

FIG. 9.1. *North Carolina Confederate Monument unveiling scene, view along Hillsborough Street, Raleigh, 1895.* (NCDAH)

The following year, amid the turbulence of military occupation, she and the Ladies Memorial Association (LMA) of Wake County established one of the first Confederate cemeteries in the South and held their first memorial ceremonies on May 10, 1867. Since that time, the LMA had erected a monument at their cemetery and sponsored ever more elaborate memorial events amid a changing political landscape. Most recently, Branch's daughter had led the North Carolina Monumental Association, formed in 1892 as an outgrowth of the LMA, in producing this public monument and ceremonial event whose scale and proud assertion of the Confederate cause would have been unimaginable in 1866.

These women and the organizations they led in the decades immediately following the Civil War assumed important new roles in southern life. As Gaines Foster shows in *Ghosts of the Confederacy,* Ladies Memorial Associations formed throughout the South in the 1860s played a crucial part in easing white southerners' adjustment to loss and helping them regain hope for the future. As sponsors of memorial events that were for the South "virtually the only cultural expression concerned with the meaning of the war," LMAs took an early and defining role in shaping public memory of the Lost Cause, nationally as well as in the South. Creating a widely accepted vision of the meaning of the Confederacy, they contributed to national reunification on largely southern terms. In North Carolina, their work also undergirded the reclamation of elite leadership in a social hierarchy disturbed by war and Reconstruction. Moreover, as historians Anne Firor Scott, Anastatia Sims, and others have demonstrated, it was through these memorial associations that southern white women first began to participate in organizational leadership in their communities: in such associations, whose purpose served the goals and had the approval of southern white men, women were not only permitted but encouraged to assume semipublic leadership roles hitherto unfamiliar in most of the South. Avowedly apolitical yet politically shrewd in their strategies, beginning promptly after the war these women used gender conventions to accomplish goals that would have been difficult or impossible for their male compatriots.[2]

The story of the Ladies Memorial Association of Wake County and the North Carolina Monumental Association illuminates several interlocking themes: the roles of the women and men who worked together in these organizations as elite women tempered by war stepped readily into leadership positions, where they combined feminine deference with executive and persuasive skills; the sometimes dramatic interaction of memorial pursuits with political events from the first years of Reconstruction through the 1890s; and the ways in which these history-minded women retold the saga of their own accomplishments to suit changing times.

In May 1866, a small group of Raleigh citizens met to organize the Ladies Memorial Association of Wake County. Several of them had recently sought out the graves of Confederate soldiers throughout the town and county and found them in sadly neglected condition. To remedy this situation, the "object of the association" was a simple one: to "protect and care for the graves of our Confederate soldiers." Despite its name, the organization, like many LMAs, included men as well as women. At their initial meeting on May 23, the members heard a prayer and a brief address by a local Presbyterian minister, then elected officers, all women. The founders recalled that they had been inspired by the example of other LMAs across the region. After the first LMA formed four months earlier in Columbus, Georgia, to plan spring memorial services, it had sent an appeal to "the ladies throughout the South" for a Confederate decoration day to be "handed down as a religious custom of the South."[3]

In 1866, Raleigh was under Federal occupation, as it had been since city leaders had peacefully surrendered to Gen. William T. Sherman's troops on April 13, 1865. The military presence, however, had been reduced to a skeleton force, and under Presidential Reconstruction a provisional state government was in effect, for the state had not yet returned to the Union. The revised state constitution eliminated slavery but did not permit suffrage for blacks. Former Confederates and former Unionists, despite bitter political conflict, were working to rebuild the economy. To a considerable degree the antebellum elite had resumed its accustomed dominance if not regained its wealth.

Like most LMAs, the Wake County organization was led by women associated with the antebellum upper classes and closely involved with the Confederate cause. The founding leaders had coped with the losses and challenges of the war and evidently welcomed the opportunity for postwar leadership and activity. By all accounts, the moving spirit behind the

LMA was Sophia Partridge (1817–81; fig. 9.2), its first secretary. A native of Vienna, New York, she came to North Carolina as a child and in 1846 established Miss Partridge's Select School for Young Ladies in Raleigh, where she taught academic subjects, arts, and deportment. Keeping her school open through the war, this adopted Southerner had her students make bandages and dressings for the men who filled the city's Confederate hospitals. "Until the close of the war, she was found in the hospitals, cheering and comforting the sick and wounded, and when these died, she saw that boards with their names were placed at the heads of their graves, and thus were the names of many preserved."[4]

After the war, according to her fellow LMA leader Peter Pescud, it was Partridge who conceived the idea of an association "for the re-interment and future care of our dead braves." She brought to the endeavor a strong sense of order and system, as shown in her ongoing determination to mark and re-mark soldiers' graves and keep records of their names and regiments. Pescud observed that "no mother ever nursed her first born with the care she gave to keeping the cemetery in good order, and to making the Memorial Association a success." He also asserted that it was "to *her* influence and persistent exertions, that the *first* Confederate cemetery in the late Confederacy . . . was organized."[5]

The group selected as president Nancy Haywood Blount Branch (1817–1903; fig. 9.3). Like many LMA presidents, she was a socially prominent widow of a Confederate officer, Gen. Lawrence O'Bryan Branch. Both were well-educated members of leading eastern North Carolina planter families. Lawrence Branch, a Princeton-educated attorney, president of the Raleigh and Gaston Railroad, and United States congressman from 1855 to 1861, enlisted in 1861 and became a brigadier general. He was killed by a sharpshooter in 1862 while serving under Gen. "Stonewall" Jackson. Nancy Branch donned black for the rest of her life (as did many Confederate widows) and gained a reputation as "one of the best informed students of war history in the South." She brought to the LMA presidency not only her status as a general's widow and her political and social connections but also, as LMA minutes suggest, the administrative skills, diplomacy, and firmness needed to pursue the association's goals in perilous times.[6]

The men and women of the LMA worked together to accomplish their mission but adhered to a traditional gender division of labor. President Branch regularly called upon the men to carry out such tasks as property negotiations, organizing heavy labor, and public speaking. She had the women focus their efforts on planning and persuasion, fund-raising, and social and ceremonial events. Men and women sometimes worked independently but often in cooperation, and Branch appointed key committees with equal numbers of men and women. At the first meeting, on May

FIG. 9.2. *Sophia Partridge, the moving spirit behind Raleigh's LMA and its first secretary, from the* Raleigh Times, *January 23, 1937.* (NCDAH)

FIG. 9.3. *Nancy Haywood Blount Branch, the first president of Raleigh's LMA, from* The Confederate Veteran, *date unknown.* (NCDAH)

23, 1866, she appointed a "Ways and Means" Committee of ten ladies and ten gentlemen, plus twenty young ladies to solicit subscriptions among the public. She asked three men to explore suitable locations for a Confederate cemetery and three women, aided by a male attorney, to draft a constitution.[7]

The committees reported promptly at the June 16, 1866, meeting. The women began the constitution with a statement that conveyed a spirit of undefeated gentility: "We may be poor, but enough is left to prove our hearts to be still rich in the treasures of gratitude and affection." Although they could not adorn their cemetery with "storied urn or sculptured pillar," its hallowed grounds would "by the strength of patriotism and love, loom up as the loftiest obelisks, on which are inscribed, the deeds of a hundred hard fought fields." During the war the Southern woman had nursed and cheered the dying soldier; now, "let her last labor of love be, to collect his remains within the sacred enclosure" and assure them proper care. The constitution went on to define the duties of the officers and board of managers (all women) and authorized the board to appoint six men to meet with them as "the President's Council."

The men of the cemetery committee reported on their visit to the burial ground near the rock quarry southeast of Raleigh, where they found four

"*A Strong Force of Ladies*" | 219

to five hundred Confederate graves. Located near the former Confederate Pettigrew Hospital taken over by Union troops at the end of the war, the grounds lay neglected, with the inscriptions on the headboards defaced and nearly effaced. The committee recommended immediate action to preserve these "mementoes of the dead" lest the names fade away entirely. The cemetery site itself would have been suitable had it not been used for burial of Union soldiers as well, whose graves now surrounded the Confederate dead. After considering the notion of planting hedges to separate the Confederates and Federals, the committee recommended establishing a new cemetery.

President Branch appointed a committee of three women and three men to select and obtain a site. They approached civic leader Henry Mordecai, asking him to donate land for the Confederate graves. They promised to form a company later to purchase and develop his adjoining property as a cemetery and park, but Mordecai responded, "the Ladies' Memorial Association are welcome to as many acres of my land as they need for such a sacred purpose, without any consideration."[8]

By autumn 1866, work was proceeding apace. The women had set about raising money, selling life subscriptions of $100 each and many small annual subscriptions, organizing a sewing circle, and planning a winter bazaar. On November 17, the LMA published an appeal for help in clearing and leveling the forested and irregular terrain. "The young men who have volunteered their services, and the citizens generally, who take any interest in the work" were asked to meet on Monday morning at the Memorial Cemetery "for the purpose of commencing work on the place. Each one is requested to bring either an axe, pick, or spade, and come prepared to remain all day." Meanwhile, Capt. George Mordecai Whiting took charge of transferring Confederate remains from the Rock Quarry Cemetery and elsewhere. He and three young women re-marked the headboards in pencil and made a list of names before the graves were opened. Plans were sketched for the layout of the cemetery, and a stone monument there was under discussion. By the beginning of 1867, preparation of the grounds had progressed substantially, but the cost of removing trees, grading and terracing, clearing walkways, and digging graves had used up all the funds.[9]

The LMA members mounted a carefully orchestrated, suitably feminine appeal to the state legislature for help. They had a friendly legislator introduce a request for $1,500, hopeful that the legislature, which included many former Confederates, would support their cause. On February 14, they published in the Raleigh *Sentinel* a report timed to appear on the day of the vote. Typical of the LMA, the report strategically blended sentiment and system aimed at the hearts as well as the heads of the legislators.

"Friends of the Ladies Memorial Association," the report began reassuringly, would be "pleased to learn" that the cemetery was nearly prepared and would be ready for reburials within eight to ten days. Claiming broad public support, the LMA hoped that "every lady in Raleigh and Wake County, will feel it to be a sacred pleasure . . . to aid in decorating the Cemetery" and along with "hundreds of little girls," would be represented by a shrub or flower "planted by their own hands." The association leaders would "*expect, and will rely* upon the young men . . . to assist in the disinterment and burial of their late comrades in arms." They explained that only because of the widespread poverty of the times and the unexpectedly high costs of grading and draining were they "constrained to appeal . . . to their friends in the Legislature" for $1,500 to complete their "labor of love."

Demonstrating their systematic approach to an immense task, the LMA explained in the *Sentinel* that 750 to 800 men had to be reburied: "Their names and register will be alphabetically arranged and numbered, and corresponding numbers will be placed on a square capped post to be placed at the head of each grave," while the remains of 170 whose names were unknown would be buried under two or more mounds "surmounted with a cannon reversed, *if allowed*." Softening the impact of the mass burial, the LMA envisioned a design that met the picturesque ideals of the era: "At each angle of the cemetery will be a thatched summer house, of hexagon or octagon shape, arranged with seats, of gothic finish, and surmounted with a cross. An osage orange hedge will be planted next the fence, and a flower bed along the borders. The monument, mounds, graves and summer houses will be approached by winding gravel walks, neatly turfed and leading from the centre mound." The report ended on a practical note: "They need 10 hands daily for several weeks, and their friends will be called upon for laborers by Superintendent Watson, who will hire hands for any who wish to assist, at 75 cts. per day."

That same day, as the bill came before the legislature, the women left nothing to chance. When the House of Commons took up the LMA petition, the request was, as the *Sentinel* reported, "backed up by a strong force of ladies in the gallery." Under the eyes of the women, the House passed the bill without opposition and sped it to the Senate, where "the rules were suspended and the resolution passed its several readings unanimously." The LMA's strategy was carefully devised to use womanly persuasion without overstepping gender conventions. Although women were precluded from speaking before the General Assembly, LMA leaders had arranged to have their bill introduced, quietly lobbied their friends, and then arrived to support their bill. This may well have been the first time North Carolina women had filled the galleries of the Capitol to encourage passage of a bill; after their success in 1866 women repeatedly used this acceptably feminine form of political expression.[10]

Events soon took an unexpected turn. In everyone's mind in mid-February was the Congressional Reconstruction bill, which was opposed by President Andrew Johnson but supported by the chairman of the House Committee on Reconstruction Thaddeus Stevens and the Radical Republican majority. In response to southern states' 1866 rejection of the Fourteenth Amendment and black suffrage, along with conservatives' success in regaining power under Presidential Reconstruction, the Congressional plan imposed stiffer voting and officeholding restrictions on former Confederates and required ratification of the Fourteenth Amendment and new state constitutions allowing blacks to vote. To enforce these policies, Congress placed the southern states under newly organized military rule, which assumed authority over state governments.[11]

In Raleigh, tensions ran high as each day brought news of developments in Washington. The Raleigh *Sentinel* counseled calm and introduced a humor column: "In these gloomy times, when men born free in a free Republic formed by Washington and the fathers, are threatened with political slavery by a despotic majority, we may as well laugh as cry, since there is no help for it, but quiet submission or removal." Viewing passage of the bill as inevitable, the editor only hoped that under the new military occupation, the Union officer assigned to Raleigh would be "a sensible, discreet man, and a thorough gentleman, such as we esteem Col. [James V.] Bomford ... to be."[12]

With national developments still pending, the local situation shifted dramatically. On February 20, the LMA Board of Managers called a special meeting: "Ways and means were discussed for the removal of the Confederate Dead, the Association having been notified that Confederate soldiers buried at the Rock Quarry Cemetery must be removed immediately to make room for the Federal Dead."[13] Spurred by the order, the LMA adopted final plans for the cemetery, using a simpler scheme than originally envisioned and deferring hopes for a monument there. The group also decided to go ahead with a public fund-raiser at the State Capitol planned for February 22: a lecture given by Confederate general R. E. Colston, superintendent of the Hillsborough Military Academy, on the life and heroism of Stonewall Jackson. Meanwhile, LMA members and Capt. George Whiting quickly organized the onerous task of moving the graves. On February 22, they urgently requested the help of "the Young, Middle-Aged, and Old Men of Wake," on the next Monday and Tuesday "and longer if necessary" to begin the removal of the Confederate remains. Gentlemen "who cannot personally attend ... can assist very much by hiring a hand or two, or sending a waggon or cart."[14]

The response was heartening, but the work proceeded slowly. On February 28, the LMA encouraged the "gallant boys ... so zealously working":

"Your brows are already crowned with wreaths of laurel, on each field from Bethel to Bentonsville, and you are now linking your names, in the memories of the fairer sex, with those martyred ones who never flinched, when duty called." "We behold in you ... that devotion to principle, which justly belongs to the sons of Carolina, and pledge ourselves to *sustain* you to the last." The task was far from over: "Be of good cheer, the more difficult the undertaking, the greater will be the cause for exultation, when the work is complete, and the last evergreen is planted to mark that sacred spot, where repose in peace the ashes of your gallant comrades." By March 6, the remains of 269 men had been moved, and it was predicted that the rest would be moved within ten days.[15]

As the workers labored against the Federal deadline, national political events continued to unfold. After the Reconstruction bill passed on March 2 over Johnson's veto, the *Sentinel* editor advised on March 6, "it is the duty of all citizens of the Southern States, who remain in them, to obey the law and conform peaceably to the requirements of those who rule over us." Defense of heritage took on new meaning: though "the 'old North State' [was] legislated out of political vitality on the 2nd day of March 1867," certain comforts remained: "We still have the prestige of a right noble old Commonwealth *that was*. We may still tell our children of the erewhile goodly old state."

In the midst of all this, LMA secretary Sophia Partridge described the stresses of the times in a letter to a friend: "I tell you I want to get away from this same old place, much as I love it. A Yankee Cem. of 15 acres a Yankee camp & hospital white and black soldiers constantly passing and repassing, fighting and cussing is a little too much for me.... Another week will see us under military rule, and Raleigh is to be the headquarters; military force increased & etc." Partridge also witnessed the collapse of some who were pushed beyond the breaking point. In one case, the unique appeal of the Ladies Memorial Association captured the disturbed imagination of William Holland Thomas, a Confederate officer who had led a famous regiment of Cherokee troops. "Suffering under mental derangement, growing out of the excitements of the times," as the *Sentinel* explained later, he had evidently been inspired by General Colston's recent LMA fund-raising lecture on Stonewall Jackson. Partridge reported:

> Col. Thomas is in Raleigh deranged. He went to the Commandant of the Post the other day and told him he expected to be arrested in a few days and warned him not to send a private ... as he should kill him said just send an officer and he would walk right down. Col Bomford said he would go himself. All right he said That's the style. He went to see Mrs Russ and told her he was going to deliver a lecture the next night for the

FIG. 9.4. *National Cemetery, Raleigh. Photograph ca. 1890s.* (NCDAH)

benefit of the Memorial Asso. His Indians would be down in the train and lecture in the Cherokee language and he would interpret. Well he was missing the next night and when found was in the capitol face & hands stained, dressed in Indian costume waiting for an audience. Now he is looking for headquarters for his 600 Indians for the protection of Raleigh. His brother in law Love, is trying to get him away. Is it not sad. I expect more of our noble patriots will go crazy at the degradation and meanness heaped upon the south.[16]

I have to go over to the Cemetery quite often. We have moved 447, all out of the Yankee line, and another week or ten days will I expect complete the work of removing all the bodies, then we will begin to set out evergreens and flowers and make improvements. Did I tell you in my last that the Yankees notified us that we must remove our dead *immediately* to make room for theirs? We felt insulted. They are making a National Cem. here and moving all their dead from other parts of the state here. Load after load of pine box coffins pass by here every day, and a great many of them are not more than 2 or three ft long, short Yankees they. I suppose though they are only pieces of them.[17]

The drama and unpleasantness of the removal etched the event into the memories of participants and made it a central theme in the creation history of the association. In 1882, Peter Pescud reiterated calmly enough how he, "aided by the ladies, received and superintended the re-interment of the remains." Then he flared out at the "heartlessness of the wretch sent by the authorities at Washington City to prepare a cemetery for the Federal dead, in which confiscated ground were interred most of our dead. The said *Nero* sent insulting messages to the Memorial Association, insisting on the removal of the Confederate dead before the cemetery was in readiness for the graves to be opened, and finally threatened that if our dead were not removed by a given day, their remains would be placed in the public road." Vindication did come, however, for when the post commandant was informed of the situation, he "severely rebuked the man in charge of the Federal cemetery."[18]

The gruesome nature of the work left the strongest memory. Years later, Pescud remembered, "when most of the coffins reached the cemetery they needed repairs. Others were half full of most offensive fluid, and as the coffins at the top leaked badly, in removing them from the wagons to the graves the persons and clothing of those thus employed were thoroughly saturated; but such was the love of our noble boys for their late companions in arms, and so heartily did they sympathize with the ladies in their work of love, that none flinched or complained."[19]

One of the "noble boys" remembered the work from a different perspective. David Whiting, then aged about fifteen, was the brother of Capt. George Whiting, who was directing the removal. Late in his life he recalled:

> I was there helping too (I always turned up if anything was doing). There were about 15 of the Raleigh boys helping and some just looking on. The negroes were free and the whites had to work. As the wagons would come in with the boxes containing the remains of some Confederate soldier we would take it out of the wagon carry it to a grave and let it in with ropes.... Some of the boxes were decaying and the bottoms would drop out and sometimes the foot end would give way but it was on the bill and to be done now we commenced it. Bill Pell put his hands under a box at the head end and I was lifting the foot end and it was lower on account of my height. When the lid slid off and the foot board came with it and the body ... started toward me, I dropped my end because the man in it scared me. His hair had grown all around his body to his feet and it was thick and as coarse as horse hair and he had a sword buckled to his waist.... I ran for home with Bill Pell trying to catch me but a flying machine could not have done it that day. I did not go back for two or three days. Brother George said I wouldn't make a soldier.... 50 years afterwards our good work is forgotten and no one knows or cares how it was done or who did it.[20]

By the end of March, the LMA had accomplished much. The transfer from the Rock Quarry Cemetery was finished, along with the reburial of nearly all the Confederate remains found elsewhere in the county. They filled more than five hundred graves, more than half with North Carolinians. "As soon as we shall be blessed with fair weather, the work of turning and ornamenting will be commenced," predicted the *Sentinel* on March 21.

As spring arrived and the "ornamenting" proceeded, resilient gentility and optimism rendered the grim removal of late winter a thing of the past. By early May, the Memorial Cemetery had become "the resort, every afternoon, of numbers of our townspeople." "Under the assiduous culture of our ladies, the grounds are daily becoming more and more beautiful and attractive. In twelve months from this time, when the flower-plants, mosses and shrubbery shall have fully developed, it will be one of the loveliest spots in all the land. Go to the Cemetery when you will, and fresh flowers may be found upon graves of sleeping heroes, here and there. Most of our young ladies have selected two or three mounds, the preservation and decoration of which are to constitute their peculiar 'labor of love.'"[21]

At the LMA meeting on May 3, President Branch's first annual report related the year's accomplishments with little hint of the tensions involved. She thanked the young men for their work, reported that many marked headboards were in place, and commended the "efficient Board of Managers and able Council of gentlemen associated with me" for being "prompt and faithful" in their duties and for their "general efficiency and zeal."[22]

But a more pressing topic occupied the May 3 gathering—that of ceremonies to honor the Confederate dead. Throughout the South that spring, LMAs were sponsoring memorial events at which they decorated Confederate graves with flowers. The Raleigh LMA negotiated carefully the limits of its capacity to honor the Confederate dead under the newly imposed Union military presence. Setting the stage, the *Sentinel* carried reports—probably supplied by the LMA—of recent observances in Georgia and other states, where businesses closed in honor of the day and "the ladies formed in procession, each bearing a floral offering, and marched to the cemetery, where memorial wreaths were deposited on the graves." Closer to home, however, it was reported, "The military authorities at Newbern prohibited the procession contemplated by the ladies of the Memorial Association of that City, on the occasion of laying the corner-stone of the Confederate mausoleum, in Cedar Grove Cemetery, on yesterday. The exercises at the Cemetery, however, were to be conducted according to the published program."[23]

At their April 24 meeting, the LMA members had discussed whether to hold any "*public* demonstration in honor of the Confederate Dead." By May 3, they were planning the "order of arrangements for the 10th of May, as the anniversary of the death of Gen. T. J. Jackson and showing appropriate honors to our Confederate Dead." A vote was taken as to "whether the ceremonies of the day should be public or strictly private. Decided they should be public so far as to meet on the capitol square or in the capitol and proceed from thence in procession to the cemetery."[24]

The decision to stage a procession and public ceremony was a politically charged one under the terms of military rule. The care with which the

LMA publicized its plans suggests the delicacy of the situation. On May 4, the *Sentinel* reported on the previous day's LMA meeting and announced, "It was decided to commemorate the 10th. of May,—the anniversary of the death of Jackson and of the formation of the Association—by becoming memorial observances. There will be no attempt at formal display." The ladies of the association would meet at the Capitol at 5 P.M. and "quietly repair to the Cemetery, for the purpose of decorating the hallowed mounds of the sleeping brave." On the day of the event, the *Sentinel* confirmed that ceremonies would be "observed as heretofore announced. . . . We are requested to say that the ladies will assemble at the Capitol *at half past 3 o'clock* with their votive offerings of flowers and evergreens, whence they will quietly proceed to the Cemetery, for the purpose of decoration and other observances." The article stressed that the spirit prompting the event was "in accordance with that holy feeling of veneration for the memory of the patriot brave and of departed friends, that prevails in all Christian lands."[25]

After the ceremony, the *Sentinel* described it as "one of the most beautiful, attractive and imposing we have ever witnessed." At the hour appointed, "hundreds of persons wended their way to the Cemetery—many in vehicles, but most on foot—fair women, little children and even many of our most prominent and venerable citizens—so that [when] the ceremonies commenced, there was probably assembled a concourse of between five and six hundred deeply moved and interested spectators." The cemetery observance proceeded with a prayer by a former chaplain of North Carolina troops, a hymn by a choir of gentlemen, and a brief oration by Seaton Gales (Civil War veteran and editor of the *Sentinel*). Gales recalled that a year ago to the day, the women had met at the Capitol and "in detached and mournful groups" placed flowers on the "dispersed and isolated" sites of Confederate graves. After that "pilgrimage of love," they had decided to gather all the remains "in one consecrated spot." Now, he proclaimed, "Looking around you, this bright and balmy afternoon," upon the cemetery they had established, "you may well feel a grateful pride, a holy satisfaction, in the consummation of your labors and your hopes"[26] (fig. 9.5).

Probably with an eye to the Federal presence, Gales spoke with resignation of the defeated cause, which "whether right or wrong, was inexpressibly dear to our hearts" as were those who had defended it. "The cause is gone;—the flag which symbolized it, is folded up and laid aside forever. We bow before the decree of that Providence which, however inscrutably to finite vision, doeth all things well." He acknowledged, "We may not build for them lofty monuments of marble or of bronze—for we are poor; we may not celebrate their prowess with pomp, with procession and with pageantry, for we are vanquished; we may not make public demonstration of

FIG. 9.5. *Confederate Cemetery, Raleigh. Photograph 1868, made for the LMA.* (NCDAH)

our sorrow or our gratitude—for that, perhaps, would be unbecoming," but he assured listeners that their devotion and floral tributes were sufficient to hallow and decorate the graves. With that, he invited the ladies to commence their "holy task"—"Go scatter those flowers, which so aptly prefigure the brightness of the resurrection morn!"[27]

In the *Sentinel* report of a large public ceremony on a beautiful day in May, only Gales's references to the lack of procession and public demonstration hinted at the political issues the participants faced. Yet the decision to have a procession, the very formality of the event, and the glowing report of its beauty in the newspaper constituted a genteel but unmistakable defiance of any sense of subjugation to the occupying force. In other cities such as New Bern, occupying officers forbade "formation of processions." Possibly President Branch and her colleagues devised a ceremony that both obeyed and flouted such regulations. Union officers in Raleigh may have been more tolerant than in some other cities. A key figure was probably Col. James V. Bomford, commandant of the Raleigh post, who earned the respect of Raleigh citizens for his "gentlemanly bearing" and fair administration of "delicate and responsible duties." Indeed, the chivalrous post commandant, according to Peter Pescud, had come with his family to the first anniversary observance. He "brought a large quantity of rare flowers to the cemetery, stood uncovered in front of the orator during the delivery of his address, and then placed the flowers over the graves of our dead." It is not hard to imagine that LMA leaders and Colonel Bomford arrived at a mutually satisfactory agreement about honoring the dead, but there is no evidence of any negotiations.[28] Peaceful at the time, this event, like the transfer of graves, gained drama as its story was retold over the decades.

With the cemetery established, the LMA continued to make improvements. In the summer of 1867, the members renewed efforts to erect a permanent monument there, but by 1869, they had raised only part of the funds. President Branch advised, before resigning her office in August of that year, that the money was "inadequate to the erection of a monument yet not to its commencement, which in my humble opinion would be judicious, as it would have a tendency to stimulate and arouse persons to action." Her method worked, for in 1870, the monument, a simple stone obelisk, was dedicated (figs. 9.6 and 9.8). It was inscribed with a poem by Capt. George Whiting, who had died that February and was buried nearby.[29]

In the ensuing decades, the LMA participated in various endeavors—publication in 1882 of their own history by Peter Pescud; reburial of North Carolina soldiers' remains from Gettysburg (1871) and Arlington (1883) in their cemetery; contributions to a local Confederate soldiers' home and to Confederate cemeteries in Virginia and elsewhere; and ceremonies honoring Jefferson Davis, whose casket lay in state in the North Carolina State Capitol en route from New Orleans to Richmond in 1893 (fig. 9.7). They also continued improvement of their cemetery, and in the mid-1870s, replaced the decaying headboards with granite markers (fig. 9.8), numbered to correspond to a list, which the ever orderly Sophia Partridge "prepared in triplicate," depositing copies with county and state officials.[30]

Each year, the LMA sponsored the May 10 ceremony, which grew more elaborate following the return to political power of former Confederate leaders. These men had organized as Conservatives to oppose the Republicans in 1867. They took the name of the national Democratic Party in

FIG. 9.6. "Monument to Confederate Dead." Half of stereograph card from "In and Around Raleigh, N.C. Oakwood Cemetery" series by Rufus Morgan, 1870s. (Courtesy of the North Carolina Collection, University of North Carolina at Chapel Hill Library)

FIG. 9.7. *Parade in Raleigh for Jefferson Davis's casket en route from New Orleans to Richmond, 1893.* (NCDAH)

FIG. 9.8. *Confederate Cemetery, obelisk and stone markers. Photograph by Anne Miller, 2000.* (NCDAH)

1876, the election that brought an end to Reconstruction and withdrawal of federal troops in 1877. Beginning in 1883, the LMA instituted a practice of having each Memorial Day speaker pay tribute to a North Carolina Confederate officer and publishing the lectures as a record of Confederate history. In time, the tenor of the memorial addresses shifted from simply honoring the dead to a broader vindication of North Carolinians' valor and the rightness of the Confederate cause.

In the 1890s, the memorial movement took a new turn, as its leaders began the effort to raise a state Confederate monument. By this time, a trend had begun throughout the South of erecting memorials on civic sites as well as in burial grounds. Veterans in North Carolina raised the idea in the mid-1880s. Democratic leader and publisher Samuel A'Court Ashe ran several articles in his Raleigh *News and Observer* promoting patriotic shrines and monuments, and at the LMA's 1885 Memorial Day oration, former newspaper editor and congressman Col. Alfred Moore Waddell proclaimed that the Confederate dead deserved "to be perpetuated otherwise than by such memorial marbles as private affection may erect." No action was taken, however, for several years.[31]

In 1892, as the nation faced economic and social turmoil and North Carolina Democrats worried that a "third party" (later the Populist Party) might divide the loyalties of the white electorate, a few prominent Democratic veterans began a campaign for a state Confederate memorial. They included Capt. Samuel A'Court Ashe, the aforementioned publisher of the *News and Observer;* Col. Edward D. Hall, state veterans organization leader; and Capt. Octavius Coke, North Carolina secretary of state, known as the "old warhorse of Democracy." Soon realizing that the monument drive required women's involvement, they sought the help of the LMA. In June, the LMA called a public meeting at the supreme court featuring a speech by Captain Coke, to which they invited all wives and daughters of Confederate soldiers and all others interested in "preserving the glorious memory of the dead."[32]

By July 1892, the North Carolina Monumental Association (NCMA) had been formed with a female "board of management" called the Lady Managers, a male "advisory board," including Ashe and Coke, and Mrs. Armistead Jones as president, Miss Meggie Cowper secretary, and Donald W. Bain (the state treasurer) as treasurer. (After Bain's death in November 1892, Col. Samuel McDowell Tate succeeded him in both positions.) Election of Nancy Branch Jones (fig. 9.9) as president cemented

FIG. 9.9. *Nancy Branch (Mrs. Armistead) Jones. Photograph early twentieth century. (Courtesy of Nancy Branch Maupin [Mrs. Charles] Neely)*

the link with the LMA, since she was not only a "leader of society" whose husband was prominent in the Democratic Party, but also the daughter of Nancy Branch, founding president of the LMA.[33]

In their first year, the NCMA leaders considered possible sites for a state Confederate monument, including Nash Square, a Raleigh civic park, and explored potential sources of designs. To boost "enthusiasm and interest" statewide, President Jones recruited female vice-presidents in nearly every county. In Raleigh, the ladies organized a September "lawn party" fundraiser at Nash Square, featuring a Confederate concert, a tent full of Confederate relics, and a reenactment of a Confederate camp scene complete with some of the "best known citizens of the city" in their old uniforms. The event proved such a hit that it ran several days longer than planned and brought in substantial contributions.[34]

By the end of 1892, however, it was clear that private fund-raising was inadequate, and the NCMA turned to the (predominantly Democratic) legislature for an appropriation of $10,000. As in 1866, the women focused full attention on the legislators when the latter convened early in 1893. "The ladies" joined the committee on appropriation before the bill was presented, and when the bill came up, they "took the House by storm"—crowding the galleries, filling the lobbies and aisles of the chamber, and even sitting on the steps of the speaker's stand, all to the immense approval of the *News and Observer:* "In the presence of so many fair patriots, for the ladies are always more devoted in their love of country than men are, there was no disposition manifested to antagonize the Monument bill." With little dissent, the appropriation was approved in both houses, with the added provisions that the monument be built of North Carolina stone and stand on the Capitol Square. The mandated position on the prime public site in the state confirmed the official identification of the state with the North Carolina Monumental Association's cause.[35]

Within the NCMA the men exerted more authority than in the Ladies Memorial Association, but the women's prominence increased after their success with the legislature. The association maintained a genteel image of harmony and deference along traditional gender lines; only occasionally did any hint of tension enter the record. On October 26, 1893—eight long months after the appropriation passed—President Jones and the Lady Managers met to receive a committee's recommendation of the site and to consider selection of the design; the minutes noted that "a number of gentlemen, members of the Association, were also present." The committee recommended the south side of the Capitol Square, but a long debate ensued as other men refused to give up on Nash Square. Finally and perhaps with some impatience, the Lady Managers settled the issue by accepting the legislated Capitol site, with the specific spot still to be determined.[36]

FIG. 9.10. *Drawing of North Carolina Confederate Monument*, Muldoon Monument Company brochure, date unknown, Louisville, Kentucky. (NCDAH)

The next topic was the choice of the design. Upon motion of one of the women, a "special committee of five of the Lady Managers was appointed to select a design." But the treasurer, Colonel Tate, swiftly suggested that a committee of "three experienced gentlemen" be appointed to "serve with" the women as "consulting members, in relation to the details of the plan." President Jones acceded and appointed Tate, Confederate general R. F. Hoke, and Col. W. J. Hicks, an architect-builder. The record is silent as to the women's reaction to Tate's insistence on the men's participation.

The eight men and women met promptly and recommended a design from the Muldoon Monument Company of Louisville, Kentucky (fig. 9.10). When the design committee met again, they "invited" Colonel Hicks "as an architect to supervise the whole," and after "close inspection and inquiry on the part of Gen. Hoke and Col. Tate," settled on the design. A contract was drawn up and signed by President Jones. With key decisions made, though with less than half of the $25,000 cost in hand and fund-raising curtailed by the national economic depression of 1893, the NCMA followed a strategy proposed by Nancy Jones's mother nearly twenty-five years earlier: "It was believed wisest to lay the corner stone, believing this would encourage the progress of the work."[37]

FIG. 9.11. *Ribbon for North Carolina Monumental Association cornerstone-laying event, 1894. The event was actually held on May 22 because May 20 was a Sunday. (North Carolina Museum of History)*

The cornerstone-laying, held on May 22, 1894, proved a "great event," with a procession of dignitaries, eloquent oratory, and military features (fig. 9.11). The women of the statewide NCMA filled half the grandstand. Confederate veterans leader Col. E. D. Hall laid the cornerstone, which the women had made into a reliquary of the Lost Cause. Several relics came with provenances that intensified their meaning: one woman contributed a box containing a lock of Gen. Robert E. Lee's hair "cut in the tent of Gen.

[James J.] Pettigrew, with his autograph card" and "a strand plucked from the tail of Gen. Lee's horse, Traveler, by Walker Anderson"; the bullet that killed General Pettigrew's horse at the Battle of Gettysburg, taken out by a Major Collins; and a piece of the apple tree from the site of Gen. Robert E. Lee's surrender at Appomattox Court House, Virginia, given by Gen. W. J. Hardee.[38]

Rhetoric of the day illustrated the emerging defense of the Confederate cause as well as the honor of the men who fought for it. Providing insight into the developing Confederate celebration, Walter Grimes, legislator for the bill, expounded on Confederate valor and explained that in the South the word "patriotism" had a meaning unique in the world: "with us it not only means love of home and love of country, but it means loyalty to the memory of those who laid down their lives for a cause that was just and honorable." This was the "patriotism," he proclaimed, that the women of the South had been instilling "into the heart ... of every child of the South for thirty years."[39]

After the event, fund-raising continued, fueled as predicted by the cornerstone-laying and led by President Jones, who took an ever more public role, sending out appeals statewide and publishing letters above her name in the newspapers. But the NCMA soon faced unprecedented challenges in the face of a rapidly changing political landscape. For years, the Republicans, including many black voters, had regularly opposed the Democrats in North Carolina, though with little success, as Democrats used racial fears and the specter of a return to Reconstruction to win often narrow victories. Amid the hard times of the early 1890s, however, the third-party Populist movement gained strength among whites, including longtime Democrats and especially farmers, frustrated by entrenched "Bourbon" Democrats who favored big business and rebuffed proposals for progressive reforms. In 1894, the Republicans and Populists joined forces as Fusionists and defeated the Democrats in a victory that surprised the winners and stunned the losers. The General Assembly that took office in 1895 was "overwhelmingly Fusionist" and included five blacks among the Republicans.[40]

For the heavily Democratic NCMA this startling defeat put the monument project in a very different position. The legislature of 1893 had "enthusiastically" appropriated $10,000, and by the end of 1894, private fund-raising had yielded an additional $5,000. But the construction of the monument was proceeding, with a projected completion date in April 1895, at which time full payment of the contract of $25,000 was expected. The NCMA turned again to the legislature for aid, in the form of a loan of $10,000.

This time, the NCMA bill faced strong opposition. "Do Not Pass It," urged the Populist Raleigh newspaper, the *Caucasian*. The editor insisted that public money would be better spent on the common schools and asserted, "It is not at all certain that any monuments ought to be built on either side to perpetuate the memories of our unnatural civil war. The sooner the rancors and hates of that unhappy struggle are forgotten by both North and South, the better it will be for the whole country." He believed that "There has not been one of these monuments inaugurated, either North or South, that has not been the occasion of stirring up sectional bitterness that would better be left to quietly perish."[41]

The women of the NCMA undertook the challenge. As the bill came up for debate, they again packed the Capitol. When the Senate took up the topic on February 23, "the galleries were crowded to their utmost capacity with the ladies and they filled the lobbies on floor of the Senate." The girls of St. Mary's College in Raleigh "graced the west lobby of the Senate," while the galleries were "packed with other lady friends of the bill." But despite the women's presence, after long and impassioned debate, the measure was defeated 28 to 8. Many of the "almost heart-broken dear ladies of the State," a friend wrote, "departed amidst the blinding tears of disappointment, sorrow, and regret."[42]

As luck would have it, an unrelated controversy had arisen a few days earlier that altered the fate of the monument bill. By tradition, legislators sometimes proposed that the body adjourn for the day in honor of notable public figures. On February 21, a black legislator had offered a resolution to adjourn in honor of Frederick Douglass, the African American leader who had died on February 20, and the House passed it. Democrats and the *News and Observer* pounced on the unexpected opportunity.

"Miscegenation Legislature Adjourns in Loving Memory of Fred Douglass," the newspaper crowed: "The affair . . . will be a vital blow in the State at the Fusionists." The *News and Observer,* recently acquired by Democratic partisan Josephus Daniels, accused legislators of honoring an "apostle of miscegenation"—a reference to Douglass's marriage to a white woman—and of thereby promoting "social equality" with its implication of interracial sexual relationships. The paper also drew patriotism into the brew, claiming (inaccurately) that the legislators had honored Douglass while refusing similar tributes to the birthdays of Lee and Washington. Other state newspapers joined the attack, and soon the national press was covering the story. The *News and Observer* relentlessly fanned the flames—"Shame, Shame, Shame" at the "General Assembly's Infamy"—and insisted that "All patriotic men must stand together to preserve the Anglo Saxon civilization."[43]

The *News and Observer* then devised the strategy of linking the Douglass resolution of February 21 with the defeat of the Confederate monument bill of February 23—at once intensifying public outrage at the Fusionists and infusing new life into the monument campaign. Although there was no inherent connection between the two events, on February 24, the *News*

FIG. 9.12. *Cartoon linking the North Carolina Confederate Monument to "Fred Douglas,"* News and Observer, *February 24, 1895.*

and Observer ran a cartoon (fig. 9.12) that tied them visually, in an image that juxtaposed white female purity and male blackness and miscegenation, with not-so-subtle hints of black dominance and white subjugation. It showed the white women kneeling beside their uncompleted monument, with one woman pleading with the racially mixed legislators, who are weeping over the coffin of "Fred Douglas." The two-part caption read: "Ladies Monumental Association to the Legislature Now in Session: 'Let us teach posterity that patriots die not in vain. A land without monuments is a land without memories. Lend us of your means to commemorate the virtues of our fallen dead'" and "The North Carolina General Assembly to the Ladies: 'It is not your dead, but our Fred over whom we weep. Bear with us, our hearts are in the coffin there with Caesar, and we must pause till they come back to us.'"

The plight of the "noble women" ill treated by the "miscegenist legislature" captured popular attention as part of the larger fracas. Legislators struggled to defend themselves in the growing firestorm of public opinion. Some insisted they had not voted for the resolution. Others defended their votes as innocent gestures of courtesy, not endorsements of miscegenation. One cited an old story that George Washington had doffed his hat and bowed to a black man "because he did not want to be outdone in polite manners by a negro" and said, "I felt that as the negroes in this House ... have for decades been pulling off their hats to my ideals, that it was not too much for me to doff mine once to theirs."[44]

Within days, many legislators came to see support for the monument as an antidote to the Douglass problem. On February 28, a new bill, this time for an appropriation rather than a loan, was placed before the Senate by Hiram Grant, a leading Republican and former Union officer who had abstained from the previous vote. A Democratic senator "congratulated the Senate on its change of sentiment." Speaker after speaker—including former opponents—lined up in support of the appropriation, while others still staunchly opposed it. One opponent insisted that "to build a monument to the Confederate dead could not rectify the mistake of that adjournment," but finally, after one senator changed his vote, the bill passed by a vote of 21 to 20. "Glory to God and the Confederate dead," cried a supporter. Upon passage of the bill, Sen. Theophilus White, a Confederate veteran from Perquimans County, crossed the aisle and shook Grant's hand, thanking God that "the time had come when there was no North, no South, no East, no West, but one common country of brothers in peace." According to the *News and Observer*, "There was prolonged cheering, and it was some time before order could be restored." The newspaper's headline rejoiced, "Blue and Gray join in honoring the Confederate dead."[45]

In the House, still raw from the Douglass furor, debate was emotional. Proponents waxed eloquent, some moving themselves and their audience to tears, while another threatened that no one "would ever be re-elected . . . who dared to vote against this bill." One representative still "opposed the bill because he said it came right upon the heels of the attacks of the *News and Observer*, that he had had many letters from his people denouncing the appropriation passed by the senate, and thought our duty was to the living and not to the dead." Another believed "the memories of the war should be buried out of sight, [and] he was in favor of digging a hole and burying all monuments (a murmur of groans)."

The women had again arrived in force, and they were not shy in making their feelings known. One speech brought loud approbation "from the galleries full of ladies, which the Speaker rapped down, saying he would allow reasonable applause, but not uproarious applause." At one point opponents moved to table the bill, and when that motion was defeated, "there was a flood of applause . . . and tears burst from the faces of some of the older mother-women while a smile swept over the faces of the gayly dressed younger women like light." Eventually the bill passed, 60 to 38. Reflecting on a triumph gained by the combined efforts of Democratic leaders, a relentless newspaper campaign, and the ladies' ostensibly apolitical appeals, the *News and Observer* exulted: "And the Women Win."[46]

With their state funds obtained, the NCMA moved toward completion of the monument, which was rising on the west side of Union Square. Almost daily, the *News and Observer* reported on its progress and the plans for the unveiling scheduled for May 20, 1895. Political tensions gave the upcoming celebration greater meaning: it not only symbolized shared reverence for the Confederate cause but also demonstrated Democrats' success in snatching victory from the Fusionists using the twin appeals of southern patriotism and white southern womanhood. The women's leadership in the memorial project perfectly suited the Democrats' need to undercut Fusionism, and the women rose to the occasion, following their legislative victory with plans for a patriotic extravaganza.

Reports building up to the unveiling shared the page with news of heated political struggles. The Fusionist legislature had authorized new charters in several cities, including Raleigh, which provided for direct local elections. As Raleigh's vote of May 6 neared, the *News and Observer* urged citizens to "leave no stone unturned to elect the Democratic ticket," unless they wished to return to the Reconstruction era's "Republican rule," "corruption," and "venality." On May 7, the newspaper announced the triumph of "pure white Democracy"—"The City Still Ours . . . No Negro Rule in Raleigh."

Meanwhile, crowds visited the monument site to watch the "dangerous and difficult work" as each section was put into place. NCMA President Jones appointed and published lists of committees, chaired by men, to handle Reception, Military, Veterans, Ways and Means, Transportation, Entertainment, Decorations, Music, and more. Immense crowds were predicted, including hundreds expected to arrive by rail, for which reduced rates had been arranged with the railroad companies. A moment of excitement came on May 8 when the "veil" was removed briefly from the completed monument for a photograph made for the Monumental Association. Two electric company linemen climbed up and removed the veil, "Mr. Wharton got in his fine work with a big camera," and soon the monument was "as closely shrouded with its white veil as ever." The "order of the march of procession" was published to encourage citizens along the route to decorate their homes and businesses.[47]

An ongoing theme was that of broad unity. "Everybody and his wife coming," ran one headline. Announcements reminded Raleigh citizens to make every veteran and visitor welcome. The message of unanimity underscored the notion that the Confederate cause had enjoyed the full support of the Southern people, dismissing from public memory both the resistance to the war, which had been bitter and strong in the state, and the more recent conflict over public support for the monument. Conveniently ignoring the fact that only the political fluke of the Douglass incident and relentless pressure had forced the legislature into funding completion of the monument, supporters created a public image of universal approbation for a noble cause.[48]

By attracting thousands of people from across the state and widespread public attention to the unveiling, the sponsors affirmed social stability and race loyalty despite widening class divisions. The emphasis on the shared Confederate tradition carried a powerful appeal to Populists to return to the Democratic fold. Thus did Julian S. Carr—Durham tobacco magnate, veterans' association leader, and Democratic supporter—publish an open invitation to "every Confederate soldier" in Durham County to join him in the procession in Raleigh "without regard to creed or party" and offered free transportation if needed.[49]

Enticing notices of social events—luncheons, afternoon receptions where the leading Confederate generals' widows would greet hundreds of veterans, a late-night ball after the unveiling—also whetted public interest. The NCMA planned a "Confederate Concert" to follow the unveiling, with a program of war songs and hymns sung by both men and women. It was to include a special "old camp scene" feature: "as the soldiers lying around on the ground, talk over the day's battle," a soloist sings "Tenting to Night," and then as reveille is heard, Miss Carrie Young "rushes into camp with a Confederate cap, singing a most enthusiastic war song," including the "Rebel yell" for which she had become famous.[50]

At the "Great Event" itself on May 20, 1895, the women of the NCMA took a visible but silent ceremonial role. At the front of the mile-long procession to the Capitol Square came carriages with the speakers and honored officials, including the officers of the Monumental Association. Behind them marched the chief marshal, contingents of military groups, local light infantry organizations, and ordered ranks of Confederate veterans, many flying the faded and battle-scarred flags of their units. "Conspicuous among those first to be escorted to the grand stand were Mrs. Armistead Jones, Mrs. Gen. W.L.O'B. Branch, Mrs. Gen. Stonewall Jackson and granddaughter Julia Jackson Christian, and Mrs. Gen. D. H. Hill and little granddaughter."

Prominently positioned on the grandstand among male dignitaries, the women sat quietly during the long ceremony, continuing their custom of having the men speak for them. Capt. Samuel A'Court Ashe welcomed the gathered crowd on behalf of the "ladies who undertook this work and whose devoted labor accomplished its completion." Another speaker saluted the women's success, providing as well a classic stereotype of woman's ideal qualities and role in public life. He expressed the wish that Mrs. President had not called upon him to speak, but had asked her executive committee instead. "But they, like the rest of the good women of North Carolina, have a way of doing as they please, and we men cannot stop them. It is good for us that we cannot, for they are always right; and we, nearly always wrong." The monument would not have been possible, he proclaimed, without the women's trait of "perseverance which never surrenders and which laughs at impossibilities and cries, 'it shall be done.'" Though "always modest, amiable and true," the daughters of the state "never retreat or surrender when once they unfurl their banner in a campaign of mercy or of love. 'Forward' is their command, and victory their goal." He acknowledged the decisive role of the women when the legislature threatened not to fund the monument: "when the voice of woman is heard ... speaking in her firm and modest way and saying that this monument shall be erected ... her low, sweet voice as enrapturing as the song of the sirens, and as mighty as the thunders of

Jupiter... startles the men from the seashore to the mountains, and behold this polished shaft as if touched by the wand of a magician leaps forth from out the rough quarry at her command."[51]

After more speeches, most expounding on the valor of North Carolina's fighting men and the patriotism of the Confederate cause, finally came the unveiling. Little Julia Jackson Christian (fig. 9.13) pulled the cord, and the veil dropped from the monument like "the garments of Elijah." Visible to the public at last, the monument of Mount Airy granite stood seventy-five feet tall. Resting upon a stepped base, a large block featured seals of the state and the Confederacy, flanked by dynamic, life-size bronze figures of an artilleryman and a cavalryman (fig. 9.14). From the block, a tall shaft rose to a Corinthian capital, upon which stood a ten-foot bronze figure of an infantryman (fig. 9.15). Realistically modeled by "Prof. Von Miller, the finest sculptor in bronze living," and cast at the Royal Foundry in Munich, these figures, like most Civil War monuments, honored the common soldier rather than high-ranking officers. The symbolic reversal of hierarchy stressed the shared experience of war and served the purposes of the organizers by promoting social unity across all classes. When darkness came, the spectacle increased as the monument was illuminated by a halo of electric lights.[52]

The "Great Event" grandly fulfilled the NCMA's hopes. It had attracted an estimated thirty thousand people and the attention of the entire state. Even the Populist newspaper lent its enthusiastic support to the event. A visiting northern officer praised the monument and commented that the South "would lose the respect of the world" if it did not thus honor its soldiers. Although many blacks came to watch the event, there was little mention in the papers of the black citizenry, except for a report that the northern officer saw "no notable difference between such a gathering here and in New England, except that the absence of the negroes would be marked in a New England procession." Outside the official stance of universal welcome, and at odds with the rhetoric seeking northern respect for southern valor, one Confederate veteran found that the ceremonies "were sadly marred, in the opinion of every ex-Confederate soldier with whom I have spoken, by a want of due consideration shown to ex-Federal soldiers, who were present for the purpose of uniting with us in doing honor to the bravest men that ever followed standard into action." For the sponsors, however, it was, as the *News and Observer* proclaimed, "a perfect success."[53]

A unique and lasting contribution was the May 20, 1895, "Woman's Edition" of the *News and Observer,* which gave the women a printed voice that served as a socially acceptable counterpoint to their customary silence on the public stage (fig. 9.16). Well in advance, the newspaper had announced that the "Monumental Issue" of the paper was to be "gotten out by the Ladies Monumental Association, under the supervision of Mesdames Ar-

FIG. 9.13. *Julia Jackson Christian, sketch*, News and Observer, *May 21, 1895. The granddaughter of Gen. "Stonewall" Jackson unveiled the monument.*

FIG. 9.14. *North Carolina Confederate Monument. Photograph 1895.* (NCDAH)

FIG. 9.15. *Statue of Confederate soldier for the top of the North Carolina Confederate Monument, uncrated prior to final placement, 1895.* (North Carolina Museum of History, Raleigh)

mistead Jones, John W. Hinsdale, and Garland Jones." The women would "write all the articles, solicit all the advertisements, correct the proof, and in every way have charge of the paper for that day" except setting the type and running the press. "The regular staff will be displaced, and a staff of lovely women, young and old, will enter the office for a day and teach us lessons in advanced journalism."[54]

The title page of the "Woman's Edition" assured readers: "A woman's noblest station is retreat, / Her fairest virtues fly from public sight." Within, the women assembled a twelve-page publication that provided an early and widely popular codification of the Lost Cause. Their articles covered every aspect of the war with emphasis on elite female heroism. One story related "How the St. Mary Girls spent the thrilling days of wartime." "The Southern Woman, The Part She Played in the Mighty Drama of War, Knitting an Hourly Business" recalled that "dainty hands, which had hitherto scorned all manner of work as degrading, now held themselves ennobled by the most menial drudgery for the soldiers. Labor of this type was regarded as a feminine type of military glory."[55]

In the "Woman's Edition" the ladies also set forth the history of their own memorial work, writing narratives that tailored events of the 1860s to fit the political climate of the 1890s. "How the Work Began, the Formation of the Wake County Ladies Memorial Association," probably written by Mrs. Garland Jones, and "The Wake County Memorial Association"

FIG. 9.16. *Cover, "Woman's Edition,"* News and Observer, *May 20, 1895.*

by Mrs. M. L. Shipp constitute a remarkable example of the adjustment of public memory. At the same time that their politically active husbands and other Democratic friends were raising the specter of Reconstruction to discredit Republican foes, the women were recasting the saga of their founding in similar terms.

"It was a very short while after the federal soldiers took possession of our town," their story began, that the mayor of Raleigh was informed that the Confederate dead must be "moved at once, that the Yankee dead might be placed there." At a town meeting, the Ladies Memorial Association was formed, and its president received a message the next day that unless the remains "were removed at once, they would be thrown in the county road." Encouraged by the women, the young men of the city, "rolling wheelbarrows through the scorching summer sun," moved the remains to the Confederate cemetery where they were "safe from Sherman's bummers, as there was scarcely a new made grave anywhere, but what was opened in search of treasures by these men." Thus the LMA founding of 1866 and the grave-moving of February and March 1867—both long after Sherman's "bummers" had left the city—were all shifted back to a single hot summer of 1865.

In the 1860s, the LMA meetings and the transfer of remains were publicly announced and highly visible, but the 1895 version further villainized the Yankees and highlighted the women's courage: "This was a more perilous undertaking than can now be imagined. Everybody was under strict surveillance—the former slaves made spies upon the actions of their owners, as well as the vigilance of the troops to find any offence, however slight, against the military laws, kept the people from expressing openly their sympathy with the Confederates, as they would be put under arrest, not even ladies being exempt from this insult, and carried before the military court."

At the initial May 10 Memorial Day observation in 1867, the LMA had devised a quiet procession and a large gathering at a formal service at the cemetery. The 1895 version acknowledged that there had been a prayer, a hymn, and a short address, but (perhaps influenced by oft-told tales of events in New Bern and elsewhere) emphasized that "No procession was allowed, unless the United States flag was carried, and as it was several years before the ladies were so much 'reconstructed' as to march under this flag, the gathering of the people was without special order or ceremony." Dramatizing the troubles and tyranny of Reconstruction and the contrast with the proud, flag-fluttering procession of the present day, the 1895 narrative formed the LMA's standard origin story and the basis of further tellings over the years.[56]

With the monument completed and unveiled and after publication of the "Woman's Edition," President Jones paid the final bill for the monument and sent to each of the vice-presidents across the state an elegant packet of mementos of the cause "dear to all true North Carolinians"—a photograph of the monument, an "authorized badge" of the association, and a copy of the Woman's Edition of the *News and Observer*. With that, she bid "adieu" to the North Carolina Monumental Association.[57]

The Ladies Memorial Association continued its regular activities, adding a stop at the Confederate monument to its annual May 10 procession to the Confederate Cemetery. Less than a year after the monument was unveiled, the usually quiet LMA engaged in a sharp controversy, which opened up the tensions at work even among the white elite, differences over the meaning of the Confederate past and its place in the present, and over the limits of women's roles in defining public ceremonies. As the Memorial Day procession lined up on May 10, 1896, the new LMA president Mrs. Garland Jones was shocked to see that one of the marching units, the cadets from the Agricultural and Mechanical College, the state land-grant school, was carrying the Stars and Stripes. She approached their instructor, a U.S. Navy officer, and requested "that this flag be dispensed with and the Confederate flag substituted." The officer "declined to accede," however, and the procession went on. Coverage in the *News and Observer* made no mention of the flag incident, but an accompanying illustration (fig. 9.17) depicted both the Confederate flag at the cemetery and the Stars and Stripes in the parade. Incensed, President Jones fired off a letter in the name of the LMA to the competing local paper, the *Press-Visitor*, objecting to the officer's "flaunting" the Federal flag and castigating the usually supportive *News and Observer* for its "burlesque" of the flag. She threatened to discontinue Memorial Day observations rather than repeat such "wanton violations of the sacred day."[58]

But President Jones found that she had gone too far. Immediate public objection appeared in a letter the *New and Observer* featured under the headline, "Stars and Stripes, The Flag of a Happy and United Country." In it, Fabius Busbee, an influential Democrat and Raleigh social leader, corporate lawyer, and veteran, wrote on behalf of other veterans to insist that the LMA letter must not be construed as "representing the view of the ex-Confederates of this city." While he cherished a "deeply seated reverence for the immortal banner" under which the old veterans appropriately marched, Busbee asserted that they were now loyal citizens of the United States, who honored the Stars and Stripes "as the emblem of a re-united country." Protesting "any criticism of the officer in command of the cadets," Busbee stated that for the college cadets, all born after the war, there could be "nothing more inappropriate than to ask that the Confederate flag shall be borne by a command, part of whose support is derived from a Federal

FIG. 9.17. *Cartoon, "Scenes in Oakwood Cemetery,"* News and Observer, *May 12, 1896.*

appropriation, and which is commanded by an officer of the United States Navy. I should not respect such officer if he were to consent to the flag, which he has sworn to uphold, [being] displaced by any other or even laid aside." He applauded "the unfaltering devotion of our women to the memory of the Confederate cause, but it should be clearly understood that these memorial observances are not intended to conflict with absolute loyalty to the government and flag of our country. If it is otherwise, then many will absent themselves."[59]

Debate flared over the next few days in a cross fire of letters in the local press. Even within the LMA, there was sharp disagreement, as some members objected to President Jones's statements and questioned her authority in writing in their names without knowing their views. After intense debate at a called meeting—six members had no objection to the use of the United States flag; one member suggested abandoning military features entirely—a slim majority endorsed President Jones's actions. The LMA also adopted a series of resolutions clarifying the meaning of the Confederate flag in their ceremonies.[60]

Three decades after the first gathering at the Confederate Cemetery on Memorial Day, 1867, flags and processions were still a powerful symbolic and political issue. In 1867, the women faced Union strictures against processions and carried no flags. By 1896, conditions had altered so greatly that parades bristling with Confederate flags were a familiar sight. Accustomed to the LMA's role as custodian of Confederate memory, President Jones had, perhaps unwittingly, stepped across a boundary. To southerners who promoted the economic and political benefits of national reunification, her objection to the American flag was inappropriate and counterproductive. It is also possible that to Confederate veterans and other men, her direct challenge to a military officer, even—or especially—in the name of their dead comrades, constituted a violation of the roles of military chivalry and of gender that they could not countenance.

In the late 1890s, the visibility of the LMA waned as the fast-growing United Daughters of the Confederacy (UDC), which began a chapter in Raleigh in 1896 and included many LMA members, assumed guardianship of the Confederate tradition. In 1897, it was announced that the UDC would join the LMA in the May 10 ceremonies, and before long the UDC dominated the event, with the LMA relegated to providing lunch to the ever-dwindling number of veterans.[61]

The Memorial Day tradition endured and even intensified amid the political strife at the end of the century. National reunion on southern terms and vindication of the valor of the southern soldier were solidified by the Spanish-American War in 1898, when northern and southern men fought together again under the same flag. In North Carolina, following a second Fusionist victory in 1896, in 1898 and 1900, Democrats resorted to a violent "white supremacy crusade," which recaptured white voters by pulling out all the stops on the old themes of "Negro domination," interracial sex, and Reconstruction horrors. In 1900, Memorial Day, an official state holiday that fell shortly before the election, was an occasion to emphasize shared values in the white populace: "the people of Raleigh of all classes and creeds, all of these will join hands and hearts tomorrow in a common cause and will decorate with the purest flowers the last resting places of the fallen soldiers."[62]

It was in this context that the origin story of the LMA gained its definitive retelling, provided by LMA president Mrs. Garland Jones for the *News and Observer* early in the election year of 1900. She stuck close to the version prepared for the "Woman's Edition" in 1895 but amended the chronology and added some new flourishes. The time grew more specific: "It was hardly more than a month after Sherman's army entered the City of Raleigh," she wrote, that the women had organized the LMA, and the Federal deadline for removal grew tighter: after taking possession of Pettigrew Hospital, the Federal officer threatened to throw the bodies in the road if they were not "removed in two days." The transfer under "scorching, summer sun" gained a "touching little incident" considerably softened by memory: "one of the coffins had been a little strained . . . allowing a long, half-curled lock of fair hair to escape, which hung down as the coffin was lifted from the wagon. This lock of hair is now in the possession of one of the ladies."[63]

Mrs. Jones also updated the account of the first memorial ceremonies by intensifying Federal officers' tyranny—possibly reflecting her own recent experience with U.S. officials and Confederate flags—and again changing the weather, this time from a sunny day to a dreary one:

> [On] the first Memorial Day, May 10, 1867 . . . the writer well remembers the meeting in the rain at the capitol square of a number of faithful men and women, who walked to the cemetery, carrying their garlands and crosses and flowers, and closely followed by several Federal officers, detailed by the military authority, who then governed the State, to see that "no procession was formed." It was believed at the time, and it has never been contradicted, that the threat was made that if the L.M.A., chiefly women and children, did form a procession, it would be fired on without further warning. On this day there were no exercises of any kind, not even a prayer, and it demanded some courage and some independence from those who walked under the dripping skies through the ankle-deep mud of the country . . . to fulfill this poor duty to the dead.

Mrs. Jones's 1900 rendition became the most widely accepted version of the LMA history. In 1938, it was reissued by the United Daughters of the Confederacy, and it became the basis for many subsequent accounts.[64]

By 1919, the days of the LMA were over. In that year, its officers asked the local chapter of the UDC to "accept our membership as its own and to take over and carry on the work in which we are now and have so long been engaged," especially the care of the Confederate Cemetery. The UDC chapter continued to maintain the Confederate Cemetery until 1998, when it was deeded to the Oakwood Cemetery management. The UDC also fended off in 1934 a proposal to remove the Confederate monument from Union Square, claiming state legislative authority and the memory of the women who weathered "those long dark days of the Sixties, and the dreadful reconstruction times . . . To tear down their labor of love and sacrifice which was the work of many long years will be an insult to their memory, and breaking faith with the dead—we cannot do it."[65]

Within the span of half a century after the Civil War, the Lost Cause had been transformed and so had the South. Through their use of symbols, ceremonies, and feminine appeals, the LMA and the NCMA played key roles in advancing and refining the Confederate tradition and reinforcing the social and political hierarchy they believed in. Ostensibly apolitical as women, they were able to accomplish what their overtly partisan men could not. Remaining above the fray yet skillfully navigating difficult political situations, they repeatedly gained state support in establishing their version of history as the official public memory.

Women's public roles had been likewise redefined by the turn of the century, as women assumed leadership in myriad causes, from educational reform to both sides of the woman suffrage issue; many women pursued these along with continued participation in the UDC and other patriotic organizations. It was the women of the LMA, girded by their experience in war and working in tandem with male friends and relatives, who had in the 1860s first stepped competently and discreetly into the unfamiliar territory of public leadership. If their cause was one that honored dead heroes and reinforced a social structure rooted in the past, they themselves were pioneers in the public realm, effectively combining feminine deference and strategic public actions in pursuit of their goals and thereby shaping the direction of the future.

NOTES

Research for this article was supported by an Archie K. Davis Fellowship from the North Caroliniana Society. For research assistance, the author would like to thank Elizabeth Reid Murray and John C. Williams, and George Stevenson and Michael Hill of the Division of Archives and History; for readings of drafts, the author is grateful to John Bishir, Jerry Cashion, Jeffrey Crow, Michael Hill, Kate Hutchins, Cynthia Mills, and Anastatia Sims.

1. Details are drawn from accounts in the *News and Observer* (Raleigh), May 20–22, 1895.

2. Gaines M. Foster, *Ghosts of the Confederacy: Defeat, the Lost Cause, and the Emergence of the New South, 1865 to 1913* (New York: Oxford University Press, 1987), 4–8, 38–45, 127–135, 43 (quotation). In North Carolina, evidence indicates that the activities of the LMA and the North Carolina Monumental Association (NCMA) were more closely related to partisan politics and the Democrats' reclamation of political power than Foster sees in the movement in general. See discussion of this process in memorials and architecture in "Landmarks of Power: Building a Southern Past, 1885–1915," chapter 10 of this volume. On the Civil War monument movement, see Kirk Savage, *Standing Soldiers, Kneeling Slaves: Race, War, and Monument in Nineteenth-Century America* (Princeton, N.J.: Princeton University Press, 1997).

On southern women's public roles, see Anastatia Sims, *The Power of Femininity in the New South: Women's Organizations and Politics in North Carolina, 1880–1930* (Columbia: University of South Carolina Press, 1997); Anne Firor Scott, *The Southern Lady: From Pedestal to Politics, 1830–1930* (Chicago: University of Chicago Press, 1970); Margaret Supplee Smith and Emily Herring Wilson, *North Carolina Women: Making History* (Chapel Hill: University of North Carolina Press, 1999). Sims points out that even in the antebellum era, "southerners applied the taboo against public activity for women selectively," and North Carolina women took a role in "benevolence, reform, and patriotism," including the church, the temperance movement, and the Mount Vernon Ladies Association (*North Carolina Women*, 15). Drew Gilpin Faust, in *Mothers of Invention: Women of the Slaveholding South in the American Civil War* (Chapel Hill: University of North Carolina Press, 1996), 251–53, depicts women's memorial work as focused on restoring their husbands' shattered morales. Evidence from the Raleigh groups suggests that men and women worked jointly to accomplish mutual goals.

3. LMA minutes, May 1866, Ladies Memorial Association Papers, privately held, Raleigh, hereinafter cited as LMA Papers; *Sentinel* (Raleigh), May 13, 1867; Margaret Wootten [Mrs. Bryan Wells] Collier, *Biographies of Representative Women of the South, 1861–1929*, 6 vols. ([College Park? Ga.]: privately published, 1929), 5:233 (last quotation). Collier relates that the Columbus association planned their first memorial day for April 26, 1866, anniversary of Gen. Joseph E. Johnston's surrender to Gen. William T. Sherman at the Bennett Place in North Carolina; in March 1866, their secretary sent an appeal to newspapers and individuals in the South. See also Foster, *Ghosts of the Confederacy*, 38. As Foster points out, although the groups were called Ladies Memorial Associations, most included men as well as women. These were independent local organizations, in contrast to the broader network organized in the 1890s by the United Daughters of the Confederacy (UDC), into which many LMAs, including the Raleigh group, subsequently merged. Foster also explains (42) that a Georgia woman conceived the southern spring memorial day idea from a German ceremony of decorating graves on All Saints' Day, and that the North "quickly adapted the southern custom to celebrate its own dead" (43).

4. Peter F. Pescud, *A Sketch of the Ladies' Memorial Association of Raleigh, N.C., Its Origin and History* (Raleigh: privately published, 1882), 2; Grady Lee Ernest Carroll Sr., *They Lived in Raleigh*, 2 vols. (Raleigh: privately printed, 1977); 1:166–67.

5. Pescud, *Ladies' Memorial Association*, 2. Pescud, longtime and leading supporter of the LMA and its work, was the owner of a Raleigh pharmacy; he served on the city council and had been among the citizens who, on April 13, 1865, accompanied the mayor of Raleigh to surrender the city to Sherman's troops in exchange for protection of its citizens and property. It is difficult to ascertain the accuracy of Pescud's claim that Raleigh's Confederate Cemetery was the first in the South. Certainly, most of the other Confederate burial grounds were in existing cemeteries or extensions of those. Because circumstances in Raleigh required an entirely new cemetery for Confederate remains in 1866 and 1867, it may well be the first of this kind. (During the war, marking of soldiers' graves had been funded by the state legislature, which authorized a plank fence around the graves and headboards marked "with their names, States, and regiments, as far as practicable." "Resolutions to Enclose the Soldiers' Burial Ground," *Laws of North Carolina, 1862–1863*, 73, courtesy of Elizabeth Reid Murray.)

6. Collier, *Representative Women of the South*, 5:175–78, 175 (quotation). Mrs. Lawrence O'Bryan Branch Papers, Private Collections, State Archives, Division of Archives and History, Raleigh, hereinafter cited as Branch Papers. *Dictionary of North Carolina Biography*, s.v. "Branch, Lawrence O'Bryan."

7. These steps and those described below are all taken from the LMA minutes, 1866–67, LMA Papers.

8. Pescud, *Ladies' Memorial Association*, 3. Until the late 1860s, Raleigh's chief burial ground was the City Cemetery on Hargett Street, established in 1798 and reaching capacity by the mid-nineteenth century. As promised, additional Mordecai land was subsequently acquired and developed as Oakwood Cemetery, a picturesque, parklike burial ground chartered in 1869 by the Raleigh Cemetery Association and still in active use. Elizabeth Reid Murray, *Wake: Capital County of North Carolina* (Raleigh: privately published, 1983), 112, 506, 567, 589.

9. *Sentinel*, November, 17, 1866 (quotation). Pescud, *Ladies' Memorial Association*, 4. There are no LMA minutes between August 1866 and January 1867.

10. *Sentinel*, February 14, 1867 (quotation). I have been unable to identify an earlier time that women filled the Capitol to lobby the legislators. However, as Guion Griffis Johnson explains, as early as the 1840s, politicians who rejected participation by women nevertheless appealed to women to use their influence in politics, and many political events were "cheered by the 'approving smiles of the fair.'" Guion Griffis Johnson, *Ante-Bellum North Carolina* (Chapel Hill: University of North

Carolina Press, 1937), 249, quoting the *North Carolina Standard* (Raleigh), October 28, 1840.

11. *Sentinel,* February–March 1867; William S. Powell, *North Carolina through Four Centuries* (Chapel Hill: University of North Carolina Press, 1989), 380–95; Allen W. Trelease, "Reconstruction: The Halfway Revolution," in *The North Carolina Experience: An Interpretive and Documentary History,* ed. Lindley S. Butler and Alan D. Watson (Chapel Hill: University of North Carolina Press, 1984), 286–94.

12. *Sentinel,* February 18, 16, 1867. Col. James V. Bomford, a native of New York, was a graduate of West Point and a career officer in the U.S. Infantry from 1832 to his retirement in 1874. He became colonel of the Eighth Infantry in 1864 and was made brevet brigadier general for "faithful and effective service." William H. Powell, comp., *List of Officers of the Army of the United States from 1779 to 1900* (New York: L. R. Hamersly and Co., 1900), 201.

13. LMA minutes, February 20, 1867, LMA Papers. Perhaps the order was in fact an unexpected and unreasonable demand, as LMA members' memoirs suggest, but it is possible that the officer in charge of the National Cemetery, facing the prospect of new shipments of Union dead, had been urging the LMA for some time to complete their move.

14. LMA minutes, February 24, 1867, LMA Papers. *Sentinel,* February 22, 1867. The fundraiser lecture, held on February 22 (Washington's birthday and founding date of the Confederacy), was given by General Colston, who had formerly taught at the Virginia Military Institute and was a colleague of Stonewall Jackson. *Sentinel,* February 9, 1867.

15. *Sentinel,* February 28, March 6, 1867.

16. [Sophia Partridge] to Fanny Lewis, March 10, 1867, Ladies Memorial Association of Wake County Papers, State Archives. The last page(s) of the letter being lost, it is unsigned, but internal evidence and handwriting indicate that it is from Partridge.

William Holland Thomas was adopted as a Cherokee chief and helped tribe members retain their land and residency after the Cherokee Removal of 1838 and thus to become the Eastern Band of the Cherokee. He served as state legislator and led a company of Confederate troops, including Cherokee soldiers who sometimes donned war paint in battle. One of many who filled the state insane asylum to capacity after the war, he spent much of his later years in the Western North Carolina Asylum (now Broughton Hospital) at Morganton. He was interviewed by James Mooney, who was collecting stories for his *Myths of the Cherokee.* See *Dictionary of North Carolina Biography,* s.v. "Thomas, William Holland," and *Sentinel,* March 12, 1867, which reported that Thomas had been "sent to the Insane Asylum. We have for days been satisfied that such a step was necessary."

17. [Sophia Partridge] to Fanny Lewis, March 10, 1867.

18. Pescud, *Ladies' Memorial Association,* 4–5.

19. Ibid., 5.

20. David B. Whiting, "Some Things That Happened in My Life," undated (early-twentieth-century) typescript, 40–41, David Brainard Whiting Papers, Private Collections, State Archives. Thanks to George Stevenson for calling my attention to this account.

21. *Sentinel,* May 3, 1867.

22. LMA minutes, May 3, 1867, LMA Papers. John Waters was the superintendent. Again, it was Sophia Partridge who took responsibility for painting the heavy planks white and marking them. Pescud, *Ladies' Memorial Association,* 5.

23. *Sentinel,* May 3, 1867. While ceremonies in Georgia were held on April 26, North Carolina selected May 10, in honor of Stonewall Jackson, and other states chose other days. See Foster, *Ghosts of the Confederacy,* 42–44.

24. LMA minutes, April 24, May 3, 1867, LMA Papers. The April 24 minutes state ambiguously that the LMA considered whether to have an address at the Capitol and a procession from there to the cemetery and decided "*not* to have no *public* demonstration." The double negative could be interpreted as expressing either intent not to have a public demonstration or a determination to have one.

25. *Sentinel,* May 4, 10, 1867.

26. *Sentinel,* May 13, 1867.

27. Ibid.

28. Pescud, *Ladies' Memorial Association,* 5. As the *Sentinel* editor had anticipated before his arrival in 1867 (see note 12 above), Colonel Bomford's handling of the military presence in Raleigh met with such approval that at his reassignment to Charleston in 1868, the Raleigh City Council passed a resolution praising his

"high soldierly qualities and gentlemanly bearing" and commending his command for "the value of its services in the preservation of order and the administration of impartial justice, which has so endeared itself to this Board and to the community generally." When he left the city on May 16, a "number of gentlemen were assembled at the Depot to bid him a respectful farewell. He has administered his delicate duties fairly, courteously, and impartially, and has always entertained and expressed the kindest consideration for our people." Murray, *Wake: Capital County*, 593–94, and *Sentinel*, May 9, 18, 1868. The conservative *Sentinel* ran many stories critical of other occupying officers, and the emphasis on Bomford's "gentlemanly" qualities indicates that he treated the Raleigh elite well and that those leaders found him to be sufficiently respectable and respectful.

29. LMA minutes, August 10, 1869, March 21, 1870, LMA Papers; George Mordecai Whiting (1842–70), marker, Confederate Cemetery, Raleigh. Whiting died of tuberculosis contracted during the war. Carroll, *They Lived in Raleigh*, 1:149. On the Federal Memorial Day in late May 1868, see Murray, *Wake: Capital County*, 588–89.

30. Pescud, *Ladies' Memorial Association*, 5 (quotation). Clippings, minutes, correspondence, 1880s–1890s, LMA Papers.

31. "A Brief Sketch of the Life and Services of Brig. Genl. George Burgwyn Anderson . . . ," May 10, 1885, Addresses, LMA Papers. Alfred Moore Waddell was the speaker and in 1895 was the main orator at the unveiling of the Confederate monument. He figured prominently in the Democratic white supremacy campaign of 1898 and in the racial riot in Wilmington, North Carolina, on November 10, 1898, in which the city's elected Republican officials were forced out of office.

32. *News and Observer*, March 24, June 15, 19, 1892, May 20, 1895. On March 24, the newspaper published a letter from "Rebel" proposing a Confederate monument at the Capitol Square, but nothing concrete occurred until summer. The idea for the meeting was initially credited to Col. Edward Dudley Hall (1823–96) of Wilmington, elderly leader of the North Carolina Division of the United Confederate Veterans (*News and Observer*, February 2, 1893), but in subsequent accounts, the younger Democratic stalwarts Octavius Coke (1840–95) and Samuel A'Court Ashe (1840–1938) were identified as having called the organizing meeting. *News and Observer*, May 24, 1894, and other accounts. See *Dictionary of North Carolina Biography*, s.v. "Ashe, Samuel A'Court," "Coke, Octavius," and "Hall, Edward Dudley." Announcements of the meeting stated that Coke was to offer remarks, but reports of the meeting were overshadowed by accounts of a rally held at the news of Grover Cleveland's nomination, at which Coke was a principal speaker. *News and Observer*, June 15, 19, 23, 1892. On Coke as "the old warhorse of democracy," see *News and Observer*, August 16, 1892.

33. *News and Observer*, July 16, 1892. The women were variously referred to as officers of the "Board of Lady Managers" and of the organization itself.

34. *News and Observer*, September 1–10, 1892. Undated clippings, Branch Papers. Although it is often called Capitol Square, the proper name for the area is Union Square, the site of the State Capitol, positioned at the meeting point of the capital's four axial streets; four secondary squares, including Nash, mark the four quadrants of the grid plan.

35. *News and Observer*, February 16–24, 1893, May 24, 1894.

36. NCMA minutes, October 26, 1893, Branch Papers.

37. NCMA minutes, November 2, 8, 1893, Branch Papers. *News and Observer*, May 20, 1895.

38. *Daily Press* (Raleigh), May 22, 1894. The event was actually held on May 22 because May 20 was a Sunday.

39. *Daily Press*, May 22, 1894.

40. Helen G. Edmonds, *The Negro and Fusion Politics in North Carolina, 1894–1901* (Chapel Hill: University of North Carolina Press, 1951), 37–38, and Allen W. Trelease, "The Fusion Legislatures of 1895 and 1897: A Roll-Call Analysis of the North Carolina House of Representatives," *North Carolina Historical Review* 57 (July 1980): 280–309.

41. *Caucasian* (Raleigh), February 21, 1895. The editor of the Populist newspaper was Marion Butler. *News and Observer*, February 26, 1895.

42. *News and Observer*, February 24, 1895; *Caucasian*, February 28, 1895. Edmonds, *The Negro and Fusion Politics*, 41–43.

43. *News and Observer*, February 22, 24, and afterward. In 1894, Josephus Daniels, in collaboration with tobacco manufacturer Julian S.

Carr, purchased the *News and Observer*, and in 1895, Daniels moved to Raleigh from Washington, D.C., to assume full control over the newspaper.

44. *News and Observer*, February 27, 1895 (quotation).

45. *News and Observer*, March 1, 2, 1895. Sen. Hiram Grant, a Republican from Wayne County who introduced the bill, was a native of Connecticut; as a Union officer he had served in North Carolina and settled in Goldsboro after the war. See *Dictionary of North Carolina Biography*, s.v. "Grant, Hiram Louis."

46. *News and Observer*, March 8, 1895.

47. *News and Observer*, April-May, 1895, May 9, 1865 (photograph quotation).

48. *News and Observer*, May 14, 1895 (quotation).

49. *News and Observer*, May 3, 1895. On Carr, see *Dictionary of North Carolina Biography*, s.v. "Carr, Julian Shakespeare."

50. *News and Observer*, May 16, 1895.

51. *News and Observer*, May 20, 21, 1895.

52. *News and Observer*, May 20, 1895. Foster, *Ghosts of the Confederacy* (127–44) explains how Confederate unveilings and other celebrations "ritually aligned the common man with the social order" (131) and fostered "social unity" and "deference to leadership" (139). This purpose, seen throughout the South, was especially important for North Carolina Democrats hoping to recapture white voters from the Populists. See Savage, *Standing Soldiers, Kneeling Slaves*, 162–208, on meanings of the use of common soldiers for northern and southern Civil War memorials. The sculptor was Ferdinand von Miller II (1842–1929).

53. *News and Observer*, May 20, 21, 1895; *Caucasian*, May 23, 1895; Fabius Busbee to *News and Observer*, May 14, 1896.

54. *News and Observer*, May 5, 1895.

55. "Woman's Edition," May 20, 1895, copy in Hinsdale Papers. Subsequent quotations are from this issue. The editors explained that all the articles were written by women except those denoting male authors. Thus, the sole article that acknowledged the magnitude of the LMA's accomplishment in completing the monument during "the greatest financial depression that the country has seen in a quarter of century,"
carried the headline, "The Work is Finished (Written by a Man)." The May 20, 1895, issue does not appear in regular runs of the *News and Observer* but only in private collections.

56. *News and Observer*, May 20, 1895. This and a subsequent retelling, while tailored to political circumstances, also share features characteristic of traditional stories in general: dramatic emphasis and exaggeration; compression of similar events into a single incident; and attachment of many incidents to a single main figure, such as Gen. William T. Sherman and his troops.

57. Bills and receipts, 1895, Confederate Monument file, Capital buildings, 1767–1919, Treasurer's and Comptroller's Papers, State Archives. One souvenir packet is in the John W. Hinsdale Papers, Special Collections Department, Duke University Library, Durham, hereinafter cited as Hinsdale Papers.

58. LMA minutes, May 15, 1896, clippings, marked "Press-Visitor, May 12th, 1896," in LMA minute book, LMA Papers; *News and Observer*, May 12, 14, 1896.

59. *News and Observer*, May 14, 1896. On Fabius Haywood Busbee, see Carroll, *They Lived in Raleigh*, i, 170–71.

60. *News and Observer*, May 14, 15, 1896; LMA minutes, May 15, 1896, undated clippings from *News and Observer* and "Press-Visitor, May 12th, 1896," clippings in LMA minute book, LMA Papers. One of the principal challengers to Mrs. Jones within the LMA was Addie Worth (Mrs. Josephus) Daniels.

61. *News and Observer*, April 8, 1897.

62. *News and Observer*, May 9, 1900.

63. *News and Observer*, March 25, 1900.

64. *News and Observer*, March 25, 1900. Charlotte Bryan Grimes Williams, ed., *History of the Wake County Ladies Memorial Association* (Raleigh: James Johnston Pettigrew Chapter, UDC, 1938), 7–10.

65. Williams, *History of the Wake County Ladies Memorial Association*, 22–23. Joe Freed (general manager of Oakwood Cemetery), telephone conservation with author, August 25, 2000. The deed from the James Johnston Pettigrew Chapter, UDC, to the Raleigh Cemetery Association was dated August 13, 1998, and registered October 23.

Ten

LANDMARKS OF POWER

BUILDING A SOUTHERN PAST, 1885–1915

In 1901, the speaker at the dedication of the Olivia Raney Library in Raleigh, North Carolina, compared the city's landmarks with those of Washington, D.C. In the national capital, "three great architectural monuments" possessed "symbolic significance": the United States Capitol, the Washington Monument, and the Library of Congress. "So in our smaller sphere," three landmarks of Raleigh stood out. First was the old State Capitol, "symbolizing the commonwealth's loyalty to constitutional liberty." Near it stood two newer landmarks. "Our handsome Confederate monument" on the Capitol grounds offered "a token of our loyalty to the memory of our fallen heroes who laid down their lives in defense of those principles for which Washington so successfully fought." And the library, given by local businessman Richard Beverly Raney in memory of his wife, provided "a memorial of the highest type of our cultured Christian womanhood"—a classically detailed building in which "the simplicity and elegance of its graceful proportions and unpretentious appearance" evoked its namesake's exemplary character, while its proximity to the war memorial recalled "that noble band of women" (including Mrs. Raney) "to whose untiring efforts we are chiefly indebted for our Confederate monument (fig. 10.1)."[1]

In this address, the Reverend M. M. Marshall of Christ Episcopal Church in Raleigh identified three important types of landmarks that gained dominion throughout the turn-of-the-century South. In addition

---

"Landmarks of Power: Building a Southern Past, 1885–1915" appeared in *Southern Cultures* inaugural issue (1993): 5–45, and is reprinted by permission of Duke University Press.

to revering antebellum buildings as survivors from a glorious past, leaders of his generation employed the twin arts of sculpture and architecture to assert their own definition of the past and its relationship to the present and the future. As Marshall's ceremonial comments illuminated, these new landmarks represented a set of interlocking beliefs, including the renewed place of the vindicated South in the American mainstream, the rightness and patriotism of the Confederate cause, and the association of classical architecture with idealized southern virtues.

Seen in the context of contemporary cultural and political events, the creation of symbolic sculpture and architecture by the southern elite functioned as part of their reclamation of regional and national power. As they placed monuments in prime civic spaces, whether commemorating the heroes of the Confederacy, the patriotic women of colonial Edenton, or the Revolutionary fighters of the Cape Fear region, these leaders spelled out chapter after chapter of a saga of patrician Anglo-Saxon continuity, of order, stability, and harmony. The location of monuments in the state's principal civic places lent authority to the version of history they represented, while at the same time the monuments claimed those public spaces and thereby defined the setting for public life. And, just as monuments com-

FIG. 10.1. *Hillsborough Street, Raleigh, looking west from Union Square, showing (left to right) Olivia Raney Library, North Carolina Confederate Monument, and Raney House. Photograph ca. 1903.* (NCDAH)

memorated specific heroes and events, so architecture commemorated and asserted the renewed continuity of the values and way of life those heroes represented. In public and institutional buildings, classicism universally reiterated the ideal of a venerable and stable hierarchy, while in residential architecture the Colonial Revival symbolizing "the big-heartedness and hospitality which are the rightful heritage of the southern people" recreated in modern terms the deferential social relations the antebellum plantation represented.

Thus, just as they took control of the political process during the decades spanning the turn of the century, the southern elite also codified a view of history that fortified their position in the present and their vision of the future. By erecting public landmarks celebrating that history and proclaiming a legitimizing continuum from the Old South to the New South, they shaped both public memory and public life. Raleigh and Wilmington, North Carolina's largest cities in 1890 and its main centers of political and cultural activity, provide case studies of this process during a defining period of crisis.[2]

THE SOUTHERN ELITE AS SHAPERS OF PUBLIC MEMORY

Throughout America in the decades just before and after 1900, political and cultural elites drew upon the imagery of past golden ages to shape public memory in ways that supported their own authority. By commissioning monumental sculpture that depicted American heroes and American virtues in classical terms, and by reviving architectural themes from colonial America as well as from classical Roman and Renaissance sources, cultural leaders affirmed the virtues of stability, harmony, and patriotism. They were responding to sweeping changes in the nation's fabric, including national reunification after the Civil War, industrial modernization, growing immigration and social tensions, and rising American nativism, nationalism, and imperialism. Leading patrons ranged from the new princes of industry, who saw America as the site of a second Renaissance, to the embattled "native" aristocrats of various regions; they worked in concert with Beaux-Arts–educated architects and artists who brought European training and ideas to their practices in burgeoning American cities. In 1893, the World's Columbian Exposition in Chicago presented a spectacular display of a set of official American ideals. An ensemble of heroic sculpture and classical architecture, laid out in the formal plan and rationally divided sectors promoted by the City Beautiful movement, offered an image of a unified, stable, hierarchical Anglo-Saxon nation asserting its place in the world, an image that soon reached into communities of the North and South.[3]

The principal shapers of public memory and patrons of public sculpture and architecture in Raleigh and Wilmington were likewise members of an established elite. They were akin to aristocrats throughout the nation, and (as Marshall's remarks at the library dedication revealed) they were well acquainted with national cultural trends and their relationship to them. They also shared among themselves certain backgrounds, experiences, and values. All were Democrats, and, with a few notable exceptions, they were members of families of long-established social and economic prominence, who had customarily participated in national and international currents of trade and taste. Many boasted colonial ancestry and had traditions of service in the Revolutionary and Confederate causes. Their families were interlaced by ties of ancestry and marriage, as well as by education—typically at the University of North Carolina at Chapel Hill for men and St. Mary's, an Episcopal school in Raleigh, for women—and by religion, for most of this group were members of the Episcopal church, a denomination long associated with the state's upper class and with the values of hierarchy and social stability.

Although they had much in common with patricians elsewhere in the nation, these North Carolinians had their own special concerns as well as their own version of history, for as southerners they alone among American elites had experienced devastating military and political defeat along with jolting impoverishment. Yet, in contrast to blue bloods in many northern cities, they managed to regain their political as well as social and cultural clout. In the last decades of the nineteenth century, they were in the process of consolidating their reclamation of power and position and reasserting their status as vindicated patriots in a reunified America. They recalled a golden age before the Civil War, when "Southern statesmen directed the policies of the nation," when "aristocratic" southern society was led by "the wisest, the strongest, the most learned," and when their families had constituted the upper tier in a hierarchical society and slavery-based economy. Although many of them had opposed secession, they nevertheless had sacrificed family members and fortunes to the Southern cause. During Reconstruction, they had seen their world turned upside down and their political power and wealth shrivel, as "democracy" replaced "aristocracy," and power passed into the hands of black and ordinary white citizens who were "not so able or cultured." In the mid-1870s, white Conservatives regained political power and soon revived the Democratic party label in North Carolina. Calling themselves "Redeemers" and led by Civil War governor Zebulon Vance, who retook the governor's office in 1876, they considered themselves saviors of the state. With a series of constitutional amendments, the Democratic legislature rolled back many of the egalitarian measures of Reconstruction and took control of local government. As one of their number recalled, "For twenty years this new system remained in force and quiet reigned."[4]

Along with recapturing political dominance, members of the old aristocracy gradually adjusted to a new economy. Some remained agriculturalists and renegotiated farm-labor arrangements, while many moved to town to engage in business and professions, where their prospects were tied increasingly to national corporate networks. Even as they adapted economically, the leading families perpetuated their customary social networks. Almost in inverse relationship to their threadbare circumstances, they revitalized elaborate social rituals and public rhetoric, which they adorned with carefully polished silver and phrases. And, like their compatriots throughout the nation, they entered into cultural and patriotic pursuits that asserted their accustomed political, economic, and social dominance.

In their hands, the creation of symbolic landmarks unfolded in two principal phases, punctuated by political events. In the 1880s and early 1890s, patrician Democrats began to call for a rehabilitation of state and southern history and the erection of civic monuments dedicated to that history, transforming the cult of defeat into the dominant culture of power regained. At the end of the century, the turbulent political campaigns of 1898 and 1900 riveted public attention and generated new themes in the Democrats' use of history. After 1900 the re-entrenched elite turned with unprecedented energy and conviction to the shaping of public memory and the creation of official symbols, which quickly established a codified tradition and transformed the setting of public life.

THE CONFEDERATE MONUMENT AND SOUTHERN PATRIOTISM

In 1883, Samuel A'Court Ashe, a Raleigh newspaper publisher, politician, and historian, returned from a trip to Boston fired up by New Englanders' commemorative zeal. As a Confederate veteran, a native of the Wilmington area, and a descendant of colonists and Revolutionary heroes of the Cape Fear region, Ashe typified North Carolina's early leaders in collecting and publishing state history. Upon his return to Raleigh, he immediately began a series of articles in his *News and Observer* urging North Carolinians to celebrate their own history and patriotic shrines.[5]

In the same spirit, and probably influenced by Ashe, Alfred Moore Waddell addressed the Raleigh Ladies Memorial Association (LMA) on Confederate Memorial Day, May 10, 1885. Waddell, likewise a former Confederate officer and a descendant of Cape Fear colonists and Revolutionary War officers, was a Wilmington resident and former congressman who had become one of the state's most popular public speakers. The sponsor of the occasion was one of the many local Ladies Memorial Associations established throughout the South in the 1860s to assure the proper burial of Confederate soldiers and the marking and decoration of their graves. In these, genteel southern women first stepped into public roles as guardians of regional memory and history. They enlisted male relatives, friends, and political figures for speeches on Confederate Memorial Day.[6] In his oration of 1885, Waddell issued a call to memorialize the state's heroes and laid out an agenda for action.

He proclaimed that the period of mourning after the war was over, as was the era of poverty that excused failure to build monuments to the state's heroes. The state, "though stripped of the sovereignty in which, with her sisters, she once robed herself, has long since put off the habiliments of mourning, and, clad in a new vesture, with renewed hope and courage, is moving majestically onward to a grand destiny." He pointed out that whereas "every civilized land" had monuments to its greatest sons to inspire and instruct natives and visitors, North Carolina had never erected memorials to her heroes and statesmen. Waddell challenged his audience:

> Go to the Capitol at Washington and enter the ... Hall of Statuary. There is a place reserved in it for two statues from each State, and these places are being rapidly filled by the marble and bronze images of distinguished soldiers and statesmen. Look around for North Carolina's contribution. It is not there. Go to any other State Capitol, and if its public grounds do not contain some statue or monument in commemoration of its great men, its legislative halls at least are hung with portraits of its Governors. Then come back here to Raleigh—go into your own State Capitol—see at the base of the rotunda those four empty niches—pass through the corridors—enter the Legislative Halls and look around! No monument, no statue, no bust, not even a portrait to remind you that North Carolina ever produced one man that she thought worthy of remembrance. Surely if her gratitude to or appreciation of her dead soldiers and statesmen is to be measured by the number of memorials which she has established in honor of them then it is safe to say that such a sentiment does not exist.

Addressing first the heroes of the recent war, Waddell acknowledged the importance of Confederate monuments already standing in cemeteries across the state, but he insisted that the memory of the Confederate dead "deserve[d] to be perpetuated otherwise than by such memorial marbles as private affection may erect." He called for public support of civic monuments to the Confederate soldier to reflect "a sentiment alike jealous of the honor of North Carolina, and tenderly grateful to her heroic sons."[7]

In the next three decades, the civic memorial movement Waddell envisioned followed precisely the course he laid out. In the 1890s, Civil War memorializing shifted from funereal markers placed in cemeteries to mon-

FIG. 10.2. *Bird's-eye view of State Capitol grounds showing Raney House and First Baptist Church (lower left), Confederate monument and Olivia Raney Library (lower center), State Capitol (center), and Christ Church (upper center). Postcard, late 1930s.* (NCDAH)

uments of southern patriotism located in such civic spaces as courthouse greens and town squares. The North Carolina Confederate Monument, on Union Square at the State Capitol, was one of the state's earliest and certainly its most imposing monument of this new type. It was the project of the North Carolina Monumental Association (NCMA) led by socially prominent women with links to the older Ladies Memorial Association (LMA). Proclaiming that "a land without monuments is a land without memories," the NCMA organized a statewide fundraising campaign. By 1895 these women, with assistance on practical matters from "experienced gentlemen," oversaw the completion of the state's official monument to the Confederate solider (see chapter 9). [8]

On May 20, 1895, some thirty thousand people gathered from across the state for the unveiling of the seventy-five-foot monument that rose at the west end of Union Square, the most prominent public site in the state. The granite column, flanked by bronze figures of a North Carolina cavalryman and artilleryman, and topped by a bronze infantryman (see figs. 9.14 and 9.15. p. 242), stood on axis with the western portico of the Capitol and faced Hillsborough Street, the premier residential avenue and one of four axial streets that defined the city plan (fig. 10.2). The NCMA's president, Nancy Branch Jones, and other dignitaries presided over elaborate ceremonies in which the seven-year-old granddaughter of Gen. Stonewall Jackson pulled the cord that let the draperies slide from the monument like "the garments of Elijah." The orator of the day was Alfred Moore Waddell.[9]

Again Waddell set forth an emerging agenda—the "true" history of the Confederate cause and North Carolina's role in that story. His hour-long oration was headlined in the *News and Observer* as "A Masterly Defence of the Cause for Which They Fought—In History's Clear Light." It featured the retelling of southern history then sweeping the region—a southern interpretation that played an essential role in the gradual reunion between North and South on southern Democrats' terms. Waddell began by observing that a southerner reading history written by northern men could not but recall "what Froude said about history generally, namely that it seemed to him 'like a child's box of letters with which we can spell any word we please. We have only to select such letters as we want, arrange them as we like, and say nothing about those which do not suit our purpose.'"

He then set forth "the plain unvarnished truth concerning the causes of and the responsibility for the war in which men to whose memory this monument is erected, were sacrificed." This was necessary because

> for thirty years past, my countrymen, kinsmen and my friends have been pilloried before the world as ignorant, barbarous, cruel traitors and rebels, who, without the slightest justification or excuse, sought to destroy the best government under the sun, and deluged a continent in blood. The charge is still made and reiterated in conversation, in school books, in magazine articles, in public speeches, in public records, and in published history.

To counter this "monstrous perversion of the truth," Waddell insisted, "self respect and a decent regard for the memory of our heroic dead" required a statement of "the facts and the proof."[10]

Waddell presented the southern cause as part of the heroic tradition of American patriotism. For the throng gathered around the monument (fig. 10.3), the message was illustrated by the inscriptions, symbols, and figures on the monument itself, and Waddell's speech reinforced the meaning of those emblems. Drawing first upon the North Carolina state seal on the monument, with its date of May 20, 1775, he lauded "the men of Mecklenburg" who "on this day one hundred twenty years ago" declared their independence from British tyranny: "[F]irst of all Americans, despite the doubting Thomases—[they] renounced allegiance to the British crown, declared themselves a free and independent people." With this Waddell invoked belief in the May 20, 1775, "Mecklenburg Declaration of Independence," an alleged event disputed by historians but popularly revered. When North Carolina seceded from the Union on May 20, 1861, the seces-

FIG. 10.3. *North Carolina Confederate Monument and the State Capitol, Raleigh. Postcard, 1909.* (NCDAH)

sion convention authorized a state flag emblazoned with the two dates to glorify the parallel between the two declarations of independence.[11] Amid the turn-of-the-century passion for southern vindication, selection of May 20, 1895, as the day to unveil the state's Confederate monument reaffirmed the linkage of the Confederate and Revolutionary causes.

Next, Waddell traced the nation's early history from a southern perspective, stressing the retention of states' rights, including secession, under the Constitution—a theme emphasized on the monument by the seal of the Confederate States with its image of George Washington. He defended the southern people—"Deo Vindice," said the Confederate motto on the monument—who had "sought peace and not a quarrel" and were "forced to defend their liberties and their homes." And, sharing in an ongoing process of affirming North Carolina's contribution to the Confederacy, he recited the saga of North Carolina's long and valiant soldiering as a source of state pride. Her men had proved themselves "worthy of their Revolutionary sires" in battles from the first to the last of the war: their motto "First at Bethel, Last at Appomattox" is writ large on the monument. He ended with an encomium to the Confederate soldier, loyal like his fathers to the Union, but compelled by love of his state to come to her defense. Surely gesturing to the bronze infantryman outlined against the sky, Waddell declaimed, "Stand then, bronze image of him who wore the gray! Thou art a triumph of Art; he was God's gift to his country. Thou shalt perish, but he shall live forever in the hearts of his people."

Waddell's oration struck sympathetic chords. Fellow Wilmingtonian and business leader James Sprunt wrote, "You were first in the hearts of your countrymen yesterday.... [O]n all sides the speech is said to be the best ever delivered in North Carolina." Little anticipating the direction of the future, Sprunt predicted that "the eloquent words of your masterful address on probably the last occasion of such public honours to the Lost Cause will be repeated from generation to generation by those who look with reverence and admiration upon the beautiful shaft in Raleigh." Democratic spokesman Henry Groves Connor of Wilson praised Waddell for his "setting forth of our side of the question," noting that "we must preserve our integrity and make our fight in the struggle now confronting us. It behooves us to purify our hearts and educate our minds to meet the common enemy."[12]

THE WHITE SUPREMACY CRUSADE

Connor alluded to political developments then gaining momentum in the state, which in the mid- and late 1890s absorbed the energy of the state's cultural and business as well as political leaders. Throughout the South, Democrats faced challenges from Populists and Republicans, but only in North Carolina did they lose control of the state.

By the 1890s, the Democrats were perceived increasingly as the allies of moneyed interests and railroad magnates. Amid nationwide economic woes, especially the worsening poverty among farmers, the Populist movement gained strength from white farmers disillusioned with Democratic policies. In 1894, after their efforts at reform were rebuffed by the Democrats, North Carolina's Populists forged a "Fusion" ticket with the Republicans. Drawing support from both white and black voters, the Fusionists took a majority of seats both in the state legislature and in Congress. In 1896 the Fusionists kept a majority in the legislature and Republican candidate Daniel Rus-

FIG. 10.4. *Cartoon, "Under Which Flag?"* News and Observer, *Nov. 1, 1898*. (NCDAH)

sell won the governor's office. As well, more Republicans (including some blacks in the eastern plantation region) and Populists took office in local and state government.[13]

To recapture political power by splitting the opposition, the Democrats, long known as "the white man's party," set upon a "White Supremacy Crusade." The crusade tore aside the veil of gentility that normally inhibited public discourse and exposed the specter of violence. Organized by Furnifold M. Simmons, chairman of the Democratic party, and led by Charles B. Aycock, Robert Glenn, and Francis Winston, the crusade inspired Democrats across the state to put aside old intraparty differences. Josephus Daniels made his recently acquired Raleigh *News and Observer* "the militant voice of White Supremacy" and "the printed voice of the campaign" (fig. 10.4). The election of 1898 proved to be so violent that, as Josephus Daniels later commented, it was "sometimes difficult for readers of *The News and Observer* to tell which was the bloodier, the war against Spain or the war to drive the Fusionists from power."[14]

The epicenter of violence was in Wilmington. Businessman James Sprunt later recalled that the port city had a growing number of black citizens "whose attitude towards the whites had become unbearable," and, since the Fusionist victory, a city council that included black and white Republicans who were "not at all responsive to enlightened opinion." Repeatedly, as the city's Democratic leaders and prominent businessmen strove to regain control of city government, they drew upon the heroic actions of their ancestors as precedent. As early as 1897, when Democrats sought unsuccessfully to have the city council removed, their attorney, John D. Bellamy, Jr., declared that "it was quite in the order of things for Wilmington to be resisting the infamous legislation by which her citizens are deprived of local self-government, for it was the citizens of this city who first resisted the odious British Stamp Act."[15]

In August 1898, an editorial in the city's black newspaper, the *Wilmington Record*, on the inflammable topic of interracial sex became a rallying point for the state's white supremacist campaign, whose leaders fanned the flames of racial and sexual fears. In Wilmington this editorial supplied the catalyst for action. As Sprunt remembered, "Hope of better days had almost faded away when a vile publication in a negro newspaper aroused the whites to action and determined them to rid the city of the pests that had been a menace to its peace and an incubus on its prosperity. It was resolved to purge the city and to displace the inefficient government."[16]

In late October 1898, as election day neared, again the precedent of history was sounded, when Alfred Moore Waddell gave a "sizzling talk" to a packed house of white men and women at the municipal theater. As a contemporary recalled, "In ordinary times Waddell was one of the most graceful and classical of speakers," but in this campaign "he was an American Robespierre." After blasting the evils of Negro domination and asserting Anglo-Saxon supremacy in the South, the nation, and the world, Waddell looked to history as he invoked the spirit of the "men of the Cape Fear" to move his compatriots to action instead of talk. "We are the sons of the men who won the first victory of the American Revolution at Moore's Creek, who stormed at midnight the rocky face of Stony Point.... We are the brothers of the men who wrote with their swords from Bethel to Bentonsville [sic] the most heroic chapters in American annals." Proclaiming that "we ourselves are men who, inspired by these memories, intend to preserve, at the cost of our lives, if necessary, the heritage that is ours," he stated that the men of the Cape Fear could no longer abide "intolerable conditions" in Wilmington: "We are resolved to change them if we have to choke the current of the Cape Fear with carcasses."[17]

Waddell's speech captured attention throughout the state. A friend in the northeastern part of the state called it "the equal of Patrick Henry's famous oration." His cousin, Rebecca Cameron of Hillsborough, a patriotic leader and Episcopal churchwoman, wrote to Waddell that she and others had been "amazed, confounded and bitterly ashamed of the acquiescence and quiescence of the men of North Carolina at the existing conditions, and more than once have asked wonderingly, Where are the white men and the shotguns?" Continuing her cousin's theme, she wrote, "We applaud to the echo your determination that our old historic river shall be choked with the bodies of our enemies, white and black, but what this state shall be redeemed. It has reached the point where bloodletting is needed for the health of the commonwealth, and when the depletion commences let it be thorough!" Sharing Waddell's history, she recalled that "the men of the Cape Fear were the first to stay ... English aggression when your great-grandfather was one of a goodly company in the proud light of day who said to the Magistry of England 'no farther.' And I am glad that it is once more our colony and our family who catch up the far back echo, and bugle forth the story." She added, "We are aflame with anger here. I wish you could see Anna, she is fairly rampant and blood thirsty. These blond women are terrible when the fighting blood is up. I hope it will not come to the last resort but when it does let it be Winchesters and buckshot at close range."[18]

In Wilmington, the election day of November 8 was peaceful. There, as throughout the state, the Democratic ticket triumphed. But in Wilmington the story had not ended. The next day, several groups of "prominent businessmen" assembled to make plans to oust the city council (which was not up for election) and rid the community of certain blacks and other Republicans. Then, on November 10, Waddell led a group to the *Wilmington Record* office, where he forced open the door, and the group destroyed the press and burned the building. In a confusing sequence of events, threats and rumors of violence sped through the city, and white men shouldered their Winchesters and shotguns and moved into the streets. The Wilmington Light Infantry, recently returned from service during the Spanish-American War, turned out in force in support of the Democrats. Sporadic violence broke out. At day's end, the conflict ceased, leaving an unconfirmed number of black men dead—Waddell put the number at twenty—and several whites and blacks wounded. That evening, Waddell and others forced the resignation of the city council and took control of the government with Waddell as mayor. The Wilmington Light Infantry patrolled the city on horseback to round up and imprison overnight those black and white Republicans whom the Democrats planned to banish from Wilmington.[19]

Although the Wilmington "race riot" was widely condemned in northern newspapers, and although many North Carolinians cringed at the violence it had unleashed, the Democrats who had led what they called the "Revolution of 1898" became heroic figures to many others. On November 13, Bennehan Cameron, a wealthy and wellborn Hillsborough planter and businessman who had been active in the white supremacy campaign, wrote to his kinsman Waddell, "As you well know, I have always admired you; & now, I am almost a hero worshiper. God bless you! for your deliverance of your good people." On the local scene, James Sprunt later recalled that "while some of the incidents were deplored by whites generally, yet when we consider the peaceful and amicable relations that have since existed, the good government established and maintained, and the prosperous, happy conditions that have marked the succeeding years, we realize that the results of the Revolution of 1898 have indeed been a blessing to the community." For his part, Waddell characterized the event as "a radical revolution accompanied by bloodshed and a thorough reorganization of social and political conditions," which "set the pace for the whole South on the question of white supremacy, and assured beyond further controversy the adoption of the Constitutional amendment in regard to negro suffrage in the state."[20]

In 1900, after winning the "Revolution of 1898," the Democrats aimed at total victory. The governorship was at stake as well as legislative seats, but the central issue was an amendment to the state constitution designed to disfranchise blacks and eliminate them from political participation. Again Democrats employed violence and intimidation to keep blacks from the polls. "You are Anglo-Saxons. You are armed and prepared and you will do your duty. . . . Go to the polls tomorrow, and if you find the negro out voting, tell him to leave the polls and if he refuses, kill him, shoot him down in his tracks. We shall win tomorrow if we have to do it with guns," proclaimed Waddell in a "fighting speech."[21]

By winning an overwhelming victory in 1900, North Carolina's Democrats, like their compatriots throughout the South, gained control of the political process itself. To many of them it seemed that a long chapter that began in defeat had finally ended in triumph; for some, the very violence of their victory was an essential catharsis of old defeat. As promised in the campaign, young Democratic leaders inaugurated an era of economic progressivism that emphasized public education, transportation, and encouragement of business. They also passed "Jim Crow" laws to legalize racial segregation, along with disfranchisement, as a modern, rational remedy to past ills that would "cleanse" public life and promote peaceful social and economic advancement.[22]

Once again the vindicating muse of history was invoked, this time by Gov. Charles B. Aycock in his inaugural address of January 1901. As he proclaimed the bright new age for a new century, the young leader looked back briefly to link recent events with the heroic past. First he compared the Democrats who had waged the "combat" of 1898 with North Carolina's early heroes of the American Revolutionary cause—"that people who fought the first fight in Alamance against bad government and wrote the first Declaration of Independence in Mecklenburg." He then likened the "revolutionary" suffrage amendment to "the war for Independence ... known as the Revolution," and tied the spirit of the disfranchisement movement to "the revolutionary spirit of 1776," which "still lives in the hearts of North Carolinians ... a glorious part of their heritage."[23]

THE CODIFICATION AND COMMEMORATION OF SOUTHERN HISTORY

It was in this highly charged context that in 1900 the state's Democratic leaders inaugurated an era of "historical awakening." Many felt that North Carolina had lagged behind while other states had progressed in historical activities; now they proceeded to remedy the situation. In the fall of 1900, in the auditorium of Raleigh's new Olivia Raney Library, prominent Democrats organized the State Literary and Historical Association. This group worked in affiliation with kindred organizations: its published reports included news from the recently formed North Carolina chapters of such hereditary and patriotic groups as the Colonial Dames of America, the Daughters of the Revolution, the Daughters of the American Revolution, the Order of the Cincinnati, the Sons of the Revolution, the United Confederate Veterans, and the United Daughters of the Confederacy. Many people belonged to more than one of these organizations. They constituted a statewide network of men and women interested in the histories of their own patrician families and of the state at large, which they usually perceived as one and the same.[24]

These men and women led a surge of patriotic, cultural, and historical activity. They collected and published historical records; published state histories and school textbooks; initiated "North Carolina Day" in the public schools; established and expanded historical museum collections; and, with equal fervor, marked and memorialized historic sites, events, and personages. These endeavors had less to do with an obsession with the past than with the belief that a proper understanding of history and state pride, like educational reform and literary production, were necessary components of a modern American state. A remarkable sense of shared purpose threaded through these pursuits. Just as members of ancestral patriotic groups traced their family lineages to colonial and Revolutionary forebears in order to affirm their place in contemporary society, so like-minded politicians and historians traced political lineage back to those heroic ancestors to affirm political legitimacy.[25]

With competing visions of the state's past, present, and future all but silenced in official discourse, these leaders shared a powerful sense that both in politics and in the culture at large, matters had been returned to their correct alignment. Again they occupied their unquestioned and proper place in a stable, racially tiered society.[26] From this perspective they codified a lasting version of the state's history that tied Old South to New, interweaving old family heritage, Anglo-Saxon supremacy, and military and political heroism. The saga began with the establishment of the "first Anglo-Saxon settlement" in the New World at Roanoke in the 1580s, focused on aristocratic families and the plantation culture they established in the colonial period, and glorified Revolutionary North Carolinians' early resistance to British tyranny. It lauded the progress of the antebellum era, sanctified the sacrifices and patriotism of North Carolina Confederates, and insisted that their cause had engaged the unified support of the populace. Finally, the story demonized the era of Reconstruction, ennobled the Democratic redemption of the state, and asserted the present era as a rebirth of southern progress and leadership in the nation.[27] As they erected memorials to the events and heroes of this narrative, Democratic leaders transformed principal civic spaces into visual illustrations of their saga. In both Wilmington and Raleigh, their memorial work moved beyond commemoration of the Confederacy to mark a continuum of patrician patriotism that wove each chapter into a single epic stretching from the colonial past to the redeemed present.

Immediately after the election of 1900, the Democrats triumphantly unveiled a giant bronze figure of their hero Zebulon Baird Vance. Sculptor Henry J. Ellicott's lifelike portrait captured Vance in a characteristic gesture of debate, a Beaux-Arts sculptural technique of depicting the subject in mid-gesture to intensify the emotional impact of the work. Standing on a

FIG. 10.5. *Vance monument and the State Capitol, Raleigh. Postcard, ca. 1911.* (NCDAH)

FIG. 10.6. *Worth Bagley monument (right), Union Square, Raleigh. Postcard, ca. 1910.* (NCDAH)

base that raised the eight-and-a-half-foot statue to a height of more than twenty-five feet, the powerful monument (fig. 10.5) took command of the eastward axis of Raleigh's Union Square. Acclaimed by Democrats as the perfect ideal of North Carolina, Vance had governed the state during the Civil War, led Redemption and won the governorship in 1876, and served in the United States Senate from 1879 until his death in 1894. Soon after his death, friends had proposed a memorial, but funding was not forthcoming, nor was the racially and politically divided legislature likely to support such a project. When Democrats again "redeemed" the legislature in 1898, they promptly appropriated funds to memorialize the heroic figure of the earlier Redemption. The unveiling on August 22, 1900, was "a fitting time," as Josephus Daniels happily observed, "for Aycock, the new Governor was to receive it." In lauding the "immortal Vance" as the ideal subject for the first memorial to a North Carolina leader on Union Square, the speaker at the unveiling also advocated another in Statuary Hall in Washington, D.C. Within a few years, Vance's marble likeness filled that long-empty niche, where in due course it was joined by a statue of Aycock in the other niche.[28]

On May 20, 1907, a bronze figure of Worth Bagley (fig. 10.6), unveiled before a huge throng on Union Square, provided a new chapter in the saga of heroic southern vindication. The monument, made by popular New York sculptor Francis H. Packer, memorialized the young North Carolinian who had been the first American officer killed in the Spanish-American War. Bagley was a member of a prominent eastern North Carolina family, and his sister Adelaide was the wife of *News and Observer* publisher Josephus Daniels. The Spanish-American War, in which northern and southern soldiers fought together under a single flag, fostered sectional reunification in the cause of American nationalism. The young southerner's death in Cuba on May 11, 1898, was hailed in the national press as sealing the "covenant of brotherhood between the north and south," for now "we are all Worth Bagley's countrymen."[29]

The 1907 commemoration further expanded the meaning of Bagley's death. On the base of his monument, the inscription—"First Fallen, 1898"—linked his heroism to the nearby Confederate monument with its motto, "First at Bethel, Last at Appomattox." And the unveiling date of May 20, as speaker Gov. Robert Glenn explained, deepened the sense of continuity: already sacred as "first marking the Declaration of Independence, second as the day on which North Carolina had turned to fight for friends and kindred," May 20 now had a third significance as "the day on which the breach of sectionalism had been healed and union had been cemented in the blood of Worth Bagley." Thus, claimed another speaker, Bagley's death signaled "a new era of Union" in which "the logical adjustment of history would again give the leadership of the nation to the South."[30]

In Wilmington as well, memorializing focused upon heroes central to city leaders' interpretation of the past and present. The Wilmington Ladies Memorial Association had already given the city its Confederate memorial at Oakdale Cemetery in 1872. Now Wilmington women led state patriotic organizations to commemorate other heroes of the Cape Fear. The city's first civic monument—the Cornelius Harnett Monument—was presented by the North Carolina Society of the Colonial Dames of America, whose officers were mainly patrician Wilmington women, including Luola Murchison Sprunt (wife of James Sprunt), Gabrielle DeRosset Waddell (wife of Alfred Moore Waddell), and her aunt, Catherine DeRosset Meares. The

FIG. 10.7. *Members of the North Carolina chapter of the Society of the Cincinnati, gathered in Wilmington on April 20, 1906, for cornerstone-laying of Harnett obelisk. Among those identified by numbers are James Sprunt, nonmember guest (1); Marshall D. Haywood (5); Bennehan Cameron (9); Bishop Joseph Blount Cheshire, Jr. (10); Samuel A. Ashe (11); Alfred Moore Waddell (15); and Julian S. Carr, nonmember guest (17).* (NCDAH)

Dames selected a prime site, a "commanding and beautiful position" in the central plaza of Market Street.[31]

The cornerstone-laying ceremony in 1906 drew a large and festive crowd that reflected the overlapping circles of political and cultural leadership. The Colonial Dames invited the North Carolina chapter of the Society of the Cincinnati to participate (fig. 10.7) and requested that the Wilmington Light Infantry, "the flower of Wilmington for more than a half-century," provide a military feature. They asked Francis Winston, Masonic as well as political leader, to lay the cornerstone, and Wilmington mayor Alfred Moore Waddell to deliver an address. Waddell extolled the "heroes and patriots of the Lower Cape Fear" and assured his listeners that despite the previous absence of monuments as "material evidence of such loyalty of sentiment," the descendants of those heroes "cling with tenacity to their traditions." The following spring the Colonial Dames presented the classical granite obelisk to Mayor Waddell. As the inscription showed, the thirty-foot memorial commemorated both Cornelius Harnett and "the memory of the colonial heroes of the lower Cape Fear," especially the 150 men "who made the first armed resistance in the American Colonies to the oppressive stamp act of the British Parliament February 19, 1766."[32]

FIG. 10.8. *George Davis monument. Photograph ca. 1911. (Courtesy of the Pearl Stevens Butler Collection, New Hanover County Public Library, Wilmington, North Carolina)*

At one level, this first civic monument in Wilmington simply commemorated local colonists who resisted the Stamp Act and led the Revolutionary cause; since the leaders of the Colonial Dames were Wilmington residents and descendants of colonial Cape Fear planters, the subject was a natural choice. Yet for these women as for most members of the audience, the recent "Revolution" in Wilmington was fresh in memory. Indeed, in 1906 a reporter from Raleigh observed that the residents of Wilmington who "participated in or who flourished at the time of the post-election burning of the negro newspaper office and in the suppression of black supremacy in the city [still] date events from the 'Revolution.' That now is heard a good many times here in the course of a day." The rhetoric of the "Revolution of 1898" repeatedly linked that event with the "heroes of the lower Cape Fear" and their resistance to the Stamp Act. By erecting this obelisk, the women marked the center of the city with a monument that evoked a continuity of heroism from their colonial ancestors to their own men of the Cape Fear. Perhaps, too, the obelisk in its commanding position also served as an inspiration or a warning that the old "tenacity to their traditions" yet lived on.[33]

Four years later a second monument on Market Street honored George Davis, a brilliant aristocrat who had served as attorney general of the Confederacy. The Cape Fear chapter of the Daughters of the Confederacy (which shared many members with the Colonial Dames) had conceived the idea of a memorial to Davis soon after his death in 1896, but was at the time devoting its energies to creating a Confederate museum, which it opened in 1898 in the Wilmington Light Infantry Armory. In 1904 the Daughters began fundraising for the monument, but donations came slowly until 1909, when their president recruited James Sprunt to spearhead a quick and effective financial campaign. In 1911 they presented to the city a life-size bronze figure sculpted by Francis H. Packer. Like the Vance memorial in Raleigh, the statue of Davis showed its subject in midgesture, "reaching forward in a characteristic gesture of the right hand, while the left rests lightly upon the flag to which he was true to the end of his life" (fig. 10.8). After the unveiling by Davis's grandsons and a historical address by Democratic leader and judge H. G. Connor, a stirring rendition of Davis's poem, "Carolina's Sons Are Ready," tied the Confederate cause to the Revolutionary War and "Mecklenburg! the proud old story!" On the base of the monument, paired seals of North Carolina and the Confederacy, the latter with its figure of George Washington, reiterated the vindication of Confederate leadership as noble and patriotic service.[34]

Memorializing continued in Wilmington and Raleigh after 1911, expanding on the intertwined themes of patriotic heroism and Democratic political accomplishments. It took several years before the impulse to glorify the Confederacy was fully satisfied. As late as 1924 a private bequest funded a Confederate memorial in downtown Wilmington (fig. 10.9), designed by architect Henry Bacon with expressive figures representing courage and sacrifice, again sculpted by Francis H. Packer. In Raleigh, where Union Square had become the focus of statewide commemorative interest, two new memorials filled out the Confederate story. On June 10, 1912, the North Carolina Division of United Daughters of the Confederacy unveiled sculptor Gutzon Borglum's dramatic bronze of Henry Lawson Wyatt (1842–61), the North Carolina private who had been the "First Confederate Soldier to Fall in Battle in the War Between the States," at Bethel Church on June 10, 1861. Two years later, again on June 10, a memorial to the North Carolina Women of the Confederacy was unveiled, the result of another private donation by a Confederate veteran. The architect for the project was Henry Bacon and the sculptor was New Yorker Augustus Lukeman. The donor, Ashley Horne, appointed a committee consisting mostly of prominent veterans to direct the project. The sculptor presented two designs for the principal figures—one "an elderly woman seated, reciting to a young girl . . . the story of the War Between the States, representing the activities of the

Women of the South in perpetuating the memories of the Confederacy," and the other showing the same woman telling the story to her grandson at her side, "inciting him to emulate the deeds of his fathers." The committee unanimously chose the latter.³⁵

Inside the State Capitol, commemoration also proceeded. In 1908 the Daughters of the Revolution dedicated the first memorial in the long-naked rotunda—a bronze plaque commemorating "Fifty-one Ladies of Edenton" who, on October 25, 1774, had signed a resolution supporting the patriot cause. This early political act by American women, which became popularly known as the "Edenton Tea Party," was especially inspiring to the Daughters as an example of feminine "patriotism and zeal." The Daughters initially planned to place their memorial in Edenton, but after Edentonian Frank Wood erected a cannon topped by a teapot on the alleged site of the "tea party," the group decided to install their memorial in the Capitol. To raise money for the plaque, in 1901 the Daughters inaugurated a popular historical series, *The North Carolina Booklet,* which featured works by political and cultural leaders and prominent historians. Leaders in planning the memorial and editing the *Booklet* were two local women, Mary Hilliard Hinton and Elvira Worth Moffitt, both members of elite political families and both deeply involved in the era's full range of patriotic and cultural work.³⁶

The unveiling of the plaque drew together the overlapping circles of aristocratic families and Democratic leaders: Lt. Gov. Francis Winston and Chief Justice Walter Clark gave addresses, Bennehan Cameron represented the Society of the Cincinnati, Marshall DeLancey Haywood represented the Sons of the Revolution, and, in a typical involvement of the rising generation in the ceremony, several children of "Revolutionary Patriots" unveiled the tablet (fig. 10.10). Within four years, the long-empty niches in the rotunda were filled with marble busts of political leaders, and these were soon followed by plaques celebrating colonial and Revolutionary heroism, and by various portraits throughout the building.³⁷

Surely the most powerful recitation of the history that took form in these years resounded through the Capitol when historian, editor, and political leader Samuel A'Court Ashe—who had sparked the commemorative movement back in 1883—delivered the dedicatory address in 1909 for a portrait of the building's architect, David Paton. Speaking in the Senate chamber, Ashe used the Capitol itself as a text by evoking the "undying memories" that pervaded its halls. He began with the accomplishments of antebellum days, then recalled the trials of the Civil War and the leadership of "the mighty Vance" before turning to the years that followed: "[T]hese mute walls are witnesses of the saturnalia of Reconstruction still awaiting some Dante to portray the scenes with realistic power." As to the recent past,

FIG. 10.9. *Confederate monument, South Third Street, Wilmington. Photograph 1924. (Courtesy of the Louis T. Moore Collection, New Hanover County Public Library)*

FIG. 10.10. *Unveiling of Daughters of the Revolution memorial to "Fifty-one Ladies of Edenton" at the State Capitol, Raleigh. Photograph 1908.* (NCDAH)

these walls have witnessed the reversal of that State policy forced on an unwilling people by the mailed hand of the conquering power, and the full restoration of Angli-Saxon [sic] control. Never in history has a people been so clearly and effectually vindicated as those gallant souls of North Carolina, who, emulating the constancy of Hamilcar, swore their children to undying opposition to those who would destroy their civilization. Let the oppressed of future ages gaze on the scene and take courage. Already hallowed are the memories that these chambers evoke. What grand occasions yet await them![38]

THE ARCHITECTURE OF THE NEW OLD SOUTH

Ashe recognized that buildings possessed the power to evoke hallowed memories and to inspire future ages. For his generation of southern leaders, the architecture of the colonial and antebellum past had special meaning, as did the construction of new buildings whose form and imagery captured in modern terms the symbols of that glorious past. The South's revival of classicism in public architecture and its embrace of the closely related Colonial Revival in residential architecture paralleled national trends, but with a distinctively southern face and meaning. Just as the monuments they erected in civic spaces commemorated past heroes and events, so in block after block of downtown buildings and in the premier residential neighborhoods where they had their homes, the southern elite's revival of classical and colonial architecture commemorated an entire way of life: the "golden age" before the war. This architecture shaped public memory of the past and defined the life of the present by asserting in ubiquitous physical form "the southern aristocracy's continuing legitimate authority as the dominant force in the region's political, social, and economic life."[39] And, moving beyond mere glorification of a past epoch, this architecture perpetuated and revitalized for modern daily use the deferential social values of the heirs and heiresses of the glorified tradition.

A vivid local explication of the new architecture appeared in a 1907 article in Josephus Daniels's *News and Observer*. The story was entitled, "A People Known by Way They Build: How Raleigh Has 'Found Herself' Architecturally and the Building That is Replacing Mistakes and Fixing Permanent Standards." Superficially, the article simply reported changing taste in Raleigh architecture. But just beneath the surface was the story of architecture as a marker of political and social events and values. Asserting that "Beauty in architecture sounds the signal in a community of stability," the writer presented a brief history of architectural evolution in terms that paralleled the publisher's own sense of recent history. Condemning previous decades' architectural "atrocities," the writer blasted that era's "pretentious frames, garbled ideas put together for the purpose of display." He contrasted these errors with recent improvements that defined a time when "the community has found itself, when the frightful begins to be pulled down; when the pretentious becomes an eyesore, when the notion is that of harmony, of fitness to use and right to be. Each has its place." He pointed to the present desire for "simplicity and timeliness" as evidence that "the callow period has passed, that the bumptious period of uncertainty has been weathered, and that there is experience as well as confidence in the air."

The city's admirable models of architecture were either antebellum landmarks or newly constructed works of classical mien. The writer praised the

State Capitol—"an anomaly of beauty [which] stood as a protest against bad taste, over-pretension, under-estimation"—and admired Christ Episcopal Church as a spiritually inspiring edifice in English Gothic style. "These two early triumphs of city-building," he asserted, "stand as the case may be as a reproach or congratulation to the city that is building about them. And in recent years there has been an effort towards the symetry [*sic*] which they speak and the form which they glorify." The writer saw evidence of "the progress of the new thoughts in the homes of the people, in the buildings that exactly or by relation speak the public mind." He singled out a new state college building "in the Greek style" as "a triumph of proportion and taste," praised the "Colonial design" of buildings at Peace and St. Mary's (schools for young women), and admired a number of churches and businesses affiliated with the local elite. "It is in the homes of Raleigh," he concluded, "that the significance of the building and architectural spirit may be best observed," for new homes showed "a notable taste and an evident building for permanency. Whether the new homes be simple cottages or, as in many cases, real mansions the note is the same, a regard for art with comfort."[40]

The architecture the *News and Observer* writer so admired shared in the national revival of symmetry and classical themes. In the late nineteenth century, most southern cities had built more or less ornate versions of the eclectic, picturesque styles popular throughout the nation, characterized by irregular outlines, exuberant machine-made ornament, and rich textures and colors. As these variegated styles faded from fashion, and tastes turned toward balance, classical motifs, and smooth pale surfaces, the southern elite went beyond the usual rejection of recent styles, vehemently demonizing the architecture of the late nineteenth century along with the political and social conditions it seemed to represent. They embraced a new architecture that blended modern technological convenience with a revival of classical imagery akin to antebellum landmarks. This architecture provided a compelling metaphor for southern leaders promoting their region as offering the best of modern reform and race relations combined with the stable social hierarchy modeled by the Old South. Thus the new classically detailed skyscrapers and columned public buildings of southern cities represented both the South's renewed prosperity and participation in the urban American mainstream, and the region's preoccupation with "harmony, fitness to use and right to be."

In residential architecture a more specifically southern image emerged, both in the nationally popular Colonial Revival style and especially in the "Southern Colonial" style. Introduced to the region in the 1890s in homes of the elite, the Colonial Revival style swiftly gained broad and lasting acceptance. Besides its appeal as a national fashion with a certain regional flavor, the strength of the Colonial Revival was also rooted in deeper impulses in society.

The American Colonial Revival gained momentum when the 1876 Centennial Exposition sparked national enthusiasm for the American past and for "Old Colonial" (especially New England) architecture. American architects recorded colonial buildings of both the North and the South and used colonial motifs in their designs. In 1893, the grandiloquent Beaux-Arts architecture of the White City of the Chicago World Exposition encouraged the shift in popular taste toward imperial classical styles, while the exposition's individual state buildings showed visitors myriad "Colonial" styles. A few, such as Virginia's Mt. Vernon, were meant as replicas (North Carolina planned but could not fund a copy of Tryon Palace), but most, such as the Connecticut, West Virginia, and Kentucky buildings, were creative assemblages of motifs inspired by colonial architecture. Initially the Colonial Revival cast a broad net, drawing upon a heritage that reached from initial white settlement to the mid-nineteenth century's industrial and picturesque architecture. "The term Old Colonial is applied to a certain style of work, a free, and in many instances a refined, treatment of Classical details rather than to any fixed period," explained one early practitioner. Increasingly after about 1915 the focus narrowed to more literal use of seventeenth- and eighteenth-century precedents. The ascendancy of the Colonial Revival was linked to rising American nationalism and Anglo-Saxon nativism in the face of labor and class turbulence and massive immigration. Popular architectural literature, especially from the 1890s through the 1910s, presented the Colonial Revival as the architecture of Americanness; of patriotism, stability, and longevity; and specifically as "the architecture of our Anglo-Saxon heritage."[41]

In the South, identification of the colonial style with Anglo-Saxon American culture appealed not only to nativist pride but also to white supremacy. Southern bonding of colonial architecture with Anglo-Saxon elite culture likewise extended from the first settlement to the Civil War, particularly emphasizing the flowering of plantation culture just before the war. Within the broader colonial style, a specific "Southern Colonial" style emerged in the form of a large and symmetrical house characterized by a portico of great white columns. The Kentucky Building at the Chicago World's Fair in 1893 presented an early use of the type and term. National architectural writers eagerly embraced the term Southern Colonial along with the ideal of southern life it symbolized. In 1895, *American Architect and Building News* described a new house in St. Louis whose massive columned portico made it "more of the southern Colonial architecture than its sister style of the Northeastern States," and "somewhat of a relief from the ordinary run of Colonial houses." The columns were "part and parcel of the southern Colonial, [which] somehow or another bear with them a certain tinge of the big-heartedness and hospitality which are the rightful heritage of the southern people." The Southern Colonial house also incorporated modern conveniences of plumbing, heating, and lighting, an apt parallel to the Democrats' carefully devised amalgam of tradition and modern reform. That the Southern Colonial house was built more often for an urban businessman than for a cotton planter only confirmed its power. Modeled around 1900 chiefly in residences of prosperous members of old families, by 1910 it gained sway among wealthy citizens of various backgrounds.[42]

In a 1903 article entitled "Revival of the Colonial Style—A Simple, Dignified Home after the Old Fashion," Charlotte architects Charles Christian Hook and Stewart Rogers laid out the meaning of the style by way of a "resume of architecture in this country in the last fifty years" on southern terms: "The civil war marked the change from good to bad architecture in the South, the reason for which is apparent. In antebellum days when a home was built of any pretensions the owner and designer as a rule was an educated gentleman of refinement," who, "familiar with the classics and having other colonial work as models took pains to preserve the proper proportions." But "after the great conflict and things being reversed in general, we find a greater reversal in architecture than any other sign of the times. Why was it? Because the illiterate and unrefined being new to wealth desired it more than purity, and the cultured and once wealthy were either too poor to build or were so busy during the reconstruction period they had no time to devote to art." In those evil times, architecture was handed over to "the most ignorant class of men, in fact, any jack-leg who could wield a hatchet and saw. All colonial details and proportions were discarded as being 'old timey' [and] the jack-leg-carpenter with the deadly jigsaw ran riot in the land." But now, they affirmed, "out of all this chaos we again have a revival of the colonial, [which] in its purity expresses more real refined sentiment and more intimate associations with our history than any [other style], for it is not only an association of English history with our own but also expresses the authentic memoirs of the American people." In this framework the architects presented their design for a colonial style house, symmetrical and pure white, with a "stately portico." The interior as well as the exterior was "strictly colonial in detail," with a paneled den, a mahogany staircase, polished hardwood floors, and white enameled walls.[43]

In both Raleigh and Wilmington, the first major residential projects in the Southern Colonial style were for patrician families for whom the architectural reclamation of continuity from glorious past to redeemed present had deep associations. Such houses reinforced a way of life in which, as one resident remembered of Raleigh in 1905, "the women were fine hostesses, not only abounding in wit and delightful chit-chat but in well-ordered

FIG. 10.11. *Dudley-Sprunt House, South Front Street, Wilmington. Postcard, ca. 1905.* (NCDAH)

households" where "the relation between old Raleighites and their black friends was beautiful," for many of the servants "never left the premises and scarcely knew they had been set free." And, as the feminine domain in an era of elaborate, large-scale entertaining, the magnified version of the antebellum plantation house offered the perfect setting for hospitality, patriotism, and ancestral distinction—all in an urban residence larger and vastly more convenient than most plantation houses had ever been.[44]

Continuity with the past was literal in some of the earliest Colonial Revival projects, in which elite couples aggrandized existing antebellum mansions. An important early example came when Wilmington civic leaders James and Luola Sprunt remodeled the downtown residence of antebellum governor Edward Dudley. James Sprunt, a Scots-born businessman and Confederate veteran, wrote local history and endowed a series of historical monographs at the University of North Carolina. As president of the North Carolina Society of Colonial Dames, Luola Murchison Sprunt led in local and state efforts to mark important colonial sites. Soon after the Sprunts bought the house in 1895, they expanded it and transformed its public visage with a monumental Corinthian portico flanked by broad porches. The resulting "handsome Colonial residence" (fig. 10.11) instantly gained acclaim as one of the city's principal landmarks and the setting for Mrs. Sprunt's Colonial Dames meetings and celebrated hospitality.[45]

In Raleigh, too, the first major statement in the Southern Colonial style appeared in the refashioning of an antebellum residence. In 1901 Bennehan and Sallie Cameron undertook an expansion of his grandfather's house on Hillsborough Street. Bennehan Cameron, whose father and grandfather had been among the richest men in the state before the Civil War, was a free-spending and progressive planter active in the 1898 and 1900 Democratic campaigns and later in promotion of better highways. Tracing lineage from Revolutionary heroes, he enthusiastically supported patriotic groups and commemorative pursuits. Sallie Taliaferro Mayo Cameron, a descendant of old Virginia families, was the daughter of Peter H. Mayo, a wealthy Richmond businessman who had been on Gen. Robert E. Lee's staff.[46] With her father's help, Sallie and Bennehan Cameron obtained remodeling plans from Richmond architect William G. Noland, a prominent practitioner of revival styles. To the rear they built a large addition with bedrooms, modern bathrooms, and a new kitchen. Sallie was especially interested in transforming the public face of the residence: her father reported that Noland was "working up the front porch drawing ... after getting your first letter about it last week. We think we can carry out your wishes." With its towering portico of Ionic columns and curved porches at each end, the Cameron mansion impressed Raleigh as "a fine old colonial-type residence" that "carried one's thoughts back to the days of large plantations and baronial rule"[47] (fig. 10.12).

The same architectural themes also appeared in new residences. The epitome of the Southern Colonial house and Raleigh's first and grandest example was built in 1902 for Richard Beverly Raney. The wealthy widower Raney had previously erected the Olivia Raney Library as a memorial to his first wife; in 1902, in preparation for his marriage to Kate Whiting Denson, he constructed a new house on Hillsborough Street (fig. 10.13)

FIG. 10.12. *Cameron House, Hillsborough Street, Raleigh. Photograph ca. 1902.* (*Courtesy of the Southern Historical Collection, Wilson Library, University of North Carolina at Chapel Hill*)

FIG. 10.13. *Raney House, Hillsborough Street. Photograph ca. 1903, from Charles Barrett,* Colonial Southern Homes *(1903).* (NCDAH)

FIG. 10.14. *Raney House, with Kate Raney and R. Beverly Raney sitting on their porch. Photograph ca. 1903, from Barrett,* Colonial Southern Homes. (NCDAH)

across from the library, thus completing a symmetrical relationship with the Confederate monument. The couple both came from old planter families that had suffered losses during the war and endured years of poverty afterward. R. Beverly Raney, son of a Granville County planter, had come to Raleigh at age eighteen in 1868 to work as a hotel clerk, had moved up rapidly, and had soon become general agent for a national life insurance company. Kate Denson came from an aristocratic Cape Fear planter family that had "lost everything" after the war; her parents had moved to Raleigh, where her father was a teacher and a leader in Confederate veterans' affairs. Although not involved in political activities, Beverly and Kate Raney (fig. 10.14) moved in the city's highest social circles, in which Raney's business success enabled them to enjoy the fruits of prosperity regained.[48]

To design their house, Raney turned to Raleigh architect Charles Barrett. Barrett was an early proponent of the Southern Colonial style, who, with his former partner William P. Rose, had published an example of "a complete modern southern home" in the *Southern Architect* in 1899. Now working on his own, Barrett designed the Raney mansion as a full-fledged exemplar of the style and immediately published it as the centerpiece of his *Colonial Southern Homes* (1903; fig. 10.15). Carrying forward many aspects of antebellum plantation houses, the symmetrically planned residence had a central hallway and flanking formal rooms—all rendered on a vaster scale and with more rooms than its antebellum predecessors. Its modern amenities included "sanitary, scientific" plumbing, heating, and electric lighting. The exterior presented the Southern Colonial at its most spectacular, with two massive Ionic porticoes addressing Hillsborough Street and the Capitol. In such a house, the imagery of the old plantation evoked family histories of lost grandeur, while its modern luxury and prominent location expressed the Raneys' position in the city where they and other children of planter families had created a new urban version of the old way of life.[49]

More and more columned residences appeared as other members of the cities' elites followed suit. Raleigh's Hillsborough Street was soon lined by a parade of pillared porticoes on both old and new houses. A mile down the street, opposite the Cameron mansion, St. Mary's School, the old Episcopal girls' school, refurbished its campus in Southern Colonial style.[50] In Wilm-

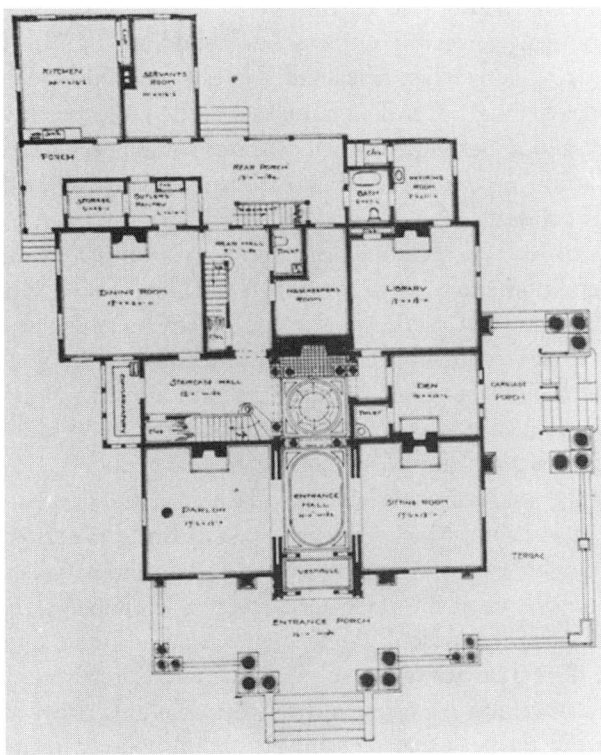

FIG. 10.15. *Plan of Raney House. From Barrett,* Colonial Southern Homes. (NCDAH)

Landmarks of Power | 283

FIG. 10.16. *Orton Plantation. Postcard, mid-twentieth century.* (NCDAH)

ington, too, local reporters rhapsodized reliably over the "modern," "convenient," "Colonial" residences wealthy citizens were building. The most flamboyant example rose in 1905 when Elizabeth Eagles Haywood Bridgers—descendant of ancient North Carolina families and the recent widow of Preston L. Bridgers, a local businessman who had been among the leaders of the 1898 "Revolution"—built a massive stone townhouse dominated by a curved portico of colossal Ionic columns and filled with the latest in luxurious modern amenities.[51] As the popularity of the style continued, an especially powerful rendition appeared in 1913 when the Cape Fear Club, bastion of the city's business and professional men, erected its new clubhouse in the form of a red brick mansion trimmed in white marble, "patterned closely after the Colonial style of architecture," and featuring "long commodious verandas, with large white columns" and reception rooms "arranged and decorated after the Colonial style of the Adams period."[52]

The Southern Colonial image also reached beyond the city into suburban enclaves. Between 1907 and 1910, Mary Bridgers, Preston Bridgers's sister, developed Carolina Heights east of Wilmington for leading industrialists and merchants, building the most imposing residences in "Colonial" style with porticoes in every classical order.[53] At the same time, on their Orton Plantation on the Cape Fear River (fig. 10.16), James and Luola Sprunt transformed another antebellum mansion into a hybrid Colonial Revival composition, keeping the classical, temple-form plantation house with its grand portico as the central element to which they added conveniently appointed wings on either side. Sprunt regarded Orton as "the most attractive of all the old colonial estates on the Cape Fear," which "still maintains its reputation of colonial days for a refined and generous hospitality" and presents "one of the finest examples of pure Colonial architecture in America... with its stately white columns gleaming in the sunshine."[54] These landmarks inaugurated a lasting pattern. As cities' changing residential trends and the proliferation of suburbs embodied growing separation among races and classes, the Colonial Revival in its myriad forms came to dominate upper- and middle-class housing throughout the South, and to be identified simply and universally with traditional domesticity, respectability, and continuity.

THE EPITOME OF THE NEW SOUTHERN ORDER

When North Carolina Democratic leaders organized the state's official presentation at the Jamestown Tercentennial Exposition of 1907, they recapitulated themes that had recently emerged in the state's life. The exposition combined a celebration of the oldest (1607) establishment of Anglo-Saxon culture in America with a southern-sponsored reunion of blue and gray, a presentation of modern southern race relations, and a certain amount of economic boosterism. Led by Gov. Robert Glenn, North Carolina set out to put on an exhibit "first-class in every respect" to attract investors and "desirable" immigrants. Business leaders presented displays touting the state's economic progress and opportunities.

Charged with creating a state history exhibit, Mary Hilliard Hinton, editor of the Daughters of the Revolution's thriving *North Carolina Booklet*, worked with other prominent women to assemble a dazzling display of the recent "historical awakening in the Old North State." The exhibit began with depictions of America's first Anglo-Saxon settlement, the Lost Colony at Roanoke, illustrated by paintings funded by Bennehan Cameron and copied from John White's 1585 and 1588 drawings of native Indian life. (Miss Hinton noted that this feature was presented simply "to start with the beginning of our state's history, and not with an ambition to antedate the first permanent English settlement at Jamestown by twenty-two years.") Displays included photographs of James Sprunt's collection of portraits of the Lords Proprietors, silver from various "aristocratic" families, pictures of celebrated plantation homes and furniture from a few of them, and a depiction of the Edenton Tea Party scene together with possessions of those patriotic colonial ladies.[55]

North Carolina's chief expenditure was on its state building. With each participating state constructing an example of its "typical Colonial" architecture, the exposition managers hoped to create a "Colonial acropolis

FIG. 10.17. *North Carolina Building, Jamestown Exposition. Photograph 1907.* (NCDAH)

restful to the eye and satisfying to sentiment," which would "result in a revival of interest in Colonial architecture, which is really the only distinctive American order of building." Virginia erected a brick and marble colonial mansion 116 feet long, while Georgia offered a Greek Revival temple modeled on President Roosevelt's mother's ancestral home as "a splendid specimen of the old colonial home." North Carolina leaders chose the Southern Colonial style that had become so popular in the state, a house built of North Carolina pine and "of large colonial design with immense columns and porches." The North Carolina Building (fig. 10.17) further promoted the style back home by inspiring citizens who visited the exposition to copy it in their own houses. And the North Carolina Architectural Association, which included many of the state's chief practitioners of the Colonial Revival, held its summer 1907 meeting at the exposition amidst the seaside "Colonial acropolis."[56]

In this official display of the state's self-image, as in the Colonial Revival architecture and commemorative monuments back home, Democratic leaders set forth the values and the heritage they intended to shape the state in the new century. Miss Hinton summed up their accomplishment:

> The keynote of American life is progress—an excellent and most powerful characteristic; yet harm and ultimate ruin will surely follow in its trail unless safeguarded by conservatism. No study so engenders and promotes the cultivation of this check to vandalism as does History. At last the dominant trait of the Anglo-Saxon race is asserting itself and we are becoming more like our relatives overseas, who guard sacredly whatever bears on their glorious past.[57]

For the Democratic elite, the book had opened on a redeemed and progressive South that reaffirmed the social order of their antebellum heyday, while embracing a program of modern economic progress. Just as they had taken control of the political process with strategies devised to dictate the present and the future, so at the same time they took control of the region's history and defined the meaning of the past in a fashion that explained and vindicated the present. By molding public memory of the past, they also shaped the direction of the future. They engaged in a process that, while sharing some features with what has been called the "invention of tradition," might best be termed the "arranging of tradition."[58] Rather than concocting a history to undergird their position, they employed precisely the same tactic that Alfred Moore Waddell had described in 1895, using the events of the past "like a child's box of letters with which we can spell any word we please. We have only to select such letters as we want, arrange them as we like, and say nothing about those which do not suit our purpose." Vital to this spelling out of the past was the creation of public, visible, lasting symbols of that past.

Thus between 1890 and 1910 elite Democratic leaders succeeded in forging a symbolic ensemble that defined North Carolina history and public life in accord with their vision of society. Within a short time, both the history they spelled out and the social and political system they had established took on an aura of permanence, which was reinforced in the form of monuments and architecture. So effective was the combined effect of cultural and political control that for many it seemed that the hierarchical, racially segregated South had always been thus, except for the brief aberration of Reconstruction, and presumably would always remain so.

In the mid-twentieth century, challenges to the racial and political structure created by the Democrats in 1900 began to change the South. Far more lasting, however, was the definition of history they had established. Although historians in the middle and late years of the twentieth century have begun to reexamine old assumptions, public memory has been slow to change. In the sagas told by memorials and by the seemingly unbroken continuity of colonial architecture, the old story persists. Through the powerful and lasting language of monuments and architecture, the guardians of the glorious past have continued to guard the past, the present, and the future.

NOTES

The author acknowledges with thanks a 1987 Henry Francis du Pont fellowship at the Winterthur Museum for initial research on this topic. The author also thanks, for critical readings and suggestions, John Bishir, Jerry Cashion, Jeffrey Crow, Catherine Hutchins, James Leloudis, Carl Lounsbury, William Price, Janet Seapker, Dell Upton, Harry Watson, Camille

Wells, and Chris Wilson; and for encouragement and assistance in obtaining illustrations and information, Claudia Brown, Ned Cooke, Michael Hill, Elizabeth Reid Murray, Beverly Tetterton, Edward Turberg, Abigail Van Slyck, Harry Warren, and R. Beverly R. Webb.

1. Rev. M. M. Marshall, "Address," in *Exercises at the Opening of the Olivia Raney Library, Held in the Library Hall on the Evening of Thursday, January Twenty-Fourth, 1901* (Capital Printing Co., 1901), 14–15.

2. Wilmington, the Cape Fear River port settled in the early eighteenth century, was from 1850 through 1900 North Carolina's largest city, with about 20,000 people (56 percent of whom were black) in 1890. Raleigh, the inland capital established in 1792, had in 1890 nearly 13,000 people (50 percent black and 50 percent white). In subsequent decades the piedmont industrial cities of Charlotte and Winston-Salem drew ahead in population.

3. This summary derives primarily from the following works: Kenneth Ames, "Introduction," in *The Colonial Revival in America*, ed. Alan Axelrod (W. W. Norton and Co., 1985); Edward L. Ayers, *The Promise of the New South: Life After Reconstruction* (Oxford University Press, 1992); John Bodnar, *Remaking America: Public Memory, Commemoration, and Patriotism in the Twentieth Century* (Princeton University Press, 1992); Michele H. Bogart, *Public Sculpture and the Civic Ideal in New York City, 1890–1930* (University of Chicago Press, 1989); Gaines M. Foster, *Ghosts of the Confederacy: Defeat, the Lost Cause, and the Emergence of the New South, 1865 to 1913* (Oxford University Press, 1987); Michael Kammen, *Mystic Chords of Memory: The Transformation of Tradition in American Culture* (Alfred A. Knopf, 1991); Robert W. Rydell, *All the World's a Fair: Visions of Empire at American International Expositions, 1876–1916* (University of Chicago Press, 1984); Christopher Wilson, *The Myth of Santa Fe* (University of New Mexico Press, 1997); Richard Guy Wilson et al., *The American Renaissance, 1876–1917* (Pantheon, 1979); and Richard Guy Wilson, "Architecture and the Reinterpretation of the Past in the American Renaissance," *Winterthur Portfolio* 18 (Spring 1983): 69–87.

4. Quotes from Charles B. Aycock, "The South Regaining Its Prestige," in *Literary and Historical Activities in North Carolina, 1900–1905* (Raleigh Publications of the Historical Commission, 1907), 1:120; and *The Biographical History of North Carolina from Colonial Times to the Present,* ed. Samuel A. Ashe (Charles L. Van Noppen, 1905), 1:36.

5. Harry S. Warren, "Colonel Frederick Augustus Olds and the Founding of the North Carolina Museum of History" (M.A. thesis, East Carolina University, 1988), 20–21. Samuel A'Court Ashe (1840–1938), a graduate of the U.S. Naval Academy and an Episcopalian, engaged in several occupations, founded the *News and Observer* in 1881, and produced *The Biographical History of North Carolina.* See *The Dictionary of North Carolina Biography,* ed. William S. Powell (University of North Carolina Press, 1979–).

6. The Raleigh Ladies Memorial Association was organized in 1866 with Mrs. General L. O'B. Branch (née Nancy Haywood Blount) as president ("Ladies Memorial Association," the *News and Observer,* 10 May 1903). North and South Carolina and some of Virginia used May 10 as Memorial Day, the anniversary of Stonewall Jackson's death (Foster, *Ghosts of the Confederacy,* 42). Alfred Moore Waddell (1834–1912), a descendant of colonial general Hugh Waddell and Revolutionary general Francis Nash, practiced law, edited newspapers in Charlotte and Wilmington, and though opposing secession, served as an officer in the war. As a "Redeemer" Conservative and Democrat, he was elected to Congress (1870–79); he wrote *Some Memories of My Life* and works of Cape Fear history (Powell, ed., *Dictionary of North Carolina Biography*).

7. Ladies Memorial Association Records, North Carolina State Archives, Division of Archives and History, Raleigh. As Waddell noted, the state had previously (1857) erected a bronze cast of Houdon's statue of George Washington on the Capitol grounds.

8. See Foster, *Ghosts of the Confederacy,* on the shift from funereal to civic memorials. According to Ralph W. Widener, Jr.'s, *Confederate Monuments* (privately published, 1982), in North Carolina only the Concord monument (1892) predates the Raleigh monument on a civic site. On the North Carolina Monumental Association, see Branch Papers, North Carolina Division of Archives and History. Officers included Mrs. Armistead Jones (president), Mrs. Garland Jones, and Mrs. John W. Hinsdale. Mrs. Armistead Jones (née Nancy Haywood Branch) was the daughter of Gen. Lawrence O'Bryan Branch (railroad president and Confederate officer) and Nancy Haywood

Blount Branch, founding president of the Ladies Memorial Association. Her husband, Armistead Jones, was a Confederate officer, Raleigh attorney, and Democratic party leader (see "Armistead Jones" in Powell, ed., *Dictionary of North Carolina Biography*). First quote, undated (February 1895) clipping, Scrapbook, Branch Papers, North Carolina Division of Archives and History.

9. *News and Observer,* 20, 21 May 1895. The granite came from Mount Airy, N.C., quarries. In contrast to the popular mass-produced soldier figures, the figures were modeled on North Carolina regiments and fashioned by Bavarian sculptor Ferdinand Von Miller. Prominent on the dais were Mrs. Armistead Jones, Mrs. Gen. Branch, Mrs. Gen. Stonewall Jackson, and Mrs. Gen. D. H. Hill. Rev. Aldert Smedes, principal of St. Mary's School, offered the prayer. Julia Jackson Christian unveiled the monument.

10. See Fred Arthur Bailey, "The Textbooks of the 'Lost Cause': Censorship and the Creation of Southern State Histories," *Georgia Historical Quarterly* 75 (Fall 1991): 507–33, for a similar 1895 speech by Stephen D. Lee to the United Confederate Veterans in Houston, part of the effort of the "South's aristocrats" to defend "not merely the South, but, more importantly, the embattled status of southern patricians" (508).

11. Richard N. Current, "That Other Declaration, May 20, 1775–May 20, 1975," *North Carolina Historical Review* 54 (April 1977): 169–91. North Carolina Confederate leaders' usage of the symbolic date paralleled the Confederate government's choice of February 22 as its founding date and the use of Washington's image on its official seal.

12. James Sprunt to Alfred Moore Waddell, 21 May 1895, and H. G. Connor to Alfred Moore Waddell, 23 May 1895, Alfred Moore Waddell Papers, Southern Historical Collection, Library of the University of North Carolina at Chapel Hill. (See political leader Henry Groves Connor and his son, historian and archivist Robert D. W. Connor, in Powell, ed., *Dictionary of North Carolina Biography*.)

13. J. Morgan Kousser, *The Shaping of Southern Politics: Suffrage Restriction and the Establishment of the One-Party South, 1880–1910* (Yale University Press, 1974); C. Vann Woodward, *Origins of the New South, 1877–1913* (Louisiana State University Press, 1971); and Paul Escott, *Many Excellent People: Power and Privilege in North Carolina, 1850–1900* (University of North Carolina Press, 1985).

14. Quotes from Josephus Daniels, *Editor in Politics* (University of North Carolina Press, 1941), 295, 283. Other first-hand accounts that capture even in retrospect the spirit of the times include Alfred Moore Waddell, *Some Memories of My Life* (Edwards and Broughton, 1908), and a 1933 interview with Furnifold Simmons in Carl Goerch, *Down Home* (Edwards and Broughton, 1943), 131–58. Charles B. Aycock and Robert Glenn later served as governors, and Francis Winston, organizer of the "White Supremacy Club" system, became lieutenant governor.

15. James Sprunt, *Chronicles of the Cape Fear River* (Edwards and Broughton, 1916), 554–55; and H. Leon Prather, *We Have Taken a City: The Wilmington Racial Massacre and Coup of 1898* (Associated University Presses, 1984), 45. In 1898 Bellamy was the successful Democratic candidate for Congress.

16. Alex Manly, publisher of the *Wilmington Record,* wrote the editorial in response to Atlanta writer Rebecca Felton's article on lynching black men for raping white women. Portions of his editorial were taken out of context and widely reprinted to exacerbate white fears. Prather, *We Have Taken a City;* and Sprunt, *Chronicles,* 554–55.

17. *Wilmington Messenger,* 25 October 1898. On 28 October 1898, at the "White Supremacy Convention" at Goldsboro, Waddell used similar language. Following a speech by William A. Guthrie of Durham (a former Populist)—who led off with an assertion of Anglo-Saxon supremacy: "Resist our march of progress and civilization and we will wipe you off the face of the earth"—Waddell described white Wilmingtonians' problems and their determination to drive out Manly, Russell, and others "if they have to throw enough dead Negro bodies in the Cape Fear to choke up its passage to the sea." This speech "electrified" the convention and, quoted across the state, made Wilmington's cause "the cause of all" (Daniels, *Editor in Politics,* 301).

18. George M. Tolson, Hertford, N.C., 27 October 1898, to Alfred Moore Waddell; and Rebecca Cameron to Alfred Moore Waddell, 26 October 1898, Waddell Papers. Miss Cameron, a cousin of both Waddell and Bennehan Cameron, was a leader in the United Daughters of the Confederacy and a founder in 1900

of the State Literary and Historical Society. "Anna" was her sister (see genealogical chart, Jean Bradley Anderson, *Piedmont Plantation: The Bennehan-Cameron Family and Lands in North Carolina* [Historic Preservation Society of Durham, 1985]).

19. Prather, *We Have Taken a City;* and Waddell, *Some Memories of My Life.*

20. Bennehan Cameron to Alfred Moore Waddell, 13 November 1898, Waddell Papers. Sprunt, *Chronicles,* 555; and Waddell, *Some Memories of My Life,* 243.

21. Waddell is quoted in Daniels, *Editor in Politics,* 368. Chief "engineers" of the state's suffrage amendment were George Rountree of Wilmington, Francis Winston of Bertie County, and Josephus Daniels. The election of 1900 was held in August rather than November to prevent possible Federal interference (Kousser, *Shaping of Southern Politics,* 190–91).

22. With the disfranchisement of blacks, the Republican party also wrote off the Negro vote and became "lily white," and factionalism promptly returned to the Democratic party. These events were entwined with such national trends as dwindling northern concern over the fate of southern blacks (as epitomized in the acceptance of separate but equal facilities in *Plessy v. Ferguson*); mounting Anglo-American nativism in the face of growing immigration from eastern and southern Europe; and expanding American imperialism in lands with non-Anglo-Saxon populations. Amidst these trends, the New South used its white supremacist "solution" to the "Negro problem" and its predominantly native-born white population to undergird a position of national leadership.

23. *Public Documents of the State of North Carolina* (Edwards and Broughton and E. M. Uzzell, 1901), vol. 1, document 1a, pp. 2, 4, 12.

24. The qualification for membership read "any white resident of the State, or North Carolinian residing out of the State, who subscribes to the purposes of the Association" (*Literary and Historical Activities in North Carolina,* 1–3, 6).

25. From these roots also emerged the state's tradition of distinguished historians as well as the fruitful relationship between historical pursuits and civic and political leaders. See William S. Price, Jr., "Plowing Virgin Fields: State Support for Southern Archives, Particularly North Carolina," *Carolina Comments* 29 (March 1991): 41–47.

26. An important dimension of this story is to be explored in dissenting views of other groups both black and white, whose stories were omitted or denied in the official codified saga written and symbolic. In Virginia, as Kirk Savage describes in "Race, Memory and Identity: The National Monuments of the Union and the Confederacy" (Ph.D. diss., University of California, Berkeley, 1990), blacks' dissenting views took a variety of forms, including both nonparticipation and pointed commentary. For example, concerning the monument to Robert E. Lee in Richmond, a local black newspaper, the *Richmond Planet,* observed on 7 June 1890 that "[t]he Negro ... put up the Lee Monument, and should the time come, will be there to take it down" (Savage 150).

27. See *Literary and Historical Activities in North Carolina* for representative rhetoric on these topics; *The North Carolina Booklet* (North Carolina Society of the Daughters of the Revolution, 1901–1926); Daniel Harvey Hill, *Young People's History of North Carolina* (Alfred Williams, 1916); and Ashe, ed., *Biographical History of North Carolina.*

28. *News and Observer,* 16, 18, 19 August 1900; *Heroes and Heroines on Union Square* (State Capitol Foundation, Inc., 1983); Daniels, *Editor in Politics,* 369; and *Literary and Historical Activities in North Carolina.* See Bogart, *Public Sculpture and the Civic Ideal,* 32, on Beaux-Arts sculptor Augustus Saint-Gaudens's influential use of gesture in his celebrated *Farragut* (1881).

29. Quotes from the *Atlanta Constitution* and *New York Tribune,* Ayers, *Promise of the New South,* 331–32. Francis H. Packer was a New York sculptor who worked with the prominent Beaux-Arts sculptor Daniel Chester French on such projects as the figure of Lincoln in Henry Bacon's Lincoln Memorial in Washington, D.C. (Tony P. Wrenn, *Wilmington, North Carolina: An Architectural and Historical Portrait* [University Press of Virginia, 1984], 203).

30. *News and Observer,* 19, 20, 21 May 1907.

31. Wrenn, *Wilmington,* 295–97; *Wilmington Star,* 2, 3 May 1907; and Rosa Chiles, "North Carolina Society of Colonial Dames in America," in Sprunt, *Chronicles,* 578–79.

32. *Wilmington Messenger,* 20, 21 April 1906, and 3 May 1907; and *Wilmington Star,* 2, 3 May 1907.

33. Fred Olds, *Wilmington Morning Star,* 28 January 1906, reprinted in the 27 January 1906

Charlotte Observer; courtesy of Harry Warren. In 1909 the Colonial Dames erected a second marker to the "Men of the Cape Fear" at Brunswick, a ruined town that was the actual site of the Stamp Act resistance, citing the 150 "armed men of the Cape Fear," led by George Moore of Orton and Cornelius Harnett. The site was part of the Murchison and Sprunt holdings; in 1952 James Laurence Sprunt donated the Brunswick Town site to the state (James Sprunt, *The Story of Orton Plantation* [published privately in Wilmington, 1958]).

34. *Presentation of the Statue Hon. George Davis to the City of Wilmington by the Daughters of the Confederacy,* 20 April 1911. The address at the cornerstone laying was by Alfred Moore Waddell; that at the unveiling by Judge H. G. Connor (Mrs. William M. Parsley, "The George Davis Monument," in Sprunt, *Chronicles,* 572–73). On Sprunt's role see Mrs. William M. Parsley to James Sprunt, 9 January and 27 March 1909. Sprunt promised to donate $1,000 and persuaded two businessmen to match his sum (Sprunt to H. Walters, 2 February 1909; Sprunt to S. P. Shotter, 4 March 1909), and others to donate smaller amounts (Sprunt to various recipients, March 1909); he also worked out arrangements with the sculptor (correspondence from the Alexander Sprunt and Sons Papers, Special Collections Library, Duke University, Durham).

35. Architect Henry Bacon had lived in Wilmington and maintained ties during an illustrious career that included the Lincoln Memorial. Horne Committee Papers, North Carolina Division of Archives and History. Other monuments on Union Square commemorate Democratic educator Charles McIver (1912); Charles B. Aycock (1924); Samuel A'Court Ashe (1940); three presidents North Carolina "gave the nation" (1948); Vietnam veterans (1987); and World Wars I and II and the Korean Conflict (1990).

36. The *Booklet* began in May 1901 under Miss Martha Helen Haywood and Mrs. Hubert Haywood; they were soon succeeded by Miss Hinton and Mrs. Moffitt. These women made the *Booklet* a long-lived success that helped define the emerging canon of state history. See Mary Hilliard Hinton (1869–1961), and Elvira Worth Moffitt (1836–1930) in Powell, ed., *Dictionary of North Carolina Biography;* Mary Hilliard Hinton Papers, Southern Historical Collection; and Elvira Worth Moffitt Papers, Southern Historical Collection).

37. *News and Observer,* 24 October 1908; *Charlotte Evening Chronicle,* 24 October 1908; and *Greensboro Daily Industrial News,* 25 October 1908.

38. *David Paton: Architect of the North Carolina State Capitol, An Address by Samuel A. Ashe* (Edwards and Broughton, 1916), 15.

39. Quoted in Bailey, "Textbooks of the 'Lost Cause,'" 508.

40. *News and Observer,* 6 June 1907. See also Charlotte V. Brown, "The Day of the Great Cities," in Catherine W. Bishir, Charlotte V. Brown, Ernest H. Wood, and Carl R. Lounsbury, *Architects and Builders in North Carolina: A History of the Practice of Building* (University of North Carolina Press, 1990), 298.

41. Glenn Brown, in "Old Colonial Work in Virginia and Maryland," *American Architect and Building News,* 22 October 1887, 198. Joy Wheeler Dow, *American Renaissance: A Review of Domestic Architecture* (William T. Comstock, 1904). Nationally the Colonial Revival was related to the creation of American period rooms in museums, the establishment of many national patriotic and ancestral organizations, and the passage of the National Origins Act in 1924; see William B. Rhoads, *The Colonial Revival* (Garland Publishing, Inc., 1977), and William B. Rhoads, "The Colonial Revival and American Nationalism," *Journal of the Society of Architectural Historians* 35 (December 1976): 239–54.

42. *American Architect and Building News,* 6 April 1895. Issues of *Southern Architect* show the incorporation of Colonial motifs into houses of a variety of forms in the late 1890s and a shift to the symmetrical house with a dominant portico in 1899.

43. *Charlotte Observer,* 20 December 1903. Similar ideas were repeated in national literature, as, for example, J. Robie Kennedy, Jr., "Examples of Georgian and Greek Revival Work in the Far South," *Architectural Record* 21 (March 1907); and Russell F. Whitehead, "The Old and the New South," *Architectural Record* 30 (July 1911).

44. Robert W. Winston, *It's A Far Cry* (Henry Holt and Co., 1937), 262–63.

45. Wrenn, *Wilmington,* 53–55. See also the *Wilmington Star,* 2 May 1902 and 4 May 1907.

After James Sprunt's death his son, J. Laurence Sprunt, replaced the portico and porches with a small, Georgian Revival entrance portico. See James Sprunt (1846–1924) in Powell, ed., *Dictionary of North Carolina Biography*. As Colonial Dames president, Luola Sprunt developed a systematic list of colonial sites to mark, which formed a basis for subsequent state programs (Sprunt, *Chronicles*, 578–85, and *Story of Orton Plantation*).

46. On Bennehan Cameron, (1854–1925), son of Paul and Anne Ruffin Cameron, see Powell, ed., *Dictionary of North Carolina Biography;* Jean Anderson, *Piedmont Plantations;* and Bennehan Cameron Papers, Southern Historical Collection.

47. P. H. Mayo to Sallie Cameron, 17 June 1901; Sallie Cameron to Bennehan Cameron, July–October, 1901; and "Alterations & Additions to Residence of Col. Bennehan Cameron," September 1901, Noland & Baskervill, Architects, Richmond (blueprints for rear extension and porch details), Bennehan Cameron Papers, Southern Historical Collection. Last quote is from Virgil St. Cloud, *Pioneer Blood* (Edwards and Broughton, 1948). Bennehan Cameron was a friend of Thomas Dixon, and unsubstantiated local tradition claims the house was the setting for Dixon's novel *The Clansman*.

48. Clippings and family memorabilia, courtesy of R. Beverly R. Webb. See Richard Beverly Raney in *Who's Who in America*, 1903 (1215). Kate's parents were Capt. Claudius B. and Mary Matilda Cowan Denson (see "Claudius Denson" in Powell, ed., *Dictionary of North Carolina Biography*). Mary Matilda was the daughter of Thomas and Mary Ashe London Cowan of Old Town Plantation on the Cape Fear. After the war, the Densons lived in reduced circumstances in Pittsboro, then moved to Raleigh in 1887 when Denson became coprincipal with Hugh Morson of the Raleigh Male Academy. On the day of the unveiling of the Confederate monument, the Densons hosted a lawn party for the Wilmington Light Infantry. Kate Denson pursued church, patriotic, and artistic interests: in 1899 when the city adopted a coat of arms and city flag to give to the U.S.S. Raleigh, which had distinguished itself in the Spanish-American War, she sewed the flag, and in 1900 she helped organize a Confederate lawn party for veterans on the occasion of the unveiling of the Vance Memorial (*News and Observer*, 16 August 1900). Kate and Beverly Raney were also members of Christ Church.

49. *Southern Architect* 10 (March 1899): 684–85; and Charles Barrett, *Colonial Southern Homes* (privately printed in Raleigh, 1903).

50. Next to the Raney House, the Johnson residence gained a tall Corinthian portico. Nearby, the Rogers family built a big new columned brick house fronted by a tall Ionic portico. In the next block rose Dr. Andrew Goodwin's frame house with an Ionic portico by William P. Rose. Across the street the antebellum residence of Gen. Lawrence O'Bryan Branch received a bowed Corinthian portico (Survey and Planning Branch Files, North Carolina Division of Archives and History). At St. Mary's, the Episcopal diocese bought the campus from its longtime owners, the Cameron family, in 1897, and soon began a building campaign. In 1903–4 a brick residence for Bishop Joseph Blount Cheshire, Jr., was built on the campus from designs by Charles Barrett. It was followed by the neoclassically detailed Eliza Battle Pittman Auditorium of 1907 (designed by C. C. Hook) and the 1910 expansion and remodeling of the main building by architect Charles E. Hartge, with a towering portico facing Hillsborough Street (Martha Stoops, *The Heritage: The Education of Women at St. Mary's College, Raleigh, North Carolina, 1842–1982* [St. Mary's College, 1984]).

51. Preston Bridgers, son of leading railroader Robert R. Bridgers, was "a merchant, manufacturer, banker, capitalist" who was "prominently identified with the 'Revolution of 1898,' when the best citizenship of the city banded together to suppress negroes and substrata agitators" and "cleans[e] the community of its viciously undesirable riff-raff" (R. H. Fisher, *Biographical Sketches of Wilmington Citizens* [Wilmington Stamp and Printing Co., 1929], 85). On the Bridgers mansion see the *Wilmington News*, 23 July 1971; Wrenn, *Wilmington,* 87; and McMillan's blueprints in the Bridgers Mansion File, Survey and Planning Branch, North Carolina Division of Archives and History.

52. Leslie N. Boney, Jr., *The Cape Fear Club, 1967–1983* (Wilmington Printing Co., 1984), 1–7. The Cape Fear Club was organized in 1866, mainly by former Confederate officers, to "promote literary and social intercourse among its members" and to reassert old social patterns in the turbulent postwar years. They built a clubhouse from designs by New York architect

Charles Pierrepont H. Gilbert (*Wilmington Evening Dispatch*, 3 November 1913).

53. Mary Bridgers (1871–1910), heiress of railroader Robert Bridgers, led in establishing the Christian Science church in Wilmington. Architect Burett Stephens, who came from Chicago in 1905, planned the Carolina Heights development and designed its principal houses. These were the homes of Atlantic coastline railroad president Thomas Emerson, Delgado Cotton Mill president Edwin C. Holt, and wholesale grocer J. W. Brooks (S. Carol Gunter, *Carolina Heights: The Preservation of an Urban Neighborhood in Wilmington* [Wilmington Department of Planning, 1982], 15; and Wrenn, *Wilmington*, 280–84).

54. Orton began as the early-eighteenth-century home of "King" Roger Moore of the powerful Moore family; it was incorporated into an imposing temple-form Greek Revival mansion in about 1840. After the war, Orton Plantation was the winter home of Col. Kenneth Murchison; after his death in 1904, his son-in-law Sprunt bought Orton and encouraged his wife to restore and expand the house (Sprunt, *Story of Orton Plantation*). Sprunt, *Chronicles*, 57–58.

55. Mary Hilliard Hinton, *The North Carolina Historical Exhibit at the Jamestown Ter-Centennial Exposition* (Edwards and Broughton, 1916), 7, 9.

56. *The Official Blue Book of the Jamestown Ter-Centennial Exposition*, ed. Charles Russéll Kelley (Colonial Publishing Co., Inc., 1909), 367–68. Lumber merchant Kenneth Howard in Dunn, North Carolina, was one who copied the North Carolina building in his residence (Davyd Foard Hood, Kenneth L. Howard House National Register nomination, Survey and Planning Branch, North Carolina Division of Archives and History). On the NCAA meeting see *Southern Architect and Building News*, 28 December 1907. Predecessor and later contemporary of the North Carolina chapter of the American Institute of Architects, the group included as founding leaders Charles Barrett (vice president), Charles McMillan, C. E. Hartge, and C. C. Hook. On the NCAA and the North Carolina American Institute of Architects, see Brown, "The Day of the Great Cities" in Bishir et al., *Architects and Builders in North Carolina*, 337–40.

57. Hinton, *North Carolina Historical Exhibit*, 7.

58. See *The Invention of Tradition*, ed. Eric Hobsbawm and Terence Ranger (Cambridge University Press, 1983).

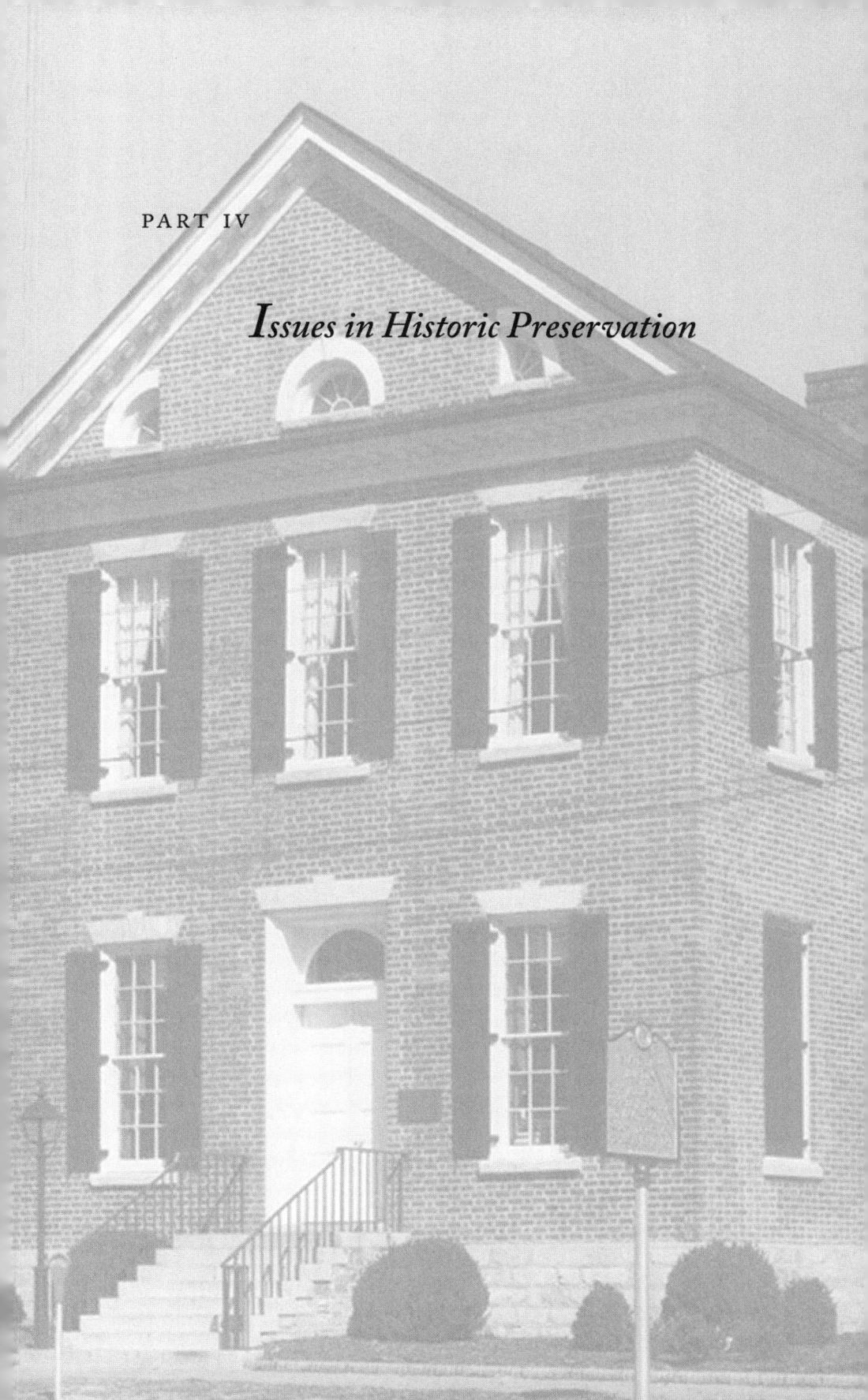

PART IV

Issues in Historic Preservation

Eleven

LOOKING AT NORTH CAROLINA'S HISTORY THROUGH ARCHITECTURE

I have heard it said, by those who know them well, that there are at least three good, different, and occasionally overlapping reasons to preserve old buildings—and corresponding ways of considering the value of those buildings.

Perhaps the most commonly admired reason is stated from the viewpoint of connoisseurship or art history: because the historic building is a more or less wonderful example of a certain style of architecture. This viewpoint tends to base evaluation upon the aesthetic quality of the physical object. Biltmore is a superb example of late-nineteenth-century Chateauesque style, the late work of a master, Richard Morris Hunt. The State Capitol in Raleigh (fig. 11.1), designed according to classical precedents, is a superb example of the Greek Revival style. Land's End in Perquimans County (fig. 11.2), with its classical portico and beautiful craftsmanship, displays the same style in a regional adaptation. If one looks at buildings strictly from this viewpoint, it may mean that one values most highly the preservation of the *best* examples of certain styles or types.

The second viewpoint is the practical or functional—the notion that some old buildings are worth saving because they are useful to today's daily life. There are good bricks and woodwork it's a shame to waste; the spaces are pleasant; they are or can be livable and marketable. This is a selling point

---

"Looking at North Carolina's History through Architecture" was originally a talk given at the annual meeting of the Federation of North Carolina Historical Societies on November 18, 1982; it appeared in *Carolina Comments* 31, no. 2 (March 1983): 51–57, and is reprinted by permission of the Historical Publications Section, North Carolina Office of Archives and History, Department of Cultural Resources, Raleigh.

FIG. 11.1. *State Capitol, 1833-40, Raleigh. Photograph by Charles Clark, 1967. The architectural centerpiece and heart of the state, among the finest Greek Revival edifices in the nation, was designed by architects William Nichols Jr., Ithiel Town and A. J. Davis, and David Paton, with assistance from William Strickland.* (NCDAH)

FIG. 11.2. *Land's End, 1830s, Hertford vicinity, Perquimans County. Photograph by Randall Page, 1973. This imposing plantation house combines bold Greek Revival details from popular pattern books with the "engaged" porch and multisloped gable roof form of regional character.* (NCDAH)

FIG. 11.3. *State Bank, 1814, Raleigh. Photograph 1970s. The former state bank, one of the few early-nineteenth-century buildings remaining in Raleigh, now houses a credit union.* (NCDAH)

for preservation that has received lots of press—and success. It's certainly a part of my daily life. I work and earn my living in a mid-nineteenth-century Greek Revival house that now functions as a state office. I keep some of my income in an early-nineteenth-century bank (fig. 11.3); I spend most of that money on an early-twentieth-century bungalow in a streetcar suburb. None of these buildings would be regarded as the top of the line from a connoisseurship viewpoint; but they are useful and well built, and I like how they enrich my life. Practical values encourage the preservation of many buildings.

A third reason to preserve old buildings is as a record of the past. Old buildings are sources of information about past ways of life, and much of this information cannot be discerned in other ways. The great soaring elegance of the Jefferson Standard Building (fig. 11.4) speaks unmistakably of Greensboro's pride, passion, and ambition in 1922 to become a city. The little cluster of mill houses at Glencoe in Alamance County (fig. 11.5) communicates something of the rural isolation of North Carolina's antebellum textile mill villages. Looking at historic buildings from this viewpoint suggests certain values about what to preserve, why, and how. Those values may sometimes overlap with connoisseurship or practicality—or they may not.

It is this third way of looking at historic buildings that I want to focus on here—first, what is rewarding about it to the amateur or professional historian, and second, some of the problems in dealing with buildings that are the record of our past.

I have no idea how many of you are in the habit of looking at architecture as a record of the past—either for fun or for profit. One thing I need to tell you is that it is fun. It enhances your daily life, at absolutely no cost,

Looking at North Carolina's History through Architecture

FIG. 11.4. *Jefferson Standard Building, 1923, Greensboro. Photograph by JoAnn Sieburg-Baker, 1975. The skyscraper, designed by architect Charles C. Hartmann, was the pride of Greensboro and for a time the tallest building in the state.* (NCDAH)

FIG. 11.5. *Glencoe Mill Village, 1880s, Burlington vicinity, Alamance County. This small, riverside mill village has been renewed as a model preservation project by Preservation North Carolina, but many mill houses, mills, and mill villages are being lost every year. Photograph by Michael T. Southern, 2002.* (NCDAH)

giving you an entirely new dimension to entertain your mind. And that, in my book, is one of the great real-life values of education and history, however seldom mentioned it may be.

I am only one of hundreds of people who began to look at architecture as a record of history and to see my town—the world—with entirely new eyes. And once you start looking at and thinking about your surroundings from a certain viewpoint, you get hooked—you can't *not* do it. If you know a modicum of geology, for example, wherever you travel you notice the rock formations—whether they be visible in highway cuts or simply the underlying landscape. "Hmm. Quite a fault there!" Or "what a nice Triassic basin!" And so it is with looking at buildings. It's not just their aesthetic appeal. Everywhere one goes, the past presents itself as it might if you were, say, driving through rural New England remarking to yourself or your companion, "Look at all those fantastic early-nineteenth-century houses. But such tiny little farms! What *were* they growing?" And then you notice the Connecticut River flowing ever so navigably into Long Island Sound. Or, driving the roads of piedmont North Carolina, you see nice farmland and only the simplest and cheapest and most conservative early houses; and you begin to wonder the reverse (fig. 11.6). And then you look at a map and note the absence of rivers navigable to any ocean ports, and you begin to understand. Or you approach Wilmington on your way to the beach. You see from a distance a middle-sized, apparently early-twentieth-century port city. But you decide to get off the highway and poke around, and soon you see more—not much colonial, that's soon clear, but instead a collection of high-style, expensive, *urban* antebellum buildings, which tells you that this place was suddenly quite a place in the mid-nineteenth century.

FIG. 11.6. *Mebane House, early nineteenth century, Greensboro vicinity, Guilford County. Photograph by H. McKelden Smith, 1977. A two-story frame house with brick chimney such as this one was considered a substantial dwelling in the nineteenth-century piedmont.* (NCDAH)

As a friend of mine once said, "What do you suppose people who don't look at buildings do on trips?"

Beyond the traveler's delight, however rewarding, there is a dimension that looking at history through architecture can represent for the serious historian—the local historian, the social historian, the cultural historian, the economic historian, the plain old regular historian—as well as the so-called architectural historian. Having learned whatever architectural history I know by looking at buildings and trying to figure out their meaning by reading documents and history books (and then finding history in turn more meaningful because of what the buildings say), I truly believe in the importance of buildings as a source of information about the past—information that complements, in the true sense of completes, what can be learned from written documents.

A historian studying the history of religious revivalism in rural areas, for example, could find out a great deal by reading in contemporary literature or interpretive history. But there is a dimension you could experience in no way other than by going to some of the camp-meeting grounds (fig. 11.7), where you would see the layout, the centrality of the arbor, the ancient concentricity of communal rows of tiny family shelters, the simplicity of construction, perhaps the use of color, and the absolute lack of "style"—but

FIG. 11.7. *Rock Springs Campground, Arbor 1832, Lincolnton vicinity, Lincoln County.* Photograph by Randall Page, 1972. *The campground still hosts summer camp meetings as it has done since the 1830s.* (NCDAH)

FIG. 11.8. *Coolmore, 1860, Tarboro vicinity, Edgecombe County. Photograph 1970. Designed by Baltimore architect E. G. Lind, the villa-style plantation house recalls the antebellum wealth and trade of the Tar River community of Tarboro.* (NCDAH)

the great power of basic design. You would recognize the need to be present when the people arrived in August, but you would also gain knowledge just by being *in the place.*

Or consider a cultural historian engaged in studying the great shift from a largely traditional rural society, which adhered to old, chiefly local modes of behavior, to a more "modern" community in which novel ideas, national models, and popular styles assumed prominence. Sources? Newspapers, letters, diaries, promotional tracts, economic records, the census—*and buildings.*

Tarboro, because many of its buildings from the nineteenth century still stand, would be a good place to work. One can see on the one hand the conservatism of its finest buildings of the first forty or fifty years of the century—even its wealthiest inhabitants erected simple frame houses, not much different from those built in the countryside for generations. But then, suddenly, sharply, in the 1850s, change. No longer the local models, but instead nationally promoted architectural styles are the standard for the elite: a grand and pretentious and utterly nonlocal suburban villa designed by an English architect for a local industrialist; a Gothic cottage promoted in architectural pattern books of the day; another villa (fig. 11.8), commissioned by a wealthy planter to be designed by a Baltimore architect, whose every bit of fine finish was ordered from Baltimore suppliers or executed by

FIG. 11.9. *Chowan County Courthouse, 1767, Edenton. Photograph by Stuart Schwartz, 1972. The only colonial courthouse standing in the state is a revered landmark.* (NCDAH)

Baltimore craftsmen. Thus, when one reads of the impact made by steamboats plying the Tar River, when one learns of the growing sophistication and emphasis upon progressive "book" farming among Edgecombe County's planters, it all begins to add up to provide a picture of the past—of what happened as thinking shifted from old and local and familiar to new and national and modern. The buildings are part of that story, offering a unique dimension.

But historians have tended to focus on written documents and to relegate the "built documents" of our history to the purview of the preservationist or the art historian. And we have tended to let the viewpoint of the connoisseur or the "practical" folks decide what should be saved. The value of historic buildings as a record of our past as a reason for saving them has received short shrift.

This brings up some difficult questions. What *are* the values used to judge the merits of historic buildings in determining public policy, creating the agendas of historical societies, and inspiring the crusades of preservationists? How do those values and policies shape and edit the very record we have of the past? Are they the values we as historians want to use to determine what we preserve as a record of our past?

We must always keep in mind that buildings, like written documents, mostly record the past of the rich, the successful, the literate, the white; and they represent the *best* of what these people did. It is by no means a balanced picture. Natural forces and ordinary human behavior tend constantly to skew the record toward the elite, to winnow out the ordinary. You do it yourself all the time to material as well as written documents of your own life—keeping the "important" stuff. The baby clothes you fold in tissue paper are the handmade beauties that the kid never actually wore much, not the knit jumpsuit with the leg snaps for diapers she wore every day for the first year. Will any of those stretched and faded jumpsuits survive to the next century, or will people of that time be forced to conclude that we still ironed embroidered dresses during the 1980s?

The buildings that stand for a century or two—and those which people naturally save—are the best ones. What do we have left from North Carolina's colonial period? Only the best, you can be assured. We have such monuments as the Chowan County Courthouse in Edenton (fig. 11.9) or nearby St. Paul's Church (see fig. 3.5, p. 75) but there is nothing standing to represent the lives of the thousands of people who lived in crude little dwelling houses. No wonder we think of it as a period of grace and order and elegance.

Or, to consider a more recent period, there were over 300,000 slaves in North Carolina on the eve of the Civil War. Of the houses owned by the large planters and slave owners—a tiny percentage of the population—dozens and dozens have survived, a goodly proportion of the total number that once stood. But slave houses? Practically zero—maybe a few dozen in the entire state, I would estimate. These structures were once legion and now are mighty few (fig. 11.10). There are not many practical reasons for saving slave houses once there are no slaves to house.

What we end up with, naturally, is not just a lot more of the grand and the glorious, preserved in inflated proportion, particularly when compared with the "ordinary," but almost exclusively the grand and the glorious and nearly none of the ordinary. Typically, the ordinary and the common are ignored until they are so few in number that they themselves become remarkable and unique. Two nineteenth-century examples are covered bridges, once a great sign of progress, and log houses with stick-and-mud chimneys, an ancient chimney form used in the construction of many slave dwellings and modest farmhouses. When I was born in 1942 there were scores and scores of these in North Carolina. They fell away unmourned for the most part as better bridges and better chimneys became attainable. At the present time there exist in all of North Carolina only three covered bridges and three or four known examples of the stick-and-mud chimney type. That's all.

In our generation, for the first time, decisions affecting the preservation of buildings are being made self-consciously as part of broad policies and procedures designed to save the patrimony of our nation and locality. These explicitly stated policies and procedures, intended to "preserve history," will shape what survives from our past to the next century.

Most policies are based on the assumption that what you ought to try to save is the best. In the National Register of Historic Places, the local historic property designation, the Historic Preservation Fund, and so on, the emphasis is on the unique, the fine, the outstanding, or perhaps the *best examples* of the typical. How often do we say, "Well, don't worry about tearing that down; those are a dime a dozen"? We assume that these values are correct. And I think they are, for they have helped us save things of great value. But are they also misleading? May they represent a confusing of the connoisseurship viewpoint (that a rare or fine object is better than a not-so-fine one) with the historian's viewpoint about buildings as a record of our past? Such well-meaning selectivity may only legitimize and intensify the natural process. Thus, with the best of intentions we ourselves may be unconsciously editing the record of the past.

Today there are fragile multitudes of structures from our recent history that are comparable to the slave houses and covered bridges that were yesterday's losses. I could mention for example log tobacco barns, rural tenant houses, and shotgun houses in urban developments. How many of these early-twentieth-century structures are there? Uncounted numbers. How are they distributed on the landscape? So broadly, so commonly, that they are taken for granted. Yet they are now outmoded and are being abandoned, replaced, and destroyed at a rapid rate. Today's legions will probably not last my lifetime. They will be just as gone as the slave houses and the covered bridges.

How important were the broad patterns of history these structures represent—the production of flue-cured tobacco in North Carolina (fig. 11.11), the rise of the tenant system, the in-migration and living patterns of many blacks in North Carolina's cities and towns? On a scale of one to ten, how might we rank these chapters in our history? Eight? Nine?

What are we—any of us—doing to keep or study these physical reminders of our past while they are still here in goodly numbers? I know of little scholarly attention to them. Things are not just in books because they are important; they also *become* important because they appear in books. There is a wealth of potential doctoral dissertations in any of these classes of things. Here's one: How did the shotgun house form (fig. 11.12)—which

FIG. 11.10. *Boyette Slave House, 1850s, Smithfield vicinity, Johnston County. Photograph 1983. A rare example (restored by the owner) of a slave dwelling, here with a wood and clay chimney, also an uncommon survival.* (NCDAH)

FIG. 11.11. *Tobacco barn, early twentieth century, Yanceyville vicinity, Caswell County. Photograph ca. 1956. Once a common sight in much of the state (at one time numbering over half a million), flue-cure tobacco barns are now an endangered breed.* (NCDAH)

one scholar traces from New Orleans back through Haiti to Africa as a black building type—find such rapid and universal translation across the American landscape between 1870 and 1900? Is it indeed predominantly a black house form? Did black residents or white developers decide to build them? Why? When? How?

And there are difficult preservation decisions to be made—the more difficult because no one has studied these matters. The buildings of ordinary people from the eighteenth and most of the nineteenth century are lost from the rural and urban landscape. But we still have many from the early twentieth century—a century with only seventeen more years to go. How do we deal with that heritage while it still stands? How do we single

FIG. 11.12. *Shotgun houses, early twentieth century, Kinston. Photograph by Collin Ingraham, 1995. Urban renewal has eliminated thousands of small worker houses in towns and cities; in a few cases they have been renovated for continued use.* (NCDAH)

FIG. 11.13. *Ricks tenant farmstead, early twentieth century, Rocky Mount vicinity, Nash County. Photograph by Richard Mattson, 1984. The built legacy of tenant farming, which was essential to the economy from the post–Civil War era into the 1960s, is disappearing throughout the countryside.* (NCDAH)

out a few "especially typical" tobacco barns or shotguns? What do you say to HUD or a local community development agency when it wants to replace worn-out, poorly built shotgun houses in a run-down neighborhood with clean, shiny, snug brick ranchers? What about these neighborhoods is vital to record or to save? Or do you let the passing of such structures go unmourned? How can you say, "Oh, dear tobacco farmer, please take out a loan to keep these wonderful and picturesque tobacco barns in the landscape—even though you can barely afford to make the payments on your mortgage and new bulk barns"? Are you kidding?

What historical society is going to research and restore as a museum the living conditions of a typical tenant house (fig. 11.13) as some have done by reproducing the glories of Hope Plantation to illustrate the gentry's way of life? Where can anyone in the future see what it might have been like to live in a neat, clean, well-kept tenant house with a washstand with a mirror over it in the kitchen, a wringer washer on the porch, gleaming linoleum floors, and chicken houses and an outhouse and a Delco plant in the yard? People remember such things now, but few of the former residents of those tenant houses had estate inventories or kept diaries or had photographs of the interiors of their houses made for magazines.

These are not landmarks that can be singled out individually for campaigns. You can put trendy shops and asparagus ferns into disused textile mills or tobacco warehouses, but there's not much call for adaptive reuse of the little log barns in which tobacco was cured.

We will probably save a few such places—a tobacco barn at Duke Homestead, perhaps a shotgun in which a black political leader was born. But what the future will miss out on is the *range* of such things. The very numerousness and commonness is part of their significance. Their variations, their distribution, the knowledge of living people about what you did in them, how life and work fit into them—these are things we can see now but will miss a generation from now.

What *are* responsible preservation decisions about such resources? How should we record such buildings when we conduct surveys of areas in which there are dozens or even hundreds of them? How can historians encourage their study and analysis while they are still here as evidence? I don't have answers. But I think the questions are worth asking.

AUTHOR'S NOTE, 2006

After more than twenty years, most of the issues discussed in this chapter still confront preservationists. Urban redevelopment and various housing programs are eliminating all but a few shotgun-plan houses, along with many other small dwellings in urban areas. Moreover, the public housing

FIG. 11.14. *Cannady Farm, ca. 1904, Raleigh vicinity, Wake County. Photograph by Michael T. Southern, 1984. Tobacco farms such as this one, and labor-intensive family farms in general, are vanishing from the landscape at a rapid rate, reflecting changes in agricultural technology and crops as well as spreading urbanization.* (NCDAH)

built according to the design ideals of the 1930s, 1940s, and 1950s as an alternative for lower income families is also being destroyed by redevelopment programs, with little objection from preservationists or historians. In the countryside, which is rapidly changing with revolutions in technology, crops, and the entire agricultural economy, the traditional tobacco barns and tenant houses are vanishing even more rapidly than we anticipated in the early 1980s.

In the early twenty-first century, the challenges have broadened. Drastic changes in manufacturing and agriculture—especially the globalization of manufacturing—have undercut the traditional pillars of the state's economy, including its chief industries (tobacco, furniture, and textiles). The closing of factories has left towns in economic trouble and many important factory buildings vacant. New uses, encouraged by preservation tax advantages, are filling many industrial buildings, but many more are empty and endangered. Preservation and economic redevelopment are working hand in hand toward new approaches.

It is not only the heritage of the New South that is endangered, but the legacy of the more recent past, the architecture of the mid-twentieth-century era when North Carolina leaders strove to make ours a progressive Southern state, and built public, industrial, corporate, and residential structures accordingly. Like the Victorian buildings that succumbed to the wrecker's ball in the mid-twentieth century, the most striking architecture of this progressive period faces a period of great vulnerability, subject to both economic pressures and the biases of current taste. Several important buildings have been lost while they were still relatively young and strong, but growing interest in preservation and public attention to this recent history may help shift the tide.

In a still broader scope we face tremendous change in the rural landscape, including the very agrarian character and the family farms that have characterized much of the state for centuries. As part of the larger picture, preservationists forge links with those who focus on the interlocking issues of farmland retention, environmental quality, transportation, economic development, and urban sprawl. Here, perhaps, is the largest challenge, in addressing not only the history and architectural heritage of an agricultural past, but the economic and social future of the state and the region.

Twelve

YUPPIES, BUBBAS, AND THE POLITICS OF CULTURE

Those of us who work in the field of historic preservation or who teach preservation-related courses often promote the belief that preservation embodies values that are objectively right and true. Many of us work to convince the rest of the world of the validity of the "preservation ethic" through "preservation education," or to regulate preservation values through local, state, and federal laws and programs. I hope to suggest that we may serve preservation goals better by recognizing that historic preservation embodies values that are far from being universal or objective. Rather, they are the values of the segment of society to which most students of vernacular architecture and most preservation professionals belong. Whatever our various disciplines—whether we are historians, folklorists, landscape historians, architectural historians, archaeologists—we are part of a class group with its own distinct values.

On a superficial level, part of this class group has been popularly labeled Young Urban Professionals—Yuppies. Dennis Rogers, a North Carolina newspaper columnist, contrasts the tastes and activities of Yuppies with those of another group he calls Bubbas—Brothers Unburdened with Briefcases, BMWs, or Aerobics. Yuppies, as Rogers reports in familiar terms, "eat green spaghetti, hang out to drink chablis and Chivas Regal in bars that have a lot of ferns, drive BMWs to health spas, and will spend enough money

---

"Yuppies, Bubbas, and the Politics of Culture" appeared in *Perspectives in Vernacular Architecture III,* eds. Thomas Carter and Bernard Herman (Columbia: University of Missouri Press, 1989), 8–15, and is reprinted by permission of the University of Missouri Press, Columbia, Missouri.

this year on jogging suits to buy a good set of recaps for a pickup." Bubbas, on the other hand, drink "sweet iced tea so dark you can't see through it," or Wild Turkey and 7-Up. They often have girlfriends or wives with two first names; they get paid every Friday; and they like Hank Williams Jr., Dolly Parton, *Smokey and the Bandit,* and a dog that rides in the back of a four-wheel-drive pickup. Rogers says that a Bubba would define a squash racket as selling vegetables in a roadside stand at inflated prices to Yuppies.[1]

In cultural terms, Yuppies are inherently and intentionally nonlocal and nonethnic; accordingly, the distinguishing characteristics of their consumer tastes are recognized throughout the nation. Bubbas, on the other hand, are specific to a Southern, white, working-class population (whether located in the cultural hearth area of the rural and small-town South or in such outposts as Detroit or California). Many other ethnic and regional groups exist as Bubba corollaries, each with its own distinctive social and aesthetic values, which, if different from those of Bubbas, share the quality of being non-Yuppie.

A third group also takes an important role in most communities. Continuing the acronym approach, they may be termed Buccoes—the Boardroom, Ultrasuede, and Country Club Crowd. Their cultural preferences shape both the character and the survival of architecture throughout much of the country. They are neither Bubbas nor Yuppies, though they can assume some of the behavior of each when it is appropriate.

But to return to Yuppies. Though easily trivialized in clichés of consumerism, Yuppies are important as part of a much larger class. As one observer put it, "The social group that includes the 'Yuppies' was labeled the 'New Class' by sociologists in the 1960s. It is that segment of the nation's upper class whose chief asset is human capital—high levels of education—rather than financial capital."[2] Sociologists and historians of social groups take the analysis further. They see this group as part of a class that emerged in the nineteenth century, the "Market Professionals."

Market professionals, as summarized in a recent study of architectural professionalism, are members of occupation groups who define their social and economic status in terms of "selling their time and intangible skills, rather than clearly defined products to their clients." They include doctors, lawyers, architects, and, not least, historians, architectural historians, folklorists, and archaeologists. Market professionals base their status on two main ideals: their specialized professional training and education and their ability to supply impartial, expert knowledge for the public or the client's good. Thus market professionals do not define their value and place in society in terms of raw labor power, as do lower-class workers, or in terms of competence in making or fixing or transporting things, as do technical or blue-collar workers, or even in terms of ownership of capital (land, slaves, factories, stocks), as do members of the upper class. Instead, the market professionals' value comes from their exclusive possession of knowledge that they are able to convince other members of society is essential and cannot be obtained from any other supplier. This is what an architect, a doctor, a historian possesses as essential stock-in-trade. This claim of exclusive and valuable professional knowledge is, if the profession defines itself successfully, what gives the professional his or her special status in society—a position above the laborer and technician but not requiring land or capital.[3]

Thus, when market professionals meet each other, the standard questions to ask as they begin to size one another up are "What do you do?" "Where do you work?" "Where did you go to school?" By contrast, for both Bubbas and Buccoes, as for most people in the world over time, the really important questions are "Where are you from?" and then a series of more subtle questions that ultimately mean "Who are you?" and specifically "Who is your family?"[4] In this latter value system, it is place and family that matter the most—*who you are*—not something as transitory and superficial as *what you do*. While professionals typically leave their hometowns eagerly to establish an identity grounded in education and individual accomplishments, Bubbas and Buccoes are attached to their sense of community, of place, of family, of being where people know who you are.

Often the market professional, firmly grounded in principles he or she believes to be absolute, finds the values of the Bubbas and Buccoes quite foreign and even offensive. Many a professional would identify with the earnest preservationist who insisted, "I've always been taught that people who define people in terms of *who you are* rather than *what you do* are *wrong.*" Thus professionals, including preservationists, come to their work not objectively but weighted with their own values, values that are necessary to their own well-being and that will necessarily affect their judgments and actions.

So what? How does an identity as a market professional affect what the preservationist does? Two aspects of preservation work suggest the impact of class values on preservation actions.

An obvious example takes place when a young professional preservationist begins work in a local community—as an architectural surveyor, a planner, an employee of a local nonprofit organization. Chances are that he or she will go into a community where Bubbas compose most of the population and where Buccoes and Bubbas share political power. It is their history and their interaction that are represented in the historic fabric the preservationist studies. And it is their views and their actions that will affect what stays and what is lost in the community. In short, it is their community. The preservationist needs to know this. He or she needs to know it in order to understand them, their history, their buildings, and their current behavior. He or she needs to know it to avoid saying stupid things. And he or she needs to know it in order to serve them and their community and the cause of preservation in a useful way. But, unfortunately, most preservationists, in their academic training, where they gain the credentials to obtain their jobs, are not likely to learn much about the importance of Bubbas' and Buccoes' values. In fact, often academic training emphasizes the very opposite point of view.

Many of us as preservation professionals have said something like this (in however tactful terms) to a local political figure or preservation buff after an introductory tour of the community: "This house you love because it was your grandmother's house isn't really all that significant, because stylistically it's marginal at best." Or, "This mansion your committee wants to save because it belonged to Colonel Ravenel and Miss Julia who had the Civil War monument erected and the library established, that's quite admirable. But let me explain to you about the greater significance of This Other Thing." This Other Thing may be a pure example of a Craftsman-style bungalow, or the only surviving slave house in the county, or a perfectly stratified Woodland site, or a center-chimney German house set over a spring, or a completely preserved textile mill village or streetcar suburb, or a sleek Moderne gas station—or whatever. In any case, the professional values This Other Thing because of its interest to his profession—rather than because of mere family ties or local sentiment. This is what he learned to value in his professional training. Besides, such things can best be interpreted through the exercise of professional abilities; their interpretation and evaluation require his participation and, in turn, assert his value and status as a professional. Thus, in making evaluations of significance, the professional may, perhaps unconsciously, place his own class values uppermost and ignore the community's values—all in the name of professionalism.

But, if the professional realizes that there really are different, equally powerful and equally valid value systems at work in the community, and that his is only one of them (and a historically new and minor one at that), it may enable him to take a broader view. This expanded viewpoint may make his work easier and more effective. For one thing, he may find the local setting a little less astonishing. More important, by acknowledging the presence of different cultures within the community, he may be able to convince community members to preserve more of their resources in the long run.

There is a second, larger arena in which the same issues appear: the public arena of government policy in historic preservation. As early as the 1930s, when the Historic American Buildings Survey (HABS) was established in part to give unemployed architects work during the Depression, and increasingly since the passage of the Historic Preservation Act of 1966, a high proportion of preservation professionals have worked in or with government. In this capacity they bring professional values into government policies.[5] This returns us to the theme suggested in my title, "Yuppies, Bubbas, and the Politics of Culture." To what extent do preservation professionals, in the name of historic preservation and the protection of cultural diversity, in fact promote the values of their own class—the values of professionalism, of Yuppiedom perhaps—as absolute rather than relative values?

As a preservationist, I first began to question the effect of my own tastes and values on my professional judgments when I heard papers by Vernacular Architecture Forum members about class-related aesthetic processes in urban areas. In her paper on "Modernizing," Elizabeth Cromley analyzed the tastes, aesthetic rules, and expressed values of mid-twentieth-century Italian working-class families through their remodelings of late nineteenth-century New York rowhouses. She examined how they used bright paint, carefully arranged metal awnings, patterns of brick facing or Permastone, and a wide range of screen-door designs to create a balance between communality and individuality. In "Making a House a Home," Alice Gray Read described how southern blacks altered their Philadelphia rowhouses. She demonstrated how on those severe, sidewalk-abutting facades, these families used such symbolic devices as Astroturf to define a space of sidewalk abutting the house, and arranged furniture, plants, concrete ornaments, and other artifacts to turn these spaces into the porches and social areas needed for proper living. These two scholars explored the philosophies, social and aesthetic needs, and personal concerns that lie behind remodelings many of us would label *tacky*.[6]

These are academic studies. The questions they raise, however, cross over into the areas of government policy where preservationists operate. In this context, a familiar preservation term such as *professional standards* may take on new and different meaning, a meaning quite different from the objectivity we usually equate with these words. Three specific areas come to mind: National Register of Historic Places eligibility, tax credit certification, and local historic district commission service.

In each of these areas, the yardsticks by which such matters as significance or appropriateness are judged are "professional standards." The regulations assure this. Professionals using professional guidelines are the ones who determine eligibility for the National Register and for tax credits at the state, regional, and federal levels. Professionals administer tax-credit rehabilitations and write and interpret the Secretary of the Interior's Standards (or "Secretary's Standards") for rehabilitation of historic properties. Professionals instigate design review boards in locally designated historic districts. And—because of regulations written by professionals—they are required as "qualified professionals" on such review boards, to assure that properly professional decisions are made. Furthermore, in most historic districts, the insistence on appropriate contemporary design for new infill construction requires by implication the employment of another professional—the architect—rather than, God forbid, a contractor who specializes in colonial homes.

What are the implications of the professionalization of these government preservation activities? Consider, for example, the integrity and thus the eligibility for admission to the National Register of a district where changes have been made by residents over time. Generally, the closer the alterations are to the taste of the architectural historian evaluating the district, the more likely he or she is to determine that the neighborhood has sufficient "integrity" to be nominated. The more antithetical the changes are to the historian's taste, the less likely. A case in point could be a late-nineteenth- or early-twentieth-century mill village composed of rows and rows of small frame houses built by a company that imposed an institutionalized design on all the buildings and maintained them for workers. Although there were hierarchical differences in size and form to distinguish worker status, the buildings were uniform within each group. Few now remain in this condition. In the mid-twentieth century, the company has sold off the houses to the residents, who now own them. They have naturally modified their houses to state their separate ownership.

If Yuppies had bought these houses, doubtless there would be tasteful color modulations in paint from one to another, Levolor blinds in the windows and unpainted wood decks and glass solaria attached to the rear, possibly solar panels on the roof of one and a clever postmodern arch inserted into the gable of another. Such modifications might well be given a design award. But the people who actually live in these places make their modifications differently. They add grapevine wrought-iron porch posts, green translucent porch awnings or carports, asbestos siding or Permastone in various colors, green Astroturf on the porches and steps, and animal statuary in the front yards. Seldom do these people change the form of their houses significantly except for adding or filling in a space to provide an indoor bathroom. Many well-meaning preservation professionals have excluded such individuated mill villages from the National Register because of such changes. In such an evaluation, the professional may be placing more importance on the taste and cultural values evident in minor surface changes than on the surviving patterns of individual house form, hierarchy among buildings, and spatial arrangements—the characteristics that are basic to the significance of the district. Thus, the professional may unintentionally allow personal taste and class values to dominate his or her evaluation of significance.

The effects of such judgments are considerable. Decisions about what is eligible for the National Register can determine what places are afforded protection from highway construction or from demolition for federally funded urban renewal, as well as what places receive an opportunity for rehabilitation through federal tax credits. Such decisions can affect the future and the very survival of neighborhoods, villages, and entire communities.

This brings us to the administration of the tax credits themselves. Here again, value judgments are involved. The Department of the Interior's Secretary's Standards—by which certifications of rehabilitation for income-producing historic property are evaluated—begin with the following statement: "'Rehabilitation' assumes that at least some repair or alteration of the historic building will need to take place in order to provide for an *efficient contemporary use* [italics added]; however, these repairs and alterations must not damage or destroy the materials and features—including their finishes—that are important in defining the building's historic character." This statement seems to be neutral and objective enough. However, in actual application of the Secretary's Standards, Yuppie values often prevail. A typical case would be a three-story brick commercial structure of around 1910, identified as a "contributing" building in a downtown National Register district. The owner, a "Bubba," wishes to obtain certification of a rehabilitation for tax credit purposes. The upper stories are intact and have modest brickwork decoration, a small bracket cornice, and arched windows, and the owner plans to repair these and leave them intact. The street-level storefront was replaced in the late 1960s, leaving no indication of its original appearance. The question arises as to what is an "appropriate" new storefront treatment that will meet the Secretary's Standards. Perhaps a sleek International style or witty postmodern design might be approved by the state and federal architectural historians or architects who review the project. But what if this owner wants to install a turquoise and red Permastone facade, with curly white ironwork around a neon-outlined picture window with a seahorse sign blinking off and on, "Bubba's Oyster Bar." Or what if he wants to put in "Katy's Kolonial Kitchen," with white balustrades, green shutters, and brickwork that repeats the architectural preferences of the entire community? These may be socially "efficient contemporary uses," but are they "appropriate," and in whose terms?

Local design review boards probably have the strongest impact in the relationships among taste, class values, and historic preservation issues. Such boards are established by local governments to protect historic areas,

KUDZU By Doug Marlette

FIG. 12.1. *"Kudzu" comic strip, July 21, 1987, by Doug Marlette*, Atlanta Constitution. *Thanks to Suzanne Pickens for calling attention to this strip.* (*Courtesy of Doug Marlette*)

usually having the power to delay demolitions and to determine whether substantial alterations are appropriate. Design review boards are typically required to include professional architects and historians as well as interested citizens and residents of the regulated areas. It is perhaps impossible to separate taste from "appropriateness," especially when the issue of new design arises. Fortunately, most review boards consist of sensible local people who know community norms and are careful not to be overzealous in imposing their own tastes. They operate within long-standing community patterns of class values involving often unstated, ongoing negotiations between Buccoes and Bubbas. It may in fact be the appearance of the Yuppie professional unaware of the need for such negotiation that creates the most trouble.

In any case, there is always tension when different cultural biases about design interact. It becomes especially intense if a predominantly Yuppie professional review board is making decisions about alterations in a Bubba or other non-Yuppie community (fig. 12.1). In one such case involving a designated neighborhood of mainly Victorian buildings, the review board turned down the application of a citizen to put a metal awning on his brick ranch house, and class issues emerged in strong terms. As local district designations expand to include more diverse neighborhoods, such tensions will probably increase. The city of Charleston has sought to establish guidelines suitable for large and ethnically diverse areas, and other cities will doubtless need to face similarly complex issues if local designation is to protect and enhance cultural diversity rather than the tastes of a single class.

David Whisnant, in *All That Is Native and Fine: The Politics of Culture in an American Region*, offers a useful perspective on the issues raised here. His study describes the work of settlement schools and other promoters of folk culture in the Appalachian region in the early twentieth century. He also treats the broader issue of "cultural 'otherness,'" the question of "how people perceive each other across cultural boundaries—especially those boundaries that correlate with cultural class." His study, as he describes it, addresses the topic of "how mostly educated, urban, middle-and-upper-class, liberal 'culture workers' perceived, manipulated (I use the word here in a purely descriptive sense), and projected the culture of the mostly rural, lower-class working people in the southern mountains during the half-century after 1890." These "culture workers," as he calls them, sought to maintain what they saw as the "traditional mountain" and even "old English" values of the Appalachian culture by convincing mountaineers to avoid adapting to industrialization, to sing only the songs that the culture workers believed to be authentic and pure, and even to learn traditional English morris dances. This phase of cultural politics in preserving a perceived American past, Whisnant states, had to do with politics, not "at the formal level of legislative act, judicial decision, or policy directive, but at the more basic level of individual values and assumptions, personal style and preference, community mores and local traditions."[7]

Today's preservationists and scholars have much in common with those early-twentieth-century culture workers, as we seek to preserve what *we* perceive as valuable from the past. A major difference is that, unlike Whisnant's culture workers, for professionals working in the public preservation sector today taste and class values are deeply—and intentionally—entwined with official policies and legislation. The impact of that entwining can be tremendous. We are, whether we like it or not, immersed daily in the "politics of culture."

As participants in the politics of culture, we as preservationists or scholars need to be aware of the impact of our own value systems on the decisions we make. If in the long run we hope to enhance and protect the cultural diversity of the American vernacular landscape, then we can serve that end better by acknowledging and respecting the plurality of cultures at work in any community and by seeing how we ourselves fit into that pattern.

NOTES

1. Dennis Rogers, "Move Over Yuppies, Here Comes Bubba in a Pickup," *Raleigh News and Observer*, 8 March 1984.

2. Martin Shefter and Benjamin Ginsburg, "Why Reaganism Will Be with Us into the 21st Century," *Washington Post National Weekly Edition*, 30 September 1985.

3. Dell Upton, "Pattern Books and Professionalism: Aspects of the Transformation of Domestic Architecture in America, 1800–1860," *Winterthur Portfolio* 19, nos. 2/3 (Summer/Autumn, 1984): 107–50, esp. 112–13. Upton cites Burton Bledstein, *The Culture of Professionalism* (New York: W. W. Norton, 1976), ix–x, 3–5.

4. John Shelton Reed cites the same dichotomy between the South and other regions in *One South* (Baton Rouge and London: Louisiana State University Press, 1982), 182.

5. I am assuming that taste is an expression of values and that the imposition of taste is therefore an imposition of values.

6. Elizabeth Collins Cromley, "Modernizing: Or 'You Never See a Screen Door on Affluent Homes,'" *Journal of American Culture* 5:2 (Summer 1982): 71–79. Alice Gray Read, "Making a House a Home in a Philadelphia Neighborhood," in *Perspectives in Vernacular Architecture, II*, ed. Camille Wells (Columbia: University of Missouri Press, 1986), 192–99.

7. David E. Whisnant, *All That Is Native and Fine: The Politics of Culture in an American Region* (Chapel Hill: University of North Carolina Press, 1983), xiii, xiv.

INDEX

Italicized page numbers refer to illustrations

Aaron (workman), 141, 155n32
Abram/Abraham (carpenter), 104n36
Adam, Robert and James, 159, 160; mantel design by, *160*
Adamesque style, 6, 159, 165, 168, 171, 173, 174, 284
Albemarle hotel (Nags Head), 203, 204
Albemarle Sound region, 75, 76, 129, 131, 135, 188, 190, 194, 200
Albert (painter), 105n48
Albert (plasterer), 69, 70, 86
Aleck (painter), 105n48
Allen (carpenter), 87
Allen, William (brickmason), 108n97
All Saints Church (Nags Head), 195
Alston, Ruina Williams, 181
Alston, Samuel, 177, 181
Alston, Samuel T., 181
Alston, Theodosia Burr, 212n18
Alston House (Halifax Co.), 181
Alston-Williams family, 165, 177; genealogical/house chart of, *163*. *See also* Williams family
American Architect and Building News (1895), 278
American Revolution, 159, 257, 258, 265, 267, 268, 271, 272
Anderson, Walker, 235
Andrew (bricklayer), 98, 99, 100
Anglo-Saxon identity, 7, 236, 255, 265, 266, 268, 275, 278, 285, 286
Anthony (sawyer), 75, 135, 136
Appalachian region, 320
Appomattox Court House (Va.), 235, 262
apprenticeships, 72, 88, 107–8n95; bond, *73*, 107n90; laws, 88
apprentice system, 12, 14, 18
architectural books, use of, 18, 19, 20, 22, 25, 28, 30, 31, 32, 37, 38, 46, 160, 298
architectural models, national, 113–20
architectural profession, development of, 19, 126, 129, 149, 152n8
Artis, Jim (carpentry contractor), 94, 95, 97

Ashe, Samuel A'Court, 231, 240, 252n32, 258, *271*, 274, 276, 288n5, 291n35
Atkins, Rodham (builder), 73, 104n40
Aycock, Gov. Charles B., 264, 267, 270, 291n35

Bacon, Henry (architect), 273, 290n29, 291n35
Badham, Miles, 140, 141, 155n32
Bagley, Worth, 270; monument to, *269*, 270
Bain, Donald W., 231
Baker, William A. (coppersmith), 125
ballast, 123
Baltimore (Md.), 164, 303
Barnes, David A., House (Murfreesboro), 18, *30*, 32; ground plan, *33*
barns, tobacco, 306, *307*, 310
Barrett, Charles (architect), 282, 283, 292n50, 293n56; *Colonial Southern Homes*, 283
barter system, 37, 42
Bartlett, Joe (bricklayer), 99
Baskerville, Dr. Robert D., 44, 45, 46, 62
Baskerville, William Rust, 42, 48, 59
Battle, Lucy, 86–87
Battle, William Horn, 107nn73–76
Baum, Wash L., 208
Beasley, Bill, 103n32
Beasley, Gilbert, 103n32
Beaufort (Carteret Co.), 190
Bellamy, John D., 95
Bellamy, John D., Jr., 264
Bellamy Mansion (Wilmington), *95*, 95
Ben (carpenter), 82–83, 103n25
Benjamin, Asher, 20, 22, 31, 131; *American Builder's Companion*, 144, 155n38; *Country Builder's Assistant*, 131, 152n10; *The Practical House Carpenter*, 20, *25*; *The Practice of Architecture*, 20, *23*
Bentley, James (carpenter), 88
Bentley, William (carpenter), 88
Bernstein, Basil, 57
Berry, Ben, 109n115
Berry, John (brick mason), 17, 50n15
Berry, John (builder), 74, 78, 104n41
Bettencourt, Ephraim, 109n115
Bicknell, A. J., 28

323

Biddle, Owen, 20, 31; design for stair, *20; Young Carpenter's Assistant,* 20
Biltmore (Asheville), 297
black artisans, 5, 69–109; contracts made by, 96; free, 87–89, 91, 92, 94, 95, 96; laws restricting, 89, 92; protest against competition, 89, 95, 96; restrictions, 94; slave owners, 89, 91
blacks, free, 69–109
Blandwood (Greensboro), 52n46
Blount, Bill, 140
Blount, Davy, 155n32
Blount, Dick, 154n28
Blount, Joseph, 146, 147
Bomford, Col. James V., 222, 223, 227, 251n12, 252n28
Bonarva, 76, 79, 148
Bond, Nathaniel, 155n32
Boon, James (carpenter), 92–93
Borglum, Gutzon (sculptor), 273
Boston (Mass.), 160, 165
Boulton, Benjamin (carpenter), 155n30
Boyd, John E., 17
Boydton (Mecklenburg Co., Va.), 17, 18; house in, *29*
Boydton Methodist Episcopal Church, *35*
Boyette Slave House (Smithfield vic.), *307*
Braddock, Israel (house joiner), 108n97
Bragg, Thomas (carpenter), 78, 105n43, 177
Branch, Gen. Lawrence O'Bryan, 218, 292n50
Branch, Nancy Haywood Blount, 215, 218, *219,* 220, 226, 227, 229, 232, 240
Brewner, Jacob (carpenter), 60
brick: importation of, 121–25; manufacture of, 121–25, 137; sources for, 122
brickmakers and bricklayers, 78, 98, 99, 138, 139; skills, 78; tasks, 98, 99
Bridgers, Elizabeth Eagles Haywood, 284
Bridgers, Mary, 284, 293n53
Bridgers, Preston L., 284, 292n51
Bridgers, Robert R., 292n51, 293n53
bridges, covered, 306
Briggs, John J. (carpenter), 72, 102n15
Brody, Adam, 149
Brown, John (carpenter), 107n80
Brown Marsh Presbyterian Church (Elizabethtown vic.), 92, *93*
Brunswick Town (Brunswick Co.), 291n33
Bryan House (New Bern), *83*
Bubbas, 312–21; cartoon, *319*
building materials, 71; imported, 137, 141, 142, 143; shipping, 122, 123
Bunnell, Rufus (architect), 95
Burgess, James (builder), 168, 170, 171, 179, 180, 186nn18–19

Burgess, John, 177
Burgess, Martha Jane Alston, 177
Burgwin, John (planter), 77, 104n36
Burgwyn, Henry K., Sr., 78, 104n39
Burlington (Alamance Co.), 300
Burnside, General, 195
Burnside (Hillsborough), 85
Burrows, Thomas (carriage maker), 37
Burton and Holmes (builders), 62
Burwell, 104n37
Burwell House (Chase City, Va. vic.), *30*
Busbee, Fabius, 245

Caesar (brickmaker), 75, 103n26
Calder, James (architect-builder), 120n11
Caledonia plantation (Halifax Co.), 151n2
Cambridge (plasterer), 105n48
Camden, Moses (carpenter), 87
Cameron, Bennehan, 266, *271,* 274, 280, 281, 285
Cameron, Duncan, 78, 104n39
Cameron, Paul, 85
Cameron, Rebecca, 265, 289n18
Cameron, Sallie Taliaferro Mayo (Mrs. Bennehan), 280, 281
Cameron House (Raleigh), *281,* 281, 283
camp-meeting grounds, 302
Cane Creek Baptist Church (Yancey Co.), 80
Cannady Farm (Raleigh vic.), *310*
Canova, Antonio, 114, 117, 119
Cape Fear Bank (Fayetteville), 149, 156n45
Cape Fear Club (Wilmington), 284, 292n52
Cape Fear region, 255, 258, 265, 270, 271
Capitol Square (Raleigh), 232, 240
Carolina Heights (Wilmington), 284, 293n53
carpenters: skills, 72, 73; tasks, 72, 73; tools, 73
Carr, Julian S., 239, 253n43, *271*
Carraway, J. D. (carpenter), 80, 104n40
Cary (driver), 69, 70
Casino, The (Nags Head), 209
Cato (carpenter), 140, 141, 155n32
Cedar Grove Cemetery (New Bern), 226
cemeteries. *See under specific names*
Chapel Hill (Orange Co.), 86
Charleston, 72, 160, 165
Chase City (Mecklenburg Co., Va.), 17, 18
Cherokee troops, 223, 251n16
Cherry Hill (Warren Co.), *28, 28*
Cheshire, Bishop Joseph Blount, Jr., *271,* 292n50
chimneys, wooden, 54, *307,* 307
Chowan County Courthouse (Edenton), *304, 305*
Christ Church (first) (Raleigh), 156n45
Christ Episcopal Church (Raleigh), 254, *260,* 277

Christian, Julia Jackson, 215, 240, 241, *242*, 260
Christianville (Mecklenburg Co., Va.), 17, 18. *See also* Chase City (Mecklenburg Co., Va.)
City Beautiful movement, 256
City Hall–Thalian Hall (Wilmington), *97*, 97
Civil War, 16, 17, 38, 119, 125, 184, 188, 190, 194, 195, 216, 249, 256, 257, 269, 274, 278, 279, 280, 305
Clark, David, 75, 135, 136
Clark, Elijah, 122, 123, 124, 125
Clark, Chief Justice Walter, 274
codes, elaborate and restricted, 57, 58
Coke, Capt. Octavius, 231, 252n32
Coleman, Dr. Littleton H., 174
Coleman-White House (Warrenton), 168, 174, *175*; windows, *175*
Collins, Josiah, 75, 76, 79, 98, 100, 103n32, 139
Colonial Dames of America, 267, 270, 271, 272, 280
Colonial Revival style, 4, 7, 256, 276, 277, 278, 279, 280, 284, 285, 291n41
Colston, Gen. R. E., 222, 223
Columbia (Tyrrell Co.), 80
Confederate Cemetery (Raleigh), 218, 219, 220, 221, 226, *228*, 229, *230*, 245, 247, 248
Confederate monument (Wilmington), 275
Confederate remains, removal of, 222–25, 244; from Gettysburg and Arlington, 229
Confederate tradition, 215–93
Connor, Henry Groves, 263, 273
construction, sequence of, 69, 76, 134–41
construction process, traditional, 71
contracts and specifications, 5, 42, 44, 45, 53, 55, 60; ending in suits, 63; English, 58, 59. *See also* specifications, examples of
Cooleemee, 51n29
Coolmore (Tarboro vic.), *303*, 303
Coper (bricklayer), 98
Corbin, Edmund, 88
Cosby, Dabney (brick contractor), 49n3, 78, 81, 86, 92, 104n42, 105n51
Cowper, Miss Meggie, 231
Cozzens, Leonard, 59
Craven County jail (New Bern), 106n60, 122
Culpepper, Hal Wood, 207
Culpepper, John, 204
"culture workers," 320
Cunningham, James (brickmaker), 137
Currituck Sound bridge, 208

Dalkeith (Warren Co.), *176*, 177, 180
Damon (carpenter), 105n48
Daniel (carpenter), 106n64
Daniels, Adelaide Bagley (Mrs. Josephus), 270
Daniels, Jonathan, 188

Daniels, Josephus, 236, 252n43, 264, 270, 276
Daniels, Moncie, 209
Darlet, William, 134, 136
Daughters of the American Revolution, 267
Daughters of the Revolution, 267, 274, 285; unveiling of memorial to "Fifty-one Ladies of Edenton," 275
Dave (carpenter), 140, 141
Davidson, Berry (millwright), 56, 57, 67n5
Davis, Alexander Jackson (architect), 52n46, 85, 117, 156n45, 298
Davis, George, 273; monument (Wilmington), *272*, 273
Davis, Jefferson, 229; parade in Raleigh for casket of, *230*
Dawes, William (mason), 63
Day, Thomas (cabinetmaker), 90, 91
Democratic Party, 229, 235, 247, 264, 287
DeRosset, Dr. A. J., 59
design process, 31–37, 46, 48, 133–34; traditional, 53–68
Dewey, Jack (carpenter), 85, 106n60, 106–7n70
Dick (bricklayer and plasterer), 76, 85, 98, 99, 103n27
Dickinson (Dickerson), Dave, 141, 144, 155n32
Diver (carpenter, sawyer, and hewer), 74
Dixon, Haywood (carpenter), *77*, 78
Dixon, Murfree (carpenter), 102n15
Donnell, John R., 82–83, 106n59
Douglass, Frederick, 236, 237, 239
Downing, A. J., 22, 28, 31; *Cottage Residences*, 22, *40*, 41
Drake, Nicholas, 177
Drane, Mrs. Frederick, 213n21
drawings, architectural, 133–34
dress, 152n7, 166, 186n13
Dudley-Sprunt House (Wilmington), *280*, 280
Duke Homestead (Durham Co.), 309

Eagle Lodge (Hillsborough), 156n45
Eaton, William, House, 20, *21*; stair hall, *22*
Edenton (Chowan Co.), 72, 75, 76, 94, 126, 129, 130, 134, 135, 137, 139, 148, 192, 255, 274, 304, 305; map of, *127*
Edenton Academy, 76, 98, 139
"Edenton Tea Party," 274; unveiling of State Capitol memorial, *275*, 285
Elgin (Warren Co.), 177, *178*, 180; entrance (detail), *179*; mantels, *181*; portico (detail), *179*; rear side, *178*; stair hall, *180*
Eli (bridge builder), 76
Elizabeth City (Pasquotank Co.), 192, 196, 206, 207
Elizabethtown (Bladen Co.), 93

Ellicott, Henry J. (sculptor), 268
Ellison, Stewart (carpenter), *84, 85,* 106n69
Emmanuel Episcopal Church (Warrenton), 41, *43*
Endly, George, 17
Engleside (Warrenton), *27,* 28, 42; mantel, *26*
Essex County (Ma.), 62
Eureka (Mecklenburg Co., Va.), 44, 46, *47,* 48, 59, 62; ground plan, *45;* rear stair hall, *47*
Evans, Carter, 108n103

factories, sash and blind, 18
Fayetteville (Cumberland Co.), 88, 94, 130
Fearing, Henrietta, 212n19; cottage (1869), 212n21
Federal style, 3, 20, 82, 83, 122, 131, 144, 159, 160, 170, 174
Finney, Robert (plasterer and carpenter), 97, 109n118
Finney, William (plasterer and brickmason), 97, 109n118
First Baptist Church (Raleigh), 260
First Presbyterian Church (Raleigh), 120n9
Fisher, Charles, 71, 101n6
flag: City of Raleigh, 292n48; Confederate, 215, 227, 245, *246,* 247, 248; U.S. (Stars and Stripes), 244, 245, 246, *246*
Flat's Band, 202
floorcloth, 146
flooring, 86
Floyd, Hardy (stonemason), 69, 71, 101n4
Fort Raleigh, 214n59
frame: balloon, 18, 38; timber, 38, 54, 171; —, specifications for, 58, 59, 60, 65, 66
French, Benjamin (plasterer), 141, 155n33
French, Daniel Chester (sculptor), 290n29
Frog, Jim, 154n28
furniture, 91, 129, 143, 155n39; imported, 144, 146, 147
Fusionists, 235, 236, 238, 247, 263

Gaddy, J. F. (carpenter), 58
Gaither family, 212n21
Gales, Seaton, 227, 228
Gautier, Joseph R., 108n101
George (carpenter), 107n80
Georgian style, 174
Gettysburg (Pa.), 229, 235
Gilbert (sawyer), 74, 135, 136
Gilbert, Charles Pierrepont H., 293n52
Gill, Richard (carpenter), 53, 63
Glencoe Mill Village (Burlington vic.), 299, 300
Glenn, Gov. Robert, 264, 270, 285

Godfrey, Clark, and His 11 Piece Swing Orchestra, 209
Gothic Revival style, 25, 131, 207, 277, 303
Gould, William H., 95
Governor's Palace (Raleigh), 113, 114, 115, *118,* 119; plan of, 117, 120n12
Grandy, Florence L., 212n19, 213n21
Grant, Hiram, 237, 238, 253n45
Grant, William (builder), 66
Gray, Stevens, 61
Greek Revival style, 16, 20, 22, 32, 34, 42, 114, 117, 120n15, 131, 143, 144, 171, 180, 181, 277, 286, 297, 298, 299
Green, James (carpenter), 108n97
Green, Paul (playwright), 214n59
Green, Rigdon (house joiner), 108n97
Greensboro (Guilford Co.), 299, 300, 301
Grice, Miss Allie (Mrs. Charles), 203
Griffin, W. W., Cottage (Nags Head), 212n21
Grimes, Walter, 235
Grove Hill (Warren Co.), 181, *183*
Gunter Creek plantation (Warren Co.), 165, 177, 181
Gurkin Cottage (Nags Head), 213n21

Halifax (Halifax Co.), 162, 164
Hall, Col. Edward D., 231, 234, 252n32
Handcock, William (carpenter), 108n97
Harnett, Cornelius, 271; monument to, 270, 271
Harriss, T. W. and Martha, 51–52n38
Harry (carpenter), 78, 86–87, 140, 141
Hartge, Charles E. (architect), 292n50, 293n56
Hartmann, Charles C. (architect), 300
Hattie Creef (sailboat) and the Wright brothers, 200, 201
Haughawort, Ned (tinner), 78, 104n41
Hawks, Francis, 122
Hawks, John (architect), 120n12, 122, 131, 152n8, 152n10
Hayes Plantation (Chowan Co.), 3, 6, 74, 75, 76, 126–56, *148;* ground plan, *130,* 131; kitchen wing, *141;* land façade, *132, 150;* land portico and stone steps, *142;* land-side entrance, *144;* library, *133,* 174; mantels, *145, 146;* stair hall, *145;* water façade, *132, 138*
Haywood, John, 79, 84, 115
Haywood, Marshall DeLancey, *271,* 274
Hazle, Robert (carpenter), 108n97
Hector (bricklayer), 99, 100, 154n28
Henry, Louis D., 107n90
Hermitage Plantation (Martin Co.), 127, 128, 151n2, 152n10
Hertford (Perquimans Co.), 191, 192
Hewes, Joseph, 152n10

Hicks, Col. W. J., 233
Hill, Mrs. Gen. D. H., 215, 240
Hillsborough (Orange Co.), 74, 78, 85, 265, 266
Hillsborough Military Academy, 222
Hill-Webb House (Hillsborough), 52n46
Hinsdale, Mrs. John, 242
Hinton, Mary Hilliard, 274, 285, 286
Historic American Buildings Survey (HABS), 2, 315
historic preservation, 297–311, 312–21; government policy in, 314–15; professional identities, 312–21
Historic Preservation Act of 1966, 2, 316
"hoi toiders," 190
Hoke, R. F., 233
Hollowell, Graham, 208, 213n31
Hollowell's Hotel (Nags Head), 204
Holt, Jacob W. (carpenter-contractor), 3, 4, 5, 11–52, 81–82; design process of, 19, 31–37, 46, 48; distribution of buildings by, *13*; family, 14; ground plan by, 42, *44*; House, *40*, 40, 41; house attributed to, *29*; workshop of, 15, 39, 81
Holt, Jacob Whitington (son of J. W.), 18
Holt, Thomas J. (architect), 14, 15, 16, 19, 38
Holt, William Howard Kenneth (builder), 18
Hook, Charles Christian (architect), 279, 293n56
Hope Plantation, 309
Hopkins, Samuel, 105n49
Horne, Ashley, 273
Hoskins, Dick, 109n122, 154n28
Houdon, 288n7
house plans, *33*, 33, 34, 37
house raising, 140
houses: shotgun, 306, *308*; tenant, 306, *308*, 309, 310. *See also specific houses by name*
housing, public, 309
Howard, William A., 14
Howe family, 94
Hunt, Richard Morris (architect), 297

insane asylum (Raleigh), 85
Iredell, James, House, 155n38
Iredell, James, Jr., 148, 149
Isaac (carpenter), 107n80
Italianate style, 16, 22, 32, 41, 42
Ives, Bishop Levi Silliman, 195

Jack (carpenter), 107n79
"jack-leg-carpenter," 279
Jackson, John H., 97
Jackson, Gen. "Stonewall," 218, 242, 260
Jackson, Mrs. Gen. "Stonewall," 215, 222, 223, 240

Jackson (Northampton Co.), 65
Jacob (carpenter), 72, 79
Jamestown Tercentennial Exposition, 285
Jefferson Standard Building (Greensboro), 299, 300
Jeffrey (bricklayer), 98, 99
Jeffreys, William, 92
Jenkins, Mr. (carpenter), 86
Jenkins, Edward (architect), 8n7
Jerry (house painter), 76, 100
Jim (bricklayer), 98, 99
Jim (house mover), 76
"Jim Crow" laws, 267
John (shoemaker, painter, and carpenter), 74
Johnson, Pres. Andrew, 222
Johnson, Martin, 200, 201
Johnston, Frances Benjamin Cathcart, 2, 127, 128, 151n2
Johnston, Gabriel (uncle of Samuel), 152n6
Johnston, James Cathcart, 75, 76, 78, 103n25, 126, *128*, 128, 129, 131, 133, 134, 135, 136, 137, 138, 139, 146, 147, 148, 149; education of, 128; estate of, 156n48; windmill project, 149, 150, 156n46
Johnston, Samuel, 126, 127, 128, 151n2, 152n10
Jones, Gen. Calvin, 113, 114, 115, 117, 119n6
Jones, Mrs. Garland, 242, 243, 247, 248
Jones, Nancy Branch (Mrs. Armistead), 215, 216, *231*, 231, 232, 233, 239, 240, 242, 245, 246, 260
Jones, William (carpenter), 69, 70, 72, 92, 101n5
Jones's Springs (Warren Co.), 164

Kearney, William (planter), 70
Kentucky Building, 278
Kevan and Lorimer (slaters), 124
Kingsbury, Russell, 64
Kinston (Lenoir Co.), 308
kitchens, description of, 64, 131, 197

Ladies Memorial Association (LMA) of Wake County, 215–49, 250n3, 258, 260, 288n6
Lafayette (plasterer), 105n48
Lafever, Minard, 20, 31; design for a front door, *23*; *The Young Builder's General Instructor*, 20, 22
Lake Erie, Battle of, 167
Lamb, E. F., Cottage (Nags Head), 212n21
Land's End (Hertford vic.), 297, *298*
Lane, Allen (stonecutter), 83–84
Lane, Frederick (carpenter), 106n60
Lane, Hardy B. (carpenter), 104n40, 106n60
Lane, Jobe (carpenter), 58
Lane, William (carpenter), 88
Latimer, Zebulon, 59
Latrobe, Benjamin Henry (architect), 113, 120n9

Lawrence, Park (carpenter), 88
Leary, Cornelius (carpenter), 155n30
Lee, Gen. Robert E., 236, 281; lock of hair, 234; monument to, in Richmond, 290n26; piece of apple tree from Appomattox Court House, 235; Traveler (horse), 235
LeGrand, Lewis (carpenter), 88
Leigh, Gilbert (joiner), 61
Lenoir, Thomas, 58
Lenox, Robert, 142, 155n34
Leonminster (Ma.), 59
LeRoy Hotel (Nags Head), 204
Lewis (bricklayer), 98, 99
libraries, 131, 156n48, 174
Lincolnton (Lincoln Co.), 302
Lind, E. G. (architect), 303
Little, William P., 74
log construction, 58, 64, 151n3, 305
Lost Cause, the, 216, 234, 235, 239, 243, 249, 258, 263
Lost Colony, 190, 214n59, 285
Louisburg (Franklin Co.), 69, 70, 71
Lucas, George, 80, 105n49
Lukeman, Augustus (sculptor), 273

Mack (bricklayer), 76, 103n27
MacMullen family, 213n21
Manly, Alex, 289n16
Manly, Gov. Charles, 83–84
Manteo (Dare Co.), 198, 209, 213n22
manumission, 89
Market House (Wilmington), 80
Marshall (bricklayer), 99
Marshall, John (carpenter), 79, 85
Marshall, Rev. M. M., 254, 255, 257
Massenburg, Nicholas, House (Louisburg vic.), 69–70, *70;* rear chimney, *70*
Mayo, Peter H., 281
McCraw, John C. (carpenter), 39
McIntire, William (carpenter), 87
McIver, Charles, 291n35
McMillan, Charles (architect), 293n56
Meares, Catherine DeRosset, 270
Mebane House (Greensboro vic.), *301*
"Meckenburg Declaration of Independence," 261, 267, 270, 273
Memorial Day, Confederate, 217, 226, 227, 228, 230, 244, 245, 247, 248, 258, 259
memory, public, 254–93
Midgett family, 212n19
Millen, Jim, 79, 109n121, 139, 140, 144
Miller, Prof. Von (sculptor), 241
Mills, Samuel N. (cabinetmaker), 37
Milton (Caswell Co.), 91

Mitchel, Elizabeth Person, 177, 179
Mitchel, Peter, 177
Mitchell, Joshua (brickmason), 106n60, 122, 124
Modlin service station (Nags Head), 209
Moffitt, Elvira Worth, 274
Montford, Donum (brick builder), 76, 91, 106n60
Montgomery, Lizzie Wilson, 15, 38, 41, 42
Montmorenci (Warren Co.), 160, *161,* 165–72, 174, 177, 182, 184–85n1; drawing room and mantels, *167,* 180; medallion, *169;* stair, 168, *169,* 170, 184–85n1, 186n14
Montmorenci–Prospect Hill School, 6, 159–87; map of, *162*
monuments and memorials, 215–75. *See also specific monuments and memorials by name*
Moore, "King" Roger, 293n54
Moore's Creek, 265
Moravians, 102n11; settlement, 72
Mordecai, Henry, 220
Mordecai House (Raleigh), 156n45
Morehead, John Motley, 52n46
Morrissette, Miss Cassie, 204
Mosby, R. H., 108n102
Moses (sawyer), 74, 75, 105n48, 135, 136
Mount Airy (Va.), 131
Mount Airy granite, 289n9
Mount Petros (Inez vic.), 174, 177, 180
Mount Vernon, 278
Muldoon Monument Company, 233
Mumford (carpenter), 79
Murchison, Col. Kenneth, 293n54
Murfreesboro (Hertford Co.), 18

Nags Head (Dare Co.), 3, 6, 188–214, *191, 195,* 213n22; bathhouse, *202;* boats to, *201;* cottages, *197, 202, 205, 206, 210,* 212–13n21; hotels, *192, 199;* island transportation, *198;* Lifesaving Station, *202;* Modlin service station, *209*
Nash, Solomon (carpenter), 94, 105n53, 109n115
National Cemetery (Raleigh), 224, 224, 316–18
National Register of Historic Places, 2, 306, 316, 317, 318; nominations to, 3
Ned (sawyer, hewer, violin player, and "part of a carpenter"), 74
Nelson (bricklayer), 76, 103n27
neoclassical style, 91, 143, 276
New Bern (Craven Co.), 6, 76, 82, 83, 85, 88, 91, 121–25, 130, 131, 135, 142, 228
New Bern Academy, 152n10
New Bern Jail (New Bern), 6, 121–25, *124. See also* Craven County jail
News and Observer (Raleigh), 206, 208, 231, 232, 236, 237, 238, 239, 241, 245, 258, 261, 264, 270,

276, 277; "Woman's Edition," 241, *243*, 243, 245, 247
Newton, Marrs (carpenter), 106n69
New York, 121, 123, 124, 126, 143, 147, 160, 164, 165
Nichols, Joe (carpenter), 78, 104n41
Nichols, William (architect-builder), 79, 117, 120n15, 126, 129, 130, 131, 133, 134, 139, 140, 141, 142, 143, 144, 147, 148, 149, 152n10, 155n30, 298; as state architect, 149, 156n45
Nichols, William, Jr. (architect), 156n45
Nixon, Francis (planter), 190
Noland, William G. (architect), 281
Norcom, Dr. James, 155n32
Norfolk (Va.), 75, 139, 162, 164, 190
Northampton County courthouse and jail, 58, 59, 65
North Carolina Booklet, The, 274, 285, 291n36
North Carolina Building, Jamestown Tercentennial Exposition, 285–86, *286*
North Carolina Confederate Monument (1870) (Raleigh), 229, 232, *233*, 237, *242*, 254, *255*, 260, 260, *262*, 262, 282; cartoon linking it to "Fred Douglas," *237*, 237; cornerstone-laying, *234*, 234; description of, 241; proposal to remove, 248; statue atop, *242*, 260; unveiling of, *216*, 238, 239, 240, 241, 260; —, black attendance at, 241
North Carolina Literary and Historical Association, 267
North Carolina Monumental Association, 216, 217, 231, 232, 235, 239, 240, 245, 249, 260

Oakdale Cemetery (Wilmington), 270
Oakland (Halifax Co.), *176*, 177, 180; entrance (detail), *179*
Oakwood Cemetery (Raleigh), *246*, 246, 247, 250n8
Ocracoke (Hyde Co.), 190
Old East (UNC–Chapel Hill), *85*, 86
Oliver, John M. (carpenter), 82, 104n40, 122
Olivia Raney Library (Raleigh), 254, *255*, 260, 267, 281
Orange County Courthouse (Hillsborough), *74*
Orton Plantation (Cape Fear River), *284*, 284–85, 293n54
Osborne (plasterer), 85, 86, 155n32
Outer Banks (N.C.), 188, 196, 198; geography of, 190, 195, 211n5; map of, *189*; settlement of, 190
Outlaw, Edward G., Sr., Cottage (1885) (Nags Head), 213n21
Outlaw, Edward G., Jr., 196, 200
Overman, R. F. and Kate, 212n19, 213n21
Oxford (Granville Co.), 69, 70

Packer, Francis H. (sculptor), 270, 273, 290n29
painting and graining, decorative, 15, 37, 39
Palladian style, 6, 131, 170, 171, 174, 177, 180, 181
Palladio, Andrea (architect), 131; *Four Books of Architecture*, 131
Parker, Marshall (brickmason), 139
Parris, Alexander (architect), 5, 113, 116, 117
Partridge, Sophia, 218, *219*, 223, 229
Paton, David (architect), 117, 274, 298
Patterson, James (builder), 80, 85, 105n49
Peace College (Raleigh), 16, 17, 277
Peale, Charles Willson, 166
penitentiary (Raleigh), 148, 156n45; plan by Nichols, 149
Percival, William (architect), 52n46, 81
Person, William, 177, 179
Pescud, Peter, 218, 224, 228, 229, 250n5
Peter (carpenter), 73, 79, 103n25
Petersburg (Va.), 18, 87, 115, 161, 162, 164, 165
Pettigrew, Ebenezer, 76, 78, 79, 80, 103n32, 134, 148, 149
Pettigrew, Gen. James J., 235
Pettigrew Hospital (Raleigh vic.), 220, 248
Philadelphia, 121, 122, 123, 124, 137, 160, 164, 165, 166, 183
Phillips, J. P. (builder), 18
piazzas, 46, 59, 99, 100, 192
plantation society, 14, 41, 128, 161, 162, 163, 164, 165, 166, 174, 177, 184, 185n10, 282, 283, 285
plastering, 100, 143; ornaments, 168, *169*
Polk, William, 72, 102n14
Ponds, Fresh (Nags Head), 199, 213n27
Pool, George, Cottage (1866) (Nags Head), 213n21
Pool, Dr. William Gaskins, 196, 212nn18–19
Pool Rock (Vance Co.), *34*
Populist Party, 231, 235, 263, 264
Porter, Benjamin (joiner), 61
Portsmouth (Carteret Co.), 190
Post, James F. (architect-contractor), 95, 97
Price, George (plasterer), 95, 97, 109n118
Prince Edward County (Va.), 13, 15, 37, 39
Prospect Hill (Airlie vic.), 168, 170–74, *172*, 177, 180, 182, 186n20; mantel, *173*; stair, *173*
Pruden cottage (Nags Head), 208

Raleigh, Sir Walter, 190
Raleigh (Wake Co.), 6, 7, 76, 78, 79, 83, 85, 92, 113, 130, 165, 182, 215, 244, 256, 268, 273, 276, 279, 282, 297
Raleigh Academy, 114
Raleigh and Gaston Railroad, 15, 16, 50n15, 218
Randall (sawyer), 75, 135
Raney, Kate Whiting Denson, 281–*82*, 292n48

Raney, Richard Beverly, 254, 281–*82*
Raney, Thomas H., 64
Raney House (Raleigh), *255, 260,* 281, *282,* 282, 283; modern amenities of, 283; plan of, *283*
Ranlett, William, 22, 25, 28, 31, 38; *The Architect,* 22, *26,* 41, *44* (ground plan), 62; "Italian villa," *45,* 46
Ravenscroft School (Asheville), 52n46
Read, James (carpenter), 155n30
"Rebel yell," 240
Reconstruction, 216, 217, 222, 223, 230, 235, 239, 244, 257, 268, 274, 279, 287
"Redeemers," 257, 269
Reedy Rill (Warren Co.), *12,* 28; mantel, *24*
Rem, Isaac (plasterer), 108n97
Republican Party, 235, 263, 264
reunification, 238, 270
Rice, Edward T. (brickmason and plasterer), 15, 34, 35
Richardson, Cicero (bricklayer), 88
Richardson, George, *New Vitruvius Britannicus,* 153n11
Richmond (Va.), 113, 115
Ricks tenant farmstead (Rocky Mount vic.), *308*
"Rip Van Winkle state," 113, 161
Roanoke Island (Dare Co.), 190, 195, 285
Roanoke Valley, 161, 162, 164, 165
Robards, Washington (carpenter), 80
Robin (shoemaker and carpenter), 74
Rock Quarry Cemetery (Raleigh), 220; transfer of remains from, 220, 222, 225
Rock Springs Campground (Lincolnton vic.), *302*
Rocky Mount (Nash Co.), 308
Rogers, Dennis, 312
Rogers, Stewart (architect), 279
Roodes, William (carpenter), 59
Roosevelt, Pres. Franklin D., 214n59
Roosevelt, Pres. Theodore, 286
Rose, G. W. (contractor), 97
Rose, William P. (architect), 282, 292n50
Rotherwood (Prince Edward Co.), 14, 20, *21,* 49n6; stair, *20*
Russell, Daniel, 264

Saint John's College (Oxford), 17
Salem (Forsyth Co.), 102n11
Salisbury (Rowan Co.), 62, 81, 89
Sam (carpenter), 73, 84, 107n81
Sammesbury, David (carpenter), 58
Sampson, James (carpenter), 91–92, 94
Sandy, Uriah (carpenter), 108n97
sawmills, 135

saws, 18, 136–37
Sawyer, Dr. C. W., 203
Sawyer, Lewis (house joiner), 108n97
Sawyer, Old Ben (bricklayer), 98, 99, 100
sawyers, 74–75, 136; tasks, 74, *135,* 135
Scotland Neck (Halifax Co.), 80
Secretary of the Interior's Standards, 316, 318
Sentinel, 220, 221, 222, 223, 225, 226, 227, 228
Shadow Lawn (Chase City, Va.), *29*
Shady Grove, 177
Shady Oaks (Warrenton vic.), 182
Sheridan, Thomas (carpenter), 92, 93, 108n101
Sheridan family, 92, 108n101
Sherman, Gen. William T., 217, 244, 248
Shipp, Mrs. M. L., 244
Shocco Springs (Warren Co.), 164, 166
shoemaking, 74
Silvester (bricklayer), 99, 100
Simmons, Furnifold M., 264
Simon (carpenter), 82
Skinner, Joseph Blount, Law Office (Edenton), 153n11, 155n38
skyscrapers, 299, 300
slave(s): artisans, 6, 69, 95, 96, 97, 105n53; badge, 94; boarding costs, 82, dealers, 87; hiring of, 79–84, 86, 94, 105n44, 135, 138, 153n18; house (example of), *307;* legal status of, 107n89; literacy of, 72, 80, 92, 94, 97, 107n80; at Nags Head, *191,* 191, 194; passes, 84, 88–89, 92–93, *93,* 94, 136; population on eve of Civil War, 305; runaway, 87; quality of work, 76, 77; skills of, 76, 77, 104n35; task system, 136, 153–54n20; teams, 78; tools, 82
Sloan, Samuel, 31; *The Model Architect, 43,* 46
Smith, Benjamin (planter), 72, 102n13
Smithfield (Johnston Co.), 307
smokehouse, description of, 64
Snowden and Wagner, 122, 123
Society of the Cincinnati, 267, *271,* 271, 274
Somerville House (Warrenton), *25,* 32; ground plan, *33;* porch and entrance, *23;* stair hall, *39*
Sons of the Revolution, 267, 274
Southern Architect, 283
Southern Colonial style, 280, 281, 282, 283, 286
Spanish-American War, 200, 247, 266, 270
specifications, examples of, 64–66
Spencer, Captain Abraham (contractor), 70
Sprunt, James, 263, 264, 266, *271,* 273, 280, 284–85
Sprunt, Luola Murchison (Mrs. James), 270, 280, 284, 292n45
Stamp Act, 264, 271, 272, 291n33
St. Andrew's-by-the-Sea (Nags Head), 207

Stanly, John Carruthers, 91, 108n99
State Bank (Fayetteville), 149, 156n45
State Bank (Raleigh), 299, 299
State Capitol (Raleigh), 119, 156n45, 215, 222, 254, 259, 260, 260, 262, 269, 274, 277, 297, 298
State House (Raleigh), 79, 114, 117, 119n4, 120n15, 156n45
Statuary Hall, U.S. Capitol, 259, 270
Steele, John, 62
Stephen (carpenter), 73
Stephens, Burett (architect), 293n53
Stepney (sawyer), 74, 135
Stevenson, Martin (carpenter), 82–83, 106n60
St. John's Church (Williamsboro), 80
St. Lawrence, Patrick, 80
St. Louis (Mo.), 278
St. Mary's College, 198, 199, 236, 257, 277, 283
St. Mary's Muse, 198
St. Matthew's Church (Hillsborough), 156n45
Stone, Silas M., 104n38
stone, imported, 142
stonework, specifications for, 60, 61
St. Paul's Episcopal Church (Edenton), 75, 76, 130, 137, 139, 305
Strickland, William (architect), 298
Stringer, George (brickmason), 108n97
Stuart, James, and Nicholas Revett, *Antiquities of Athens*, 131, 153n11
Sully, Thomas, 114, 119
Sumner Cottage (1868) (Nags Head), 212n21
Sunnyside (Littleton vic.), 51–52n38
Swain, Gov. David L., 86

Tarboro (Edgecombe Co.), 85 303
taste, 40, 92, 113, 115, 117, 129, 130, 141, 143, 147, 152n6, 164, 173, 257, 276, 311, 316, 318, 319, 320
Tate, Col. Samuel McDowell, 231, 233
Taylor, Archibald, House (Franklin Co.), 36; stair hall, 39
Taylor, Henry (carpenter), 95
Thalian Hall. *See* City Hall–Thalian Hall (Wilmington)
Thomas, William Holland, 223, 224, 251n16
Thorne, Henry Hill, 177
Thorne, Temperance Davis, 171
Thorne, William Williams, 168, 171, 174, 177, 186n20
Throop, George Higby, 191, 192, 193; *Nags Head: or Two Months among "The Bankers." A Story of Sea-Shore Life and Manners*, 191
Tillett, Marshall Field, 207
Tillett, Samuel, 196
Tillett, Tilghman, 198

Tillett family, 213n24
timber, types of, 58, 59, 60, 65, 66, 134
tools, carpentry, 82; imported from New York, 140
Town, Ithiel (architect), 117, 156n45, 298
Townsend, James (housewright), 58, 59, 62, 63
Treadwell and Thorne, 137
Trimble, John M. (architect), 97
Trinity College (Asheboro vic.), 17
Trinity Episcopal Church (Scotland Neck vic.), 79
Trotter, Thomas (mechanic), 156n46
Tryon, William, 121, 131
Tryon Palace (New Bern), 120n12, 131, 152n10, 278
Tucker House (Raleigh), *81*
Turner, Thomas (slater), 125
Turner Cottage. *See* Pool, George, Cottage
Tuscan-Doric style, 22
Tusculum (Arcola vic.), 181, *182*; stair (detail), *182*
Twine, S. J. (builder), 204, 206–8, *207*, 211, 214n50; description of cottages built by, 207–8

Ulysses (plasterer), 76, 103n28
Union Hill plantation (Warren Co.), 165, 167
Union Square (Raleigh), 260, 269, 270, 273. *See also* Capitol Square (Raleigh)
Union Tavern (Milton), 90
United Confederate Veterans, 267
United Daughters of the Confederacy (UDC), 247, 248, 249, 267, 273
University of North Carolina at Chapel Hill, 80, 86, 114, 128, 164, 257, 280

Vance, Zebulon Baird, 257, 268, 269, 274; monument to, 268, *269*, 270, 273
Vaux, Calvert, 31
Vine Hill (Franklin Co.), 32, 51n37; entrance, *27*; ground plan, *33*
Vinson House (Murfreesboro), *31*

Waddell, Col. Alfred Moore, 231, 252n31, 258, 259, 261, 263, 264, 265, 266, *271*, 271, 287, 288n6
Waddell, Gabrielle DeRosset (Mrs. Alfred), 270
Waddell, John A. (carpenter-builder), 39
Wadesboro (Anson Co.), 59
Wake Forest (Wake Co.), 119n6
Walker, John, 141, 144, 155n32
Walpole, Horace, *Encyclopedia*, 131
Ward, Benjamin (carpenter), 53, 63

War of 1812, 113, 114, 119n6
Warren County Courthouse (Warrenton), *34*, 41
Warren County Jail (Warrenton), 60; plan of, *61*
Warrenton (Warren Co.), 14, 15, 16, 17, 20, 22, 24, 26, 27, 28, 40, 41, 42, 81, 162, 164, 174, 179, 182
Warrenton Presbyterian Church, *35*, 41
Wash (stonemason), 69, 70, 79
Washington (carpenter), 105n48
Washington, George, 114, 117, 119, 166, 236, 237, 254, 262, 273, 288n7
Washington (Beaufort Co.), 85, 94
Waterside Theater, 214n59
Waverly (Mecklenburg Co., Va.), ground plan, *44*
Webber, Caty (cake woman), 88
Webbs Brothers (architects), 8n7
Welcome, Joe (bricklayer), 76, 79, 98, 99, 100, 103n32, 139, 140
Welcome, Old (bricklayer), 98, 99, 103n32
Wellford, Robert, composition ornaments of, 166–67, 186n15
Wessington (Edenton), 51n29
Whedbee Cottage (Nags Head), 213n21
White, Cornelius, 63
White, John (artist), 285
White, Sen. Theophilus, 238
White Rock (Halifax vic.), 174; stair, *175*
"White Supremacy Crusade," 264, 265, 266, 267, 278, 289n17
Whitfield, Macon, house for, 53, 54, 63
Whiting, David, account of removal of Confederate remains, 225
Whiting, Capt. George Mordecai, 220, 222, 225, 229
Wickham House (Richmond, Va.), 5, 113–20, *118*; description of, 116; ground plan, *115*, 115, 116. *See also* Woodlawn (Halifax Co.)
Wiggins, Mason, 181
Wiley (carpenter), 165
Wilkins, W. W., 135, 136
Williams, Caroline Alston, 174
Williams, Charity Alston, 177
Williams, Delia Haywood, 165, 166
Williams, Elizabeth (Betsey), 166, 177
Williams, Elizabeth Alston, 165, 166
Williams, John A., 177
Williams, Joseph John, II, 165, 166
Williams, Joseph John, III, 174, 177
Williams, Mary K. Davis, 82, 174, 177
Williams, Melissa, 167
Williams, Melissa Jane Burgess, 165, 166, 177, 186n13
Williams, Dr. Solomon, 174

Williams, William, 160, 165, 168, 171, 174, 177, 183
Williams family, 174; genealogical/house chart of, 163
Williamsboro (Vance Co.), 80
Williamston (Martin Co.), 128
Willis (carpenter), 72, 105n48
Willis (stonemason), 69, 70, 79
Wilmington (New Hanover Co.), 7, 59, 72, 80, 85, 87, 91–92, 94, 96, 97, 256, 264, 265, 266, 268, 272, 273, 279, 288n2, 301; building trades in, 108–9n105; steam-powered sawmills in, 135
Wilmington Herald, 96
Wilmington Ladies Memorial Association, 270
Wilmington Light Infantry, 266, 271
Wilmington "Race Riot" (1898), 265, 272, 284
Wilmington Record, 264
Wilson (sawyer), 75, 135, 136
Wilson, T. E., House (Warrenton), entrance, *24*
Windsor (Bertie Co.), 53, 54, 63, 134
Winston, Mrs. Duncan, 212n21
Winston, Lt. Gov. Francis, 264, 271, 274
Winterthur, Henry duPont, Museum. *See* Montmorenci
Wise, Gen. Henry A., 195
women: in public life, 216, 218, 240, 243, 249, 259; at State Capitol, 221, 232, 233, 236
Wood, Edward, 150, 155n32
Wood, Frank, 274
Wood, John Coffin (builder), 59
Wood, Martha, Cottage. *See* Gurkin Cottage (Nags Head)
Wood, Robert Barclay (builder), 59, 97
Woodlawn (Halifax Co.), 181
Woodson, Francis (brickmason and plasterer), 15, 34, 35
Worcester (Ma.), 62
World's Columbian Exposition (Chicago), 256, 278
World War I, 205
World War II, 188
Worthington cottage (Nags Head), 213n21
Wright brothers, 201
Wright Brothers National Memorial, 214n59
Wurster, William (architect), 8n7
Wyatt, Henry Lawson, 273

Yancey, Bartlett, House (Yanceyville vic.), stair, *90*
Yanceyville (Caswell Co.), 90, 307
Yarborough House hotel (Raleigh), 92
Yuppies, 312–21; characteristics of, 312–13

Ziegler Cottage (Nags Head), 205